The Prince

Or, Why Constantinop.

Lew Wallace

Alpha Editions

This edition published in 2024

ISBN 9789362096548

Design and Setting By

Alpha Editions

www.alphaedis.com

Email - info@alphaedis.com

Contents

BOOK IV
THE PALACE OF BLACHERNE (Continued)

CHAPTER XI
THE PRINCESS HEARS FROM THE WORLD

The sun shone clear and hot, and the guests in the garden were glad to rest in the shaded places of promenade along the brooksides and under the beeches and soaring pines of the avenues. Far up the extended hollow there was a basin first to receive the water from the conduit supposed to tap the aqueduct leading down from the forest of Belgrade. The noise of the little cataract there was strong enough to draw a quota of visitors. From the front gate to the basin, from the basin to the summit of the promontory, the company in lingering groups amused each other detailing what of fortune good and bad the year had brought them. The main features of such meetings are always alike. There were games by the children, lovers in retired places, and old people plying each other with reminiscences. The faculty of enjoyment changes but never expires.

An array of men chosen for the purpose sallied from the basement of the palace carrying baskets of bread, fruits in season, and wine of the country in water-skins. Dispersing themselves through the garden, they waited on the guests, and made distribution without stint or discrimination. The heartiness of their welcome may be imagined; while the thoughtful reader will see in the liberality thus characterizing her hospitality one of the secrets of the Princess's popularity with the poor along the Bosphorus. Nor that merely. A little reflection will lead up to an explanation of her preference for the Homeric residence by Therapia. The commonalty, especially the unfortunate amongst them, were a kind of constituency of hers, and she loved living where she could most readily communicate with them.

This was the hour she chose to go out and personally visit her guests. Descending from the portico, she led her household attendants into the garden. She alone appeared unveiled. The happiness of the many amongst whom she immediately stepped touched every spring of enjoyment in her being; her eyes were bright, her cheeks rosy, her spirit high; in a word, the beauty so peculiarly hers, and which no one could look on without consciousness of its influence, shone with singular enhancement.

News that she was in the garden spread rapidly, and where she went everyone arose and remained standing. Now and then, while making acknowledgments to groups along the way, she recognized acquaintances, and for such, whether men or women, she had a smile, sometimes a word. Upon her passing, they pursued with benisons, "God bless you!" "May the Holy Mother keep her!" Not unfrequently children ran flinging flowers at her feet, and mothers knelt and begged her blessing. They had lively recollection of a sickness or other overtaking by sorrow, and of her boat drawing to the landing laden with delicacies, and bringing what was quite as welcome, the charm of her presence, with words inspiring hope and trust. The vast, vociferous, premeditated Roman ovation, sonorously the Triumph, never brought a Consular hero the satisfaction this Christian woman now derived.

She was aware of the admiration which went with her, and the sensation was of walking through a purer and brighter sunshine. Nor did she affect to put aside the triumph there certainly was in the demonstration; but she accounted it the due of charity—a triumph of good work done for the pleasure there was in the doing.

At the basin mentioned as the landward terminus of the garden the progress in that direction stopped. Thence, after gracious attentions to the women and children there, the Princess set out for the summit of the promontory. The road taken was broad and smooth, and on the left hand lined from bottom to top with pine trees, some of which are yet standing.

The summit had been a place of interest time out of mind. From its woody cover, the first inhabitants beheld the Argonauts anchor off the town of Amycus, king of the Bebryces; there the vengeful Medea practised her incantations; and descending to acknowledged history, it were long telling the notable events of the ages landmarked by the hoary height. When the builder of the palace below threw his scheme of improvement over the brow of the hill, he constructed water basins on different levels, surrounding them with raised walls artistically sculptured; between the basins he pitched marble pavilions, looking in the distance like airy domes on a Cyclopean temple; then he drew the work together by a tesselated pavement identical with the floor of the house of Caesar hard by the Forum in Rome.

Giving little heed to the other guests in occupancy of the summit, the attendants of the Princess broke into parties sight seeing; while she called Sergius to her, and conducted him to a point commanding the Bosphorus for leagues. A favorite lookout, in fact, the spot had been provided with a pavement and a capacious chair cut from a block of the coarse brown limestone native to the locality. There she took seat, and the ascent, though all in shade, having been wearisome, she was glad of the blowing of the fresh upper air.

From a place in the rear Sergius had witnessed the progress to the present halt. Every incident and demonstration had been in his view and hearing. The expressions of affection showered upon the Princess were delightful to him; they seemed so spontaneous and genuine. As testimony to her character in the popular estimate at least, they left nothing doubtful. His first impression of her was confirmed. She was a woman to whom Heaven had confided every grace and virtue. Such marvels had been before. He had heard of them in tradition, and always in a strain to lift those thus favored above the hardened commonplace of human life, creatures not exactly angels, yet moving in the same atmosphere with angels. The monasteries, even those into whose gates women are forbidden to look, all have stories of womanly excellence which the monks tell each other in pauses from labor in the lentil patch, and in their cells after vesper prayers. In brief, so did Sergius' estimate of the Princess increase that he was unaware of impropriety when, trudging slowly after the train of attendants, he associated her with heroines most odorous in Church and Scriptural memories; with Mothers Superior famous for sanctity; with Saints, like Theckla and Cecilia; with the Prophetess who was left by the wayside in the desert of Zin, and the later seer and singer, she who had her judgment-seat under the palm tree of Deborah.

Withal, however, the monk was uncomfortable. The words of his Hegumen pursued him. Should he tell the Princess? Assailed by doubts, he followed her to the lookout on the edge of the promontory.

Seating herself, she glanced over the wide field of water below; from the vessels there, she gazed across to Asia; then up at the sky, full to its bluest depth with the glory of day. At length she asked:

"Have you heard from Father Hilarion?"

"Not yet," Sergius replied.

"I was thinking of him," she continued. "He used to tell me of the primitive church—the Church of the Disciples. One of his lessons returns to me. He seems to be standing where you are. I hear his voice. I see his countenance. I remember his words: 'The brethren while of one faith, because the creed was too simple for division, were of two classes, as they now are and will always be'—ay, Sergius, as they will always be!—'But,' he said, 'it is worthy remembrance, my dear child, unlike the present habit, the rich held·their riches with the understanding that the brethren all had shares in them. The owner was more than owner; he was a trustee charged with the safe-keeping of his property, and with farming it to the best advantage, that he might be in condition to help the greatest number of the Christian brotherhood according to their necessities.' I wondered greatly at the time, but not now. The delight I have today confirms the Father; for it is not in my palace and garden, nor in my gold, but in the power I derive from them to give respite from the grind of poverty to so many less fortunate than myself. 'The divine order was not to desist from getting wealth'—thus the Father continued—'for Christ knew there were who, labor as they might, could not accumulate or retain; circumstances would be against them, or the genius might be wanting. Poor without fault, were they to suffer, and curse God with the curse of the sick, the cold, the naked, the hungry? Oh, no! Christ was the representative of the Infinitely Merciful. Under his dispensation they were to be partners of the more favored.' Who can tell, who can begin to measure the reward there is to me in the laughter of children at play under the trees by the brooks, and in the cheer and smiles of women whom I have been able to draw from the unvarying routine of toil like theirs?"

There was a ship with full spread sail speeding along so close in shore Sergius could have thrown a stone on its deck. He affected to be deeply interested in it. The ruse did not avail him.

"What is the matter?"

Receiving no reply, she repeated the question.

"My dear friend, you are not old enough in concealment to deceive me. You are in trouble. Come sit here.... True, I am not an authorized confessor; yet I know the principle on which the Church defends the confessional. Let me share your burden. Insomuch as you give me, you shall be relieved."

It came to him then that he must speak.

"Princess," he began, striving to keep his voice firm, "you know not what you ask."

"Is it what a woman may hear?"

A step nearer brought him on the tesselated square.

"I hesitate, Princess, because a judgment is required of me. Hear, and help me first."

Then he proceeded rapidly:

"There is one just entered holy service. He is a member of an ancient and honorable Brotherhood, and by reason of his inexperience, doubtless, its obligations rest the heavier on his conscience. His superior has declared to him how glad he would be had he a son like him, and confiding in his loyalty, he intrusted him with gravest secrets; amongst others, that a person well known and greatly beloved is under watch for the highest of religious crimes. Pause now, O Princess, and consider the obligations inseparable from the relation and trust here disclosed.... Look then to this other circumstance. The person accused condescended to be the friend and patron of the same neophyte, and by vouching for him to the head of the Church, put him on the road to favor and quick promotion. Briefly, O

Princess, to which is obligation first owing? The father superior or the patron in danger?"

The Princess replied calmly, but with feeling: "It is not a supposition, Sergius."

Though surprised, he returned: "Without it I could not have your decision first."

"Thou, Sergius, art the distressed neophyte."

He held his hands out to her: "Give me thy judgment."

"The Hegumen of the St. James' is the accuser."

"Be just, O Princess! To which is the obligation first owing?"

"I am the accused," she continued, in the same tone.

He would have fallen on his knees. "No, keep thy feet. A watchman may be behind me now."

He had scarcely resumed his position before she asked, still in the quiet searching manner: "What is the highest religious crime? Or rather, to men in authority, like the Hegumen of your Brotherhood, what is the highest of all crimes?"

He looked at her in mute supplication.

"I will tell you—HERESY."

Then, compassionating his suffering, she added: "My poor Sergius! I am not upbraiding you. You are showing me your soul. I see it in its first serious trial.... I will forget that I am the denounced, and try to help you. Is there no principle to which we can refer the matter—no Christian principle? The Hegumen claims silence from you; on the other side, your conscience—I would like to say preference—impels you to speak a word of warning for the benefit of your patroness. There, now, we have both the dispute and the disputants. Is it not so?"

Sergius bowed his head.

"Father Hilarion once said to me: 'Daughter, I give you the ultimate criterion of the divineness of our religion—there cannot be an instance of human trial for which it does not furnish a rule of conduct and consolation.' A profound saying truly! Now is it possible we have here at last an exception? I do not seek to know on which side the honors lie. Where are the humanities? Ideas of honor are of men conventional. On the other hand, the humanities stand for Charity. If thou wert the denounced, O Sergius, how wouldst thou wish to be done by?"

Sergius' face brightened.

"We are not seeking to save a heretic—we are in search of quiet for our consciences. So why not ask and answer further: What would befall the Hegumen, did you tell the accused all you had from him? Would he suffer? Is there a tribunal to sentence him? Or a prison agape for him? Or torture in readiness? Or a King of Lions? In these respects how is it with the friend who vouched for you to the head of the Church? Alas!"

"Enough—say no more!" Sergius cried impulsively. "Say no more. O Princess, I will tell everything—I will save you, if I can—if not, and the worst come, I will die with you."

Womanlike the Princess signalized her triumph with tears. At length she asked: "Wouldst thou like to know if I am indeed a heretic?"

"Yes, for what thou art, that am I; and then"—

"The same fire in the Hippodrome may light us both out of the world."

There was a ring of prophecy in the words.

"God forbid!" he ejaculated, with a shiver.

"God's will be done, were better! ... So, if it please you," she went on, "tell me all the Hegumen told you about me."

"Everything?" he asked doubtfully.

"Why not?"

"Part of it is too wicked for repetition."

"Yet it was an accusation."

"Yes."

"Sergius, you are no match in cunning for my enemies. They are Greeks trained to diplomacy; you are"—she paused and half smiled—"only a pupil of Hilarion's. See now—if they mean to kill me, how important to invent a tale which shall rob me of sympathy, and reconcile the public to my sacrifice. They who do much good, and no harm"—she cast a glance at the people swarming around the pavilions—"always have friends. Such is the law of kindness, and it never failed but once; but today a splinter of the Cross is worth a kingdom."

"Princess, I will hold nothing back."

"And I, Sergius—God witnessing for me—will speak to each denunciation thou givest me."

"There were two matters in the Hegumen's mind," Sergius began, but struck with the abruptness, he added apologetically: "I pray you, Princess, remember I speak at your insistence, and that I am not in any sense an accuser. It may be well to say also the Hegumen returned from last night's Mystery low in spirits, and much spent bodily, and before speaking of you, declared he had been an active partisan of your father's. I do not think him your personal enemy."

A mist of tears dimmed her eyes while the Princess replied: "He was my father's friend, and I am grateful to him; but alas! that he is naturally kind and just is now of small consequence."

"It grieves me"—

"Do not stop," she said, interrupting him.

"At the Father's bedside I received his blessing; and asked leave to be absent a few days. 'Where?' he inquired, and I answered: 'Thou knowest I regard the Princess Irene as my little mother. I should like to go see her.'"

Sergius sought his auditor's face at this, and observing no sign of objection to the familiarity, was greatly strengthened.

"The Father endeavored to persuade me not to come, and it was with that purpose he entered upon the disclosures you ask.... 'The life the Princess leads'—thus he commenced—'and her manners, are outside the sanctions of society.'"

Here, from resting on her elbow, the listener sat upright, grasping the massive arm of the chair.

"Shall I proceed, O Princess?"

"Yes."

"This place is very public"—he glanced at the people above them.

"I will hear you here."

"At your pleasure.... The Hegumen referred next to your going about publicly unveiled. While not positively wrong, he condemned the practice as a pernicious example; besides which there was a defiant boldness in it, he said, tending to make you a subject of discussion and indelicate remark."

The hand on the stony arm trembled.

"I fear, O Princess," Sergius continued, with downcast look, "that my words are giving you pain."

"But they are not yours. Go on."

"Then the Father came to what was much more serious."

Sergius again hesitated.

"I am listening," she said.

"He termed it your persistence in keeping up the establishment here at Therapia."

The Princess grew red and white by turns.

"He said the Turk was too near you; that unmarried and unprotected your proper place was in some house of God on the Islands, or in the city, where you could have the benefit of holy offices. As it was, rumor was free to accuse you of preferring guilty freedom to marriage."

The breeze fell off that moment, leaving the Princess in the centre of a profound hush; except for the unwonted labor of her heart, the leaves overhead were not more still. The sight of her was too oppressive—Sergius turned away. Presently he heard her say, as if to herself: "I am indeed in danger. If my death were not in meditation, the boldest of them would not dare think so foul a falsehood.... Sergius," she said.

He turned to her, but she broke off diverted by another idea. Had this last accusation reference to the Emperor's dream of making her his wife? Could the Emperor have published what took place between them? Impossible!

"Sergius, did the Hegumen tell you whence this calumny had origin?"

"He laid it to rumor merely."

"Surely he disclosed some ground for it. A dignitary of his rank and profession cannot lend himself to shaming a helpless woman without reason or excuse."

"Except your residence at Therapia, he gave no reason."

Here she looked at Sergius, and the pain in the glance was pitiful. "My friend, is there anything in your knowledge which might serve such a rumor?"

"Yes," he replied, letting his eyes fall.

"What!" and she lifted her head, and opened her eyes.

He stood silent and evidently suffering.

"Poor Sergius! The punishment is yours. I am sorry for you—sorry we entered on this subject—but it is too late to retire from it. Speak bravely. What is it you know against me? It cannot be a crime; much I doubt if it be a sin; my walk has been very strait and altogether in God's view. Speak!"

"Princess," he answered, "coming down from the landing, I was stopped by a concourse studying a brass plate nailed to the right-hand pillar of your gate. It was inscribed, but none of them knew the import of the inscription. The hamari came up, and at sight of it fell to saluting, like the abject Eastern he is. The bystanders chaffered him, and he retorted, and, amongst other things, said the brass was a safeguard directed to all Turks, notifying them that this property, its owner, and inmates were under protection of the Prince Mahommed. Give heed now, I pray you, O Princess, to this other thing of the man's saying. The notice was the Prince Mahommed's, the inscription his signature, and the Prince himself fixed the plate on the pillar with his own hand."

Sergius paused.

"Well," she asked.

"The inferences—consider them."

"State them."

"My tongue refuses. Or if I must, O Princess, I will use the form of accusation others are likely to have adopted. 'The Princess Irene lives at Therapia because Prince Mahommed is her lover, and it is a convenient place of meeting. Therefore his safeguard on her gate.'"

"No one could be bold enough to"—

"One has been bold enough."

"One?"

"The Hegumen of my Brotherhood."

The Princess was very pale.

"It is cruel—cruel!" she exclaimed. "What ought I to do?"

"Treat the safeguard as a discovery of to-day, and have it removed while the people are all present." She looked at him searchingly. On her forehead between the brows, he beheld a line never there before. More surprising was the failure of self-reliance observable in her request for counsel. Heretofore her courage and sufficiency had been remarkable. In all dealings with him she had proved herself the directress, quick yet decided. The change astonished him, so little was he acquainted with the feminine nature; and in reply he spoke hastily, hardly knowing what he had said. The words were not straightforward and honest; they were not becoming him any more than the conduct suggested was becoming her; they lingered in his ear, a wicked sound, and he would have recalled them—but he hesitated.

Here a voice in fierce malediction was heard up at the pavilions, together with a prodigious splashing of water. Laughter, clapping of hands, and other expressions of delight succeeded.

"Go, Sergius, and see what is taking place," said the Princess.

Glad of the opportunity to terminate the painful scene, he hastened to the reservoirs and returned.

"Your presence will restore quiet at once."

The people made way for their hostess with alacrity. The hamari, it appeared, had just arrived from the garden. Observing Lael in the midst of the suite of fair ladies, he advanced to her with many strange salutations. Alarmed, she would have run away had not Joqard broken from his master, and leaped with a roar into the water. The poor beast seemed determined to enjoy the bath. He swam, and dived, and played antics without number. In vain the showman, resorting to every known language, coaxed and threatened by turns—Joqard was self-willed and happy, and it were hard saying which appreciated his liberty most, he or the spectators of the scene.

The Princess, for the time conquering her pain of heart, interceded for the brute; whereupon the hamari, like a philosopher used to making the best of surprises, joined in the sport until Joqard grew tired, and voluntarily returned to control.

CHAPTER XII
LAEL TELLS OF HER TWO FATHERS

Word passed from the garden to the knots of people on the height: "Come down quickly. They are making ready for the boat race." Directly the reservoirs, the pavilions, and the tesselation about them were deserted.

The Princess Irene, with her suite, made the descent to the garden more at leisure, knowing the regatta would wait for her. So it happened she was at length in charge of what seemed a rear guard; but how it befell that Sergius and Lael drew together, the very last of that rear guard, is not of such easy explanation.

Whether by accident or mutual seeking, side by side the two moved slowly down the hill, one moment in the shade of the kingly pines, then in the glowing sunshine. The noises of the celebration, the shouting, singing, calling, and merry outcries of children ascended to them, and through the verdurousness below, lucent as a lake, gleams of color flashed from scarfs, mantles, embroidered jackets, and flaming petticoats.

"I hope you are enjoying yourself," he said to Lael, upon their meeting.

"Oh, yes! How could I help it—everything is delightful. And the Princess— she is so good and gracious. Oh, if I were a man, I should go mad with loving her!"

She spoke with enthusiasm; she even drew her veil partially aside; yet Sergius did not respond; he was asking himself if it were possible the girl could be an impostor. Presently he resolved to try her with questions.

"Tell me of your father. Is he well?"

At this she raised her veil entirely, and in turn asked: "Which father do you mean?"

"Which father," he repeated, stopping.

"Oh, I have the advantage of everybody else! I have two fathers."

He could do no more than repeat after her: "Two fathers!"

"Yes; Uel the merchant is one of them, and the Prince of India is the other. I suppose you mean the Prince, since you know him. He accompanied me to the landing this morning, and seated me in the boat. He was then well."

There was no concealment here. Yet Sergius saw the disclosure was not complete. He was tempted to go on.

"Two fathers! How can such thing be?"

She met the question with a laugh. "Oh! If it depended on which of them is the kinder to me, I could not tell you the real father."

Sergius stood looking at her, much as to say: "That is no answer; you are playing with me."

"See how we are falling behind," she then said. "Come, let us go on. I can talk while walking."

They set forward briskly, but it was noticeable that he moved nearer her, stooping from his great height to hear further.

"This is the way of it," she continued of her own prompting. "Some years ago, my father, Uel, the merchant, received a letter from an old friend of his father's, telling him that he was about to return to Constantinople after a long absence in the East somewhere, and asking if he, Uel, would assist the servant who was bearer of the note in buying and furnishing a house. Uel did so, and when the stranger arrived, his home was ready for him. I was then a little girl, and went one day to see the Prince of India, his residence being opposite Uel's on the other side of the street. He was studying some big books, but quit them, and picked me up, and asked me who I was? I told him Uel was my father. What was my name? Lael, I said. How old was I? And when I answered that also, he kissed me, and cried, and, to my wonder, declared how he had once a child named Lael; she looked like me, and was just my age when she died"—

"Wonderful!" exclaimed Sergius.

"Yes, and he then said Heaven had sent me to take her place. Would I be his Lael? I answered I would, if Uel consented. He took me in his arms, carried me across the street and talked so Uel could not have refused had he wanted to."

The manner of the telling was irresistible. At the conclusion, she turned to him and said, with emotion: "There, now. You see I really have two fathers, and you know how I came by them: and were I to recount their goodness to me, and how they both love me, and how happy each one of them is in believing me the object of the other's affection, you would understand just as well how I know no difference between them."

"It is strange; yet as you tell it, little friend, it is not strange," he returned, seriously. They were at the instant in a bar of brightest sunlight projected across the road; and had she asked him the cause of the frown on his face, he could not have told her he was thinking of Demedes.

"Yes, I see it—I see it, and congratulate you upon being so doubly blessed. Tell me next who the Prince of India is."

She looked now here, now there, he watching her narrowly.

"Oh! I never thought of asking him about himself."

She was merely puzzled by an unexpected question.

"But you know something of him?"

"Let me think," she replied. "Yes, he was the intimate of my father Uel's father, and of his father before him."

"Is he so old then?"

"I cannot say how long he has been a family acquaintance. Of my knowledge he is very learned in everything. He speaks all the languages I ever heard of; he passes the nights alone on the roof of his house"—

"Alone on the roof of his house!"

"Only of clear nights, you understand. A servant carries a chair and table up for him, and a roll of papers, with pen and ink, and a clock of brass and gold. The paper is a map of the heavens; and he sits there watching the stars, marking them in position on the map, the clock telling him the exact time."

"An astronomer," said Sergius.

"And an astrologer," she added; "and besides these things he is a doctor, but goes only amongst the poor, taking nothing from them. He is also a chemist; and he has tables of the plants curative and deadly, and can extract their qualities, and reduce them from fluids to solids, and proportionate them. He is also a master of figures, a science, he always terms it, the first of creative principles without which God could not be God. So, too, he is a traveller—indeed I think he has been over the known world. You cannot speak of a capital or of an island, or a tribe which he has not visited. He has servants from the farthest East. One of his attendants is an African King; and what is the strangest to me, Sergius, his domestics are all deaf and dumb."

"Impossible!"

"Nothing appears impossible to him."

"How does he communicate with them?"

"They catch his meaning from the motion of his lips. He says signs are too slow and uncertain for close explanations."

"Still he must resort to some language."

"Oh, yes, the Greek."

"But if they have somewhat to impart to him?"

"It is theirs to obey, and pantomime seems sufficient to convey the little they have to return to him, for it is seldom more than, 'My Lord, I have done the thing you gave me to do.' If the matter be complex, he too resorts to the lip-speech, which he could not teach without first being proficient in it himself. Thus, for instance, to Nilo"—

"The black giant who defended you against the Greek?"

"Yes—a wonderful man—an ally, not a servant. On the journey to Constantinople, the Prince turned aside into an African Kingdom called Kash-Cush. I cannot tell where it is. Nilo was the King, and a mighty hunter and warrior. His trappings hang in his room now—shields, spears, knives, bows and arrows, and among them a net of linen threads. When he took the field for lions, his favorite game, the net and a short sword were all he cared for. His throne room, I have heard my father the Prince say, was carpeted with skins taken by him in single combats."

"What could he do with the net, little Princess?"

"I will give you his account; perhaps you can see it clearly—I cannot. When the monster makes his leap, the corners of the net are tossed up in the air, and he is in some way caught and tangled... Well, as I was saying, Nilo, though deaf and dumb, of choice left his people and throne to follow the Prince, he knew not where."

"Oh, little friend! Do you know you are talking the incredible to me? Who ever heard of such thing before?"

Sergius' blue eyes were astare with wonder.

"I only speak what I have heard recounted by my father, the Prince, to my other father, Uel.... What I intended saying was that directly the Prince established himself at home he began teaching Nilo to converse. The work was slow at first; but there is no end to the master's skill and patience; he and the King now talk without hindrance. He has even made him a believer in God."

"A Christian, you mean."

"No. In my father's opinion the mind of a wild man cannot comprehend modern Christianity; nobody can explain the Trinity; yet a child can be taught the almightiness of God, and won to faith in him."

"Do you speak for yourself or the Prince?"

"The Prince," she replied.

Sergius was struck with the idea, and wished to go further with it, but they were at the foot of the hill, and Lael exclaimed, "The garden is deserted. We may lose the starting of the race. Let us hurry."

"Nay, little friend, you forget how narrow my skirts are. I cannot run. Let us walk fast. Give me a hand. There now—we will arrive in time."

Near the palace, however, Sergius dropped into his ordinary gait; then coming to a halt, he asked: "Tell me to whom else you have related this pretty tale of the two fathers?"

His look and tone were exceedingly grave, and she studied his face, and questioned him in turn: "You are very serious—why?"

"Oh, I was wondering if the story is public?" More plainly, he was wondering whence Demedes had his information.

"I suppose it is generally known; at least I cannot see why it should not be."

The few words swept the last doubt from his mind; yet she continued: "My father Uel is well known to the merchants of the city. I have heard him say gratefully that since the coming of the Prince of India his business has greatly increased. He used to deal in many kinds of goods; now he sells nothing but precious stones. His patrons are not alone the nobles of Byzantium; traders over in Galata buy of him for the western markets, especially Italy and France. My other father, the Prince, is an expert in such things, and does not disdain to help Uel with advice."

Lael might have added that the Prince, in course of his travels, had ascertained the conveniency of jewels as a currency familiar and acceptable to almost every people, and always kept a store of them by him, from which he frequently replenished his protege's stock, allowing him the profits. That she did not make this further disclosure was probably due to ignorance of the circumstances; in other words, her artlessness was extreme enough to render her a dangerous confidant, and both her fathers were aware of it.

"Everybody in the bazaar is friendly to my father Uel, and the Prince visits him there, going in state; and he and his train are an attraction"—thus Lael proceeded. "On his departure, the questions about him are countless, and Uel holds nothing back. Indeed, it is more than likely he has put the whole mart and city in possession of the history of my adoption by the Prince."

In front of the palace she broke off abruptly: "But see! The landing is covered with men and women. Let us hurry."

Presently they issued from the garden, and were permitted to join the Princess.

CHAPTER XIII
THE HAMARI TURNS BOATMAN

The boatmen had taken up some of the marble blocks of the landing, and planting long oars upright in the ground, and fixing other oars crosswise on them, constructed a secure frame covered with fresh sail-cloth. From their vessels they had also brought material for a dais under the shelter thus improvised; another sail for carpet, and a chair on the dais completed the stand whence the Princess was to view and judge the race.

A way was opened for her through the throng, and with her attendants, she passed to the stand; and as she went, all the women near reached out their hands and reverently touched the skirt of her gown—so did their love for her trench on adoration.

The shore from the stand to the town, and from the stand again around the promontory on the south, was thronged with spectators, while every vantage point fairly in view was occupied by them; even the ships were pressed into the service; and somehow the air over and about the bay seemed to give back and tremble with the eagerness of interest everywhere discernible.

Between Fanar, the last northern point of lookout over the Black Sea, and Galata, down on the Golden Horn, there are about thirty hamlets, villages and cities specking the European shore of the Bosphorus. Each of them has its settlement of fishermen. Aside from a voluminous net, the prime necessity for successful pursuit of the ancient and honorable calling is a boat. Like most things of use amongst men, the vessel of preferred model here came of evolution. The modern tourist may yet see its kind drawn up at every landing he passes.

Proper handling, inclusive of running out and hauling in the seine, demanded a skilful crew of at least five men; and as whole lives were devoted to rowing, the proficiency finally attained in it can be fancied. It was only natural, therefore, that the thirty communities should each insist upon having the crew of greatest excellence—the crew which could outrow any other five on the Bosphorus; and as every Byzantine Greek was a passionate gambler, the wagers were without end. Vauntings of the sort, like the Black Sea birds of unresting wings, went up and down the famous waterway.

At long intervals occasions presented for the proof of these men of pride; after which, for a period there was an admitted champion crew, and a consequent hush of the babble and brawl.

In determining to conclude the fete with a boat-race open to all Greek comers from the capital to the Cyanian rocks, the Princess Irene did more than secure a desirable climax; unconsciously, perhaps, she hit upon the measure most certain to bring peace to the thirty villages.

She imposed but two conditions on the competitors—they should be fishermen and Greeks.

The interval between the announcement of the race and the day set for it had been filled with boasting, from which one would have supposed the bay of Therapia at the hour of starting would be too contracted to hold the adversaries. When the hour came there were six crews present actually prepared to contest for the prize—a tall ebony crucifix, with a gilded image, to be displayed of holidays on the winning prow. The shrinkage told the usual tale of courage oozed out. There was of course no end of explanation.

About three o'clock, the six boats, each with a crew of five men, were held in front of the Princess' stand, representative of as many towns. Their prows were decorated with banderoles large enough to be easily distinguished at a distance—one yellow, chosen for Yenimahale; one blue, for Buyukdere; one white, for Therapia; one red, for Stenia; one green, for Balta-Liman; and one half white and half scarlet, for Bebek. The crews were in their seats—fellows with knotted arms bare to the shoulder; white shirts under jackets the color of the flags, trousers in width like petticoats. The feet were uncovered that, while the pull was in delivery, they might the better clinch the cleats across the bottom of the boat.

The fresh black paint with which the vessels had been smeared from end to end on the outside was stoned smoothly down until it glistened like varnish. Inside there was not a superfluity to be seen of the weight of a feather.

The contestants knew every point of advantage, and, not less clearly, they were there to win or be beaten doing their best. They were cool and quiet; much more so, indeed, than the respective clansmen and clanswomen.

From these near objects of interest, the Princess directed a glance over the spreading field of dimpled water to a galley moored under a wooded point across on the Asiatic shore. The point is now crowned with the graceful but neglected Kiosk of the Viceroy of Egypt. That galley was the thither terminus of the race course, and the winners turning it, and coming back to the place of starting, must row in all about three miles.

A little to the right of the Princess' stand stood a pole of height to be seen by the multitude as well as the rival oarsmen, and a rope for hoisting a white flag to the top connected it with the chair on the dais. At the appearance of the flag the boats were to start; while it was flying, the race was on.

And now the competitors are in position by lot from right to left. On bay and shore the shouting is sunk to a murmur. A moment more—but in that critical period an interruption occurred.

A yell from a number of voices in sharpest unison drew attention to the point of land jutting into the water on the north side not inaptly called the toe of Therapia, and a boat, turning the point, bore down with speed toward the sail-covered stand. There were four rowers in it; yet its glossy sides and air of trimness were significant of a seventh competitor for some reason behind time. The black flag at the prow and the black uniform of the oarsmen confirmed the idea. The hand of the Princess was on the signal rope; but she paused.

As the boat-hook of the newcomers fell on the edge of the landing, one of them dropped upon his knees, crying: "Grace, O Princess! Grace, and a little time!"

The four were swarthy men, and, unlike the Greeks they were seeking to oppose, their swart was a peculiarity of birth, a racial sign. Recognizing them, the spectators near by shouted: "Gypsies! Gypsies!" and the jeer passed from mouth to mouth far as the bridge over the creek at the corner of the bay; yet it was not ill-natured. That these unbelievers of unknown origin, separatists like the Jews, could offer serious opposition to the chosen of the towns was ridiculous. Since they excited no apprehension, their welcome was general.

"Why the need of grace? Who are you?" the Princess replied, gravely.

"We are from the valley by Buyukdere," the man returned.

"Are you fishermen?"

"Judged by our catches the year through, and the prices we get in the market, O Princess, it is not boasting to say our betters cannot be found, though you search both shores between Fanar and the Isles of the Princes."

This was too much for the bystanders. The presence they were in was not sufficient to restrain an outburst of derision.

"But the conditions of the race shut you out. You are not Greeks," the judge continued.

"Nay, Princess, that is according to the ground of judgment. If it please you to decide by birth and residence rather than ancestry, then are we to be preferred over many of the nobles who go in and out of His Majesty's gates unchallenged. Has not the sweet water that comes down from the hills seeking the sea through our meadow furnished drink for our fathers hundreds of years? And as it knew them, it knows us."

"Well answered, I must admit. Now, my friend, do as wisely with what I ask next, and you shall have a place. Say you come out winners, what will you do with the prize? I have heard you are not Christians."

The man raised his face the first time.

"Not Christians! Were the charge true, then, argument being for the hearing, I would say the matter of religion is not among the conditions. But I am a petitioner, not lawyer, and to my rude thinking it is better that I hold on as I began. Trust us, O Princess! There is a plane tree, wondrous old, and with seven twin trunks, standing before our tents, and in it there is a hollow which shelters securely as a house. Attend me now, I pray. If happily we win, we will convert the tree into a cathedral, and build an altar in it, and set the prize above the altar in such style that all who love the handiworks of nature better than the artfulness of men may come and worship there reverently as in the holiest of houses, Sancta Sophia not excepted."

"I will trust you. With such a promise overheard by so many of this concourse, to refuse you a part in the race were a shame to the Immaculate Mother. But how is it you are but four?"

"We were five, O Princess; now one is sick. It was at his bidding we come; he thought of the hundreds of oarsmen who would be here one at least could be induced to share our fortune."

"You have leave to try them."

The man arose, and looked at the bystanders, but they turned away.

"A hundred noumiae for two willing hands!" he shouted.

There was no reply. "If not for the money, then in honor of the noble lady who has feasted you and your wives and children."

A voice answered out of the throng: "Here am I!" and presently the hamari appeared with the bear behind him.

"Here," he said, "take care of Joqard for me. I will row in the sick man's place, and"—

The remainder of the sentence was lost in an outburst of gibing—and laughter. Finally the Princess asked the rowers if they were satisfied with the volunteer.

They surveyed him doubtfully.

"Art thou an oarsman?" one of them asked.

"There is not a better on the Bosphorus. And I will prove it. Here, some of you—take the beast off my hands. Fear not, friend, Joqard's worst growl is inoffensive as thunder without lightning. That's a good man."

And with the words the hamari released the leading strap, sprang into the boat, and without giving time for protest or remonstrance, threw off his jacket and sandals, tucked up his shirt-sleeves, and dropped into the vacant fifth seat. The dexterity with which he then unshipped the oars and took them in hand measurably quieted the associates thus audaciously adopted; his action was a kind of certificate that the right man had been sent them.

"Believe in me," he said, in a low tone. "I have the two qualities which will bring us home winners—skill and endurance." Then he spoke to the Princess: "Noble lady, have I your consent to make a proclamation?"

The manner of the request was singularly deferential. Sergius observed the change, and took a closer look at him while the Princess was giving the permission.

Standing upon the seat, the hamari raised his voice: "Ho, here—there—every one!" and drawing a purse from his bosom, he waved it overhead, with a louder shout, "See!—a hundred noumiae, and not all copper either. Piece against piece weighed or counted, I put them in wager! Speak one or all. Who dares the chance?"

Takers of the offer not appearing on the shore, he shook the purse at his competitors.

"If we are not Christians," he said to them, "we are oarsmen and not afraid. See—I stake this purse—if you win, it is yours."

They only gaped at him.

He put the purse back slowly, and recounting the several towns of his opponents by their proper names in Greek, he cried: "Buyukdere, Therapia, Stenia, Bebek, Balta-Liman, Yenimahale—your women will sing you low to-night!" Then to the Princess: "Allow us now to take our place seventh on the left."

The bystanders were in a maze. Had they been served with a mess of brag, or was the fellow really capable? One thing was clear—the interest in the race had taken a rise perceptible in the judge's stand not less than on the crowded shore.

The four Gypsies, on their part, were content with the volunteer. In fact, they were more than satisfied when he said to them, as their vessel turned into position:

"Now, comrades, be governed by me; and besides the prize, if we win, you shall have my purse to divide amongst you man and man. Is it agreed?" And they answered, foreman and all, yes. "Very well," he returned. "Do you watch, and get the time and force from me. Now for the signal."

The Princess sent the starting flag to the top of the pole, and the boats were off together. A great shout went up from the spectators—a shout of men mingled with the screams of women to whom a hurrah or cheer of any kind appears impossible.

To warm the blood, there is nothing after all like the plaudits of a multitude looking on and mightily concerned. This was now noticeable. The eyes of all the rowers enlarged; their teeth set hard; the arteries of the neck swelled; and even in their tension the muscles of the arms quivered.

A much better arrangement would have been to allow the passage of the racers broadside to the shore; for then the shiftings of position, and the strategies resorted to would have been plain to the beholders; as it was, each foreshortened vessel soon became to them a black body, with but a man and one pair of oars in motion; and sometimes provokingly indistinguishable, the banderoles blew backward squarely in a line with the direction of the movement. Then the friends on land gave over exercising their throats; finally drawn down to the water's edge, and pressing on each other, they steadied and welded into a mass, like a wall.

Once there was a general shout. Gradually the boats had lost the formation of the start, and falling in behind each other, assumed an order comparable to a string. While this change was going on, a breeze unusually strong blew from the south, bringing every flag into view at the same time: when it was perceived that the red was in the lead. Forthwith the clansmen of Stenia united in a triumphant yell, followed immediately, however, by another yet louder. It was discovered, thanks to the same breeze, that the black banderole of the Gypsies was the last of the seven. Then even those who had been most impressed by the bravado of the hamari, surrendered themselves to laughter and sarcasm.

"See the infidels!" "They had better be at home taking care of their kettles and goats!" "Turn the seven twins into a cathedral, will they? The devil will turn them into porpoises first!" "Where is the hamari now—where? By St.

Michael, the father of fishermen, he is finding what it is to have more noumiae than brains! Ha, ha, ha!"

Nevertheless the coolest of the thirty-five men then scudding the slippery waterway was the hamari—he had started the coolest—he was the coolest now.

For a half mile he allowed his crew to do their best, and with them he had done his best. The effort sufficed to carry them to the front, where he next satisfied himself they could stay, if they had the endurance. He called to them:

"Well done, comrades! The prize and the money are yours! But ease up a little. Let them pass. We will catch them again at the turn. Keep your eyes on me."

Insensibly he lessened the dip and reach of his oars; at last, as the thousands on the Therapian shore would have had it, the Gypsy racer was the hinderling of the pack. Afterwards there were but trifling changes of position until the terminal galley was reached.

By a rule of the race, the contestants were required to turn the galley, keeping it on the right; and it was a great advantage to be a clear first there, since the fortunate party could then make the round unhindered and in the least space. The struggle for the point began quite a quarter of a mile away. Each crew applied itself to quickening the speed—every oar dipped deeper, and swept a wider span;—on a little, and the keepers of the galley could hear the half groan, half grunt with which the coming toilers relieved the extra exertion now demanded of them;—yet later, they saw them spring to their feet, reach far back, and finish the long deep draw by falling, or rather toppling backward to their seats.

Only the hamari eschewed the resort for the present. He cast a look forward, and said quickly: "Attend, comrades!" Thereupon he added weight to his left delivery, altering the course to an angle which, if pursued, must widen the circle around the galley instead of contracting it.

On nearing the goal the rush of the boats grew fiercer; each foreman, considering it honor lost, if not a fatal mischance, did he fail to be first at the turning-point, persisted in driving straight forward—a madness which the furious yelling of the people on the marker's deck intensified. This was exactly what the hamari had foreseen. When the turn began five of the opposing vessels ran into each other. The boil and splash of water, breaking of oars, splintering of boatsides; the infuriate cries, oaths, and blind striving of the rowers, some intent on getting through at all hazards, some turned combatants, striking or parrying with their heavy oaken blades; the sound of blows on breaking heads; plunges into the foaming brine; blood trickling down faces and necks, and reddening naked arms—such was the catastrophe seen in its details from the overhanging gunwale of the galley. And while it went on, the worse than confused mass drifted away from the ship's side, leaving a clear space through which, with the first shout heard from him during the race, the hamari urged his crew, and rounded the goal.

On the far Therapian shore the multitude were silent. They could dimly see every incident at the turn—the collision, fighting, and manifold mishaps, and the confounding of the banderoles. Then the Stenia colors flashed round the galley, with the black behind it a close second.

"Is that the hamari's boat next the leader?"

Thus the Princess, and upon the answer, she added: "It looks as if the Holy One might find servants among the irreclaimables in the valley."

Had the Gypsies at last a partisan?

The two rivals were now clear of the galley. For a time there was but one cry heard—"Stenia! Stenia!" The five oarsmen of that charming town had been carefully selected; they were vigorous, skilful, and had a chief well-balanced in judgment. The race seemed theirs. Suddenly—it was when the homestretch was about half covered—the black flag rushed past them.

Then the life went out of the multitude. "St. Peter is dead!" they cried—"St. Peter is dead! It is nothing to be a Greek now!" and they hung their heads, refusing to be comforted.

The Gypsies came in first; and amidst the profoundest silence, they dropped their oars with a triumphant crash on the marble revetment. The hamari wiped the sweat from his face, and put on his jacket and sandals; pausing then to toss his purse to the foreman, and say: "Take it in welcome, my friends. I am content with my share of the victory," he stepped ashore. In front of the judge's stand, he knelt, and said: "Should there be a dispute touching the prize, O Princess, be a witness unto thyself. Thine eyes have seen the going and the coming; and if the world belie thee not—sometimes it can be too friendly—thou art fair, just and fearless."

On foot again, his courtierly manner vanished in a twinkling.

"Joqard, Joqard? Where are you?"

Some one answered: "Here he is."

"Bring him quickly. For Joqard is an example to men—he is honest, and tells no lies. He has made much money, and allowed me to keep it all, and spend it on myself. Women are jealous of him, but with reason—he is lovely enough to have been a love of Solomon's; his teeth are as pearls of great price; his lips scarlet as a bride's; his voice is the voice of a nightingale

- 25 -

singing to the full moon from an acacia tree fronded last night; in motion, he is now a running wave, now a blossom on a swaying branch, now a girl dancing before a king—all the graces are his. Yes, bring me Joqard, and keep the world; without him, it is nothing to me."

While speaking, from a jacket pocket he brought out the fan Lael had thrown him from the portico, and used it somewhat ostentatiously to cool himself. The Princess and her attendants laughed heartily. Sergius, however, watched the man with a scarcely defined feeling that he had seen him. But where? And he was serious because he could not answer.

Taking the leading strap, when Joqard was brought, the hamari scrupled not to give the brute a hearty cuff, whereat the fishermen shook the sails of the pavilion with laughter; then, standing Joqard up, he placed one of the huge paws on his arm, and, with the mincing step of a lady's page, they disappeared.

CHAPTER XIV
THE PRINCESS HAS A CREED

"I shall ask you, Sergius, to return to the city to-night, for inquiry about the fete will be lively tomorrow in the holy houses. And if you have the disposition to defend me"—

"You doubt me, O Princess?"

"No."

"O little mother, let me once for all be admitted to your confidence, that in talking to me there may never be a question of my loyalty."

This, with what follows, was part of a conversation between the Princess Irene and Sergius of occurrence the evening of the fete in the court heretofore described, being that to which she retired to read the letter of introduction brought her by the young monk from Father Hilarion.

From an apartment adjoining, the voices of her attendants were occasionally heard blent with the monotonous tinkle of water overflowing the bowls of the fountain. In the shadowy depths of the opening above the court the stars might have been seen had not a number of lamps suspended from a silken cord stretched from wall to wall flooded the marble enclosure with their nearer light.

There was a color, so to speak, in the declaration addressed to her—a warmth and earnestness—which drew a serious look from the Princess— the look, in a word, with which a woman admits a fear lest the man speaking to her may be a lover.

To say of her who habitually discouraged the tender passion, and the thought of it, that she moved in an atmosphere charged with attractions irresistible to the other sex sounds strangely: yet it was true; and as a consequence she had grown miraculously quick with respect to appearances.

However, she now dismissed the suspicion, and replied:

"I believe you, Sergius, I believe you. The Holy Virgin sees how completely and gladly."

She went on presently, a tremulous light in her eyes making him think of tears. "You call me little mother. There are some who might laugh, did they hear you, yet I agree to the term. It implies a relation of trust without embarrassment, and a promise of mutual faithfulness warranting me to call you in return, Sergius, and sometimes 'dear Sergius.' ... Yes, I think it better that you go back immediately. The Hegumen will want to speak to you in the morning about what you have seen and heard to-day. My boatmen can take you down, and arrived there, they will stay the night. My house is always open to them."

After telling her how glad he was for the permission to address her in a style usual in his country, he moved to depart, but she detained him.

"Stay a moment. To-day I had not time to deal as I wished with the charges the Hegumen prefers against me. You remember I promised to speak to you about them frankly, and I think it better to do so now; for with my confessions always present you cannot be surprised by misrepresentations, nor can doubt take hold of you so readily. You shall go hence possessed of every circumstance essential to judge how guilty I am."

"They must do more than talk," the monk returned, with emphasis.

"Beware, Sergius! Do not provoke them into argument—or if you must talk, stop when you have set them to talking. The listener is he who can best be wise as a serpent.... And now, dear friend, lend me your good sense. Thanks to the generosity of a kinsman, I am mistress of a residence in the city and this palace; and it is mine to choose between them. How healthful and charming life is with surroundings like these—here, the gardens; yonder, the verdurous hills; and there, before my door, a channel of the seas always borrowing from the sky, never deserted by men. Guilt seeks exclusion, does it not? Well, whether you come in the day or the night, my gate is open; nor have I a warder other than Lysander; and his javelin is but a staff with which to steady his failing steps. There are no prohibitions shutting me in. Christian, Turk, Gypsy—the world in fact—is welcome to see what all I have; and as to danger, I am defended better than with guards. I strive diligently to love my neighbors as I love myself, and they know it.... Coming nearer the accusation now. I find here a freedom which not a religious house in the city can give me, nor one on the Isles, not Halki itself. Here I am never disturbed by sectaries or partisans; the Greek and the Latin wrangle before the Emperor and at the altars; but they spare me in this beloved retiracy. Freedom! Ah, yes, I find it in this retreat—this escape from temptations—freedom to work and sleep, and praise God as seems best to me—freedom to be myself in defiance of deplorable social customs—and there is no guilt in it.... Coming still nearer the very charge, hear, O Sergius, and I will tell you of the brass on my gate, and why I suffer it to stay there; since you, with your partialities, account it a witness against me, it is in likelihood the foundation of the calumny associating me with the Turk. Let me ask first, did the Hegumen mention the name of one such associate?"

"No."

The Princess with difficulty repressed her feelings.

"Bear with me a moment," she said; "you cannot know the self-mastery I require to thus defend myself. Can I ever again be confident of my judgment? How doubts and fears will beset me when hereafter upon my own responsibility I choose a course, whatever the affair! Ah, God, whom I have sought to make my reliance, seems so far away! It will be for Him in the great day to declare if my purpose in living here be not escape from guiltiness in thought, from wrong and temptation, from taint to character. For further security, I keep myself surrounded with good women, and from the beginning took the public into confidence, giving it privileges, and inviting it to a study of my daily life. And this is the outcome! ... I will proceed now. The plate on the gate is a safeguard"—

"Then Mahommed has visited you?"

The slightest discernible pallor overspread her face.

"Does it surprise you so much? ... This is the way it came about. You remember our stay at the White Castle, and doubtless you remember the knight in armor who received us at the landing—a gallant, fair-speaking, chivalrous person whom we supposed the Governor, and who prevailed upon us to become his guests while the storm endured. You recollect him?"

"Yes. He impressed me greatly."

"Well, let me now bring up an incident not in your knowledge. The eunuch in whose care I was placed for the time with Lael, daughter of the Prince of India, as my companion, to afford us agreeable diversion, obtained my consent to introduce an Arab story-teller of great repute among the tribes of the desert and other Eastern people. He gave us the name of the man— Sheik Aboo-Obeidah. The Sheik proved worthy his fame. So entertaining was he, in fact, I invited him here, and he came."

"Did I understand you to say the entertainment took place in Lael's presence?"

"She was my companion throughout."

"Let us be thankful, little mother."

"Ay, Sergius, and that I have witnesses down to the last incident. You may have heard how the Emperor and his court did me the high honor of a visit in state."

"The visit was notorious."

"Well, while the royal company were at table, Lysander appeared and announced Aboo-Obeidah, and, by permission of the Emperor, the story-teller was admitted, and remained during the repast. Now I come to the surprising event—Aboo-Obeidah was Mahommed!"

"Prince Mahommed—son of the terrible Amurath?" exclaimed Sergius. "How did you know him?"

"By the brass plate. When he went to his boat, he stopped and nailed the plate to the pillar. I went to look at it, and not understanding the inscription, sent to town for a Turk who enlightened me."

"Then the hamari was not gasconading?"

"What did he say?"

"He confirmed your Turk."

She gazed awhile at the overflowing of the fountain, giving a thought perhaps to the masquerader and his description of himself what time he was alone with her on the portico; presently she resumed:

"One word more now, and I dismiss the brass plate.... I cannot blind myself, dear friend, to the condition of my kinsman's empire. It creeps in closer and closer to the walls of Constantinople. Presently there will be nothing of it left save the little the gates of the capital can keep. The peace we have is by the grace of an unbeliever too old for another great military enterprise; and when it breaks, then, O Sergius, yon safeguard may be for others besides myself—for many others—farmers, fishermen and townspeople caught in the storm. Say such anticipation followed you, Sergius—what would you do with the plate?"

"What would I do with it? O little mother, I too should take counsel of my fears."

"You approve my keeping it where it is, then? Thank you.... What remains for explanation? Ah, yes—my heresy. That you shall dispose of yourself. Remain here a moment."

She arose, and passing through a doorway heavily draped with cloth, left him to the entertainment of the fountain. Returning soon, she placed a roll of paper in his hand.

"There," she said, "is the creed which your Hegumen makes such a sin. It may be heresy; yet, God helping me, and Christ and the Holy Mother lending their awful help, I dare die for it. Take it, dear Sergius. You will find it simple—nine words in all—and take this cover for it."

He wrapped the parcel in the white silken cover she gave him, making mental comparison, nevertheless, with the old Nicaean ordinances.

"Only nine words—O little mother!"

"Nine," she returned.

"They should be of gold."

"I leave them to speak for themselves."

"Shall I return the paper?"

"No, it is a copy.... But it is time you were going. Fortunately the night is pleasant and starlit; and if you are tired, the speeding of the boat will rest you. Let me have an opinion of the creed at your leisure."

They bade each other good-night.

* * * * *

About eight o'clock next morning Sergius awoke. He had dropped on his cot undressed, and slept the sweet sleep of healthful youth; now, glancing about, he thought of the yesterday and the spacious garden, of the palace in the garden, of the Princess Irene, and of the conversation she held with him in the bright inner court. And the creed of nine words! He felt for it, and found it safe. Then his thought flew to Lael. She had exonerated herself. Demedes was a liar—Demedes, the presumptuous knave! He was to have been at the fete, but had not dared go. There was a limit to his audacity; and in great thankfulness for the discovery, Sergius tossed an arm over the edge of the narrow cot, and struck the stool, his solitary item of furniture. He raised his head, and looked at the stool, wondering how it came there so close to his cot. What was that he saw? A fan?—And in his chamber? Somebody had brought it in. He examined it cautiously. Whose was it? Whose could it be?—How!—No—but it *was* the very fan he had seen Lael toss to the hamari from the portico! And the hamari?

A bit of folded paper on the settle attracted his attention. He snatched it up, opened, and read it, and while he read his brows knit, his eyes opened to their full.

"PATIENCE—COURAGE—JUDGMENT!

"Thou art better apprised of the meaning of the motto than thou wert yesterday.

"Thy seat in the Academy is still reserved for thee.

"Thou mayst find the fan of the Princess of India useful; with me it is embalmed in sentiment.

"Be wise. THE HAMARI."

He read the scrap twice, the second time slowly; then it fell rustling to the floor, while he clasped his hands and looked to Heaven. A murmur was all he could accomplish.

Afterwards, prostrate on the cot, his face to the wall, he debated with himself, and concluded:

"The Greek is capable of any villany he sets about—of abduction and murder—and now indeed must Lael beware!"

CHAPTER XV
THE PRINCE OF INDIA PREACHES GOD TO THE GREEKS

We will now take the liberty of reopening the audience chamber of the palace of Blacherne, presuming the reader holds it in recollection. It is the day when, by special appointment, the Prince of India appears before the Emperor Constantine to present his idea of a basis for Universal Religious Union. The hour is exactly noon.

A report of the Prince's former audience with His Majesty had awakened general curiosity to see the stranger and hear his discourse. This was particularly the feeling in spiritual circles; by which term the most influential makers of public opinion are meant. A sharp though decorous rivalry for invitations to be present on the occasion ensued.

The Emperor, in robes varied but little from those he wore the day of the Prince's first audience, occupied the throne on the dais. On both sides of him the company sat in a semicircular arrangement which left them all facing the door of the main entrance, and permitted the placement of a table in a central position under every eye.

The appearance of the assemblage would have disappointed the reader; for while the court was numerously represented, with every functionary in his utmost splendor of decoration, it was outnumbered by the brethren of the Holy Orders, whose gowns, for the most part of gray and black material unrelieved by gayety in color, imparted a sombreness to the scene which the ample light of the chamber could not entirely dissipate, assisted though it was by refractions in plenitude from heads bald and heads merely tonsured.

It should be observed now that besides a very striking exterior, the Emperor fancied he discerned in the Prince of India an idea enriched by an extraordinary experience. At loss to make him out, impressed, not unpleasantly, with the mystery the stranger had managed, as usual, to leave behind him, His Majesty had looked forward to this second appearance with interest, and turned it over with a view to squeezing out all of profit there might be in it. Why not, he asked himself, make use of the opportunity to bring the chiefs of the religious factions once more together? The explosive tendency which it seemed impossible for them to leave in their cells with their old dalmatics had made it politic to keep them apart widely and often as circumstances would permit; here, however, he thought the danger might be averted, since they would attend as auditors from whom speech or even the asking a question would be out of order unless by permission. The imperial presence, it was also judged, would restrain the boldest of them from resolving himself into a disputant.

The arrangement of the chamber for the audience had been a knotty problem to our venerable acquaintance, the Dean; but at last he submitted his plan, giving every invitee a place by ticket; the Emperor, however, blotted it out mercilessly. "Ah, my old friend," he said, with a smile which assuaged the pang of disapproval, "you have loaded yourself with unnecessary trouble. There was never a mass performed with stricter observance of propriety than we will now have. Fix the chairs thus"—and with a finger-sweep he described a semicircle—"here the table for the Prince. Having notified me of his intention to read from some ancient books, he must have a table—and let there be no reserved seat, except one for the Patriarch. Set a sedilium, high and well clothed, for him here on my right—and forget not a stool for his feet; for now to the bitterness of controversy long continued he has added a constriction of the lungs, and together they are grievous to old age."

"And Scholarius?"

"Scholarius is an orator; some say he is a prophet; I know he is not an official; so of the seats vacant when he arrives, let him choose for himself."

The company began coming early. Every Churchman of prominence in the city was in attendance. The reception was unusually ceremonious. When the bustle was over, and His Majesty at ease, the pages having arranged the folds of his embroidered vestments, he rested his hand lightly on the golden cone of the right arm of the throne, and surveyed the audience with a quiet assurance becoming his birth in the purple, looking first to the Patriarch, and bowing to him, and receiving a salute in return. To the others on the right he glanced next, with a gracious bend of the head, and then to those on the left. In. the latter quarter he recognized Scholarius, and covertly smiled; if Gregory had taken seat on the left, Scholarius would certainly have crossed to the right. There was no such thing as compromise in his intolerant nature.

One further look the Emperor gave to where, near the door, a group of women was standing, in attendance evidently upon the Princess Irene, who was the only one of them seated. Their heads were covered by veils which had the appearance of finely woven silver. This jealous precaution, of course, cut off recognition; nevertheless such of the audience as had the temerity to cast their eyes at the fair array were consoled by a view of jewelled hands, bare arms inimitably round and graceful, and figures in drapery of delicate colors, and of designs to tempt the imagination without offence to modesty—a respect in which the Greek costume has never been excelled. The Emperor recognized the Princess, and slightly inclined his head to her. He then spoke to the Dean:

"Wait on the Prince of India, and if he is prepared, accompany him hither."

Passing out a side door, the master of ceremonies presently reappeared with Nilo in guidance. The black giant was as usual barbarously magnificent in attire; and staring at him, the company did not observe the burden he brought in, and laid on the table. He retired immediately; then they looked, and saw a heap of books and MSS. in rolls left behind him—quaint, curious volumes, so to speak, yellow with age and exposure, and suggestive of strange countries, and a wisdom new, if not of more than golden worth. And they continued to gaze and wonder at them, giving warrant to the intelligent forethought of the Prince of India which sent Nilo in advance of his own entry.

Again the door was thrown open, and this time the Dean ushered the Prince into the chamber, and conducted him toward the dais. Thrice the foreigner prostrated himself; the last time within easy speaking distance of His Majesty, who silently agreed with the observant lookers-on, that he had never seen the salutations better executed.

"Rise, Prince of India," the Emperor said, blandly, and well pleased.

The Prince arose, and stood before him, his eyes downcast, his hands upon his breast—suppliancy in excellent pantomime.

"Be not surprised, Prince of India, at the assemblage you behold." Thus His Majesty proceeded. "Its presence is due, I declare to you, not so much to design of mine as to the report the city has had of your former audience, and the theme of which you then promised to discourse." Without apparently noticing the low reverence in acknowledgment of the compliment, he addressed himself to the body of listeners. "I regard it courtesy to our noble Indian guest to advise you, my Lords of the Court, and you, devotees of Christ and the Father, whose prayers are now the chief stay of my empire, that he is present by my appointment. On a previous occasion, he interested us—I speak of many of my very honorable assistants in Government—he interested us, I say, with an account of his resignation of the Kingship in his country, moved by a desire to surrender himself exclusively to study of religion. Under my urgency, he bravely declared he was neither Jew, Moslem, Hindoo, Buddhist nor Christian; that his travels and investigation had led him to a faith which he summed up by pronouncing the most holy name of God; giving us to understand he meant the God to whom our hearts have long been delivered. He also referred to the denominations into which believers are divided, and said his one motive in life was the bringing them together in united brotherhood; and as I cannot imagine a result more desirable, provided its basis obtain the sanction of our conscience, I will now ask him to proceed, if it be his pleasure, and speak to us freely."

Again the visitor prostrated himself in his best oriental manner; after which, moving backward, he went to the table and took a few minutes arranging the books and rolls. The spectators availed themselves of the opportunity to gratify their curiosity well as they could from mere inspection of the man; and as the liberty was within his anticipations, it gave him but slight concern.

We about know how he appeared to them. We remember his figure, low, slightly stooped, and deficiently slender;—we remember the thin yet healthful looking face, even rosy of cheek;—we can see him in his pointed red slippers, his ample trousers of glossy white satin, his long black gown, relieved at the collar and cuffs with fine laces, his hair fallen on his shoulders, beard overflowing his breast;—we can even see the fingers, transparent, singularly flexible in operation, turning leaves, running down pages and smoothing them out, and placing this roll or that book as convenience required, all so lithe, swift, certain, they in a manner exposed the mind which controlled them. At length, the preliminaries finished, the Prince raised his eyes, and turned them slowly about—those large, deep, searching eyes—wells from which, without discoverable effort, he drew magnetism at his pleasure.

He began simply, his voice distinct, and cast to make itself heard, and not more.

"This"—his second finger was on a page of the large volume heretofore described—"this is the Bible, the most Holy of Bibles. I call it the rock on which your faith and mine are castled." There was a stretching of necks to see, and he did not allow the sensation to pass.

"And more—it is one of the fifty copies of the Bible translated by order of the first Constantine, under supervision of his minister Eusebius, well known to you for piety and learning."

It seemed at first every Churchman was on his feet, but directly the Emperor observed Scholarius and the Patriarch seated, the latter diligently crossing himself. The excitement can be readily comprehended by considering the assemblage and its composition of zealots and relic-worshippers, and that, while the tradition respecting the fifty copies was familiar, not a man there could have truly declared he had ever seen one of them—so had they disappeared from the earth.

"These are Bibles, also," the speaker resumed, upon the restoration of order—"Bibles sacred to those unto whom they were given as that imperishable monument to Moses and David is to us; for they too are Revelations from God—ay, the very same God! This is the *Koran*—and these, the *Kings* of the Chinese—and these, the *Avesta* of the Magians of Persia—and these, the *Sutras* well preserved of Buddha—and these, the *Vedas* of the patient Hindoos, my countrymen."

He carefully designated each book and roll by placing his finger on it.

"I thank Your Majesty for the gracious words of introduction you were pleased to give me. They set before my noble and most reverend auditors my history and the subject of my discourse; leaving me, without wrong to their understanding, or waste of time or words, to invite them to think of the years it took to fit myself to read these Books—for so I will term them—years spent among the peoples to whom they are divine. And when that thought is in mind, stored there past loss, they will understand what I mean by Religion, and the methods I adopted and pursued for its study. Then also the value of the assertions I make can be intelligently weighed.... This first—Have not all men hands and eyes? We may not be able to read the future in our palms; but there is no excuse for us if we do not at least see God in them. Similarity is law, and the law of Nature is the will of God. Keep the argument with you, O my Lord, for it is the earliest lesson I had from my travels.... Animals when called to, the caller being on a height over them, never look for him above the level of their eyes; even so some men are incapable of thinking of the mysteries hidden out of sight in the sky; but it is not so with all; and therein behold the partiality of God. The reason of the difference between the leaves of trees not of the same species, is the reason of the inequality of genius among races of men. The Infinite prefers variety because He is more certainly to be perceived in it. At this stop now, my Lord, mark the second lesson of my travels. God, wishing above all things to manifest Himself and His character to all humanity, made choice amongst the races, selecting those superior in genius, and intrusted them with special revelations; whence we have the two kinds of religion, natural and revealed. Seeing God in a stone, and worshipping it, is natural religion; the consciousness of God in the heart, an excitant of love and gratitude inexpressible except by prayer and hymns of praise—that, O my Lord, is the work and the proof of revealed religion.... I next submit the third of the lessons I have had; but, if I may have your attention to the distinction, it is remarkable as derived from my reading"—here he covered all the books on the table with a comprehensive gesture—"my reading more than my travels; and I call it the purest wisdom because it is not sentiment, at the same time that it is without so much as a strain of philosophy, being a fact clear as any fact deducible from history—yes, my Lord, clearer, more distinct, more positive, most undeniable—an incident of the love the Universal Maker has borne his noblest creatures from their first morning—a Godly incident which I have had from the study of these Bibles in comparison with each other. In brief, my Lord, a revelation not intended for me above the generality of men; nevertheless a revelation to me, since I went seeking it—or shall I call it a recompense for the crown and throne I voluntarily gave away?"

The feeling the Prince threw into these words took hold of his auditors. Not a few of them were struck with awe, somewhat as if he were a saint or prophet, or a missionary from the dead returned with secrets theretofore locked up fast in the grave. They waited for his next saying—his third lesson, as he termed it—with anxiety.

"The Holy Father of Light and Life," the speaker went on, after a pause referable to his consummate knowledge of men, "has sent His Spirit down to the world, not once merely, or unto one people, but repeatedly, in ages sometimes near together, sometimes wide apart, and to races diverse, yet in every instance remarkable for genius."

There was a murmur at this, but he gave it no time.

"Ask you now how I could identify the Spirit so as to be able to declare to you solemnly, as I do in fear of God, that in the several repeated appearances of which I speak it was the very same Spirit? How do you know the man you met at set of sun yesterday was the man you saluted and had salute from this morning? Well, I tell you the Father has given the Spirit features by which it may be known—features distinct as those of the neighbors nearest you there at your right and left hands. Wherever in my reading Holy Books, like these, I hear of a man, himself a shining example of righteousness, teaching God and the way to God, by those signs I say to my soul: 'Oh, the Spirit, the Spirit! Blessed is the man appointed to carry it about!'"

Again the murmur, but again he passed on.

"The Spirit dwelt in the Holy of Holies set apart for it in the Tabernacle; yet no man ever saw it there, a thing of sight. The soul is not to be seen; still less is the Spirit of the Most High; or if one did see it, its brightness would kill him. In great mercy, therefore, it has always come and done its good works in the world veiled; now in one form, now in another; at one time, a voice in the air; at another, a vision in sleep; at another, a burning bush; at another, an angel; at another, a descending dove"—

"Bethabara!" shouted a cowled brother, tossing both hands up.

"Be quiet!" the Patriarch ordered.

"Thus always when its errand was of quick despatch," the Prince continued. "But if its coming were for residence on earth, then its habit has been to adopt a man for its outward form, and enter into him, and speak by him; such was Moses, such Elijah, such were all the Prophets, and such"—he paused, then exclaimed shrilly—"such was Jesus Christ!"

In his study at home, the Prince had undoubtedly thought out his present delivery with the care due an occasion likely to be a turning-point in his projects, if not his life; and it must at that time have required of him a supreme effort of will to resolve upon this climax; as it was, he hesitated, and turned the hue of ashes; none the less his unknowing auditors renewed their plaudits. Even the Emperor nodded approvingly. None of them divined the cunning of the speaker; not one thought he was pledging himself by his applause to a kindly hearing of the next point in the speech.

"Now, my Lord, he who lives in a close vale shut in by great mountains, and goes not thence so much as to the top of one of the mountains, to him the vastness and beauty of the world beyond his pent sky-line shall be secret in his old age as they were when he was a child. He has denied himself to them. Like him is the man who, thinking to know God, spends his days reading one Holy Book. I care not if it be this one"—he laid his finger on the *Avesta*—"or this one"—in the same manner he signified the *Vedas*—"or this one"—touching the *Koran*—"or this one"—laying his whole hand tenderly palm down on the most Holy Bible. "He shall know God—yes, my Lord, but not all God has done for men.... I have been to the mountain's top; that is to say, I know these books, O reverend brethren, as you know the beads of your rosaries and what each bead stands for. They did not teach me all there is in the Infinite—I am in too much awe for such a folly of the tongue—yet through them I know His Spirit has dwelt on earth in men of different races and times; and whether the Spirit was the same Spirit, I fear not leaving you to judge. If we find in those bearing it about likenesses in ideas, aims, and methods—a Supreme God and an Evil One, a Heaven and a Hell, Sin and a Way to Salvation, a Soul immortal whether lost or saved—what are we to think? If then, besides these likenesses, we find the other signs of divine authority, acknowledged such from the beginning of the world—Mysteries of Birth, Sinlessness, Sacrifices, Miracles done—which of you will rise in his place, and rebuke me for saying there were Sons of God in Spirit before the Spirit descended upon Jesus Christ? Nevertheless, that is what I say."

Here the Prince bent over the table pretending to be in search of a page in the most Holy Book, while—if the expression be pardonable—he watched the audience with his ears. He heard the rustle as the men turned to each other in mute inquiry; he almost heard their question, though they but looked it; otherwise, if it had been dark, the silence would have been tomb-like. At length, raising his head, he beheld a tall, gaunt, sallow person, clad in a monkish gown of the coarsest gray wool, standing and looking at him; the eyes seemed two lights burning in darkened depths; the air was haughty and menacing; and altogether he could not avoid noticing the man. He waited, but the stranger silently kept his feet.

"Your Majesty," the Prince began again, perfectly composed, "these are but secondary matters; yet there is such light in them with respect to my main argument, that I think best to make them good by proofs, lest my reverend brethren dismiss me as an idler in words.... Behold the Bible of the Bodhisattwa"—he held up a roll of broad-leafed vellum, and turned it dextrously for better exhibition—"and hear, while I read from it, of a Birth, Life and Death which took place a thousand and twenty-seven years before Jesus Christ was born." And he read:

"'Strong and calm of purpose as the earth, pure in mind as the water-lily, her name figuratively assumed, Maya, she was in truth above comparison. On her in likeness as the heavenly queen the Spirit descended. A mother, but free from grief or pain, she was without deceit.'" The Prince stopped reading to ask: "Will not my Lord see in these words a Mary also 'blessed above other women'?" Then he read on: ...'"And now the queen Maya knew her time for the birth had come. It was the eighth day of the fourth moon, a serene and agreeable season. While she thus religiously observed the rules of a pure discipline, Bodhisattwa was born from her right side, come to deliver the world, constrained by great pity, without causing his mother pain or anguish.'" Again the Prince lifted his eyes from the roll. "What is this, my Lord, but an Incarnation? Hear now of the Child: ... 'As one born from recumbent space, and not through the gates of life, men indeed regarded his exceeding great glory, yet their sight remained uninjured; he allowed them to gaze, the brightness of his person concealed for a time, as when we look upon the moon in heaven. His body nevertheless was effulgent with light, and, like the sun which eclipses the shining of the lamp, so the true gold-like beauty of Bodhisattwa shone forth and was everywhere diffused. Upright and firm, and unconfused in mind, he deliberately took seven steps, the soles of his feet resting evenly upon the ground as he went, his footmarks remained bright as seven stars. Moving like the lion, king of beasts, and looking earnestly toward the four quarters, penetrating to the centre the principles of truth, he spoke thus with the fullest assurance: This birth is in the condition of Buddha; after this I have done with renewed birth; *now only am I born this once, for the purpose of saving all the world.*'" A third time the Prince stopped, and, throwing up his hand to command attention, he asked: "My Lord, who will say this was not also a Redeemer? See now what next ensued"—and he read on: "'And now from the midst of Heaven there descended two streams of pure water, one warm, the other cold, and baptized his head.'" Pausing again, the speaker searched the faces of his auditors on the right and left, while he exclaimed in magnetic repetition: "Baptism—*Baptism*—BAPTISM AND MIRACLE!"

Constantine sat, like the rest, his attention fixed; but the gray-clad monk still standing grimly raised a crucifix before him as if taking refuge behind it.

"My Lord is seeing the likenesses these things bear to the conception, birth and mission of Jesus Christ, the later Blessed One, who is nevertheless his first in love. He is comparing the incidents of the two Incarnations of the Spirit or Holy Ghost; he is asking himself: 'Can there have been several Sons of God?' and he is replying: 'That were indeed merciful—Blessed be God!'"

The Emperor made no sign one way or the other.

"Suffer me to help my Lord yet a little more," the Prince continued, apparently unobservant of the lowering face behind the crucifix. "He remembers angels came down the night of the nativity in the cave by Bethlehem; he cannot forget the song they sung to the shepherds. How like these honors to the Bodhisattwa!"—and he read from the roll: ... "'Meanwhile the Devas'—angels, if my Lord pleases—'the Devas in space, seizing their jewelled canopies, attending, raise in responsive harmony their heavenly songs to encourage him.' Nor was this all, my Lord," and he continued reading: "'On every hand the world was greatly shaken.... The minutest atoms of sandal perfume, and the hidden sweetness of precious lilies, floated on the air, and rose through space, and then commingling came back to earth.... All cruel and malevolent kinds of beings together conceived a loving heart; all diseases and afflictions amongst men, without a cure applied, of themselves were healed; the cries of beasts were hushed; the stagnant waters of the river courses flowed apace; no clouds gathered on the heavens, while angelic music, self-caused, was heard around.... So when Bodhisattwa was born, he came to remove the sorrows of all living things. Mara alone was grieved.' O my reverend brethren!" cried the Prince, fervently, "who was this Mara that he should not share in the rejoicing of all nature else? In Christian phrase, Satan, and Mara alone was grieved."

"Do the likenesses stop with the births, my brethren are now asking. Let us follow the Bodhisattwa. On reaching the stage of manhood, he also retired into the wilderness. 'The valley of the Se-na was level and full of fruit trees, with no noxious insects,' say these Scriptures: 'and there he dwelt under a sala tree. And he fasted nigh to death. The Devas offered him sweet dew, but he rejected it, and took but a grain of millet a day.' Now what think you of this as a parallel incident of his sojourn in the wilderness?" And he read: ... "'Mara Devaraga, enemy of religion, alone was grieved, and rejoiced not.

He had three daughters, mincingly beautiful, and of a pleasant countenance. With them, and all his retinue, he went to the grove of "fortunate rest," vowing the world should not find peace, and there'"—the Prince forsook the roll—"'and there he tempted Bodhisattwa, and menaced him, a legion of devils assisting.' The daughters, it is related, were changed to old women, and of the battle this is written: ... 'And now the demon host waxed fiercer, and added force to force, grasping at stones they could not lift, or lifting them they could not let them go; their flying spears stuck fast in space refusing to descend; the angry thunder-drops and mighty hail, with them, were changed into five-colored lotus flowers; while the foul poison of the dragon snakes was turned into spicy-breathing air'—and Mara fled, say the Scriptures, fled gnashing his teeth, while Bodhisattwa reposed peacefully under a fall of heavenly flowers." The Prince, looking about him after this, said calmly: "Now judge I by myself; not a heart here but hears in the intervals of its beating, the text: 'Then was Jesus led up by the Spirit into the wilderness to be tempted of the devil'—and that other text: 'Then the devil leaveth him, and behold, angels came and ministered unto him.' Verily, my Lord, was not the Spirit the same Spirit, and did it not in both incarnations take care of its own?"

Thereupon the Prince again sought for a page on the roll, watching the while with his ears, and the audience drew long breaths, and rested from their rigor of attention. Then also the Emperor spoke to the Prince.

"I pray you, Prince of India, take a little rest. Your labor is of the kind exhaustive to mind and body: and in thought of it, I ordered refreshments for you and these, my other guests. Is not this a good time to renew thyself?"

The Prince, rising from a low reverence, replied:

"Indeed Your Majesty has the kingly heart; but I pray you, in return, hear me until I have brought the parallel, my present point of argument, to an end; then I will most gladly avail myself of your great courtesy; after which—your patience, and the goodwill of these reverend fathers, holding on—I will resume and speedily finish my discourse."

"As you will. We are most interested. Or"—and the Emperor, glancing over toward the monk on his feet, said coldly: "Or, if my declaration does not fairly vouch the feeling of all present, those objecting have permission to retire upon the adjournment. We will hear you, Prince."

The ascetic answered by lifting his crucifix higher. Then, having found the page he wanted, the Prince, holding his finger upon it, proceeded:

"It would not become me, my Lord, to assume an appearance of teaching you and this audience, most learned in the Gospels, concerning them, especially the things said by the Blessed One of the later Incarnation, whom we call The Christ. We all know the Spirit for which he was both habitation and tongue, came down to save the world from sin and hell; we also know what he required for the salvation. So, even so, did Bodhisattwa. Listen to him now—he is talking to his Disciples: ... 'I will teach you,' he said, to the faithful Ananda, 'a way of Truth, called the Mirror of Truth, which, if an elect disciple possess, he may himself predict of himself, "Hell is destroyed for me, and rebirth as an animal, or a ghost, or any place of woe. I am converted. I am no longer liable to be reborn in a state of suffering, and am assured of final salvation."'... Ah, Your Majesty is asking, will the parallel never end? Not yet, not yet! For the Bodhisattwa did miracles as well. I read again: ... 'And the Blessed One came once to the river Ganges, and found it overflowing. Those with him, designing to cross, began to seek for boats, some for rafts of wood, while some made rafts of basket-work. Then the Blessed One, as instantaneously as a strong man would stretch forth his arm and draw it back again when he had stretched it forth, vanished from this side of the river, and stood on the further bank with the company of his brethren.'"

The stir the quotation gave rise to being quieted, the Prince, quitting the roll, said: "Like that, my Lord, was the Bodhisattwa's habit on entering assemblies of men, to become of their color—he, you remember, was from birth of the color of gold just flashed in the crucible—and in a voice like theirs instructing them. Then, say the Scriptures, they, not knowing him, would ask, Who may this be that speaks? A man or a God? Then he would vanish away. Like that again was his purifying the water which had been stirred up by the wheels of five hundred carts passing through it. He was thirsty, and at his bidding his companion filled a cup, and lo! the water was clear and delightful. Still more decided, when he was dying there was a mighty earthquake, and the thunders of heaven broke forth, and the spirits stood about to see him until there was no spot, say the Scriptures, in size even as the pricking of the point of the tip of a hair not pervaded with them; and he saw them, though they were invisible to his disciples; and then when the last reverence of his five hundred brethren was paid at his feet, the pyre being ready, it took fire of itself, and there was left of his body neither soot nor ashes—only the bones for relics. Then, again, as the pyre had kindled itself, so when the body was burned up streams of water descended from the skies, and other streams burst from the earth, and extinguished the fire. Finally, my Lord, the parallel ends in the modes of death. Bodhisattwa chose the time and place for himself, and the circumstances of his going were in harmony with his heavenly character. Death was never arrayed in such beauty. The twin Sala trees, one at the head of his couch, the other at the foot, though out of season, sprinkled him with their flowers, and the sky rained powder of sandal-wood, and trembled softly with the incessant music and singing of the floating Gandharvis. But he whose soul was the Spirit, last incarnate, the Christ"—the Prince stopped—the blood forsook his face—he took hold of the table to keep from falling—and the audience arose in alarm.

"Look to the Prince!" the Emperor commanded.

Those nearest the ailing man offered him their arms, but with a mighty effort he spoke to them naturally: "Thank you, good friends—it is nothing." Then he said louder: "It is nothing, my Lord—it is gone now. I was about to say of the Christ, how different was his dying, and with that ends the parallel between him and the Bodhisattwa as Sons of God.... Now, if it please Your Majesty, I will not longer detain your guests from the refreshments awaiting them."

A chair was brought for him; and when he was seated, a long line of servants in livery appeared with the collation.

In a short time the Prince was himself again. The mention of the Saviour, in connection with his death, had suddenly projected the scene of the Crucifixion before him, and the sight of the Cross and the sufferer upon it had for the moment overcome him.

CHAPTER XVI
HOW THE NEW FAITH WAS RECEIVED

It had been better for the Prince of India if he had not consented to the intermission graciously suggested by the Emperor. The monk with the hollow eyes who had arisen and posed behind his crucifix, like an exorcist, was no other than George Scholarius, whom, for the sake of historical conformity, we shall from this call Gennadius; and far from availing himself of His Majesty's permission to retire, that person was observed to pass industriously from chair to chair circulating some kind of notice. Of the refreshments he would none; his words were few, his manner earnest; and to him, beyond question, it was due that when order was again called, the pleasure the Prince drew from seeing every seat occupied was dashed by the scowling looks which met him from all sides. The divining faculty, peculiarly sharpened in him, apprised him instantly of an influence unfriendly to his project—a circumstance the more remarkable since he had not as yet actually stated any project.

Upon taking the floor, the Prince placed the large Judean Bible before him opened, and around it his other references, impressing the audience with an idea that in his own view the latter were of secondary importance.

"My Lord, and Reverend Sirs," he began, with a low salutation to the Emperor, "the fulness of the parallel I have run between the Bodhisattwa, Son of Maya, and Jesus Christ, Son of Mary, may lead to a supposition that they were the only Blessed Ones who have appeared in the world honored above men because they were chosen for the Incarnation of the Spirit. In these Scriptures," unrolling the *Sutra* or *Book of the Great Decease*—"frequent statements imply a number of Tathagatas or Buddhas of irregular coming. In this"—putting a finger on a Chinese *King*—"time is divided into periods termed *Kalpas*, and in one place it is said ninety-eight Buddhas illuminated one Kalpa [Footnote: EAKIN'S Chinese Buddhism, 14.]—that is, came and taught as Saviours. Nor shall any man deny the Spirit manifest in each of them was the same Spirit. They preached the same holy doctrine, pointed out the same road to salvation, lived the same pure unworldly lives, and all alike made a declaration of which I shall presently speak; in other words, my Lord, the features of the Spirit were the same in all of them.... Here in these rolls, parts of the Sacred Books of the East, we read of Shun. I cannot fix his days, they were so long ago. Indeed, I only know he must have been an adopted of the Spirit by his leaving behind him the Tao, or Law, still observed among the Chinese as their standard of virtue.... Here also is the *Avesta*, most revered remains of the Magi, from whom, as many suppose, the Wise Men who came up to Jerusalem witnesses of the birth of the new King of the Jews were sent." This too he identified with his finger. "Its teacher is Zarathustra, and, in my faith, the Spirit descended upon him and abode with him while he was on the earth. The features all showed themselves in him—in his life, his instruction, and in the honors paid him through succeeding generations. His religion yet lives, though founded hundreds of years before your gentle Nazarene walked the waters of Galilee.... And here, O my Lord, is a book abhorred by Christians"—he laid his whole hand on the Koran—"How shall it be judged? By the indifferent manner too many of those ready to die defending its divine origin observe it? Alas! What religion shall survive that test? In the visions of Mahomet I read of God, Moses, the Patriarchs—nay, my Lord, I read of him called the Christ. Shall we not beware lest in condemning Mahomet we divest this other Bible"—he reverently touched the great Eusebian volume—"of some of its superior holiness? He calls himself a Prophet. Can a man prophesy except he have in him the light of the Spirit?"

The question awoke the assemblage. A general signing of the Cross was indulged in by the Fathers, and there was groaning hard to distinguish from growls. Gennadius kept his seat, nervously playing with his rosary. The countenance of the Patriarch was unusually grave. In all his experience it is doubtful if the Prince ever touched a subject requiring more address than this dealing with the Koran. He resumed without embarrassment:

"Now, my Lord, I shall advance a step nearer my real subject. Think not, I pray, that the things I have spoken of the Bodhisattwa, of Shun, of Zarathustra, of Mahomet, likening them in their entertainment of the Spirit to Jesus, was to excite comparisons; such as which was the holiest, which did the most godly things, which is most worthy to be accounted the best beloved of the Father; for I come to bury all strife of the kind.... I said I had been to the mountain's top; and now, my Lord, did you demand of me to single out and name the greatest of the wonders I thence beheld, I should answer: Neither on the sea, nor on the land, nor in the sky is there a wonder like unto the perversity which impels men to invent and go on inventing religions and sects, and then persecute each other on account of them. And when I prayed to be shown the reason of it, I thought I heard a voice, 'Open thine eyes—See!' ... And the first thing given me to see was that the Blessed Ones who went about speaking for the Spirit which possessed them were divine; yet they walked the earth, not as Gods, but witnesses of God; asking hearing and belief, not worship; begging men to come unto them as guides sent to show them the only certain way to everlasting life in glory—only that and nothing more.... The next thing I saw, a bright light in a white glass set on a dark hill, was the waste of worship men are guilty of in bestowing it on inferior and often unworthy objects. When Jesus prayed, it was to our Father in Heaven, was it not?—meaning not to himself, or anything human, or anything less than human.... One other thing I was permitted to see; and the reserving it last is because it lies nearest the proposal I have come a great distance to submit to my Lord and these most reverend brethren in holiness. Every place I have been in which men are not left to their own imaginings of life and religion—in every land and island touched by revelation—a supreme God is recognized, the same in qualities—Creator, Protector, Father—Infinite in Power, Infinite in Love—the Indivisible One! Asked you never, my Lord, the object he had in intrusting his revelation to us, and why the Blessed Ones, his Sons in the Spirit, were bid come here and go yonder by stony paths? Let me answer with what force is left me. There is in such permissions but one intention which a respectful mind can assign to a being great and good as God—one altar, one worship, one prayer, and He the soul of them. With a flash of his beneficent thought he saw in one religion peace amongst men. Strange—most strange! In human history no other such marvel! There has been nothing so fruitful of bickering, hate, murder and war. Such is the seeming, and so I thought, my Lord, until on the mountain's highest peak, whence all concerns lie in view below, I opened my eyes and perceived the wrestling of tongues and fighting were not about God, but about forms, and immaterialities, more especially the Blessed Ones to whom he had intrusted his Spirit. From the Ceylonesian: 'Who is worthy praise but Buddha?' 'No,' the Islamite answers: 'Who but Mahomet?' And from the Parsee; 'No—Who but Zarathustra?' 'Have done with your vanities,' the Christian thunders: 'Who has told the truth like Jesus?' Then the flame of swords, and the cruelty of blows—all in God's name!"

This was bold speaking.

"And now, my Lord," the Prince went on, his appearance of exceeding calmness belied only by the exceeding brightness of his eyes, "God wills an end to controversy and wars blasphemously waged in his name, and I am sent to tell you of it; and for that the Spirit is in me."

Here Gennadius again arose, crucifix in hand.

"I am returned from visiting many of the nations," the Prince continued, nothing daunted. "They demanded of me a faith broad enough for them to stand upon while holding fast the lesser ideas grown up in their consciences; and, on my giving them such a faith, they said they were ready to do the will, but raised a new condition. Some one must move first. 'Go find that one,' they bade me, 'and we will follow after.' In saying now I am ambassador appointed to bring the affair to Your Majesty and Your Majesty's people, enlightened enough to see the will of the Supreme Master, and of a courage to lead in the movement, with influence and credit to carry it peacefully forward to a glorious end, I well know how idle recommendation and entreaty are except I satisfy you in the beginning that they have the sanction of Heaven; and thereto now.... I take no honor to myself as author of the faith presented in answer to the demand of the nations. In old cities there are houses under houses, along streets underlying streets, and to find them, the long buried, men dig deep and laboriously; that did I, until in these old Testaments"—he cast a loving glance at all the Sacred Books—"I made a precious discovery. I pray Your Majesty's patience while I read from them.... This from the Judean Bible: 'And God said unto Moses, I AM THAT I AM: and he said, This shalt thou say unto the children of Israel, I AM hath sent me unto you.' Thus did God, of whom we have no doubt, name himself to one chosen race.... Next from a holy man of China who lived nearly five hundred years before the Christ was born: 'Although any one be a bad man, if he fasts and is collected, he may indeed offer sacrifices unto God.' [Footnote: FABER'S *Mind of Mencius*]... And from the *Avesta*, this of the creed of the Magi: 'The world is twofold, being the work of Ahura Mazda and Angra Mainyu: all that is good in the world comes from the First Principle (which is God) and all that is bad from the latter (which is Satan). Angra Mainyu invaded the world after it was made by Ahura Mazda and polluted it, but the conflict will some day end.' [Footnote: Sir William Jones.] The First Principle here is God. But most marvellous, because of the comparison it will excite, hearken to this from the same Magian creed: 'When the time is full, a son of the lawgiver still unborn, named Saoshyant, will appear; then Angra Mainyu (Satan) and Hell will be destroyed, men will arise from the dead, and everlasting happiness reign over the world.' Here again the Lawgiver is God; but the Son—who is he? Has he come? Is he gone? ... Next, take these several things from the *Vedas*: 'By One Supreme Ruler is the universe pervaded, even every world in the whole circle of nature. There is One Supreme Spirit which nothing can shake, more swift than the thought of man. The Primeval Mover even divine intelligence cannot reach; that Spirit, though unmoved, infinitely transcends others, how rapid soever their course; it is distant from us, yet very near; it pervades the whole system of worlds, yet is infinitely beyond it.' [Footnote: *Ibid.* Vol. XIII.] Now, my Lord, and very reverend sirs, do not the words quoted come to us clean of mystery? Or have you the shadow of a doubt whom they mean, accept and consider the prayer I read you now from the same *Vedas:* 'O Thou who givest sustenance to the world, Thou sole mover of all, Thou who restrainest sinners, who pervadest yon great luminary which appearest as the Son of the Creator; hide thy struggling beams and expand thy spiritual brightness that I may view thy most auspicious, most glorious, real form. OM, remember me, divine Spirit! OM, remember my deeds! Let my soul return to the immortal Spirit of God, and then let my body, which ends in ashes, return to dust.' Who is OM? Or is my Lord yet uncertain, let him heed this from the *Holiest Verse of the Vedas*: 'Without hand or foot, he runs rapidly, and grasps firmly; without eyes, he sees; without ears, he hears all; he knows whatever can be known, but there is none who knows him: Him the wise call the Great, Supreme, Pervading Spirit.' [Footnote: Sir William Jones. Vol. XIII.] ... Now once more, O my Lord, and I am done with citation and argument. Ananda asked the Bodhisattwa what was the Mirror of Truth, and he had this answer: 'It is the consciousness that the elect disciple is in this world possessed of faith in Buddha, believing the Blessed One to be the Holy One, the Fully Enlightened One, Wise, Upright, Happy, World-knowing, Supreme, the bridler of men's wayward hearts, the Teacher of Gods and men—the Blessed Buddha.' [Footnote: REHYS DAVID'S *Buddhist Sutras*.] Oh, good my Lord, a child with intellect barely to name the mother who bore him, should see and say, Here God is described!" ...

The Prince came to a full stop, and taking a fine silken cloth from a pocket in his gown, he carefully wiped the open pages of the Eusebian Bible, and shut it. Of the other books he made a separate heap, first dusting each of them. The assemblage watched him expectantly. The Fathers had been treated to strange ideas, matter for thought through many days and nights ahead; still each of them felt the application was wanting. "The purpose—give it us—and quickly!" would have been a fair expression of their impatience. At length he proceeded:

"Dealing with children, my Lord, and reverend sirs," he began, "it is needful to stop frequently, and repeat the things we have said; but you are men trained in argument: wherefore, with respect to the faith asked of me as I have told you by the nations, I say simply it is God; and touching his sanction of it, you may wrest these Testaments from me and make ashes of them, but you shall not now deny his approval of the Faith I bring you. It is not in the divine nature for God to abjure himself. Who of you can conceive him shrunk to so small a measure?"

The dogmatic vehemence amazed the listeners.

"Whether this idea of God is broad enough to accommodate all the religions grown up on the earth, I will not argue; for I desire to be most respectful"—thus the speaker went on in his natural manner. "But should you accept it as enough, you need not be at loss for a form in which to put it. 'Master,' the lawyer asked, 'which is the great commandment in the law?' And the Master answered: 'Thou shalt love the Lord thy God with all thy heart, and with all thy soul, and with all thy mind;' and he added: 'This is the first and great commandment.' My Lord, no man else ever invented, nor shall any man ever invent an expression more perfectly definitive of the highest human duty—the total of doctrine. I will not tell you who the master uttering it was; neither will I urge its adoption; only if the world were to adopt it, and abide by it, there would be an end to wars and rumors of war, and God would have his own. If the Church here in your ancient capital were first to accept it, what happiness I should have carrying the glad tidings to the peoples"—

The Prince was not allowed to finish the sentence.

"What do I understand, O Prince, by the term 'total of doctrine'?"

It was the Patriarch speaking.

"Belief in God."

In a moment the assemblage became uproarious, astounding the Emperor; and in the midst of the excitement, Gennadius was seen on tip-toe, waving his crucifix with the energy of command.

"Question—a question!" he cried.

Quiet was presently given him.

"In thy total of doctrine, what is Jesus Christ?"

The voice of the Patriarch, enfeebled by age and disease, had been scarcely heard; his rival's penetrated to the most distant corner; and the question happening to be the very thought pervading the assemblage, the churchmen, the courtiers, and most of the high officials arose to hear the reply.

In a tone distinct as his interlocutor's, but wholly without passion, the master actor returned:

"A Son of God."

"And Mahomet, the Father of Islam—what is he?"

If the ascetic had put the name of Siddartha, the Bodhisattwa, in his second question, his probing had not been so deep, nor the effect so quick and great; but Mahomet, the camel-driver! Centuries of feud, hate, crimination, and wars—rapine, battles, sieges, massacres, humiliations, lopping of territory, treaties broken, desecration of churches, spoliation of altars, were evoked by the name Mahomet.

We have seen it a peculiarity of the Prince of India never to forget a relation once formed by him. Now behind Constantine he beheld young Mahommed waiting for him—Mahommed and revenge. If his scheme were rejected by the Greeks, very well—going to the Turks would be the old exchange with which he was familiar, Cross for Crescent. To be sure there was little time to think this; nor did he think it—it appeared and went a glare of light—and he answered:

"He will remain, in the Spirit another of the Sons of God."

Then Gennadius, beating the air with his crucifix: "Liar—impostor—traitor! Ambassador of Satan thou! Behind thee Hell uncurtained! Mahomet himself were more tolerable! Thou mayst turn black white, quench water with fire, make ice of the blood in our hearts, all in a winking or slowly, our reason resisting, but depose the pure and blessed Saviour, or double his throne in the invisible kingdom with Mahomet, prince of liars, man of blood, adulterer, monster for whom Hell had to be enlarged—that shalt thou never! A body without a soul, an eye its light gone out, a tomb rifled of its dead—such the Church without its Christ! ... Ho, brethren! Shame on us that we are guests in common with this fiend in cunning! We are not hosts to bid him begone; yet we can ourselves begone. Follow me, O lovers of Christ and the Church! To your tents, O Israel!"

The speaker's face was purple with passion; his voice filled the chamber; many of the monks broke from their seats and rushed howling and blindly eager to get nearer him. The Patriarch sat ashy white, helplessly crossing himself. Constantine excellently and rapidly judging what became him as Emperor and host, sent four armed officers to protect the Prince, who held his appointed place apparently surprised but really interested in the scene—to him it was an exhibition of unreasoning human nature replying to an old-fashioned impulse of bigotry.

Hardly were the guards by the table, when Gennadius rushed past going to the door, the schismatics at his heels in a panic. The pulling and hauling, the hurry-skurry of the mad exit must be left to the imagination. It was great enough to frighten thoroughly the attendants of the Princess Irene. Directly there remained in the chamber with His Majesty, the attaches of the court, the Patriarch and his adherents. Then Constantine quietly asked:

"Where is Duke Notaras?"

There was much looking around, but no response.

The countenance of the monarch was observed to change, but still mindful, he bade the Dean conduct the Prince to him.

"Be not alarmed, Prince. My people are quick of temper, and sometimes they act hastily. If you have more to say, we are of a mind to hear you to the end."

The Prince could not but admire the composure of his august host. After a low reverence, he returned:

"Perhaps I tried the reverend Fathers unreasonably; yet it would be a much greater grief to me if their impatience extended to Your Majesty. I was not alarmed; neither have I aught to add to my discourse, unless it pleases you to ask of anything in it which may have been left obscure or uncertain."

Constantine signed to the Patriarch and all present to draw nearer.

"Good Dean, a chair for His Serenity."

In a short time the space in front of the dais was occupied.

"I understand the Prince of India has submitted to us a proposal looking to a reform of our religion," His Majesty said, to the Patriarch; "and courtesy requiring an answer, the violence to which we have just been subjected, and the spirit of insubordination manifested, make it imperative that you listen to what I now return him, and with attention, lest a misquotation or false report lead to further trouble.... Prince," he continued, "I think I comprehend you. The world is sadly divided with respect to religion, and out of its divisions have proceeded the mischiefs to which you have referred. Your project is not to be despised. It reminds me of the song, the sweetest ear ever listened to—'Peace and good will toward men.' Its adoption, nevertheless, is another matter. I have not power to alter the worship of my empire. Our present Creed was a conclusion reached by a Council too famous in history not to be conspicuously within your knowledge. Every word of it is infinitely sacred. It fixed the relations between God the Father, Christ the Son, and men to my satisfaction, and that of my subjects. Serenity, do thou say if I may apply the remark to the Church."

"Your Majesty," the Patriarch replied, "the Holy Greek Church can never consent to omit the Lord Jesus Christ from its worship. You have spoken well, and it had been better if the brethren had remained to hear you."

"Thanks, O most venerated—thanks," said the Emperor, inclining his head. "A council having established the creed of the Church," he resumed, to the Prince of India, "the creed is above change to the extent of a letter except by another council solemnly and authoritatively convoked. Wherefore, O Prince, I admit myself wiser of the views you have presented; I admit having been greatly entertained by your eloquence and rhetoric; and I promise myself further happiness and profit in drawing upon the stores of knowledge with which you appear so amply provided, results doubtless of your study and travel—yet you have my answer."

The faculty of retiring his thoughts and feelings deeper in his heart as occasion demanded, was never of greater service to the Prince than now; he bowed, and asked if he had permission to retire; and receiving it, he made the usual prostrations, and began moving backwards.

"A moment, Prince," said Constantine. "I hope your residence is permanently fixed in our capital."

"Your Majesty is very gracious, and I thank you. If I leave the city, it will be to return again, and speedily."

At the door of the palace the Prince found an escort waiting for him, and taking his chair, he departed from Blacherne.

CHAPTER XVII
LAEL AND THE SWORD OF SOLOMON

Alone in his house, the Prince of India was unhappy, but not, as the reader may hurriedly conclude, on account of the rejection by the Christians of his proposal looking to brotherhood in the bonds of religion. He was a trifle sore over the failure, but not disappointed. A reasonable man, and, what times his temper left him liberty to think, a philosopher, he could not hope after the observations he brought from Mecca to find the followers of the Nazarene more relaxed in their faith than the adherents of Mahomet. In short, he had gone to the palace warned of what would happen.

It was not an easy thing for him to fold up his grand design preparatory to putting it away forever; still there was no choice left him; and now he would move for vengeance. Away with hesitation.

Descending the heights of Blacherne, he had felt pity for Constantine who, though severely tried in the day's affair, had borne himself with dignity throughout; but it was Mahommed's hour. Welcome Mahommed!

Between the two, the Prince's predilections were all for the Turk, and they had been from the meeting at the White Castle. Besides personal accomplishments and military prestige, besides youth, itself a mighty preponderant, there was the other argument—separating Mahommed from the strongest power in the world, there stood only an ancient whose death was a daily expectation. "What opportunities the young man will have to offer me! I have but to make the most of his ambition—to loan myself to it—to direct it."

Thus the Seer reasoned, returning from Blacherne to his house.

At the door, however, he made a discovery. There the first time during the day he thought of her in all things the image of the Lael whom he had buried under the great stone in front of the Golden Gate at Jerusalem. We drop a grain in the ground, and asking nothing of us but to be let alone, it grows, and flowers, and at length amazes us with fruit. Such had been the outcome of his adoption of the daughter of the son of Jahdai.

The Prince called Syama.

"Make ready the chair and table on the roof," he said.

While waiting, he ate some bread dipped in wine: then walked the room rubbing his hands as if washing them.

He sighed frequently. Even the servants could see he was in trouble.

At length he went to the roof. Evening was approaching. On the table were the lamp, the clock, the customary writing materials, a fresh map of the heavens, and a perfect diagram of a nativity to be cast.

He took the map in his hand, and smiled—it was Lael's work. "How she has improved!—and how rapidly!" he said aloud, ending a retrospect which began with the hour Uel consented to her becoming his daughter. She was unlettered then, but how helpful now. He felt an artist's pride in her growth in knowledge. There were tedious calculations which she took off his hands; his geometrical drawings of the planets in their Houses were frequently done in haste; she perfected them next day. She had numberless daughterly ways which none but those unused to them like him would have observed. What delight she took in watching the sky for the first appearance of the stars. In this work she lent him her young eyes, and there was such enthusiasm in the exclamations with which she greeted the earliest wink of splendor from the far-off orbs. And he had ailing days; then she would open the great Eusebian Scriptures at the page he asked for, and read—sometimes from Job, sometimes from Isaiah, but generally from Exodus, for in his view there was never man like Moses. The contest with Pharaoh—how prodigious! The battles in magic—what glory in the triumphs won! The luring the haughty King into the Red Sea, and bringing him under the walls of water suddenly let loose! What majestic vengeance!

Of the idle dreams of aged persons the possibility of attaching the young to them in sentimental bonds of strength to insure resistance to every other attachment is the idlest. Positive, practical, experienced though he was, the childless man had permitted this fantasy to get possession of him. He actually brought himself to believe Lael's love of him was of that enduring kind. With no impure purpose, yet selfishly, and to bring her under his influence until of preference she could devote her life to him, with its riches of affection, admiration, and dutiful service, he had surrendered himself to her; therefore the boundless pains taken by him personally in her education, the surrounding her with priceless luxuries which he alone could afford—in brief, the attempt to fasten himself upon her youthful fancy as a titled sage and master of many mysteries. So at length it came to pass, while he was happy in his affection for her, he was even happier in her affection for himself; indeed he cultivated the latter sentiment and encouraged it in winding about his being until, in utter unconsciousness, he belonged to it, and, in repetition of experiences common to others, instead of Lael's sacrificing herself for him, he was ready to sacrifice everything for her. This was the discovery he made at the door of his house.

The reader should try to fancy him in the chair by the table on the roof. Evening has passed into night. The city gives out no sound, and the stars have the heavens to themselves. He is lost in thought—or rather, accepting the poetic fancy of a division of the heart into chambers, in that apartment of the palpitating organ of the Prince of India supposed to be the abode of the passions, a very noisy parliament was in full session. The speaker—that is, the Prince himself—submitted the question: Shall I remain here, or go to Mahommed?

Awhile he listened to Revenge, whose speech in favor of the latter alternative may be imagined; and not often had its appeals been more effective. Ambition spoke on the same side. It pointed out the opportunities offered, and dwelt upon them until the chairman nodded like one both convinced and determined. These had an assistant not exactly a passion but a kinsman collaterally—Love of Mischief—and when the others ceased, it insisted upon being heard.

On the other side, Lael led the opposition. She stood by the president's chair while her opponents were arguing, her arms round his neck; when they were most urgent, she would nurse his hand, and make use of some trifling endearment; upon their conclusion, she would gaze at him mutely, and with tears. Not once did she say anything.

In the midst of this debate, Lael herself appeared, and kissed him on the forehead.

"Thou here!" he said.

"Why not?" she asked.

"Nothing—only"—

She did not give him time to finish, but caught up the map, and seeing it fresh and unmarked, exclaimed:

"You did so greatly to-day, you ought to rest."

He was surprised.

"Did so greatly?"

"At the palace."

"Put the paper down. Now, O my Gul Bahar"—and he took her hand, and carried it to his cheek, and pressed it softly there—"deal me no riddle. What is it you say? One may do well, yet come out badly."

"I was at the market in my father Uel's this afternoon," she began, "when Sergius came in."

A face wonderfully like the face of the man he helped lead out to Golgotha flashed before the Prince, a briefest passing gleam.

"He heard you discourse before the Emperor. How wickedly that disgusting Gennadius behaved!"

"Yes," the Prince responded darkly, "a sovereign beset with such spirits is to be pitied. But what did the young man think of my proposal to the Emperor?"

"But for one verse in the Testament of Christ"—

"Nay, dear, say Jesus of Nazareth."

"Well, of Jesus—but for one verse he could have accepted your argument of many Sons of God in the Spirit."

"What is the verse?"

"It is where a disciple speaks of Jesus as the only begotten. Son."

The Wanderer smiled.

"The young man is too literal. He forgets that the Only Begotten Son may have had many Incarnations."

"The Princess Irene was also present," Lael went on. "Sergius said she too could accept your argument did you alter it"—

"Alter it!"—A bitter look wrung the Prince's countenance—"Sergius, a monk not yet come to orders, and Irene, a Princess without a husband. Oh, a small return for my surrender! ... I am tired—very tired," he said impatiently—"and I have so much, so much to think of. Come, good night."

"Can I do nothing for you?"

"Yes, tell Syama to bring me some water."

"And wine?"

"Yes, some wine."

"Very well. Good night."

He drew her to his breast.

"Good night. O my Gul Bahar!"

She went lightly away, never dreaming of the parliament to which she left him.

When she was gone, he sat motionless for near an hour, seeing nothing in the time, although Syama set water and wine on the table. And it may be questioned if he heard anything, except the fierce debate going on in his heart. Finally he aroused, looked at the sky, arose, and walked around the table; and his expression of face, his actions, were those of a man who had been treading difficult ground, but was safely come out of it. Filling a small crystal cup, and holding the red liquor, rich with garnet sparkles, between his eyes and the lamp, he said:

"It is over. She has won. If there were for me but the years of one life, the threescore and ten of the Psalmist, it had been different. The centuries will bring me a Mahommed gallant as this one, and opportunities great as he offers; but never another Lael. Farewell Ambition! Farewell Revenge! The world may take care of itself. I will turn looker-on, and be amused, and sleep.... To hold her, I will live for her, but in redoubled state. So will I hurry her from splendor to splendor, and so fill her days with moving incidents, she shall not have leisure to think of another love. I will be powerful and famous for her sake. Here in this old centre of civilization there shall be two themes for constant talk, Constantine and myself. Against his rank and patronage, I will set my wealth. Ay, for her sake! And I will begin to-morrow."

The next day he spent in making drawings and specifications for a palace. The second day he traversed the city looking for a building site. The third day he bought the site most to his fancy. The fourth day he completed a design for a galley of a hundred oars, that it might be sea-going far as the Pillars of Hercules. Nothing ever launched from the imperial docks should surpass it in magnificence. When he went sailing on the Bosphorus, Byzantium should assemble to witness his going, and with equal eagerness wait the day through to behold him return. And for the four days, Lael was present and consulted in every particular. They talked like two children.

The schemes filled him with a delight which would have been remarkable in a boy. He packed his books and put away his whole paraphernalia of study—through Lael's days he would be an actor in the social world, not a student.

Of course he recurred frequently to the engagements with Mahommed. They did not disturb him. The Turk might clamor—no matter, there was the ever ready answer about the unready stars. The veteran intriguer even laughed, thinking how cunningly he had provided against contingencies. But there was a present practical requirement begotten of these schemes— he must have money—soldans by the bag full.

Very early in the morning of the fifth day, having studied the weather signs from his housetop, he went with Nilo to the harbor gate of Blacherne, seeking a galley suitable for an outing of a few days on the Marmora. He found one, and by noon she was fitted out, and with him and Nilo aboard, flying swiftly around Point Serail.

Under an awning over the rudder-deck, he sat observing the brown-faced wall of the city, and the pillars and cornices of the noble structures towering above it. As the vessel was about passing the Seven Towers, now a ruin with a most melancholy history, but in that day a well-garrisoned fortress, he conversed with the master of the galley.

"I have no business in the strict meaning of the term," he said, in good humor. "The city has become tiresome to me, and I have fancied a run on the water would be bracing to body and restful to mind. So keep on down the sea. When I desire a change of direction, I will tell you." The mariner was retiring. "Stay," the Prince continued, his attention apparently caught by two immense gray rocks rising bluffly out of the blue rippling in which the Isles of the Princes seemed afloat—"What are those yonder? Islands, of course, but their names?"

"Oxia and Plati—the one nearest us is Oxia."

"Are they inhabited?"

"Yes and no," the captain replied, smiling. "Oxia used to have a convent, but it is abandoned now. There may be some hermits in the caves on the other side, but I doubt if the poor wretches have noumias to keep their altars in candles. It was so hard to coax visitors into believing God had ever anything to do with the dreary place that patrons concluded to give it over to the bad. Plati is a trifle more cheerful. Three or four monks keep what used to be the prison there; but they are strays from unknown orders, and live by herding a few starving goats and cultivating snails for the market."

"Have you been on either of them recently?"

"Yes, on Plati."

"When?"

"Within the year."

"Well, you excite my curiosity. It is incredible that there can be two such desolations in such close vicinity to yon famous capital. Turn and row me around them."

The captain was pleased to gratify his passenger, and stood by him while the galley encircled Oxia, telling legends, and pointing out the caves to which celebrated anchorites had lent their names. He gave in full the story of Basil and Prusien, who quarrelled, and fought a duel to the scandal of the Church; whereupon Constantine VIII., then emperor, exiled them, the former to Oxia, the latter to Plati, where their sole consolation the remainder of their lives was gazing at each other from the mouths of their respective caverns. For some reason, Plati, to which he next crossed, was of more interest to the Prince than its sister isle. What a cruel exterior the prison at the north end had! Wolves and bats might live in it, but men— impossible! He drew back horrified when told circumstantially of the underground cells.

While yet on the eastern side, the passenger said he would like to go up to the summit.

"There," he exclaimed, pointing to a part of the bluff which appeared to offer a climb, "put me on that shelving rock. I think I can go up by it."

The small boat was lowered, and directly he set foot on the identical spot which received him when, in the night fifty-six years before, he made the ascent with the treasures of Hiram King of Tyre.

Almost any other man would have given at least a thought to that adventure; the slice out of some lives would have justified a tear; but he was too intent thinking about the jewels and the sword of Solomon.

His affected awkwardness in climbing amused the captain, watching him from the deck, but at last he gained the top of the bluff.

The plain there was the same field of sickly weeds and perishing vines, with here and there a shrub, and yonder a stunted olive tree, covered trunk and branches with edible snails. If it brought anything in the market, the crop, singular only to the Western mind, was plenteous enough to be profitable to its farmers. There too was the debris of the tower. With some anxiety he went to the stone which the reader will probably remember as having to be rolled away from the mouth of the hiding-place. It had not been disturbed. These observations taken, he descended the bluff, and was received aboard the galley.

A very cautious man was the Prince of India. In commercial parlance, he was out to cash a draft on the Plati branch of his quadruple bank. He was not down to assist the captain of the galley to partnership with him in the business. So, after completing the circuit of Plati, the vessel bore away for Prinkipo and Halki, which Greek wealth and taste had converted into dreamful Paradises. There it lay the night and next day, while the easy-going passenger, out for air and rest, amused himself making excursions to the convents and neighboring hills.

The second night, a perfect calm prevailing, he took the small boat, and went out on the sea drifting, having provided himself with wine and water, the latter in a new gurglet bought for the trip. The captain need not be uneasy if he were late returning, he said on departing. Nilo was an excellent sailor, and had muscle and spirit to contend against a blow.

The tranquil environments of Prinkipo were enlivened by other parties also drifting. Their singing was borne far along the starlit sea. Once beyond sight and hearing, Nilo plied the oars diligently, bringing up an hour or two after midnight at the shelving rock under the eastern bluff of Plati. The way to the ruined tower was then clear.

Precisely as at the first visit when burial was the object, the concealing stone was pushed aside; after which the Prince entered the narrow passage crawling on his hands and knees. He was anxious. If the precious stones had been discovered and carried away, he would have to extend the voyage to Jaffa in order to draw from the Jerusalem branch of his bank. But the sword of Solomon—that was not in the power of man to duplicate—its loss would be irreparable.

The stones were mouldy, the passage dark, the progress slow. He had literally to feel every inch in front of him, using his hands as a caterpillar uses its antennae; but he did not complain—the difficulties were the inducements which led him to choose the hiding-place in the first instance. At length he went down a broken step, and, rising to his knees, slipped his left hand along the face of the wall until his fingers dropped into a crack between rocks. It was the spot he sought; he knew it, and breathed easily. In murky lamplight, with mallet and chisel—ah, how long ago!—he had worked a shelf there, finishing it with an oblong pocket in the bottom. To mask the hole was simple. Three or four easy-fitting blocks were removed, and thrusting a hand in, he drew forth the sheepskin mantle of the elder Nilo.

In spite of the darkness, he could not refrain from unrolling the mildewed cover. The sword was safe! He drew the blade and shot it sharply back into the scabbard, then kissed the ruby handle, thinking again of the purchasing power there was in the relic which was yet more than a relic. The leather of the water-gurglet, stiff as wood, responded to a touch. The jewels were also safe, the great emerald with the rest. He touched the bags, counting from one to nine inclusively. Then remembering the ten times he had crawled into the passage to put the treasures away, he began their removal, and kept at it until every article was safely deposited in the boat.

On the way back to the galley he made new packages, using his mantle as a wrap for the sword, and the new gurglet for the bags of jewels.

"I have had enough," he exclaimed to the captain, dropping wearily on the deck about noon. "Take me to the city." After a moment of reflection, he added: "Land me after nightfall."

"We will reach the harbor before sundown."

"Oh, well! There is the Bosphorus—go to Buyukdere, and come back."

"But, my Lord, the captain of the gate may decline to allow you to pass."

The Prince smiled, and rejoined, with a thought of the bags in the gurglet thrown carelessly down by him: "Up with the anchor."

The sailor's surmise was groundless. Disembarking about midnight, he whispered his name to the captain at the gate of Blacherne, and, leaving a soldan in the official palm, was admitted without examination. On the street there was nothing curious in an old man carrying a mantle under his arm, followed by a porter with a half-filled gurglet on his shoulder. Finally, the adventure safely accomplished, the Prince of India was home again, and in excellent humor.

One doubt assailed him—one only. He had just seen the height of Candilli, an aerial wonder in a burst of moonlight, and straightway his fancy had crowned it with a structure Indian in style, and of material to shine afar delicate as snow against the black bosomed mountain behind it. He was not a Greek to fear the Turks. Nay, in Turkish protection there was for him a guaranty of peaceable ownership which he could not see under Constantine. And as he was bringing now the wherewith to realize his latest dream, he gave his imagination a loosened rein.

He built the house; he heard the tinkling of fountains in its courts, and the echoes in the pillared recession of its halls; free of care, happy once more, with Lael he walked in gardens where roses of Persia exchanged perfumes with roses of Araby, and the daylong singing of birds extended into noon of night; yet, after all, to the worn, weary, droughted heart nothing was so soothing as the fancy which had been his chief attendant from the gate of Blacherne—that he heard strangers speaking to each other: "Have you seen the Palace of Lael?" "No, where is it?" "On the crest of Candilli." The Palace of Lael! The name confirmed itself sweeter and sweeter by repetition. And the doubt grew. Should he build in the city or amidst the grove of Judas trees on the crest of Candilli?

Just as he arrived before his door, he glanced casually across the street, and was surprised by observing light in Uel's house. It was very unusual. He would put the treasure away, and go over and inquire into the matter. Hardly was he past his own lintel when Syama met him. The face of the faithful servant showed unwonted excitement, and, casting himself at his master's feet, he embraced his knees, uttering the hoarse unintelligible cries with which the dumb are wont to make their suffering known. The Master felt a chill of fear—something had happened—something terrible—but to whom? He pushed the poor man's head back until he caught the eyes.

"What is it?" he asked.

Syama arose, took the Prince's hand, and led him out of the door, across the street, and into Uel's house. The merchant, at sight of them, rushed forward and hid his face in the master's breast, crying:

"She is gone—lost!—The God of our fathers be with her!"

"Who is gone? Who lost?"

"Lael, Lael—our child—our Gul Bahar."

The blood of the elder Jew flew to his heart, leaving him pale as a dead man; yet such was his acquired control of himself, he asked steadily: "Gone!—Where?"

"We do not know. She has been snatched from us—that is all we know."

"Tell me of it—and quickly."

The tone was imperious, and he pushed Uel from him.

"Oh! my friend—and my father's friend—I will tell you all. You are powerful, and love her, and may help where I am helpless." Then by piecemeal he dealt out the explanation. "This afternoon she took her chair and went to the wall in front of the Bucoleon—sunset, and she was not back. I saw Syama—she was not in your house. He and I set out in search of her. She was seen on the wall—later she was seen to descend the steps as if starting home—she was seen in the garden going about on the terrace— she was seen coming out of the front gate of the old palace. We traced her down the street—then she returned to the garden, through the Hippodrome, and there she was last seen. I called my friends in the market to my aid—hundreds are now looking for her."

"She went out in her chair, did you say?"

The steady voice of the Prince was in singular contrast with his bloodless face.

"Yes."

"Who carried it?"

"The men we have long had."

"Where are they?"

"We sought for them—they cannot be found."

The Prince kept his eyes on Uel's face. They were intensely, fiercely bright. He was not in a rage, but thinking, if a man can be said to think when his mind projects itself in a shower. Lael's disappearance was not voluntary; she was in detention somewhere in the city. If the purpose of the abduction were money, she would be held in scrupulous safety, and a day or two would bring the demand; but if—he did not finish the idea—it overpowered him. Pure steel in utmost flexion breaks into pieces without warning; so with this man now. He threw both hands up, and cried hoarsely: "Lend me, O God, of thy vengeance!" and staggering blindly, he would have fallen but for Syama.

CHAPTER XVIII
THE FESTIVAL OF FLOWERS

The Academy of Epicurus was by no means a trifle spun for vainglory in the fertile fancy of Demedes; but a fact just as the Brotherhoods of the City were facts, and much more notorious than many of them.

Wiseacres are generally pessimistic. Academy of Epicurus indeed! For once there was a great deal in a name. The class mentioned repeated it sneeringly; it spoke to them, and loudly, of some philosophical wickedness.

Stories of the miraculous growth of the society were at first amusing; then the announcement of its housing excited loud laughter; but when its votaries attached the high sounding term *Temple* to their place of meeting, the clergy and all the devoutly inclined looked sober. In their view the word savored of outright paganism. Temple of the Academy of Epicurus! Church had been better—Church was at least Christian.

At length, in ease of the increasing interest, notice was authoritatively issued of a Festival of Flowers by the Academicians, their first public appearance, and great were the anticipations aroused by the further advertisement that they would march from their Temple to the Hippodrome.

The festival took place the afternoon of the third day of the Prince of India's voyage to Plati. More particularly, while that distinguished foreigner on the deck of the galley was quietly sleeping off the fatigue and wear of body and spirit consequent on the visit to the desolate island, the philosophers were on parade with an immense quota of Byzantines of both sexes in observation. About three thousand were in the procession, and from head to foot it was a mass of flowers.

The extravaganza deserved the applause it drew. Some of its features nevertheless were doubtfully regarded. Between the sections into which the column was divided there marched small groups, apparently officers, clad in gowns and vestments, carrying insignia and smoking tripods well known to have belonged to various priesthoods of mythologic fame. When the cortege reached the Hippodrome every one in the galleries was reminded of the glory the first Constantine gained from his merciless forays upon those identical properties.

In the next place, the motto of the society—Patience, Courage, Judgment—was too frequently and ostentatiously exhibited not to attract attention. The words, it was observed, were not merely on banners lettered in gold, but illustrated by portable tableaux of exquisite appositeness and beauty. They troubled the wiseacres; for while they might mean a world of good, they might also stand for several worlds of bad. Withal, however, the youthfulness of the Academicians wrought the profoundest sensation upon the multitude of spectators. The march was three times round the interior, affording excellent opportunity to study the appearances; and the sober thinking, whom the rarity and tastefulness of the display did not hoodwink, when they discovered that much the greater number participating were beardless lads, shook their heads while saying to each other, At the rate these are going what is to become of the Empire? As if the decadence were not already in progress, and they, the croakers, responsible for it!

At the end of the first round, upon the arrival of the sections in front of the triple-headed bronze serpent, one of the wonders of the Hippodrome then as now, the bearers of the tripods turned out, and set them down, until at length the impious relic was partially veiled in perfumed smoke, as was the wont in its better Delphian days.

Nothing more shocking to the religionists could have been invented; they united in denouncing the defiant indecency. Hundreds of persons, not all of them venerable and frocked, were seen to rise and depart, shaking the dust from their feet. In course of tile third circuit, the tripods were coolly picked up and returned to their several places in the procession.

From a seat directly over the course, Sergius beheld the gay spectacle from its earliest appearance through the portal of the Blues to its exit by the portal of the Greens. [Footnote: The Blues and the Greens—two celebrated factions of Constantinople. See Gibbon, vii. pp. 79-89. Four gates, each flanked with towers, gave entrance to the Hippodrome from the city. The northwestern was called the gate of the Blues; the northeastern of the Greens; the southeastern gate bore the sullen title, "Gate of the Dead."—Prof. Edwin A. Grosvenor.] His interest, the reader will bear reminding, was peculiar. He had been honored by a special invitation to become a member of the Academy—in fact, there was a seat in the Temple at the moment reserved for him. He had the great advantage, moreover, of exact knowledge of the objects of the order. Godless itself, it had been organized to promote godlessness. He had given much thought to it since Demedes unfolded the scheme to him, and found it impossible to believe persons of sound sense could undertake a sin so elaborate. If for any reason the State and Church were unmindful of it, Heaven certainly could not be.

Aside from the desire to satisfy himself of the strength of the Academy, Sergius was drawn to the Hippodrome to learn, if possible, the position Demedes held in it. His sympathy with the venerable Hegumen, with whom mourning for the boy astray was incessant, and sometimes pathetic as the Jewish king's, gradually became a grief for the prodigal himself, and he revolved plans for his reformation. What happiness could he one day lead the son to the father, and say: "Your prayers and lamentations have been heard; see—God's kiss of peace on his forehead!"

And then in what he had seen of Demedes—what courage, dash, and audacity—what efficiency—what store of resources! The last play of his—attending the fete of the Princess Irene as a bear tender—who but Demedes would have thought of such a role? Who else could have made himself the hero of the occasion, with none to divide honors with him except Joqard? And what a bold ready transition from bear tender to captain in the boat race! Demedes writhing in the grip of Nilo over the edge of the wall, death in the swish of waves beneath, had been an object of pity tinged with contempt—Demedes winner of the prize at Therapia was a very different person.

This feeling for the Greek, it is to be said next, was dashed with a lurking dread of him. If he had a design against Lael, what was there to prevent him from attempting it? That he had such a design, Sergius could not deny. How often he repeated the close of the note left on the stool after the Fisherman's fete. "Thou mayst find the fan of the Princess of India useful; with me it is embalmed in sentiment." He shall write with a pen wondrous fine who makes the difference between love and sentiment clear. Behind the fete, moreover, there was the confession heard on the wall, illustrated by the story of the plague of crime. Instead of fading out in the Russian's mind it had become better understood—a consequence of the brightening process of residence in the city.

Twice the procession rounded the great curriculum. Twice Sergius had opportunity to look for the Greek, but without avail. So were the celebrants literally clothed in flowers that recognition of individuals was almost impossible. The first time, he sought him in the body of each passing section; the second time, he scanned the bearers of the standards and symbols; the third time, he was successful.

At the head of the parade, six or eight persons were moving on horseback. It was singular Sergius had not looked for Demedes amongst them, since the idea of him would have entitled the Greek to a chief seat in the Temple and a leading place when in the eye of the public. As it was, he could not repress an exclamation on making the discovery.

Like his associates, Demedes was in armor *cap-a-pie*. He also carried an unshod lance, a shield on arm, and a bow and quiver at his back; but helmet, breastplate, shield, lance and bow were masked in flowers, and only now and then a glint betrayed the underdress of polished steel. The steed he bestrode was housed in cloth which dragged the ground; but of the color of the cloth or its material not a word can be said, so entirely was it covered with floral embroidery of diverse hues and figures.

The decoration contributed little of grace to man or beast; nevertheless its richness was undeniable. To the spendthrifts in the galleries the effect was indescribably attractive. They studied its elaboration, conjecturing how many gardens along the Bosphorus, and out in the Isles of the Princes, had been laid under contribution for the accomplishment of the splendor. Thus in the saddle, Demedes could not have been accused of diminutiveness; he appeared tall, even burly; indeed, Sergius would never have recognized him had he not been going with raised visor, and at the instant of passing turned his face up, permitting it to be distinctly seen.

The exclamation wrung from the monk was not merely because of his finding the man; in sober truth, it was an unconventional expression provoked by finding him in the place he occupied, and a quick jump to the logical conclusion that the foremost person in the march was also the chief priest—if such were the title—in the Academy.

Thenceforward Sergius beheld little else of the show than Demedes. He forgot the impiety of the honors to the bronze serpent. There is no enigma to us like him who is broadly our antipodes in moral being, and whether ours is the good or the bad nature does not affect the saying. His feelings the while were strangely diverse. The election of the evil genius to the first place in the insidious movement was well done for the Academy; there would be no failure with him in control; but the poor Hegumen!

And now, the last circuit completed, the head of the bright array approached the Gate of the Greens. There the horsemen drew out and formed line on the right hand to permit the brethren to march past them. The afternoon was going rapidly. The shadow of the building on the west crept more noticeably across the carefully kept field. Still Sergius retained his seat watchful of Demedes. He saw him signal the riders to turn out—he saw the line form, and the sections begin to march past it—then an incident occurred of no appreciable importance at the moment, but replete with significancy a little later.

A man appeared on the cornice above the Gate—the Grate on the interior having a face resembling a very tall but shallow portico resting on slender pillars—and commenced lowering himself as if he meant to descend. The danger of the attempt drew all eyes to him. Demedes looked up, and hastily rode through the column toward the spot where the adventurer must alight. The spectators credited the young chief with a generous intent to be of assistance; but agile as a cat, and master of every nerve and muscle, the man gained one of the pillars and slid to the ground. The galleries of the Hippodrome found voice immediately.

While the acrobat hung from the cornice striving to get hold of the pillar with his feet and legs, Sergius was wrestling with the question, what could impel a fellow being to tempt Providence so rashly? If a messenger with intelligence for some one in the procession, why not wait for him outside? In short, the monk was a trifle vexed; but doubly observant now, he saw the man hasten to Demedes, and Demedes bend low in the saddle to receive a communication from him. The courier then hurried away through the Gate, while the chief returned to his place; but, instructed probably by some power of divination proceeding from sympathy and often from suspicion, one of the many psychological mysteries about which we keep promising ourselves a day of enlightenment, Sergius observed a change in the latter. He was restless, impatient, and somewhat too imperative in hastening the retirement of the brethren. The message had obviously excited him.

Now Sergius would have freely given the best of his earthly possessions to have known at that moment the subject of the communication delivered by a route so extraordinary; but leaving him to his conjectures, there is no reason why the reader should not be more confidentially treated.

"Sir," the messenger had whispered to Demedes, "she has left her father's, and is coming this way."

"How is she coming?"

"In her sedan."

"Who is with her?"

"She is alone."

"And her porters?"

"The Bulgarians."

"Thank you. Go now—out by the Gate—to the keeper of the Imperial Cistern. Tell him to await me under the wall in the Bucoleon garden with my chair. He will understand. Come to the Temple tomorrow for your salary."

CHAPTER XIX
THE PRINCE BUILDS CASTLES FOR HIS GUL BAHAR

The words between Demedes and his courier may have the effect of additionally exciting the reader's curiosity; for better understanding, therefore, we will take the liberty of carrying him from the Hippodrome to the house of Uel the merchant.

Much has been said about the Prince of India's affection for Lael; so much indeed that there is danger of its being thought one sided. A greater mistake could scarcely be. She returned his love as became a daughter attentive, tender and obedient. Without knowing anything of his past life except as it was indistinctly connected with her family, she regarded him a hero and a sage whose devotion to her, multiform and unwearied, was both a delight and an honor. She was very sympathetic, and in everything of interest to him responded with interest. His word in request or direction was law to her. Such in brief was the charming mutuality between them.

The night before he started for Plati, Lael sat with him on the roof. He was happy of his resolution to stay with her. The moonlight was ample for them. Looking up into his face, her chin in a palm, an elbow on his knee, she listened while he talked of his plans, and was the more interested because he made her understand she was the inspiration of them all.

"The time for my return home is up," he said, forgetting to specify where the home was, "and I should have been off before this but for my little girl—my Gul Bahar"—and he patted her head fondly. "I cannot go and leave her; neither can I take her with me, for what would then become of father Uel? When she was a child it might not have been so hard for me to lose sight of her, but now—ah, have I not seen you grow day by day taller, stronger, wiser, fairer of person, sweeter of soul, until you are all I fancied you would be—until you are my ideal of a young woman of our dear old Israel, the loveliness of Judah in your eyes and on your cheek, and of a spirit to sit in the presence of the Lord like one invited and welcome? Oh, I am very happy!"

He kept silence awhile, indulging in retrospect. If she could have followed him! Better probably that she could not.

"It is a day of ease to me, dear, and I cannot see any unlawfulness in extending the day into months, or a year, or years indefinitely, and in making the most of it. Can you?" he asked, smiling at her.

"I am but a handmaiden, and my master's eyes are mine," she replied.

"That was well said—ever so well said," he returned. "The words would have become Ruth speaking to her lord who was of the kindred of Elimelech... Yes, I will stay with my Gul Bahar, my most precious one. I am resolved. She loves me now, but can I not make her love me still more— Oh, doubt not, doubt not! Her happiness shall be the measure of her love for me. That is the right way, is it not?"

"My father is never wrong," Lael answered, laughing.

"Flatterer!" he exclaimed, pressing her cheeks between his hands.... "Oh, I have it marked out already! In the dry lands of my country, I have seen a farmer, wanting to lead water to a perishing field, go digging along the ground, while the stream bubbled and leaped behind him, tame and glad as a petted lamb. My heart is the field to be watered—your love, O my pretty, pretty Gul Bahar, is the refreshing stream, and I will lead it after me—never fear!... Listen, and I will tell you how I will lead it. I will make you a Princess. These Greeks are a proud race, but they shall bow to you; for we will live amongst them, and you shall have things richer than their richest— trinkets of gold and jewels, a palace, and a train of women equal to that of the Queen who went visiting Solomon. They praise themselves when they look at their buildings, but I tell you they know nothing of the art which turns dreams into stones. The crags and stones have helped them to their models. I will teach them better—to look higher—to find vastness with grace and color in the sky. The dome of Sancta Sophia—what is it in comparison with the Hindoo masterpieces copied from the domes of God on the low-lying clouds in the distance opposite the sun?"

Then he told her of his palace in detail—of the fronts, no two of them alike—the pillars, those of red granite, those of porphyry, and the others of marble—windows which could not be glutted with light—arches such as the Western Kaliphs transplanted from Damascus and Bagdad, in form first seen in a print of the hoof of Borak. Then he described the interior, courts, halls; passages, fountains: and when he had thus set the structure before her, he said, softly smoothing her hair:

"There now—you have it all—and verily, as Hiram, King of Tyre, helped Solomon in his building, he shall help me also."

"How can he help you?" she asked, shaking her finger at him. "He has been dead this thousand years, and more."

"Yes, dear, to everybody but me," he answered, lightly, and asked in turn: "How do you like the palace?"

"It will be wonderful!"

"I have named it. Would you like to hear the name?"

"It is something pretty, I know."

"The Palace of Lael."

Her cry of delighted surprise, given with clasped hands and wide-open eyes, would have been tenfold payment were he putting her in possession of the finished house.

The sensation over, he told her of his design for a galley.

"We know how tiresome the town becomes. In winter, it is cheerless and damp; in summer, it is hot, dusty and in every way trying. Weariness will invade our palace—yes, dear, though we hide from it in the shady heart of our Hall of Fountains. We can provide against everything but the craving for change. Not being birds to fly, and unable to compel the eagles to lend us their wings, the best resort is a galley; then the sea is ours—the sea, wide, mysterious, crowded with marvels. I am never so near the stars as there. When a wave is bearing me up, they seem descending to meet me. Times have been when I thought the Pleiades were about to drop into my palm.... Here is my galley. You see, child, the palace is to be yours, the galley mine."

Thereupon he described a trireme of a hundred and twenty oars, sixty on a side, and ended, saying: "Yes, the peerless ship will be mine, but every morning it shall be yours to say Take it here or there, until we have seen every city by the sea; and there are enough of them, I promise, to keep us going and going forever were it not that the weariness which drove us from our palace will afterwhile drive us back to it. How think you I have named my galley?"

"Lael," she answered.

"No, try again."

"The world is too full of names for me. Tell me."

"Gul Bahar," he returned.

Again she clasped her hands, and gave the little cry in his ears so pleasant.

Certainly the Prince was pleading with effect, and laying up happiness in great store to cheer him through unnumbered sterile years inevitably before him after time had resolved this Lael into a faint and fading memory, like the other Lael gone to dust under the stone at Jerusalem.

The first half of the night was nearly spent when he arose to conduct her across the street to Uel's house. The last words at the head of the steps were these: "Now, dear, to-morrow I must go a journey on business which will keep me three days and nights—possibly three weeks. Tell father Uel what I say. Tell him also that I have ordered you to stay indoors while I am absent, unless he can accompany you. Do you hear me?"

"Three weeks!" she cried, protestingly. "Oh, it will be so lonesome! Why may I not go with Syama?"

"Syama would be a wisp of straw in the hands of a ruffian. He could not even call for help."

"Then why not with Nilo?"

"Nilo is to attend me."

"Oh, I see," she said, with a merry laugh. "It is the Greek, the Greek, my persecutor! Why, he has not recovered from his fright yet; he has deserted me."

He answered gravely: "Do you remember a bear tender, one of the amusements at the fisherman's fete?"

"Oh, yes."

"He was the Greek."

"He!" she cried, astonished.

"Yes. I have it from Sergius the monk; and further, my child, he was there in pursuit of you."

"Oh, the monster! I threw him my fan!"

The Prince knew by the tremulous voice she was wounded, and hastened to say: "It was nothing. He deceived everybody but Sergius. I spoke of the pestilent fellow because you wanted a reason for my keeping you close at home. Perhaps I exacted too much of you. If I only knew certainly how long I shall be detained! The three weeks will be hard—and it may be Uel cannot go with you—his business is confining. So if you do venture out, take your sedan—everybody knows to whom it belongs—and the old Bulgarian porters. I have paid them enough to be faithful to us. Are you listening, child?"

"Yes, yes—and I am so glad!"

He walked down the stairs half repenting the withdrawal of his prohibition.

"Be it so," he said, crossing the street. "The confinement might be hurtful. Only go seldom as you can; then be sure you return before sunset, and that you take and keep the most public streets. That is all now."

"You are so good to me!" she said, putting her arm round his neck, and kissing him. "I will try and stay in the house. Come back early. Farewell."

Next day about noon the Prince of India took the galley, and set out for Plati.

The day succeeding his departure was long with Lael. She occupied herself with her governess, however, and did a number of little tasks such as women always have in reserve for a more convenient season.

The second day was much more tedious. The forenoon was her usual time for recitations to the Prince; she also read with him then, and practised talking some of the many languages of which he was master. That part of the day she accordingly whiled through struggling with her books.

She was earnest in the attempt at study; but naturally, the circumstances considered, she dropped into thinking of the palace and galley. What a delightful glorious existence they prefigured! And it was not a dream! Her father, the Prince of India, as she proudly and affectionately called him, did not deal in idle promises, but did what he said. And besides being a master of design in many branches of art, he had an amazing faculty of describing the things he designed. That is saying he had the mind's eye to see his conceptions precisely as they would appear in finished state. So in talking his subjects always seemed before him for portraiture. One can readily perceive the capacity he must have had for making the unreal appear real to a listener, and also how he could lead Lael, her hand in his, through a house more princely than anything of the kind in Constantinople, and on board a ship such as never sailed unless on a painted ocean—a house like the Taj Mahal, a vessel like that which burned on the Cydnus. She decided what notable city by the sea she wanted most to look at next, and in naming them over, smiled at her own indecision.

The giving herself to such fancies was exactly what the Prince intended; only he was to be the central figure throughout. Whether in the palace or on the ship, she was to think of him alone, and always as the author of the splendor and the happiness. Of almost any other person we would speak compassionately; but he had lived long enough to know better than dream so childishly—long enough at least to know there is a law for everything except the vagaries of a girl scarcely sixteen.

After all, however, if his scheme was purely selfish, perhaps it may be pleasing to the philosophers who insist that relations cannot exist without carrying along with them their own balance of compensations, to hear how Lael filled the regal prospect set before her with visions in which Sergius, young, fair, tall and beautiful, was the hero, and the Prince only a paternal contributor. If the latter led her by the hand here and there, Sergius went with them so close behind she could hear his feet along the marble, and in the voyages she took, he was always a passenger.

The trial of the third day proved too much for the prisoner. The weather was delightfully clear and warm, and in the afternoon she fell to thinking of the promenade on the wall by the Bucoleon, and of the waftures over the Sea from the Asian Olympus. They were sweet in her remembrance, and the longing for them was stronger of a hope the presence of which she scarcely admitted to herself—a hope of meeting Sergius. She wanted to ask him if the bear-tender at the fete could have been the Greek. Often as she thought of that odious creature with her fan, she blushed, and feared Sergius might seriously misunderstand her.

About three o'clock she ordered her chair brought to father Uel's door at exactly four, having first dutifully run over the conditions the Prince had imposed upon her. Uel was too busy to be her escort. Syama, if he went, would be no protection; but she would return early. To be certain, she made a calculation. It would take about half an hour to get to the wall; the sun would set soon after seven; by starting home at six she could have fully an hour and a half for the airing, which meant a possible hour and a half with Sergius.

At four o'clock the sedan was set down before the merchant's house, and, for a reason presently apparent, the reader to whom vehicles of the kind are unfamiliar is advised to acquaint himself somewhat thoroughly with them. In idea, as heretofore observed, this one was a box constructed with a seat for a single passenger; a door in front allowed exit and entrance; besides the window in the door, there was a smaller opening on each side. For portage, it was affixed centrally and in an upright position to two long poles; these, a porter in front and another behind grasped at the ends, easing the burden by straps passed over the shoulders. The box was high enough for the passenger to stand in it.

Lest this plain description should impose an erroneous idea of the appearance of the carriage, we again advert to its upholstery in silk-velvet orange-tinted; to the cushions covering the seat; to the lace curtaining the windows in a manner to permit view from within while screening the occupant from obtrusive eyes without; and to the elaborate decoration of the exterior, literally a mosaic of vari-colored woods, mother-of-pearl and gold, the latter in lines and flourishes. In fine, to such a pitch of gorgeousness had the Prince designed the chair, intending the public should receive it as an attestation of his love for the child to whom it was specially set apart, that it became a notoriety and avouched its ownership everywhere in the city.

The reader would do well in the next place to give a glance at the men who brought the chair to the door—two burly fellows, broad-faced, shock-headed, small-eyed, sandalled, clad in semi-turbans, gray shirts, and gray trousers immensely bagged behind—professional porters; for the service demanded skill. A look by one accustomed to the compound of races hived in Constantinople would have determined them Bulgarians in extraction, and subjects of the Sultan by right of recent conquest. They had settled upon the Prince of India in a kind of retainership. As the chair belonged to Lael, from long employment as carriers they belonged to the chair. Their patron dealt very liberally with them, and for that reason had confidence in their honesty and faithfulness. That they should have pride in the service, he dressed them in a livery. On this occasion, however, they presented themselves in every-day costume—a circumstance which would not have escaped the Prince, or Uel, or Syama.

The only witness of the departure was the governess, who came out and affectionately settled her charge in the chair, and heard her name the streets which the Bulgarians were to pursue, all of them amongst the most frequented of the city. Gazing at her through the window the moment the chair was raised, she thought Lael never appeared lovelier and was herself pleased and lulled with the words she received at parting:

"I will be home before sunset."

The carriers in going followed instructions, except that upon arrival at the Hippodrome, observing it already in possession of a concourse of people waiting for the Epicureans, they passed around the enormous pile, and entered the imperial gardens by a gate north of Sancta Sophia.

Lael found the promenade thronged with habitues, and falling into the current moving toward Point Serail, she permitted her chair to become part of it; after which she was borne backward and forward from the Serail to the Port of Julian, stopping occasionally to gaze at the Isles of the Princes seemingly afloat and drifting through the purple haze of the distance.

Where, she persisted in asking herself, is Sergius? Lest he might pass unobserved, she kept the curtains of all the windows aside, and every long gown and tall hat she beheld set her heart to fluttering. Her eagerness to meet the monk at length absorbed her.

The sun marked five o'clock—then half after five—then, in more rapid declension, six, and still she went pendulously to and fro along the wall—six o'clock, the hour for starting home; but she had not seen Sergius. On land the shadows were lengthening rapidly; over the sea, the brightness was dulling, and the air perceptibly freshening. She awoke finally to the passage of time, and giving up the hope which had been holding her to the promenade, reluctantly bade the carriers take her home. "Shall we go by the streets we came?" the forward man asked, respectfully.

"Yes," she returned.

Then, as he closed the door, she was startled by noticing the promenade almost deserted; the going and coming were no longer in two decided currents; groups had given place to individual loiterers. These things she noticed, but not the glance the porters threw to each other telegraphic of some understanding between them.

At the foot of the stairs descending the wall she rapped on the front window.

"Make haste," she said, to the leading man; "make haste, and take the nearest way."

This, it will be perceived, left him to choose the route in return, and he halted long enough to again telegraph his companion by look and nod.

Between the eastern front of the Bucoleon and the sea-wall the entire space was a garden. From the wall the ascent to the considerable plateau crowned by the famous buildings was made easy by four graceful terraces, irregular in width, and provided with zigzag roads securely paved.

Roses and lilies were not the only products of the terraces; vines and trees of delicate leafage and limited growth flourished upon them in artistic arrangement. Here and there were statues and lofty pillars, and fountains in the open, and fountains under tasteful pavilions, planted advantageously at the angles. Except where the trees and shrubbery formed groups dense enough to serve as obstructions, the wall commanded the whole slope. Time was when all this loveliness was jealously guarded for the lords and ladies of the court; but when Blacherne became the Very High Residence the Bucoleon lapsed to the public. His Majesty maintained it; the people enjoyed it.

Following the zigzags, the carriers mounted two of the terraces without meeting a soul. The garden was deserted. Hastening on, they turned the Y at the beginning of the third terrace. A hundred or more yards along the latter there was a copse of oleander and luxuriant filbert bushes over-ridden by fig trees. As the sedan drew near this obstruction, its bearers flung quick glances above and below them, and along the wall, and descrying another sedan off a little distance but descending toward them, they quickened their pace as if to pass the copse first. In the midst of it, at the exact point where the view from every direction was cut off, the man in the rear stumbled, struggled to recover himself, then fell flat. His ends of the poles struck the pavement with a crash—the chair toppled backward—Lael screamed. The leader slipped the strap from his shoulder, and righted the carriage by letting it go to the ground, floor down. He then opened the door.

"Do not be scared," he said to Lael, whose impulse was to scramble out. "Keep your seat—my comrade has had a fall—that is nothing—keep your seat. I will get him up, and we will be going on in a minute."

Lael became calm.

The man walked briskly around, and assisted his partner to his feet. There was a hurried consultation between them, of which the passenger heard only the voices. Presently they both came to the door, looking much mortified.

"The accident is more than I thought," the leader said, humbly.

By this time the chill of the first fear was over with Lael, and she asked: "Can we go on?"

"If the Princess can walk—yes."

She turned pale.

"What is it? Why must I walk?"

"Our right-hand pole is broken, and we have nothing to tie it with."

And the other man added: "If we only had a rope!"

Now the mishap was not uncommon, and remembering the fact, Lael grew cooler, and bethought herself of the silken scarf about her waist. To take it off was the work of a moment.

"Here," she said, rather pleased at her presence of mind; "you can make a rope of this."

They took the scarf, and busied themselves, she thought, trying to bandage the fractured shaft. Again they stood before the door.

"We have done the best we can. The pole will hold the chair, but not with the Princess. She must walk—there is nothing else for her."

Thereupon the assistant interposed a suggestion: "One of us can go for another chair, and overtake the Princess before she reaches the gate."

This was plausible, and Lael stepped forth. She sought the sun first; the palace hid it, yet she was cheered by its last rays redly enlivening the heights of Scutari across the Bosphorus, and felicitated herself thinking it still possible to get home before the night was completely fallen.

"Yes, one of you may seek another"—

That instant the sedan her porters had descried before they entered the copse caught her eyes. Doubt, fear, suspicion vanished; her face brightened:

"A chair! A chair!—and no one in it!" she cried, with the vivacity of a child. "Bring it here, and let us be gone."

The carriage so heartily welcomed was of the ordinary class, and the carriers were poorly clad, hard-featured men, but stout and well trained. They came at call.

"Where are you going?"

"To the wall."

"Are you engaged?"

"No, we hoped to find some one belated there."

"Do you know Uel the merchant?"

"We have heard of him. He has a stall in the market, and deals in diamonds."

"Do you know where his house is?"

"On the street from St. Peter's Gate, under the church by the old cistern."

"We have a passenger here, his daughter, and want you to carry her home. One of our poles is broken."

"Will she pay us our price?"

"How much do you want?"

Here Lael interposed: "Stand not on the price. My father will pay whatever they demand."

The Bulgarians seemed to consider a moment.

"It is the best we can do," the leader said.

"Yes, the very best," the other returned.

Thereupon the first one went to the new sedan, and opened the door. "If the Princess will take seat," he said, respectfully, "we will pick up, and follow close after her."

Lael stepped in, saying as the door closed upon her: "Make haste, for the night is near."

The strangers without further ado faced about, and started up the road.

"Wait, wait," she heard her old leader call out.

There was a silence during which she imagined the Bulgarians were adjusting the straps upon their shoulders; then there came a quick: "Now go, and hurry, or we will pass you."

These were the last words she heard from them, for the new men put themselves in motion. She missed the cushions of her own carriage, but was content—she was returning home, and going fast. This latter she judged by the slide and shuffle of the loose-sandalled feet under her, and the responsive springing of the poles.

The reaction of spirit which overtook her was simply the swing of nature back to its normal lightness. She ceased thinking of the accident, except as an excuse for the delay to which she had been subjected. She was glad the Prince's old retainer had escaped without injury. There was no window back through which she could look, yet she fancied she heard the feet of the faithful Bulgarians; they said nothing, therefore everything was proceeding well. Now and then she peered out through the side windows to notice the deepening of the shades of evening. Once a temporary darkness filled the narrow box, but it gave her no uneasiness—the men were passing out of the garden through a covered gate. Now they were in a street, and the travelling plain.

Thus assured and tranquil, maiden-like, she again fell to thinking of Sergius. Where could he have been? What kept him from the promenade? He might have known she would be there. Was the Hegumen so exacting? Old people are always forgetting they cannot make young people old like themselves; and it was so inconvenient, especially now she wanted to hear of the bear tender. Then she adverted to the monk more directly. How tall he was! How noble and good of face! And his religion—she wished ever so quietly that he could be brought over to the Judean faith—she wished it, but did not ask herself why. To say truth, there was a great deal more feeling in undertone, as it were, touching these points than thought; and while she kept it going, the carriers forgot not to be swift, nor did the night tarry.

Suddenly there was an awakening. From twilight deeply shaded, she passed into utter darkness. While, with her face to a window, she tried to see where she was and make out what had happened, the chair stopped, and next moment was let drop to the ground. The jar and the blank blackness about renewed her fears, and she called out:

"What is the matter? Where are we? This is not my father Uel's."

And what time an answer should have been forthcoming had there been good faith and honesty in the situation, she heard a rush of feet which had every likeness to a precipitate flight, and then a banging noise, like the slamming to of a ponderous door.

She had time to think of the wisdom of her father, the Prince of India, and of her own wilfulness—time to think of the Greek—time to call once on

Sergius—then a flutter of consciousness—an agony of fright—and it was as if she died.

CHAPTER XX
THE SILHOUETTE OF A CRIME

A genius thoroughly wicked—such was Demedes.

Quick to see the disgust the young men of Constantinople had fallen into for the disputes their elders were indulging about the Churches, he proposed that they should discard religion, and reinstate philosophy; and at their request he formulated the following:

"Nature is the lawgiver; the happiness of man is the primary object of Nature: hence for youth, Pleasure; for old age, Repentance and Piety, the life hereafter being a respectable conjecture."

The principles thus tersely stated were eagerly adopted, and going forward with his scheme, it may be said the Academy was his design, and its organization his work. In recognition of his superior abilities, the grateful Academicians elected him their High Priest.

We have seen how the public received the motto of the society. Patience, Courage, Judgment looked fair and disclosed nothing wrong; but there was an important reservation to it really the only secret observed. This was the motto in full, known only to the initiated—Patience, Courage, Judgment *in the pursuit of Pleasure.*

From the hour of his installation as High Priest, Demedes was consumed by an ambition to illustrate the motto in its entirety, by doing something which should develop the three virtues in connection with unheard of daring and originality.

It is to be added here that to his own fortune, he had now the treasury of the Academy to draw upon, and it was full. In other words, he had ample means to carry out any project his *judgment* might approve.

He pondered the matter long. One day Lael chanced to fall under his observation. She was beautiful and the town talk. Here, he thought, was a subject worth studying, and speedily two mysteries presented themselves to him: Who was the Prince of India? And what was her true relationship to the Prince?

We pass over his resorts in unravelling the mysteries; they were many and cunning, and thoroughly tried the first virtue of the Academical motto; still the sum of his finding with respect to the Prince was a mere theory—he was a Jew and rich—beyond this Demedes took nothing for his pains.

He proceeded next to investigate Lael. She too was of Jewish origin, but unlike other Jewesses, wonderful to say, she had two fathers, the diamond merchant and the Prince of India.

Nothing better could be asked—so his judgment, the third virtue of the motto, decreed. In Byzantine opinion, Jews were socially outside decent regard. In brief, if he should pursue the girl to her ruin, there was little to fear from an appeal by either of her fathers to the authorities. Exile might be the extremest penalty of discovery.

He began operations by putting into circulation the calumny, too infamous for repetition, with which we have seen him attempt to poison Sergius. Robbing the victim of character would deprive her of sympathy, and that, in the event of failure, would be a half defence for himself with the public.

He gave himself next to finding what to do with the little Princess, as he termed her. All his schemes respecting her fell short in that they lacked originality. At last the story of the Plague of Crime, stumbled on in the library of the St. James', furnished a suggestion novel, if not original, and he accepted it.

Proceeding systematically, he first examined the cistern, paddling through it in a boat with a flambeau at the bow. He sounded the depth of the water, counted the pillars, and measured the spaces between them; he tested the purity of the air; and when the reconnoissance was through, he laughed at the simplicity of the idea, and embodied his decision in a saying eminently becoming his philosophic character—the best of every new thing is that it was once old.

Next he reduced the affair to its elements. He must steal her—such was the deed in simplest term—and he must have assistants, but prudence whispered just as few of them as possible. He commenced a list, heading it with the keeper of the cistern, whom he found poor, necessitous, and anxious to better his condition. Upon a payment received, that worthy became warmly interested, and surprised his employer with suggestions of practical utility.

Coming then to the abduction, he undertook a study of her daily life, hoping it would disclose something available. A second name was thereupon entered in his list of accomplices.

One day a beggar with sore eyes and a foot swollen with elephantiasis—an awful object to sight—set a stool in an angle of the street a few doors from Uel's house; and thenceforward the girl's every appearance was communicated to Demedes, who never forgot the great jump of heart with which he heard of the gorgeous chair presented her by the Prince, and of the visit she forthwith made to the wall of the Bucoleon.

Soon as he satisfied himself that the Bulgarians were in the Prince's pay, he sounded them. They too were willing to permit him to make them comfortable the remainder of their days, especially as, after the betrayal asked of them, they had only to take boat to the Turkish side of the Bosphorus, beyond pursuit and demand. His list of assistants was then increased to four.

Now indeed the game seemed secure, and he prepared for the hour which was to bring the Jewess to him.

The keeper of the cistern was the solitary occupant of a house built round a small court from which a flight of stone steps admitted to the darkened water. He had a felicitous turn for mechanics, and undertook the building of a raft with commodious rooms on it. Demedes went with him to select a place of anchorage, and afterward planned the structure to fit between four of the pillars in form thus:

[Illustration]

Seeing the design on paper, Demedes smiled—it was so like a cross; the part in lines being the landing, and the rest a room divisible at pleasure into three rooms. A boat was provided for communication, and to keep it hid from visitors, a cord was fixed to a pillar off in the darkness beyond ken, helped though it might be by torches; so standing on the stone steps, one could draw the vessel to and fro, exactly as a flag is hoisted or lowered on a staff.

The work took a long time, but was at last finished. The High Priest of the Epicureans came meantime to have something akin to tender feeling for his intended victim. He indulged many florid dreams of when she should grace his bower in the Imperial Cistern; and as the time of her detention might peradventure extend into months, he vowed to enrich the bower until the most wilful spirit would settle into contentment.

Neither the money nor the time spent in this part of the preparation was begrudged; on the contrary, Demedes took delight in the occupation; it was exercise for ingenuity, taste, and judgment, always a pleasure to such as possess the qualities. In fact, the whole way through he likened himself to a bird building a nest for its mate.

After all, however, the part of the project most troublesome of arrangement by the schemer, was getting the Princess into the cistern keeper's house—that is, without noise, scuffle, witnesses, or a clew left behind. To this he gave more hours of reflection than to the rest altogether. The method we have seen executed was decided upon when he arrived at two conclusions; that the attempt was most likely to succeed in the garden of the Bucoleon, and that the Princess must be lured from her chair into another less conspicuous and not so well known. Greatly to his regret, but of necessity, he then saw himself compelled to increase his list of accessories to six. Yet he derived peace remembering none of them, with exception of the keeper, knew aught of the affair beyond their immediate connection with it. The porters, for instance, who dropped the unfortunate and fled, leaving her in the sedan to intents dead, had not the slightest idea of what was to become of her afterwards.

The conjunctions needful to success in the enterprise were numerous; yet the Greek accepted the waiting they put him to as a trial of the Patience to which the motto pledged him. He believed in being ready. When the house was built and furnished, he drilled the Bulgarians with such particularity that the scene in the garden may be said to have been literally to order. Probably the nearest approach to the mythical sixth sense is the power of casting one's mind forward to a coming event, and arranging its occurrence; and whether some have it a gift of nature, while others derive it from cultivation, this much is certain—without it, no man will ever create anything originally.

Now, if the reader pleases, Demedes was too liberally endowed with the faculty, trait or sense of which we have just spoken to permit the sedan to be broken; such an accident would have been very inconvenient at the critical moment succeeding the exchange of chairs. The prompter ever at the elbow of a bad man instructed him that, aside from what the Prince of India could not do, it was in his power to arouse the city, and set it going hue and cry; and then the carriage, rich, glittering, and known to so many, would draw pursuit, like a flaming torch at night. So it occurred to Demedes, the main object being to conceal the going to the cistern keeper's, why not use the sedan to deceive the pursuers? He scored the idea with an exultant laugh.

Returning now to the narrative of the enactment, directly the strange porters moved out of the copse with their unsuspecting passenger, the Bulgarians slung the poles to their shoulders, and followed up the zigzag to the Y of the fourth terrace; there they turned, and retraced their steps to the promenade; whence, after reaching Point Serail, they doubled on their track, descended the wall, traversed the garden, and, passing the gate by which they came, paraded their empty burden around the Hippodrome and down a thronged street. And again doubling, they returned to the wall, and finding it forsaken, and the night having fallen, they abandoned the chair at a spot where the water on the seaward side was deep and favorable for whatever violence theory might require. In the course of this progress they were met by numberless people, many of whom stopped to observe the gay turnout, doubting not that the little Princess was within directing its movements. Finally, their task thoroughly done, the Bulgarians hurried to where a boat was in readiness, and crossing to Scutari, lost themselves in the growing dominions of their rightful Lord, the Sultan.

One casually reading this silhouette of a crime in act is likely to rest here, thinking there was nothing more possible of doing either to forward the deed or facilitate the escape of those engaged in it; yet Demedes was not content. There were who had heard him talk of the girl—who knew she had been much in his thought—to whom he had furnished ground for suspecting him of following her with evil intent—Sergius amongst others. In a word, he saw a necessity for averting attention from himself in the connection. Here also his wit was willing and helpful. The moment the myrmidon dropped from the portico with news that the Princess was out in her chair unattended, he decided she was proceeding to the wall.

"The gods are mindful of me!" he said, his blood leaping quick. "Now is the time ripe, and the opportunity come!"

Looking at the sun, he fixed the hour, and reflected:

"Five o'clock—she is on the wall. Six o'clock—she is still there. Half after six—making up her mind to go home. Oh, but the air will be sweet, and the sea lovely! Seven o'clock—she gives order, and the Bulgarians signal my men on the fourth terrace. Pray Heaven the Russian keep to his prayers or stay hearkening for my father's bell!... Here am I seen of these thousands. Later on—about the time she forsakes the wall—my presence shall be notorious along the streets from the Temple to Blacherne. Then what if the monk talks? May the fiend pave his path with stumbling-blocks and breaknecks! The city will not discredit its own eyes."

The Epicureans, returning from the Hippodrome, reached their Temple about half after five o'clock. The dispersal occupied another hour; shortly after, the regalia having been put away, and the tripods and banners stored, Demedes called to his mounted assistants:

"My brothers, we have worked hard, but the sowing has been bounteous and well done. Philosophy in flowers, religion in sackcloth—that is the comparison we have given the city. There will be no end to our harvest. To-morrow our doors open to stay open. To-day I have one further service for you. To your horses and ride with me to the gate of Blacherne. We may meet the Emperor."

They answered him shouting: "Live the Emperor!"

"Yes," cried Demedes, when the cheering was over, "by this time he should be tired of the priests; and what is that but the change of heart needful to an Epicurean?"

Laughing and joking, they mounted, eight of them, in flowers as when in the Hippodrome. The sun was going down, but the streets were yet bright with day. It was the hour when balconies overhanging the narrow thoroughfares were crowded with women and children, and the doors beset with servants—the hour Byzantine gossips were abroad filling and unfilling their budgets. How the wooden houses trembled while the cavalcade went galloping by! What thousands of bright eyes peered down upon the cavaliers, attracted by the shouting and laughter! Now and then some person would be a little late in attempting to cross before him; then with what grace Demedes would spur after him, his bow and bowstring for whip! And how the spectators shrieked with delight when he overtook the culprit, and wore the flowers out flogging him! And when a balcony was low, and illuminated with a face fairer than common, how the gallant young riders plucked roses from their helms and shields, and tossed them in shouting:

"Largesse, Lady—largesse of thy smiles!"

"Look again! Another rose for another look!"

"From the brave to the fair!"

Thus to the gate of Blacherne. There they drew up, and saluted the officer of the guard, and cheered: "Live Constantine! To the good Emperor, long life!"

All the way Demedes rode with lifted visor. Returning through the twilight, earlier in the close streets than in the open, he led his company by the houses of Uel and the Prince of India. Something might be learned of what was going on with the little Princess by what was going on there; and the many persons he saw in the street signified alarm and commotion.

"Ho, here!" he shouted, drawing rein. "What does this mean? Somebody dead or dying?"

"Uel, the master of the house, is afraid for his child. She should have been home before sundown. He is sending friends out to look for her."

There was a whole story in the answer, and the conspirator repressed a cry of triumph, and rode on.

CHAPTER XXI
SERGIUS LEARNS A NEW LESSON

Syama, always thoughtful, took care of the treasure brought from Plati, and standing by the door watched his master through the night, wondering what the outcome of his agitation would be.

It were useless attempting to describe how the gloomy soul of the Jew exercised itself. His now ungovernable passions ran riot within him. He who had seen so much of life, who had made history as the loomsmen of Bokhara make carpets, who dealt with kings and kingdoms, and the superlatives of every kind canonized in the human imagination—he to be so demeaned! Yet it was not the disrespect to himself personally that did the keenest stinging, nor even the enmity of Heaven denying him the love permitted every other creature, bird, beast, crawling reptile, monster of the sea—these were as the ruffling of the weather feathers of a fighting eagle, compared with the torture he endured from consciousness of impotency to punish the wrongdoers as he would like to punish them.

That Lael was immured somewhere in the city, he doubted not; and he would find her, for what door could stand shut against knocking by a hand with money in it? But might it not be too late? The flower he could recover, but the fragrance and purity of bloom—what of them? How his breast enlarged and shrank under the electric touch of that idea! The devil who did the deed might escape him, for hell was vast and deep; yet the city remained, even the Byzantium ancient of days like himself, and he would hold it a hostage for the safe return of his Gul Bahar.

All the night long he walked without pause; it seemed unending to him; at length the faintest rosy tint, a reflection from morning's palette of splendor, lodged on the glass of his eastern window, and woke him from his misery. At the door he found Syama.

"Syama," he said, kindly, "bring me the little case which has in it my choicest drugs."

It was brought him, an oblong gold box encrusted with brilliants. Opening it, he found a spatula of fine silver on a crystal lid, and under the lid, in compartments, pellets differently colored, one of which he selected, and dropped in his throat.

"There, put it back," he said, returning the box to Syama, who went out with it. Looking then at the brightness brighter growing through the window, "Welcome," he continued, speaking to the day as it were a person:

"Thou wert slow coming, yet welcome. I am ready for this new labor imposed on me, and shall not rest, or sleep, or hunger, or thirst until it is done. Thou shalt see I have not lived fourteen centuries for nothing; that in a hunt for vengeance I have not lost my cunning. I will give them till thou hast twice run thy course; then, if they bring her not, they will find the God they worship once more the Lord God of Israel."

Syama returned.

"Thou art a faithful man, Syama, and I love thee. Get me a cup of the Cipango leaves—no bread, the cup alone."

While waiting, the Prince continued his silent walk; but when the tea was brought, he said: "Good! It shall go after the meat of the poppies"—adding to Syama—"While I drink, do thou seek Uel, and bring him to me."

When the son of Jahdai entered, the Prince looked at him a moment, and asked: "Hast thou word of her?"

"Not a word, not one word," and with the reply the merchant's face sunk until the chin rested on his breast. The hopelessness observable in the voice, joined to the signs of suffering apparent in the manner, was irresistibly touching. Another instant, then the elder advanced to him, and took his hand.

"We are brothers," he said, with exceeding gentleness. "She was our child—ours—thine, yet mine. She loved us both. We loved her, thou not more, I not less. She went not willingly from us; we know that much, because we know she loved us, me not less, thee not more. A pitfall was digged for her. Let us find it. She is calling for us from the bottom—I hear her—now thy name, now mine—and there is no time to be lost. Wilt thou do as I say?"

"You are strong, and I weak; be it entirely as you say," Uel answered, without looking up, for there were tears in his eyes, and a great groan growing in his throat.

"Well, see thou now. We will find the child, be the pit ever so deep; but—it is well bethinking—we may not find her the undefiled she was, or we may find her dead. I believe she had a spirit to prefer death to dishonor—but dead or dishonored, wilt thou merge thy interest in her into mine?"

"Yes."

"I alone am to decide then what best becomes us to do. Is it agreed?"

"Yes—such faith have I in you."

"Oh, but understand thee, son of Jahdai! I speak not merely as a father, but as an Israelite."

Uel looked at the speaker's face, and was startled. The calm voice, low and evenly toned, to which he had been listening, had not prepared him for the livid pursing he saw under the eyes, and the pupils lurid and unnaturally dilated—effects we know, good reader, of the meat of the poppies assisted by the friendly Cipango leaves. Yet the merchant replied, strong in the other's strength: "Am not I, too, an Israelite?—Only do not take her from me."

"Fear not. Now, son of Jahdai, let us to work. Let us first find our pretty child."

Again Uel was astonished. The countenance was bright and beaming with confidence. A world of energy seemed to have taken possession of the man. He looked inspired—looked as if a tap of his finger could fetch the extremities of the continent rolling like a carpet to his feet.

"Go now, my brother Uel, and bring hither all the clerks in the market."

"All of them—all? Consider the expense."

"Nay, son of Jahdai, be thou a true Israelite. In trade, this for that, consider the profits and stand on them closely, getting all thou canst. But here is no trade—here is honor—our honor—thine, mine. Shall a Christian beat us, and wear the virtue of our daughter as it were a leman's favor? No, by Abraham—by the mother of Israel"—a returning surge of passion blackened his face again, and quickened his speech—"by Rachael and Sarah, and all the God-loving asleep in Hebron, in this cause our money shall flow like water—even as the Euphrates in swollen tide goes bellowing to the sea, it shall flow. I will fill the mouths and eyes as well as the pockets of this Byzantium with it, until there shall not be a dune on the beach, a cranny in the wall, a rathole in its accursed seven hills unexamined. Yes, the say is mine—so thou didst agree—deny it not! Bid the clerks come, and quickly—only see to it that each brings his writing material, and a piece of paper large as his two hands. This house for their assemblage. Haste. Time flies—and from the pit, out of the shadows in the bottom of the pit, I hear the voice of Lael calling now to thee, now to me."

Uel was not deficient in strength of purpose, nor for that matter in judgment; he went and in haste; and the clerks flocked to the Prince, and wrote at his dictation. Before half the breakfasts in the city were eaten, vacant places at the church doors, the cheeks of all the gates, and the fronts of houses blazed with handbills, each with a reader before it proclaiming to listening groups:

"BYZANTINES!

"FATHERS AND MOTHERS OF BYZANTIUM!

"Last evening the daughter of Uel the merchant, a child of sixteen, small in stature, with dark hair and eyes, and fair to see, was set upon in the garden of the Bucoleon, and stolen out of her sedan chair. Neither she, nor the Bulgarians carrying her have been heard of since.

"REWARDS.

"Out of love of the child, whose name was Lael, I will pay him who returns her to me living or dead

"6,000 BEZANTS IN GOLD.

"And to him who brings me the abductor, or the name of any one engaged in the crime, with proof to convict him,

"5,000 BEZANTS IN GOLD.

"Inquire of me at Uel's stall in the Market.

"PRINCE OF INDIA."

Thus the Jew began his campaign of discovery, meaning to follow it up with punishment first, and then vengeance, the latter in conditional mood.

Let us not stop to ask about motives. This much is certain, the city arose with one mind. Such a running here and there had never been known, except possibly the times enemies in force sat down before the gates. The walls landwardly by the sea and harbor, and the towers of the walls above and below; old houses whose solitariness and decay were suspicious; new houses and their cellars; churches from crypt to pulpit and gallery; barracks and magazines, even the baker's ovens attached to them; the wharves and vessels tied up and the ships at anchor—all underwent a search. Hunting parties invaded the woods. Scorpions were unnested, and bats and owls made unhappy by daylight where daylight had never been before. Convents and monasteries were not exempt. The sea was dragged, and the great moat from the Golden Gate to the Cynegion raked for traces of a new-made grave. Nor less were the cemeteries overhauled, and tombs and sarcophagi opened, and Saints' Rests dug into and profaned. In short, but one property in Byzantium was respected—that of the Emperor. By noon the excitement had crossed to Galata, and was at high tide in the Isles of the Princes. Such power was there in the offer of bezants in gold—six thousand for the girl, five thousand for one of her captors—singly, a fortune to stir the cupidity of a Duke—together, enough to enlist a King in the work. And everywhere the two questions—Has she been found? and who is the Prince of India? Poor Uel had not space to think of his loss or yield to sorrow; the questions kept him so busy.

It must not be supposed now in this all but universal search, nobody thought of the public cisterns. They were visited. Frequently through the day parties followed each other to the Imperial reservoir; but the keeper was always in his place, cool, wary, and prepared for them. He kept open door and offered no hindrance to inspection of his house. To interrogators he gave ready replies:

"I was at home last night from sunset to sunrise. At dark I closed up, and no one could have come in afterwards without my seeing him.... I know the chair of the merchant's daughter. It is the finest in the city. The Bulgarians have carried it past my house, but they never stopped.... Oh, yes, you are welcome to do with the cistern what you please. There is the doorway to the court, and in the court is the descent to the water." Sometimes he would treat the subject facetiously: "If the girl were here, I should know it, and if I knew it—ha, ha, ha!—are bezants in gold by the thousand more precious to you than to me? Do you think I too would not like to be rich?—I who live doggedly on three noumias, helped now and then by scanty palm-salves from travellers?"

This treatment was successful. One party did insist on going beyond the court. They descended the steps about half way, looked at the great gray pillars in ghostly rows receding off into a blackness of silence thick with damps and cellar smells, each a reminder of contagion; then at the motionless opaque water, into which the pillars sank to an unknown depth: and they shivered, and cried: "Ugh! how cold and ugly!" and hastened to get out.

Undoubtedly appearances helped save the ancient cistern from examination; yet there were other influences to the same end. Its vastness was a deterrent. A thorough survey required organization and expensive means, such as torches, boats, fishing tongs and drag-nets; and why scour it at all, if not thoroughly and over every inch? Well, well—such was the decision—the trouble is great, and the uncertainty greater. Another class was restrained by a sentiment possibly the oldest and most general amongst men; that which casts a spell of sanctity around wells and springs, and stays the hand about to toss an impurity into a running stream; which impels the North American Indian to replace the gourd, and the Bedouin to spare the bucket for the next comer, though an enemy. In other words, the cistern was in daily use.

One can imagine the scene at the Prince's through the day. To bring a familiar term into service, his house was headquarters.

About eight o'clock the sedan was brought home empty, and without a sign of defacement inside or out. It told no tale.

Noon, and still no clew.

In the afternoon there was an observable cessation of vigor in the quest. Thousands broke off, and went about their ordinary business, giving the reason.

"Which way now?" would be asked them.

"Home."

"What! Has she been found?"

"Not that we know."

"Ah, you have given up."

"Yes."

"Why?"

"We are satisfied the Bulgarians stole the girl. The Turks have her; and now for a third part of either of the rewards he offers, the Prince of India, whoever he is, can ransom her. He will have plenty of time. There is no such thing as haste in a harem."

By lamplighting in the evening, the capital resumed its customary quiet, and of the turmoil of the day, the rush and eager halloo, the promiscuous delving into secret places, and upturning of things strange and suspicious, there remained nothing but a vast regret—vast in the collective sense—for the rewards lost.

Quiet crept into headquarters. To the Prince's insistence that the hunt go on, he was advised to prosecute the inquest on the other side of the Bosphorus. The argument presented him was plausible; either—thus it ran—the Bulgarians carried the child away with them or she was taken from them. They were stout men, yet there is no sign of a struggle. If they were killed, we should find their bodies; if they are alive and innocent, why are they not here? They would be entitled to the rewards along with the best of us.

Seeing the drift, the Prince refrained from debate. He only looked more grim and determined. When the house was cleared, he took the floor again fiercely restless as before. Later on Uel came in, tired, spirit-worn, and apparently in the last stage of despondency.

"Well, son of Jahdai, my poor brother," said the Prince, much moved, and speaking tenderly. "It is night, and what bringest thou?"

"Alas! Nothing, except the people say the Bulgarians did it."

"The Bulgarians! Would it were so; for look thee, in their hands she would be safe. Their worst of villany would be a ransom wrung from us. Ah, no! They might have been drawn into the conspiracy; but take her, they did not. How could they have passed the gates unseen? The night was against them. And besides, they have not the soul to devise or dare the deed. This is no common criminal, my brother. When he is found—and he will be, or hell hath entered into partnership with him—thou wilt see a Greek of title, bold from breeding and association, behind him an influence to guarantee him against the law and the Emperor. Of the classes in Byzantium to-day, who are the kings? Who but the monks? And here is a morsel of wisdom, true, else my experience is a delusion: In decaying and half-organized states, the boldest in defying public opinion are they who have the most to do in making it."

"I do not understand you," Uel interposed.

"Thou art right, my brother. I know not why I am arguing; yet I ought not to leave thee in the dark now; therefore I will go a step further. Thou art a Jew—not a Hebrew, or an Israelite, mark thee—but in the contemptuous Gentile sense, a Jew. She, our gentle Gul-Bahar, hath her beating of heart from blood thou gavest her. I also am a Jew. Now, of the classes in Byzantium, which is it by whom hate of Jews is the article of religion most faithfully practised? Think if it be not the same from whose shops proceed the right and wrong of the time—the same I myself scarce three days gone saw insult and mortify the man they chose Emperor, and not privately, in the depths of a monastery or chapel, but publicly, his court present.... Ah, now thou seest my meaning! In plainest speech, my brother, when he who invented this crime is set down before us, look not for a soldier, or a sailor, or one of thy occupation—look not for a beggar, or a laborer, or an Islamite—look rather for a Greek, with a right from relationship near or remote to summon the whole priestly craft to hold up his hands against us, Jews that we are. But I am not discouraged. I shall find her, and the titled outlaw who stole her. Or—but threats now are idle. They shall have tomorrow to bring her home. I pray pardon for keeping thee from rest and sleep. Go now. In the morning betimes see thou that the clerks come back to me here. I will have need of them again, for"—he mused a moment—"yes, if that I purpose must be, then, the worst betiding us, they shall not say I was hard and merciless, and cut their chances scant."

Uel was at the door going, when the Prince called him back.

"Wait—I do not need rest. Thou dost. Is Syama there?"

"Yes."

"Send him to me."

When the slave was come, "Go," the master said, "and bring me the golden case."

And when it was brought, he took out a pellet, and gave it to Uel.

"There—take it, and thou shalt sleep sound as the dead, and have never a dream—sound, yet healthfully. To-morrow we must work. To-morrow," he repeated when Uel was gone—"to-morrow! Till then, eternity."

Let us now shift the scene to the Monastery of the St. James'.

It is eight o'clock in the morning—about the time the empty sedan was being brought to the Prince's house. Sergius had been hearkening for the Hegumen's bell, and at the moment we look in upon him, he is with the venerable superior, helping him to breakfast, if a meal so frugal deserves the name.

The young Russian, it is to be said, retired to his cell immediately upon the conclusion of the Festival of Flowers the evening before. Awaking early, he made personal preparation for the day, and with the Brotherhood in the chapel, performed the matinal breviary services, consisting of lauds, psalms, lections and prayers. Then he took seat by his superior's door. By and by the bell called him in, and thenceforward he was occupied in the kitchen or at the elder's elbow. In brief, he knew nothing of the occurrence which had so overwhelmed the merchant and the Prince of India.

The Hegumen sat on a broad armless chair, very pale and weak—so poorly, indeed, that the brethren had excused him from chapel duties. Having filled a flagon with water, Sergius was offering it to him, when the door opened without knock, or other warning, and Demedes entered. Moving silently to his father, he stooped, and kissed his hand with an unction which brought a smile to the sunken face.

"God's benison on you, my boy. I was thinking of the airs of Prinkipo or Halki, and that they might help me somewhat; but now you are here, I will put them off. Bring the bench to my right hand, and partake with me, if but to break a crust."

"The crust has the appearance of leaven in it, and you know the party to which I belong. I am not an *azymite*."

There was scarcely an attempt to conceal the sneer with which the young man glanced at the brown loaf gracing the platter on the Hegumen's knees. Seeing then a look of pain on the paternal countenance, he continued: "No, I have had breakfast, and came to see how you are, and to apprise you that the city is being stirred from the foam on top to the dregs at the bottom, all because of an occurrence last evening, so incredible, so strange, so audacious, and so wicked it weakens confidence in society, and almost forces one to look up and wonder if God does not sometimes sleep."

The Hegumen and his attendant were aroused. Both gazed at Demedes looking the same question.

"I hesitate to tell you, my dear father, of the affair, it is so shocking. The chill of the first hearing has not left me. I am excited body and mind, and you know how faithfully I have tried to school myself against excitement—it is unbecoming—only the weak suffer it. Rather than trust myself to the narrative—though as yet there are no details—I plucked a notice from a wall while coming, and as it was the first I had of the news, and contains all I know, I brought it along; and if you care to hear, perhaps our friend Sergius will kindly give you the contents. His voice is better than mine, and he is perfectly calm."

"Yes, Sergius will read. Give him the paper."

Thereupon Demedes passed to Sergius one of the handbills with which the Prince of India had sown the city. After the first line, the monk began stammering and stumbling; at the close of the first sentence, he stopped. Then he threw a glance at the Greek, and from the gaze with which he was met, he drew understanding and self-control. "I ask thy grace, Father," he said, raising the paper, and looking at the signature. "I am acquainted with Uel the merchant, and with the child said to be stolen. I also know the man whose title is here attached. He calls himself Prince of India, but by what right I cannot say. The circumstance is a great surprise to me; so, with thy pardon, I will try the reading again."

Sergius finished the paper, and returned it to Demedes.

The Hegumen folded his hands, and said: "Oh, the flow of mercy cannot endure forever!"

Then the young men looked at each other.

To be surprised when off guard, is to give our enemy his best opportunity. This was the advantage the Greek then had. He was satisfied with the working of his scheme; yet one dread had disturbed him through the night. What would the Russian do? And when he read the Prince's proclamation, and saw the rewards offered, in amounts undreamt of, he shivered; not, as he told the Hegumen, from horror at the crime; still less from fear that the multitude might blunder on discovery; and least of all from apprehension of betrayal from his assistants, for, with exception of the cistern-keeper, they were all in flight, and a night's journey gone. Be the mass of enemies ever so great, there is always one to inspire us with liveliest concern. Here it was Sergius. He had come so recently into the world—descent from a monastery in the far north was to the metropolitan much like being born again—there was no telling what he might do. Thus moved and uncertain, the conspirator resolved to seek his adversary, if such he were, and boldly try him. In what spirit would he receive the news? That was the thought behind the gaze Demedes now bent on the unsophisticated pupil of the saintly Father Hilarion.

Sergius returned the look without an effort to hide the pain he really felt. His utmost endeavor was to control his feelings. With no idea of simulation, he wanted time to think. Altogether it would have been impossible for him to have chosen a course more perplexing to Demedes, who found himself driven to his next play.

"You know now," he said to his father, "why I decline to break a crust with you. I must go and help uncover this wicked deed. The rewards are great"—he smiled blandly—"and I should like to win one of them at least—the first one, for I have seen the girl called Lael. She interested me, and I was in danger from her. On one occasion"—he paused to throw a glance to Sergius—"I even made advances to become acquainted with her, but she repulsed me. As the Prince of India says, she was fair to see. I am sure I have your permission to engage in the hunt."

"Go, and God speed you," the Hegumen responded.

"Thank you; yet another request."

He turned to the Russian.

"Now is Sergius here tall, and, if his gown belie him not, stout, and there may be need of muscle as well as spirit; for who can tell where our feet will take us in a game like this, or what or whom we may confront? I ask you to permit him to go with me."

"Nay," said the Hegumen, "I will urge him to go."

Sergius answered simply:

"Not now. I am under penance, and to-day bound to the third breviary prayers. When they are finished, I will gladly go."

"I am disappointed," Demedes rejoined. "But I must make haste."

He kissed the Hegumen's hand and retired; after which, the meal speedily concluded, Sergius gathered the few articles of service on the platter, and raised it, but stopped to say: "After prayers, with your consent, reverend Father, I will take part in this affair."

"Thou hast my consent."

"It may take several days."

"Give thyself all the time required. The errand is of mercy."

And the holy man extended his hand, and Sergius saluted it reverently, and went out.

If the young monastic kept not fast hold of the holy forms prescribed immemorially for the third hour's service, there is little doubt he was forgiven in the higher court before which he was supposed present, for never had he been more nearly shaken out of his better self than by the Prince's proclamation. He had managed to appear composed while under Demedes' observation. In the language of the time, some protecting Saint prompted him to beware of the Greek, and keeping the admonition, he had come well out of the interview; but hardly did the Hegumen's door close behind him before Lael's untoward fate struck him with effect. He hurried to his cell, thinking to recover himself; but it was as if he were pursued by a voice calling him, and directly the voice seemed hers, sharp and piercing from terror. A little later he took to answering the appeal—I hear, but where art thou? His agitation grew until the bell summoned him to the chapel, and the sound was gladdening on account of the companionship it promised. Surely the voice would be lost in the full-toned responses of the brethren. Not so. He heard it even more clearly. Then, to place himself certainly beyond it, he begged an ancient worshipper at his side to loan him his triptych. For once, however, the sorrowful figure of the Christ on the central tablet was of no avail, hold it close as he might; strange to say, the face of the graven image assumed her likeness; so he was worse off than before, for now her suffering look was added to her sorrowful cry.

At last the service was over. Rushing back to his cell he exchanged his black gown for the coarse gray garment with which he had sallied from Bielo-Osero. Folding the veil, and putting it carefully away in his hat, he went forth, a hunter as the multitude were hunters; only, as we shall presently see, his zeal was more lasting than theirs, and he was owner of an invaluable secret.

On the street he heard everywhere of the rewards, and everywhere the question, Has she been found? The population, women and children included, appeared to have been turned out of their houses. The corners were possessed by them, and it will be easy for readers who have once listened to Greeks in hot debate to fancy how on this occasion they were heard afar. Yet Sergius went his way unobservant of the remarks drawn by the elephantine ears of his outlandish hood, his tall form, and impeded step.

Had one stopped him to ask, Where are you going? it is doubtful if he could have told. He had no plan; he was being pulled along by a pain of heart rather than a purpose—moving somnolently through a light which was also a revelation, for now he knew he loved the lost girl—knew it, not by something past, such as recollections of her sweetness and beauty, but by a sense of present bereavement, an agonizing impulsion, a fierce desire to find the robber, a murderous longing the like of which had never assailed him. The going was nearest an answer he could make to the voice calling him, equivalent to, I am coming.

He sped through the Hippodrome outwalking everybody; then through the enclosure of Sancta Sophia; then down the garden terraces—Oh, that the copse could have told him the chapter it had witnessed!—then up the broad stairway to the promenade, and along it toward Port St. Julian, never pausing until he was at the bench in the angle of the wall from which he had overheard Demedes' story of the Plague of Crime.

Now the bench was not in his mind when he started from the monastery; neither had he thought of it on the way, or of the dark history it had helped him to; in a freak, he took the seat he had formerly occupied, placed his arm along the coping of the parapet, and closed his eyes. And strange to say, the conversation of that day repeated itself almost word for word. Stranger still, it had now a significancy not then observed; and as he listened, he interpreted, and the fever of spirit left him.

About an hour before noon, he arose from the bench like one refreshed by sleep, cool, thoughtful, capable. In the interval he had put off boyishness, and taken on manhood replete with a faculty for worldly thinking that would have alarmed Father Hilarion. In other words, he was seeing things as they were; that bad and good, for instance, were coexistent, one as much a part of the plan of creation as the other; that religion could only regulate and reform; that the end of days would find good men striving with bad men—in brief, that Demedes was performing the role to which his nature and aptitude assigned him, just as the venerable Hegumen, his father, was feebly essaying a counterpart. Nor was that all. The new ideas to which he had been converted facilitated reflection along the lines of wickedness. In the Plague of Crime, told the second time, he believed he had found what had befallen Lael. Demedes, he remembered, gave the historic episode to convince his protesting friend how easy it would be to steal and dispose of her. The argument pointed to the Imperial cistern as the hiding-place.

Sergius' first prompting was to enlist the aid of the Prince of India, and go straight to the deliverance; but he had arisen from the bench a person very different from a blind lover. Not that his love had cooled—ah, no! But there were things to be done before exposing his secret. Thus, his curiosity had never been strong enough to induce him to look into the cistern. Was it not worth while to assure himself of the possibility of its conversion to the use suspected? He turned, and walked back rapidly—down the stairway, up the terraces, and through the Hippodrome. Suddenly he was struck with the impolicy of presenting himself to the cistern-keeper in his present costume—it would be such a help to identification by Demedes. So he continued on to the monastery, and resumed the black gown and tall hat.

The Hegumen's door, which he had to pass in going out again, served him with another admonition. If Demedes were exposed through his endeavor, what of the father? If, in the conflict certain of precipitation, the latter sided with his son—and what could be more natural?—would not the Brotherhood follow him? How then could he, Sergius, a foreigner, young, and without influence, combat a fraternity powerful in the city and most powerful up at Blacherne?

At this, it must be confessed, the young man's step lost its elasticity; his head sunk visibly, and the love just found was driven to divide its dominion with a well-grounded practical apprehension. Yet he walked on, out of the gate, and thence in the direction of the cistern.

Arrived there, he surveyed the wooden structure doubtfully. The door was open, and just inside of it the keeper sat stick in hand drumming upon the brick pavement, a man of medium height and rather pleasant demeanor.

"I am a stranger here," Sergius said to him. "The cistern is public, I believe; may I see it?"

"It is public, and you may look at it all you want. The door there at the end of the passage will let you into the court. If you have trouble in finding the stairway down, call me."

Sergius dropped some small coin into the keeper's hand.

The court was paved with yellow Roman brick, and moderately spacious. An oblong curbing in the centre without rails marked the place of descent to the water. Overhead there was nothing to interfere with the fall of light from the blue sky, except that in one corner a shed had been constructed barely sufficient to protect a sedan chair deposited there, its poles on end leant against the wall. Sergius noticed the chair and the poles, then looked down over the curbing into a doorway, and saw four stone steps leading to a platform three or four feet square. Observing a further descent, he went down to the landing, where he paused long enough to be satisfied that the whole stairway was built into the eastern wall of the cistern. The light was already dim. Proceeding carefully, for the stones were slippery, he counted fourteen steps to another landing, the width of the first but quite ten feet long, and slightly submerged with water. Here, as he could go no further, he stopped to look about him.

It is true there was not much to be seen, yet he was at once impressed with a sense of vastness and durability. A dark and waveless sheet lay stretched before him, merging speedily into general blackness. About four yards away and as many apart, two gigantic pillars arose out of the motionless flood stark and ghostly gray. Behind them, suggestive of rows with an aisle between, other pillars were seen, mere upright streaks of uncertain hue fainter growing in the shadowy perspective. Below there was nothing to arrest a glance. Raising his eyes to the roof above him, out of the semi-obscurity, he presently defined a brick vault springing boldly from the Corinthian capitals of the nearest pillars, and he knew straightway the roof was supported by a system of vaults susceptible of indefinite extension. But how was he, standing on a platform at the eastern edge of the reservoir, mighty in so many senses, to determine its shape, width, length? Stooping he looked down the vista straining his vision, but there was no opposite wall—only darkness and impenetrability. He filled his lungs trying the air, and it was damp but sweet. He stamped with force—there was a rumble in the vault overhead—that was all. He called: "Lael, Lael"—there was no answer, though he listened, his soul in his ears. Therewith he gave over trying to sound the great handmade cavern, and lingered awhile muttering:

"It is possible, it is possible! At the end of this row of pillars"—he made a last vain effort to discover the end—"there may be a house afloat, and she"—he clinched his hands, and shook with a return of murderous passion—"God help her! Nay, God help me! If she is here, as I believe, I will find her."

In the court he again noticed the sedan in the corner.

"I am obliged to you," he said to the keeper by the door. "How old is the cistern?"

"Constantine begun it, and Justinian finished it, they say."

"Is it in use now?"

"They let buckets down through traps in the roof."

"Do you know how large it is?" [Footnote: Yere Batan Serai, or the Underground Palace, the ancient Royal Cistern, or cistern of Constantine, is in rank, as well as in interest and beauty, the chief Byzantine cistern. It is on the right-hand side of the tramway street, west of St. Sophia. The entrance is in the yard of a large Ottoman house in last street on the right of tramway street before the tramway turns abruptly west (to right) after passing St. Sophia.

This cistern was built by Constantine the Great, and deepened and enlarged by Justinian the Great in 527, the first year of his reign. It has been in constant use ever since. The water is supplied from unknown and subterranean sources, sometimes rising nearly to the capitals of the columns. It is still in admirable preservation: all its columns are in position, and almost the entire roof is intact. The columns are arranged in twelve rows of twenty-eight, there being in all three hundred and thirty-six, which are twelve feet distant from each other or from the wall. Some of the capitals are Corinthian; others plain, hardly more than truncated pyramids. The roof consists of a succession of brick vaults.

On left side in yard of the large Ottoman house already mentioned is a trap-door. One is let down over a rickety ladder about four feet to the top of four high stone steps, which descend on the left to a platform about three and one-half feet square which projects without railing over the water. Thence fourteen steps, also without railing, conduct to another platform below, about three and one-half feet wide and ten feet long. Sometimes this lower platform and the nearer steps are covered with water, though seldom in summer and early fall. These steps are uneven—in places are broken and almost wanting; and they as well as both platforms are exceedingly slippery. The place is absolutely dark save for the feeble rays which glimmer from the lantern of the guide. One should remember there is no railing or barrier of any sort, and not advance an inch without seeing where he puts his foot. Then there is no danger. Moreover, the platform below is less slippery than the steps or the platform above. Visitors will do well to each bring his own candle or small lantern, not for illumination but for safety. When the visitors have arrived on the lower platform, which is near the middle of the eastern side against the wall, the guide, who has not descended the steps, lights a basket of shavings or other quick combustible on the platform above. The effect is instantaneous and magical. Suddenly from an obscurity so profound that only the outline of the nearest columns can be faintly discerned by the flicker of a candle, the entire maze of columns flashes into being resplendent and white. The roof and the water send the light back to each other. Not a sound is heard save distant splashes here and there as a bucket descends to supply the necessities of some house above. Nowhere can be beheld a scene more weird and enchanting. It will remain printed on the memory when many another experience of Stamboul is dim or forgotten.

PROFESSOR GROSVENOR. CONSTANTINOPLE.]

The keeper laughed, and pommelled the pavement vigorously: "I was never through it—haven't the courage—nor do I know anybody who has been. They say it has a thousand pillars, and that it is supplied by a river. They tell too how people have gone into it with boats, and never come out, and that it is alive with ghosts; but of these stories I say nothing, because I know nothing."

Sergius thereupon departed.

CHAPTER XXII
THE PRINCE OF INDIA SEEKS MAHOMMED

All the next night, Syama, his ear against his master's door, felt the jar of the machine-like tread in the study. At intervals it would slow, but not once did it stop. The poor slave was himself nearly worn out. Sympathy has a fashion of burdening us without in the least lightening the burden which occasions it.

To-morrows may be long coming, but they keep coming. Time is a mill, and to-morrows are but the dust of its grinding. Uel arose early. He had slept soundly. His first move was to send the Prince all the clerks he could find in the market, and shortly afterwards the city was re-blazoned with bills.

"BYZANTINES!

"Fathers and mothers of Byzantium!

"Lael, the daughter of Uel the merchant, has not been found. Wherefore I now offer 10,000 bezants in gold for her dead or alive, and 6,000 bezants in gold for evidence which will lead to the discovery and conviction of her abductors.

"The offers will conclude with to-day.

"PRINCE OF INDIA."

There was a sensation when the new placards had been generally read; yet the hunt of the day before was not resumed. It was considered exhausted. Men and women poured into the streets and talked and talked—about the Prince of India. By ten o'clock all known of him and a great deal more had gone through numberless discussions; and could he have heard the conclusions reached he had never smiled again. By a consensus singularly unanimous, he was an Indian, vastly rich, but not a Prince, and his interest in the stolen girl was owing to forbidden relations. This latter part of the judgment, by far the most cruel, might have been traced to Demedes.

In all the city there had not been a more tireless hunter than Demedes. He seemed everywhere present—on the ships, on the walls, in the gardens and churches—nay, it were easier telling where he had not been. And by whomsoever met, he was in good spirits, fertile in suggestions, and sure of success. He in fact distinguished himself in the search, and gave proof of a knowledge of the capital amazing to the oldest inhabitants. Of course his role was to waste the energy of the mass. In every pack of beagles it is said there is one particularly gifted in the discovery of false scents. Such was Demedes that first day, until about two o'clock. The results of the quest were then in, and of the theories to which he listened, nothing pleased him like the absence of a suggestion of the second sedan. There were witnesses to tell of the gorgeous chair, and its flitting here and yonder through the twilight; none saw the other. This seems to have sufficed him, and he suddenly gave up the chase; appearing in the garden of the Bucoleon, he declared the uselessness of further effort. The Jewess, he said, was not in Byzantium; she had been carried off by the Bulgarians, and was then on the road to some Turkish harem. From that moment the search began to fall off, and by evening it was entirely discontinued.

Upon appearance of the placards the second day, Demedes was again equal to the emergency. He collected his brethren in the Temple, organized them into parties, and sent them everywhere—to Galata, to the towns along the Bosphorus, down the western shore of the Marmora, over to the Islands, and up to the forest of Belgrade—to every place, in short, except the right one. And this conduct, apparently sincere, certainly energetic, bore its expected fruit; by noon he was the hero of the occasion, the admiration of the city.

When very early in the second day the disinclination of the people to renew the search was reported to the Prince of India, he looked incredulous, and broke out:

"What! Not for ten thousand bezants!—more gold than they have had in their treasury at one time in ten years!—enough to set up three empires of such dwindle! To what is the world coming?"

An hour or so later, he was told of the total failure of his second proclamation. The information drove him with increased speed across the floor.

"I have an adversary somewhere," he was saying to himself—"an adversary more powerful than gold in quantity. Are there two such in Byzantium?"

An account of Demedes' action gave him some comfort.

About the third hour, Sergius asked to see him, and was admitted. After a simple expression of sympathy, the heartiness of which was attested by his sad voice and dejected countenance, the monk said: "Prince of India, I cannot tell you the reasons of my opinion; yet I believe the young woman is a prisoner here in this city. I will also beg you not to ask me where I think she is held, or by whom. It may turn out that I am mistaken; I will then feel better of having had no confidant. With this statement—submitted with acknowledged uncertainty—can you trust me?"

"You are Sergius, the monk?"

"So they call me; though here I have not been raised to the priesthood."

"I have heard the poor child speak of you. You were a favorite with her."

The Prince spoke with trouble.

"I am greatly pleased to hear it."

The trouble of the Prince was contagious, but Sergius presently recovered.

"Probably the best certificate of my sincerity, Prince—the best I can furnish you—is that your gold is no incentive to the trial at finding her which I have a mind to make. If I succeed, a semblance of pay or reward would spoil my happiness."

The Jew surveyed him curiously. "Almost I doubt you," he said.

"Yes, I can understand. Avarice is so common, and disinterestedness, friendship, and love so uncommon."

"Verily, a great truth has struck you early."

"Well, hear what I have to ask."

"Speak."

"You have in your service an African"—

"Nilo?"

"That is his name. He is strong, faithful, and brave, qualities I may need more than gold. Will you allow him to go with me?"

The Prince's look and manner changed, and he took the monk's hand. "Forgive me," he said warmly—"forgive me, if I spoke doubtfully—forgive me, if I misunderstood you."

Then, with his usual promptitude, he went to the door, and bade Syama bring Nilo.

"You know my method of speech with him?" the Prince asked.

"Yes," Sergius replied.

"If you have instructions for him, see they are given in a good light, for in the dark he cannot comprehend."

Nilo came, and kissed his master's hand. He understood the trouble which had befallen.

"This," the Prince said to him, "is Sergius, the monk. He believes he knows where the little Princess is, and has asked that you may go with him. Are you willing?"

The King looked assent.

"It is arranged," the master added to Sergius. "Have you other suggestion?"

"It were better he put off his African costume."

"For the Greek?"

"The Greek will excite less attention."

"Very well."

In a short time Nilo presented himself in Byzantine dress, with exception of a bright blue handkerchief on his head.

"Now, I pray you, Prince, give me a room. I wish to talk with the man privately."

The request was granted, the instructions given, and Sergius reappeared to take leave.

"Nilo and I are good friends, Prince. He understands me."

"He may be too eager. Remember I found him a savage."

With these words, the Prince and the young Russian parted.

After this nobody came to the house. The excitement had been a flash. Now it seemed entirely dead, and dead without a clew. When Time goes afoot his feet are of lead; and in this instance his walk was over the Prince's heart. By noon he was dreadfully wrought up.

"Let them look to it, let them look to it!" he kept repeating, sometimes shaking a clinched hand. Occasionally the idea to which he thus darkly referred had power to bring him to a halt. "I have an adversary. Who is he?" Ere long the question possessed him entirely. It was then as if he despaired of recovering Lael, and had but one earthly object—vengeance. "Ah, my God, my God! Am I to lose her, and never know my enemy? Action, action, or I will go mad!" Uel came with his usual report: "Alas! I have nothing." The Prince scarcely heard or saw him. "There are but two places where this enemy can harbor," he was repeating to himself—"but two; the palace and"—he brought his hands together vehemently—"the church. Where else are they who have power to arrest a whole people in earnest movement? Whom else have I offended? Ay, there it is! I preached God; therefore the child must perish. So much for Christian pity!"

All the forces in his nature became active.

"Go," he said to Uel, "order two men for my chair. Syama will attend me."

The merchant left him on the floor patting one hand with another.

"Yes, yes, I will try it—I will see if there is such thing as Christian pity—I will see. It may have swarmed, and gone to hive at Blacherne." In going to the palace, he continually exhorted the porters:

"Faster, faster, my men!"

The officer at the gate received him kindly, and came back with the answer, "His Majesty will see you."

Again the audience chamber, Constantine on the dais, his courtiers each in place; again the Dean in his role of Grand Chamberlain; again the prostrations. Ceremony at Blacherne was never remitted. There is a poverty which makes kings miserable.

"Draw nearer, Prince," said Constantine, benignly. "I am very busy. A courier arrived this morning from Adrianople with report that my august friend, the Sultan Amurath, is sick, and his physicians think him sick unto death. I was not prepared for the responsibilities which are rising; but I have heard of thy great misfortune, and out of sympathy bade my officer bring thee hither. By accounts the child was rarely intelligent and lovely, and I did not believe there was in my capital a man to do her such inhuman wrong. The progress of the search thou didst institute so wisely I have watched with solicitude little less than thine own. My officials everywhere have orders to spare no effort or expense to discover the guilty parties; for if the conspiracy succeed once, it will derive courage and try again, thus menacing every family in my Empire. If thou knowest aught else in my power to do, I will gladly hear it."

The Emperor, intent upon his expressions, failed to observe the gleam which shone in the Wanderer's eyes, excited by mention of the condition of the Sultan.

"I will not try Your Majesty's patience, since I know the responsibilities to which you have referred concern the welfare of an Empire, while I am troubled not knowing if one poor soul be dead or alive; yet she was the world to me"—thus the Prince began, and the knightly soul of the Emperor was touched, for his look softened, and with his hand he gently tapped the golden cone of the right arm of his throne.

"That which brought me to your feet," the Prince continued, "is partly answered. The orders to your officers exhaust your personal endeavor, unless—unless"—

"Speak, Prince."

"Your Majesty, I shrink from giving offence, and yet I have in this terrible affair an enemy who is my master. Yesterday Byzantium adopted my cause, and lent me her eyes and hands; before the sun went down her ardor cooled; to-day she will not go a rood. What are we to think, what do, my Lord, when gold and pity alike lose their influence? ... I will not stop to say what he must be who is so much my enemy as to lay an icy finger on the warm pulse of the people. When we who have grown old cast about for a hidden foe, where do we habitually look? Where, except among those whom we have offended? Whom have I offended? Here in the audience you honored me with, I ventured to argue in favor of universal brotherhood in faith, and God the principle of agreement; and there were present some who dealt me insult, and menaced me, until Your Majesty sent armed men to protect me from their violence. They have the ear of the public—they are my adversaries. Shall I call them the Church?"

Constantine replied calmly: "The head of the Church sat here at my right hand that day, Prince, and he did not interrupt you; neither did he menace you. But say you are right—that they of whom you speak are the Church— what can I do?"

"The Church has thunders to terrify and subdue the wicked, and Your Majesty is the head of the Church."

"Nay, Prince, I fear thou hast studied us unfairly. I am a member—a follower—a subscriber to the faith—its thunders are not mine."

A despairing look overcast the countenance of the visitor, and he trembled. "Oh, my God! There is no hope further—she is lost—lost!" But recovering directly, he said: "I crave pardon for interrupting Your Majesty. Give me permission to retire. I have much work to do."

Constantine bowed, and on raising his head, declared with feeling to his officers: "The wrong to this man is great."

The Wanderer moved backward slowly, his eyes emitting uncertain light; pausing, he pointed to the Emperor, and said, solemnly: "My Lord, thou hadst thy power to do justice from God; it hath slipped from thee. The choice was thine, to rule the Church or be ruled by it; thou hast chosen, and art lost, and thy Empire with thee."

He was at the door before any one present could arouse from surprise; then while they were looking at each other, and making ready to cry out, he came back clear to the dais, and knelt. There was in his manner and countenance so much of utter hopelessness, that the whole court stood still, each man in the attitude the return found him.

"My Lord," he said, "thou mightest have saved me—I forgive thee that thou didst not. See—here"—he thrust a hand in the bosom of his gown, and from a pocket drew the great emerald—"I will leave thee this talisman—it belonged to King Solomon, the son of David—I found it in the tomb of Hiram, King of Tyre—it is thine, my Lord, so thou fitly punish the robber of the lost daughter of my soul, my Gul Bahar. Farewell."

He laid the jewel on the edge of the dais, and rising, betook himself to the door again, and disappeared before the Dean was sufficiently mindful of his duty.

"The man is mad," the Emperor exclaimed.

"Take up the stone"—he spoke to the Dean—"and return it to him tomorrow." [Footnote: This identical stone, or one very like it, may be seen in the "Treasury" which is part of the old Serail in Stamboul. It is in the first room of entrance, on the second shelf of the great case of curios, right-hand side.] For a time then the emerald was kept passing from hand to hand by the courtiers, none of whom had ever seen its peer for size and brilliance; more than one of them touched it with awe, for despite a disposition to be incredulous in the matter of traditions incident to precious stones, the legend here, left behind him by the mysterious old man, was accepted—this was a talisman—it had belonged to Solomon—it had been found by the Prince of India—and he was a Prince—nobody but Indian Princes had such emeralds to give away. But while they bandied the talisman about, the Emperor sat, his chin in the palm of his right hand, the elbow on the golden cone, not seeing as much as thinking, nor thinking as much as silently repeating the strange words of the stranger: "Thou hadst thy power to do justice from God; it hath slipped from thee. The choice was thine to rule the Church or be ruled by it. Thou hast chosen, and art lost, and thy Empire with thee." Was this prophetic? What did it mean? And by and by he found a meaning. The first Constantine made the Church; now the Church will unmake the last Constantine. How many there are who spend their youth yearning and fighting to write their names in history, then spend their old age shuddering to read them there!

The Prince of India was scarcely in his study, certainly he was not yet calmed down from the passion into which he had been thrown at Blacherne, when Syama informed him there was a man below waiting to see him.

"Who is he?"

The servant shook his head.

"Well, bring him here."

Presently a gypsy, at least in right of his mother, and tent-born in the valley of Buyukdere, slender, dark-skinned, and by occupation a fisherman, presented himself. From the strength of the odor he brought with him, the yield of his net during the night must have been unusually large.

"Am I in presence of the Prince of India?" the man asked, in excellent Arabic, and a manner impossible of acquisition except in the daily life of a court of the period.

The Prince bowed.

"The Prince of India who is the friend of the Sultan Mahommed?" the other inquired, with greater particularity. "Sultan Mahommed? Prince Mahommed, you mean."

"No—Mahommed the Sultan."

A flash of joy leaped from the Prince's eyes—the first of the kind in two days.

The stranger addressed himself to explanation.

"Forgive my bringing the smell of mullet and mackerel into your house. I am obeying instructions which require me to communicate with you in disguise. I have a despatch to tell who I am, and more of my business than I know myself."

The messenger took from his head the dirty cloth covering it, and from its folds produced a slip of paper; with a salute of hand to breast and forehead, declarative of a Turk to the habit born, he delivered the slip, and walked apart to give opportunity for its reading. This was the writing in free translation:

"Mahommed, Son of Amurath, Sultan of Sultans, to the Prince of India.

"I am about returning to Magnesia. My father—may the prayers of the Prophet, almighty with God, preserve him from long suffering!—is fast falling into weakness of body and mind. Ali, son of Abed-din the Faithful, is charged instantly the great soul is departed on its way to Paradise to ride as the north wind flies, and give thee a record which Abed-din is to make on peril of his soul, abating not the fraction of a second. Thou wilt understand it, and the purpose of the sending."

The Prince of India, with the slip in his hand, walked the floor once from west to east to regain the mastery of himself.

"Ali, son of Abed-din the Faithful," he then said, "has a record for me."

Now the thongs of Ali's sandals were united just below the instep with brass buttons; stooping he took off that of the left sandal, and gave it a sharp twist; whereupon the top came off, disclosing a cavity, and a ribbon of the finest satin snugly folded in it. He gave the ribbon to the Prince, saying:

"The button of the plane tree planted has not in promise any great thing like this I take from the button of my sandal. Now is my mission done. Praised be Allah!" And while the Prince read, he recapped the button, and restored it in place.

The bit of yellow satin, when unfolded, presented a diagram which the Prince at first thought a nativity; upon closer inspection, he asked the courier:

"Son of Abed-din, did thy father draw this?"

"No, it is the handiwork of my Lord, the Sultan Mahommed."

"But it is a record of death, not of birth."

"Insomuch is my Lord, the Sultan Mahommed, wiser in his youth than many men in their age"—Ali paused to formally salute the opinion. "He selected the ribbon, and drew the figure—did all you behold, indeed, except the writing in the square; that he intrusted to my father, saying at the time: 'The Prince of India, when he sees the minute in the square, will say it is not a nativity; have one there to tell him I, Mahommed, avouch, 'Twice in his life I had the throne from my august father; now has he given it to me again, this third time with death to certify it mine in perpetuity; wherefore it is but righteous holding that the instant of his final secession must be counted the beginning of my reign; for often as a man has back the property he parted from as a loan, is it not his? What ceremony is then needed to perfect his title?"

"If one have wisdom, O son of Abed-din, whence is it except from Allah? Let not thy opinion of thy young master escape thee. Were he to die to-morrow"—

"Allah forbid!" exclaimed Ali.

"Fear it not," returned the Prince, smiling at the young man's earnestness: "for is it not written, 'A soul cannot die unless by permission of God, according to a writing definite as to time'? [Footnote: Koran, III. 139.]—I was about to say, there is not in his generation another to lie as close in the bosom of the Prophet. Where is he now?"

"He rides doubtless to Adrianople. The moment I set out hither, which was next minute after the great decease, a despatch was started for him by Khalil the Grand Vizier."

"Knowest thou the road he will take?"

"By Gallipoli."

"Behold, Ali!"—from his finger the Prince took a ring. "This for thy good news. Now to the road again, the White Castle first. Tell the Governor there to keep ward to-night with unlocked gates, for I may seek them in haste. Then put thyself in the Lord Mahommed's way coming from Gallipoli, and when thou hast kissed his sandals for me, and given him my love and duty, tell him I have perfect understanding of the nativity, and will meet him in Adrianople. Hast thou eaten and drunk?"

"Eaten, not drunk, my Lord."

"Come then, and I will put thee in the way to some red wine; for art thou not a traveller?"

The son of Abed-din saluted, saying simply: "*Meshallah!*" and was presently in care of Syama; after which the Prince took the ribbon to the table, spread it out carefully, and stood over it in the strong light, studying the symbols and writing in the square of

[Illustration: THE DIAGRAM.]

"It is the nativity of an Empire, [Footnote: Since the conquest of Constantinople by Mahommed, Turkey has been historically counted an Empire.] not a man," the Prince said, his gaze still on the figure—"an Empire which I will make great for the punishment of these robbers of children."

He stood up at the last word, and continued, excitedly: "It is the word of God, else it had not come to me now nigh overcome and perishing in bitter waters; and it calls me to do His will. Give over the child, it says—she is lost to thee. Go up now, and be thou my instrument this once again—I AM THE I AM whom Moses knew, the Lord God of Israel who covenanted with Abraham, and with whom there is no forgetting—no, not though the world follow the leaf blown into the mouth of a roaring furnace. I hear, O God! I hear—I am going!"

This, it will be observed, is the second of the two days of grace the Prince appears to have given the city for the return of Lael; and as it is rapidly going without a token of performance, our curiosity increases to know the terrible thing in reserve of which some of his outbursts have vaguely apprised us.

A few turns across the floor brought him back to apparent calmness; indeed, but for the fitful light in his eyes and the swollen veins about his temples, it might be supposed he had been successful in putting his distresses by. He brought Syama in, and, for the first time in two days, took a seat.

"Listen, and closely," he said; "for I would be sure you comprehend me. Have you laid the Sacred Books in the boxes?"

Syama, in his way, answered, yes.

"Are the boxes secure? They may have to go a long journey."

"Yes."

"Did you place the jewels in new bags? The old ones were well nigh gone."

"Yes."

"Are they in the gurglet now?"

"Yes."

"You know we will have to keep it filled with water."

"Yes."

"My medicines—are they ready for packing?"

"Yes."

"Return them to their cases carefully. I cannot afford to leave or lose them. And the sword—is it with the books?"

"Yes."

"Very well. Attend again. On my return from the voyage I made the other day for the treasure you have in care"—he paused for a sign of comprehension—"I retained the vessel in my service, and directed the captain to be at anchor in the harbor before St. Peter's gate"—another pause—"I also charged him to keep lookout for a signal to bring the galley to the landing; in the day, the signal would be a blue handkerchief waved; at night, a lantern swung four times thus"—he gave the illustration. "Now to the purpose of all this. Give heed. I may wish to go aboard to-night, but at what hour I cannot tell. In preparation, however, you will get the porters who took me to the palace to-day, and have them take the boxes and gurglet of which I have been speaking to St. Peter's gate. You will go with them, make the signal to the captain, and see they are safely shipped. The other servants will accompany you. You understand?"

Syama nodded.

"Attend further. When the goods are on the galley, you will stay and guard them. All the other property you will leave in the house here just as it is. You are certain you comprehend?"

"Yes."

"Then set about the work at once. Everything must be on the ship before dark."

The master offered his hand, and the slave kissed it, and went softly out.

Immediately that he was alone, the Prince ascended to the roof. He stood by the table a moment, giving a thought to the many times his Gul Bahar had kept watch on the stars for him. They would come and go regularly as of old, but she?—He shook with sudden passion, and walked around taking what might have answered for last looks at familiar landmarks in the wide environment—at the old church near by and the small section of Blacherne in the west, the heights of Galata and the shapely tower northwardly, the fainter glimpses of Scutari in the east. Then he looked to the southwest where, under a vast expanse of sky, he knew the Marmora was lying asleep; and at once his face brightened. In that quarter a bank of lead-colored clouds stretched far along the horizon, sending rifts lighter hued upward like a fan opening toward the zenith. He raised his hand, and held it palm thitherward, and smiled at feeling a breath of air. Somehow the cloud associated itself with the purpose of which he was dreaming, for he said audibly, his eyes fiercely lighted:

"O God, the proud are risen against me, and the assemblies of violent men have sought after my soul, and have not set thee before them. But now hast thou thy hand under my head; now the wind cometh, and their punishment; and it is for me to scourge them."

He lingered on the roof, walking sometimes, but for the most part seated. The cloud in the southwest seemed the great attraction. Assured it was still coming, he would drop awhile into deep thought. If there were calls at the street door, he did not hear them. At length the sun, going down, was met and covered out of sight by the curtain beyond the Marmora. About the same time a wave of cold February air rolled into the city, and to escape it he went below.

The silence there was observable; for now Syama had finished, and the house was deserted. Through the rooms upper and lower he stalked gloomy and restless, pausing now and then to listen to a sufflation noisier and more portentous than its predecessors; and the moans with which the intermittent blast turned the corners and occasionally surged through the windows he received smilingly, much as hospitable men welcome friends, or as conspirators greet each other; and often as they recurred, he replied to them in the sonorous words of the Psalm, and the refrain, "Now the wind cometh, and the punishment."

When night was fallen, he crossed the street to Uel's. After the first greeting, the conversation between the two was remarkable chiefly for its lapses. It is always so with persons who have a sorrow in common—the pleasure is in their society, not in exchange of words.

In one thing the brethren were agreed—Lael was lost. By and by the Prince concluded it time for him to depart. There was a lamp burning above the table; he went to it, and called Uel; and when he was come, the elder drew out a sealed purse, saying:

"Our pretty Gul Bahar may yet be found. The methods of the Lord we believe in are past finding out. If it should be that I am not in the city when she is brought home, I would not she should have cause to say I ceased thinking of her with a love equal to yours—a father's love. Wherefore, O son of Jahdai, I give you this. It is full of jewels, each a fortune in itself. If she comes, they are hers; if a year passes, and she is not found, they are yours to keep, give or sell, as you please. You have furnished me happiness which this sorrow is not strong enough to efface. I will not pay you, for acceptance in such kind were shameful to you as the offer would be to me; yet if she comes not in the year, break the seal. We sometimes wear rings in help of pleasant memories."

"Is your going so certain?" Uel asked.

"O my youngest brother, I am a traveller even as you are a merchant, with the difference, I have no home. So the Lord be with you. Farewell."

Then they kissed each other tenderly.

"Will I not hear from you?" Uel inquired.

"Ah, thank you," and the Wanderer returned to him and said, as if to show who was first in his very farewell thought:

"Thank you for the reminder. If peradventure you too should be gone when she is found, she will then be in want of a home. Provide against that; for she is such a sweet stranger to the world."

"Tell me how, and I will keep your wish as it were part of the Law."

"There is a woman in Byzantium worthy to have Good follow her name whenever it is spoken or written."

"Give me her name, my Lord."

"The Princess Irene."

"But she is a Christian!"

Uel spoke in surprise.

"Yes, son of Jahdai, she is a Christian. Nevertheless send Lael to her. Again I leave you where I rest myself—with God—our God."

Thereupon he went out finally, and between gusts of wind regained his own house. He stopped on entering, and barred the door behind him; then he groped his way to the kitchen, and taking a lamp from its place, raked together the embers smothering in a brazier habitually kept for retention of fire, and lighted the lamp. He next broke up some stools and small tables, and with the pieces made a pile under the grand stairway to the second floor, muttering as he worked: "The proud are risen against me; and now the wind cometh, and punishment."

Once more he walked through the rooms, and ascended to the roof. There, just as he cleared the door, as if it were saluting him, and determined to give him a trial of its force, a blast leaped upon him, like an embodiment out of the cloud in full possession of both world and sky, and started his gown astream, and twisting his hair and beard into lashes whipped his eyes and ears with them, and howled, and snatched his breath nearly out of his mouth. Wind it was, and darkness somewhat like that Egypt knew what time the deliverer, with God behind him, was trying strength with the King's sorcerers—wind and darkness, but not a drop of rain. He grasped the door-post, and listened to the crashing of heavy things on the neighboring roofs, and the rattle of light things for the finding of which loose here and there the gust of a storm may be trusted where eyes are useless. And noticing that obstructions served merely to break the flying forces into eddies, he laughed and shouted by turns so the inmates of the houses near might have heard had they been out as he was instead of cowering in their beds: "The proud are risen against me, and the assembly of violent men have sought after my soul; and now—ha, ha, ha!—the wind cometh and the punishment!"

Availing himself of a respite in the blowing, he ran across the roof and looked over into the street, and seeing nothing, neither light nor living thing, he repeated the refrain with a slight variation: "And the wind—ha, ha!—the wind *is* come, and the punishment!"—then he fled back, and down from the roof.

And now the purpose in reserve must have revelation.

The grand staircase sprang from the floor open beneath like a bridge. Passing under it, he set the lamp against the heap of kindling there, and the smell of scorching wood spread abroad, followed by smoke and the crackle and snap of wood beginning to burn.

It was not long until the flames, gathering life and strength, were beyond him to stay or extinguish them, had he been taken with sudden repentance. From step to step they leaped, the room meantime filling fast with suffocating gases. When he knew they were beyond the efforts of any and all whom they might attract, and must burst into conflagration the instant they reached the lightest of the gusts playing havoc outside, he went down on his hands and knees, for else it had been difficult for him to breathe, and crawled to the door. Drawing himself up there, he undid the bar, and edged through into the street; nor was there a soul to see the puff of smoke and murky gleam which passed out with him.

His spirit was too drunken with glee to trouble itself with precautions now; yet he stopped long enough to repeat the refrain, with a hideous spasm of laughter: "And now—ha, ha!—the wind *is* come, and the fire, and the punishment." Then he wrapped his gown closer about his form bending to meet the gale, and went leisurely down the street, intending to make St. Peter's gate.

Where the intersections left openings, the Jew, now a fugitive rather than a wanderer—a fugitive nevertheless who knew perfectly where he was going, and that welcome awaited him there—halted to scan the cloudy floor of the sky above the site of the house he had just abandoned. A redness flickering and unsteady over in that quarter was the first assurance he had of the growth of the flame of small beginning under the grand staircase.

"Now the meeting of wind and fire!—Now speedily these hypocrites and tongue-servers, bastards of Byzantium, shall know Israel has a God in whom they have no lot, and in what regard he holds conniving at the rape of his daughters. Blow, Wind, blow harder! Rise, Fire, and spread—be a thousand lions in roaring till these tremble like hunted curs! The few innocent are not more in the account than moths burrowed in woven wool and feeding on its fineness. Already the guilty begin to pray—but to whom? Blow, O Wind! Spread and spare not, O Fire!"

Thus he exulted; and as if it heard him and were making answer to his imprecations, a column, pinked by the liberated fire below it, a burst of sparks in its core, shot up in sudden vastness like a Titan rushing to seizure of the world; but presently the gale struck and toppled it over toward Blacherne in the northwest.

"That way points the punishment? I remember I offered him God and peace and good-will to men, and he rejected them. Blow, Winds! Now are ye but breezes from the south, spice-laden to me, but in his ears be as chariots descending. And thou, O Fire! Forget not the justice to be done, and whose servant thou art. Leave Heaven to say which is guiltier; they who work at the deflowerment of the innocent, or he who answers no to the Everlasting offering him love. Unto him be thou as banners above the chariots!"

Now a noise began—at first faint and uncertain, then, as the red column sprang up, it strengthened, and ere long defined itself—Fire, Fire!

It seemed the city awoke with that cry. And there was peering from windows, opening of doors, rushing from houses, and hurrying to where the angry spot on the floor of the cloud which shut Heaven off was widening and deepening. In a space incredibly quick, the streets—those leading to the corner occupied by the Jew as well—became rivulets flowing with people, and then blatant rivers.

"My God, what a night for a fire!"

"There will be nothing left of us by morning, not even ashes."

"And the women and children—think of them!"

"Fire—fire—fire!"

Exchanges like these dinned the Jew until, finding himself an obstruction, he moved on. Not a phase of the awful excitement escaped him—the racing of men—half-clad women assembling—children staring wild-eyed at the smoke extending luridly across the fifth and sixth hills to the seventh— white faces, exclamations, and not seldom resort to crucifixes and prayers to the Blessed Lady of Blacherne—he heard and saw them all—yet kept on toward St. Peter's gate, now an easy thing, since the thoroughfares were so aglow he could neither stumble nor miss the right one. A company of soldiers running nearly knocked him down; but finally he reached the portal, and passed out without challenge. A brief search then for his galley; and going aboard, after replying to a few questions about the fire, he bade the captain cast off, and run for the Bosphorus.

"It looks as if the city would all go," he said; and the mariner, thinking him afraid, summoned his oarsmen, and to please him made haste, as he too well might, for the light of the burning projected over the wall, and, flung back from the cloud overhead far as the eye could penetrate, illuminated the harbor as it did the streets, bringing the ships to view, their crews on deck, and Galata, wall, housetops and tower, crowded with people awestruck by the immensity of the calamity.

When the galley outgoing cleared Point Serail, the wind and the long swells beating in from the Marmora white with foam struck it with such force that keeping firm grip of their oars was hard for the rowers, and they began to cry out; whereupon the captain sought his passenger.

"My Lord," he said, "I have plied these waters from boyhood, and never saw them in a night like this. Let me return to the harbor."

"What, is it not light enough?"

The sailor crossed himself, and replied: "There is light enough—such as it is!" and he shuddered. "But the wind, and the running sea, my Lord"—

"Oh! for them, keep on. Under the mountain height of Scutari the sailing will be plain."

And with much wonder how one so afraid of fire could be so indifferent to danger from flood and gale, the captain addressed himself to manoeuvring his vessel.

"Now," said the Jew, when at last they were well in under the Asiatic shore—"now bear away up the Bosphorus."

The light kept following him the hour and more required to make the Sweet Waters and the White Castle; and even there the reflection from the cloud above the ill-fated city was strong enough to cast half the stream in shadow from the sycamores lining its left bank.

The Governor of the Castle received the friend of his master, the new Sultan, at the landing; and from the wall just before retiring, the latter took a last look at the signs down where the ancient capital was struggling against annihilation. Glutted with imaginings of all that was transpiring there, he clapped his hands, and repeated the refrain in its past form:

"Now have the winds come, and the fire, and the punishment. So be it ever unto all who encourage violence to children, and reject God."

An hour afterwards, he was asleep peacefully as if there were no such thing as conscience, or a misery like remorse.

* * * * *

Shortly after midnight an officer of the guard ventured to approach the couch of the Emperor Constantine; in his great excitement he even shook the sacred person.

"Awake, Your Majesty, awake, and save the city. It is a sea of fire."

Constantine was quickly attired, and went first to the top of the Tower of Isaac. He was filled with horror by what he beheld; but he had soldierly qualities—amongst others the faculty of keeping a clear head in crises. He saw the conflagration was taking direction with the wind and coming straight toward Blacherne, where, for want of aliment, it needs must stop. Everything in its line of progress was doomed; but he decided it possible to prevent extension right and left of that line, and acting promptly, he brought the entire military force from the barracks to cooperate with the people. The strategy was successful.

Gazing from the pinnacle as the sun rose, he easily traced a blackened swath cut from the fifth hill up to the eastward wall of the imperial grounds; and, in proof of the fury of the gale, the terraces of the garden were covered inches deep with ashes and scoriac-looking flakes of what at sunset had been happy homes. And the dead? Ascertainment of the many who perished was never had; neither did closest inquiry discover the origin of the fire. The volume of iniquities awaiting exposure Judgment Day must be immeasurable, if it is of the book material in favor among mortals.

The Prince of India was supposed to have been one of the victims of the fire, and not a little sympathy was expended for the mysterious foreigner. But in refuge at the White Castle, that worthy greedily devoured the intelligence he had the Governor send for next day. One piece of news, however, did more than dash the satisfaction he secretly indulged—Uel, the son of Jahdai, was dead—and dead of injuries suffered the night of the catastrophe.

A horrible foreboding struck the grim incendiary. Was the old destiny still pursuing him? Was it still a part of the Judgment that every human being who had to do with him in love, friendship or business, every one on whom he looked in favor, must be overtaken soon or late with a doom of some kind? From that moment, moved by an inscrutable prompting of spirit, he began a list of those thus unfortunate—Lael first, then Uel. Who next?

The reader will remember the merchant's house was opposite the Prince's, with a street between them. Unfortunately the street was narrow; the heat from one building beat across it and attacked the other. Uel managed to get out safely; but recollecting the jewels intrusted to him for Lael, he rushed back to recover them. Staggering out again blind and roasting, he fell on the pave, and was carried off, but with the purse intact. Next day he succumbed to the injuries. In his last hour, he dictated a letter to the Princess Irene, begging her to accept the guardianship of his daughter, if God willed her return. Such, he said, was his wish, and the Prince of India's; and with the missive, he forwarded the jewels, and a statement of the property he was leaving in the market. They and all his were for the child—so the disposition ran, concluding with a paragraph remarkable for the confidence it manifested in the Christian trustee. "But if she is not returned alive within a year from this date, then, O excellent Princess, I pray you to be my heir, holding everything of mine yours unconditionally. And may God keep you!"

CHAPTER XXIII
SERGIUS AND NILO TAKE UP THE HUNT

We have seen the result of Sergius' interview with the Prince of India, and remember that it was yet early in the morning after Lael's disappearance when, in company with Nilo, he bade the eccentric stranger adieu, and set forth to try his theory respecting the lost girl.

About noon he appeared southwest of the Hippodrome in the street leading past the cistern-keeper's abode. Nilo, by arrangement, followed at a distance, keeping him in sight. By his side there was a fruit peddler, one of the every-day class whose successors are banes of life to all with whom in the modern Byzantium a morning nap is the sweetest preparation for the day.

The peddler carried a huge basket strapped to his forehead. He was also equipped with a wooden platter for the display of samples of his stock; and it must be said the medlars, oranges, figs of Smyrna, and the luscious green grapes in enormous clusters freshly plucked in the vineyards on the Asiatic shore over against the Isles of the Princes, were very tempting; especially so as the hour was when the whole world acknowledges the utility of lunching as a stay for dinner.

It is not necessary to give the conversation between the man of fruits and the young Russian. The former was endeavoring to sell. Presently they reached a point from which the cistern-keeper was visible, seated, as usual, just within the door pommelling the pavement. Sergius stopped there, and affected to examine his companion's stock; then, as if of a mind, he said:

"Oh, well! Let us cross the street, and if the man yonder will give me a room in which I can eat to my content, I will buy of you. Let us try him."

The two made their way to the door.

"Good day, my friend," Sergius said, to the keeper, who recognized him, and rising, returned the salutation pleasantly enough.

"You were here yesterday," he said, "I am glad to see you again. Come in."

"Thank you," Sergius returned. "I am hungry, and should like some of this man's store; but it is uncomfortable eating in the street; so I thought you might not be offended if I asked a room for the purpose; particularly as I give you a hearty invitation to share the repast with me."

In support of the request the peddler held the platter to the keeper. The argument was good, and straightway, assuming the air of a connoisseur, the master of the house squeezed a medlar, and raising an orange to his nose smelt it, calculated its weight, and answered: "Why, yes—come right along to my sitting-room. I will get some knives; and when we are through, we will have a bowl of water, and a napkin. Things are not inviting out here as they might be."

"And the peddler?" Sergius inquired.

"Bring him along. We will make him show us the bottom of his basket. I believe you said you are a stranger?"

Sergius nodded.

"Well, I am not," the keeper continued, complacently. "I know these fellows. They all have tricks. Bring him in. I have no family. I live alone."

The monk acknowledged the invitation, but pausing to allow the peddler to enter first, he at the same time lifted his hat as if to readjust it; then a moment was taken to make a roll of the long fair hair, and tuck it securely under the hat. That finished, he stepped into the passage, and pursued after his host through a door on the left hand; whereupon the passage to the court was clear.

Now the play with the hat was a signal to Nilo. Rendered into words, it would have run thus: "The keeper is employed, and the way open. Come!" And the King, on the lookout, answered by sauntering slowly down, mindful if he hurried he might be followed, there being a number of persons in the vicinity.

At the door, he took time to examine the front of the house; then he, too, stepped into the passage and through it, and out into the court, where, with a glance, he took everything in—paved area, the curbing about the stairway to the water, the faces of the three sides of the square opposite that of the entrance, all unbroken by door, window, or panel, the sedan in the corner, the two poles lashed together and on end by the sedan. He looked behind him—the passage was yet clear—if seen coming in, he was not pursued. There was a smile on his shining black face; and his teeth, serrated along the edges after the military fashion in Kash-Cush, displayed themselves white as dressed coral. Evidently he was pleased and confident. Next he went to the curb, shot a quick look down the steps far as could be seen; thence he crossed to the sedan, surveyed its exterior, and opened the door. The interior appearing in good order, he entered and sat down, and closing the door, arranged the curtain in front, drew it slightly aside and peeped out, now to the door admitting from the passage, then to the curbing. Both were perfectly under view.

When the King issued from the chair, his smile was broader than before, and his teeth seemed to have received a fresh enamelling. Without pausing again, he proceeded to the opening of the cistern, and with his hands on the curbing right and left, let himself lightly down on the four stones of the first landing; a moment, and he began descent of the steps, taking time to inspect everything discernible in the shadowy space. At length he stood on the lower platform.

He was now in serious mood. The white pillars were wondrous vast, and the darkness—it may be doubted if night in its natural aspects is more impressive to the savage than the enlightened man; yet it is certain the former will take alarm quicker when shut in by walls of artful contrivance. His imagination then peoples the darkness with spirits, and what is most strange, the spirits are always unfriendly. To say now that Nilo, standing on the lower platform, was wholly unmoved, would be to deny him the sensibilities without which there can be none of the effects usually incident to courage and cowardice. The vastness of the receptacle stupefied him. The silence was a curtain he could feel; the water, deep and dark, looked so suggestive of death that the superstitious soul required a little time to be itself again. But relief came, and he watched intently to see if there was a current in the black pool; he could discover none; then, having gained all the information he could, he ascended the steps and lifted himself out into the court. A glance through the passage—another at the sky—and he entered the sedan, and shut himself in.

The discussion of the fruit in the keeper's sitting-room meantime was interesting to the parties engaged in it. With excellent understanding of Nilo's occupation in the court, Sergius exerted himself to detain his host—if the term be acceptable—long as possible.

Fortunately no visitors came. Settling the score, and leaving a profusion of thanks behind him, he at length made his farewell, and spent the remainder of the afternoon on a bench in the Hippodrome.

Occasionally he went back to the street conducting to the cistern, and walked down it far enough to get a view of the keeper still at the door.

In the evening he ate at a confectionery near by, prolonging the meal till near dusk, and thence, business being suspended, he idled along the same thoroughfare in a manner to avoid attracting attention.

Still later, he found a seat in the recess of an unused doorway nearly in front of the house of such interest to him.

The manoeuvres thus detailed advise the reader somewhat of the particulars of the programme in execution by the monk and Nilo; nor that only—they notify him of the arrival of a very interesting part of the arrangement. In short, it is time to say that, one in the recess of the door, the other shut up in the sedan, they are both on the lookout for Demedes. Would he come? And when?

Anticipating a little, we may remark, if he comes, and goes into the cistern, Nilo is to open the street door and admit Sergius, who is then to take control of the after operations.

A little before sunset the keeper shut his front door. Sergius heard the iron bolt shoot into the mortice. He believed Demedes had not seen Lael since the abduction, and that he would not try to see her while the excitement was up and the hunt going forward. But now the city was settled back into quiet—now, if she were indeed in the cistern, he would come, the night being in his favor. And further, if he merely appeared at the house, the circumstance would be strongly corroborative of the monk's theory; if he did more—if he actually entered the cistern, there would be an end of doubt, and Nilo could keep him there, while Sergius was bringing the authorities to the scene. Such was the scheme; and he who looks at it with proper understanding must perceive it did not contemplate unnecessary violence. On this score, indeed, the Prince of India's significant reminder that he had found Nilo a savage, had led Sergius to redoubled care in his instructions.

The first development in the affair took place under the King's eye.

Waiting in ambush was by no means new to him. He was not in the least troubled by impatience. To be sure, he would have felt more comfortable with a piece of bread and a cup of water; yet deprivations of the kind were within the expectations; and while there was a hope of good issue for the enterprise, he could endure them indefinitely. The charge given him pertained particularly to Demedes. No fear of his not recognizing the Greek. Had he not enjoyed the delight of holding him out over the wall to be dropped to death?

He was eager, but not impatient. His chief dependence was in the sense of feeling, which had been cultivated so the slightest vibration along the ground served him in lieu of hearing. The closing of the front door by the keeper—felt, not heard—apprised him the day was over.

Not long afterward the pavement was again jarred, bringing a return of the sensations he used to have when, stalking lions in Kash-Cush, he felt the earth thrill under the galloping of the camelopards stampeded.

He drew the curtain aside slightly, just as a man stepped into the court from the passage. The person carried a lighted lamp, and was not Demedes.

The cistern-keeper—for he it was—went to the curbing slowly, for the advance airs of the gale were threatening his lamp, and dropped dextrously through the aperture to the upper landing.

In ambush the King never admitted anything like curiosity. Presently he felt the pavement again jar. Nobody appeared at the passage. Another tremor more decided—then the King stepped softly from the sedan, and stealing barefooted to the curbing looked down the yawning hole.

The lamp on the platform enabled him to see a boat drawn up to the lower step, and the stranger in the act of stepping into it. Then the lamp was shifted to the bow of the boat—oars taken in hand—a push off, and swift evanishment.

We, with our better information of the devices employed, know what a simple trick it was on the keeper's part to bring the vessel to him—he had but to pull the right string in the right direction—but Nilo was left to his astonishment. Stealing back to his cover, he drew the door to, and struggled with the mystery.

Afterwhile, the mist dissipated, and a fact arose plainer to him than the mighty hand on his knee. The cistern was inhabited—some person was down there to be communicated with. What should the King do now?

The quandary was trying. Finally he concluded to stay where he was. The stranger might bring somebody back with him—possibly the lost child— such Lael was in his thoughts of her.

Afterwhile—he had no idea of time—he felt a shake run along the pavement, and saw the stranger appear coming up the steps, lamp in hand. Next instant the person crawled out of the curbing, and went into the house through the passage doorway. The King never took eye from the curbing—nobody followed after—the secret of the old reservatory was yet a secret.

Again Nilo debated whether to bring Sergius in, and again he decided to stay where he was.

Meantime the cloud which the Prince of India had descried from the roof of his house arrived on the wings of the gale. Ere long Sergius was shivering in the recess of the door. For relief he counted the beads of his rosary, and there was scarcely a Saint in the calendar omitted from his recitals. If there was potency in prayers the angels were in the cistern ministering to Lael.

The street became deserted. Everything living which had a refuge sought it; yet the gale increased: it howled and sang dirges; it started the innumerable loose trifles in its way to waltzing over the bowlders; every hinged fixture on the exposed house-fronts creaked and banged. Only a lover would voluntarily endure the outdoors of such a night—a lover or a villain unusually bold.

Near midnight—so Sergius judged—a dull redness began to tinge the cloud overhead, and brightening rapidly, it ere long cast a strong reflection downward. At first he was grateful for the light; afterwhile, however, he detected an uproar distinguishable from the wind; it had no rest or lulls, and in its rise became more and more a human tone. When shortly people rushed past his cover crying fire, he comprehended what it was. The illumination intensified. The whole city seemed in danger. There were women and children exposed; yet here he was waiting on a mere hope; there he could do something. Why not go?

While he debated, down the street from the direction of the Hippodrome he beheld a man coming fast despite the strength of the gusts. A cloak wrapped him from head to foot, somewhat after the fashion of a toga, and the face was buried in its folds; yet the air and manner suggested Demedes. Instantly the watcher quit arguing; and forgetful of the fire, and of the city in danger, he shrank closer into the recess.

The thoroughfare was wider than common, and the person approaching on the side opposite Sergius; when nearer, his low stature was observable. Would he stop at the cistern-keeper's?

Now he was at the door!

The Russian's heart was in his mouth.

Right in front of the door the man halted and knocked. The sound was so sharp a stone must have been used. Immediately the bolt inside was drawn, and the visitor passed in.

Was it Demedes? The monk breathed again—he believed it was—anyhow the King would determine the question, and there was nothing to do meantime but bide the event.

The sedan, it hardly requires saying, was a much more comfortable ambush than the recess of the door. Nilo merely felt the shaking the gale now and then gave the house. So, too, he bade welcome to the glare in the sky for the flushing it transmitted to the court. Only a wraith could have come from or gone into the cistern unseen by him.

The clapping to of the front door on the street was not lost to the King. Presently the person he had seen in the boat at the foot of the steps again issued from the passage, lamp in hand as before; but as he kept looking back deferentially, a gust leaped down, and extinguished the flame, compelling him to return; whereupon another man stepped out into the court, halting immediately. Nilo opened a little wider the gap in the curtain through which he was peeping.

It may be well to say here that the newcomer thus unwittingly exposing himself to observation was the same individual Sergius had seen admitted into the house. The keeper had taken him to a room for the rearrangement of his attire. Standing forth in the light now filling the court, he was still wrapped in the cloak, all except the head, which was jauntily covered with a white cap, in style not unlike a Scotch bonnet, garnished with two long red ostrich feathers held in place by a brooch that shot forth gleams of precious stones in artful arrangement. Once the man opened the cloak, exposing a vest of fine-linked mail, white with silver washing, and furnished with epaulettes or triangular plates, fitted gracefully to the shoulders. A ruff, which was but the complement of a cape of heavy lace, clothed the neck.

To call the feeling which now shot through the King's every fibre a sudden pleasure would scarcely be a sufficient description; it was rather the delight with which soldiers old in war acknowledge the presence of their foemen. In other words, the brave black recognized Demedes, and was strong minded enough to understand and appreciate the circumstances under which the discovery was made. If the savage arose in him, it should be remembered he was there to revenge a master's wrongs quite as much as to rescue a stolen girl. Moreover, the education he had received from his master was not in the direction of mercy to enemies.

The two—Demedes and the keeper—lost no time in entering the cistern, the latter going first. When the King thought they had reached the lower platform, he issued from the chair barefooted, and bending over the curbing beheld what went on below.

The Greek was holding the lamp. The occupation of his assistant was beyond comprehension until the boat moved slowly into view. Demedes then set the lamp down, divested himself of his heavy wrap, and taking the rower's seat, unshipped the oars. There was a brief conference; at the conclusion the subordinate joined his chief; whereupon the boat pushed off.

Thus far the affair was singularly in the line of Sergius' anticipations; and now to call him in!

There is little room for doubt that Nilo was in perfect recollection of the instructions he had received, and that his first intention was to obey them; for, standing by the curbing long enough to be assured the Greek was indeed in the gloomy cavern, whence escape was impossible except by some unknown exit, he walked slowly away, and was in the passage door when, looking back, he saw the keeper leaping out into the court.

To say truth, the King had witnessed the departure of the boat with misgivings. Catching the robbers was then easy; yet rescue of the girl was a different thing. What might they not do with her in the meantime? As he understood his master, her safety was even more in purpose than their seizure; wherefore his impulse was to keep them in sight without reference to Sergius. He could swim—yes, but the water was cold, and the darkness terrible to his imagination. It might be hours before he found the hiding-place of the thieves—indeed, he might never overtake them. His regret when he stepped into the passage was mighty; it enables us, however, to comprehend the rush of impetuous joy which now took possession of him. A step to the right, and he was behind the cheek of the door.

All unsuspicious of danger, the keeper came on; a few minutes, and he would be in bed and asleep, so easy was he in conscience. The ancient cistern had many secrets. What did another one matter? His foot was on the lintel—he heard a rustle close at his side—before he could dart back—ere he could look or scream, two powerful hands were around his throat. He was not devoid of courage or strength, and resisted, struggling for breath. He merely succeeded in drawing his assailant out into the light far enough to get a glimpse of a giant and a face black and horrible to behold. A goblin from the cistern! And with this idea, he quit fighting, and sank to the floor. Nilo kept his grip needlessly—the fellow was dead of terror.

Here was a contingency not provided for in the arrangement Sergius had laid out with such care.

And what now?

It was for the King to answer.

He dragged the victim out in the court, and set a foot on his throat. All the savage in him was awake, and his thoughts pursued Demedes. Hungering for that life more than this one, he forgot the monk utterly. Had he a plank—anything in the least serviceable as a float—he would go after the master. He looked the enclosure over, and the sedan caught his eye, its door ajar. The door would suffice. He took hold of the limp body of the keeper, drew it after him, set it on the seat, and was about wrenching the door away, when he saw the poles. They were twelve or fourteen feet long and lashed together. On rafts not half so good he had in Kash-Cush crossed swollen streams, paddling with his hands. To take them to the cistern—to descend the steps with them—to launch himself on them—to push out into the darkness, were as one act, so swiftly were they accomplished. And going he knew not whither, but scorning the thought of another man betaking himself where he dared not, sustained by a feeling that he was in pursuit, and would have the advantage of a surprise when at last he overtook the enemy, we must leave the King awhile in order to bring up a dropped thread of our story.

CHAPTER XXIV
THE IMPERIAL CISTERN GIVES UP ITS SECRET

The reader will return—not unwillingly, it is hoped—to Lael.

The keeper, on watch for her, made haste to bar the door behind the carriers of the sedan, who, on their part, made greater haste to take boat and fly the city. From his sitting-room he brought a lamp, and opening the chair found the passenger in a corner to appearance dead. The head was hanging low; through the dishevelled hair the slightest margin of forehead shone marble white; a scarce perceptible rise and fall of the girlish bosom testified of the life still there. A woman at mercy, though dumb, is always eloquent.

"Here she is at last!" the keeper thought, while making a profane survey of the victim.... "Well, if beauty was his object—beauty without love—he may be satisfied. That's as the man is. I would rather have the bezants she has cost him. The market's full of just such beauty in health and strength—beauty matured and alive, not wilted like this! ... But every fish to its net, every man to his fate, as the infidels on the other shore say. To the cistern she must go, and I must put her there. Oh, how lucky! Her wits are out—prayers, tears, resistance would be uncomfortable. May the Saints keep her!" Closing the door of the sedan, he hurried out into the court, and thence down the cistern stairs to the lower platform, where he drew the boat in, and fixed it stationary by laying the oars across the gunwale from a step. The going and return were quick.

"The blood of doves, or the tears of women—I am not yet decided which is hardest on a soul.... Come along!... There is a palace at the further end of the road."...

He lifted her from the chair. In the dead faint she was more an inconvenient burden than a heavy one.

At the curbing he sat her down while he returned for the lamp. The steps within were slippery, and he dared take no risks. To get her into the boat was trying: yet he was gentle as possible—that, however, was from regard for the patron he was serving. He laid her head against a seat, and arranged her garments respectfully.

"O sweet Mother of Blacherne!" he then said, looking at the face for the first time fully exposed. "That pin on the shoulder—Heavens, how the stone flashes! It invites me." Unfastening the trinket, he secured it under his jacket, then ran on: "She is so white! I must hurry—or drop her overboard. If she dies"—his countenance showed concern, but brightened immediately. "Oh, of course she jumped overboard to escape!"

There was no further delay. With the lamp at the bow, he pushed off, and rowed vigorously. Through the pillared space he went, with many quick turns. It were vain saying exactly which direction he took, or how long he was going; after a time, the more considerable on account of the obstructions to be avoided, he reached the raft heretofore described as in the form of a cross and anchored securely between four of the immense columns by which the roof of the cistern was upheld. Still Lael slept the merciful sleep.

Next the keeper carried the unresisting body to a door of what in the feeble light seemed a low, one-storied house—possibly hut were a better word—thence into an interior where the blackness may be likened to a blindfold many times multiplied. Yet he went to a couch, and laid her upon it.

"There—my part is done!" he muttered, with a long-drawn breath.... "Now to illuminate the Palace! If she were to awake in this pitch-black"—something like a laugh interrupted the speech—"it would strangle her—oil from the press is not thicker."

He brought in the light—in such essential midnight it was indispensable, and must needs be always thought of—and amongst the things which began to sparkle was a circlet of furbished metal suspended from the centre of the ceiling. It proved to be a chandelier, provided with a number of lamps ready for lighting; and when they were all lit, the revelation which ensued while a lesson in extravagance was not less a tribute to the good taste of the reckless genius by which it was conceived.

It were long reading the inventory of articles he had brought together there for the edification and amusement of such as might become his idols. They were everywhere apparently—books, pictures, musical instruments—on the floor, a carpet to delight a Sultana mother—over the walls, arras of silk and gold in alternate threads—the ceiling an elaboration of wooden panels.

By referring to the diagram of the raft, it will be seen one quarter was reserved for a landing, while the others supported what may be termed pavilions, leaving an interior susceptible of division into three rooms. Standing under the circlet of light, an inmate could see into the three open quarters, each designed and furnished for a special use; this at the right hand, for eating and drinking; that at the left, for sleeping; the third, opposite the door, for lounging and reading. In the first one, a table already set glittered with ware in glass and precious metals; in the second, a mass of pink plush and fairy-like lace bespoke a bed; in the third were chairs, a lounge, and footrests which had the appearance of having been brought from a Ptolemaic palace only yesterday; and on these, strewn with an eye to artistic effect, lay fans and shawls for which the harem-queens of Persia and Hindostan might have contended. The "crown-jewel" of this latter apartment, however, was undoubtedly a sheet of copper burnished to answer the purpose of a looking-glass with a full-length view. On stands next the mirror, was a collection of toilet necessaries.

Elsewhere we have heard of a Palace of Love lying as yet in the high intent of Mahommed; here we have a Palace of Pleasure illustrative of Epicureanism according to Demedes. The expense and care required to make it an actuality beget the inference that the float, rough outside, splendid within, was not for Lael alone. A Princess of India might inaugurate it, but others as fair and highborn were to come after her, recipients of the same worship. Whosoever the favorite of the hour might be, the three pavilions were certainly the assigned limits of her being; while the getting rid of her would be never so easy—the water flowing, no one knew whence or whither, was horribly suggestive. Once installed there, it was supposed that longings for the upper world would go gradually out. The mistress, with nothing to wish for not at hand, was to be a Queen, with Demedes and his chosen of the philosophic circle for her ministers. In other words, the Academic Temple in the upper world was but a place of meeting; this was the Temple in fact. There the gentle priests talked business; here they worshipped; and of their psalter and litany, their faith and ceremonial practices, enough that the new substitute for religion was only a reembodiment of an old philosophy with the narrowest psychical idea for creed; namely, that the principle of Present Life was all there was in man worth culture and gratification.

The keeper cared little for the furnishments and curios. He was much more concerned in the restoration of his charge, being curious to see how she would behave on waking. He sprinkled her face with water, and fanned her energetically, using an ostrich wing of the whiteness of snow, overlaid about the handle with scarab-gems. Nor did he forget to pray.

"O Holy Mother! O sweet Madonna of Blacherne! Do not let her die. Darkness is nothing to thee. Thou art clothed in brightness. Oh, as thou lovest all thy children, descend hither, and open her eyes, and give her speech!"

The man was in earnest.

Greatly to his delight, he beheld the blood at length redden the pretty mouth, and the eyelids begin to tremble. Then a long, deep inhalation, and an uncertain fearful looking about; first at the circlet of the lamps, and next at the keeper, who, as became a pious Byzantine, burst into exclamation:

"Oh Holy Mother! I owe you a candle!"

Directly, having risen to a sitting posture, Lael found her tongue:

"You are not my father Uel, or my father the Prince of India?"

"No," he returned, plying the fan.

"Where are they? Where is Sergius?"

"I do not know."

"Who are you?"

"I am appointed to see that no harm comes to you."

This was intended kindly enough; it had, however, the opposite effect. She arose, and with both hands holding the hair from her eyes, stared wildly at objects in the three rooms, and fell to the couch again insensible. And again the water, the ostrich-wing, and the prayer to the Lady of Blacherne—again an awakening.

"Where am I?" she asked.

"In the Palace of"—

He had not time to finish; with tears, and moans, and wringing of hands she sat up: "Oh, my father! Oh, that I had heeded him! ... You will take me to him, will you not? He is rich, and loves me, and he will give you gold and jewels until you are rich. Only take me to him.... See—I am praying to you!"—and she cast herself at his feet.

Now the keeper was not used to so much loveliness in great distress, and he moved away; but she tried to follow him on her knees, crying: "Oh, as you hope mercy for yourself, take me home!" And beginning to doubt his strength, he affected harshness.

"It is useless praying to me. I could not take you out if your father rained gold on me for a month—I could not if I wished to.... Be sensible, and listen to me."

"Then you did not bring me here."

"Listen to me, I say.... You will get hungry and thirsty—there are bread, fruit, and water and wine—and when you are sleepy, yonder is the bed. Use your eyes, and you are certain to find in one room or the other everything you can need; and whatever you put hand on is yours. Only be sensible, and quit taking on so. Quit praying to me. Prayer is for the Madonna and the Blessed Saints. Hush and hear. No? Well, I am going now."

"Going?—and without telling me where I am? Or why I was brought here? Or by whom? Oh, my God!"

She flung herself on the floor distracted; and he, apparently not minding, went on:

"I am going now, but will come back for your orders in the morning, and again in the evening. Do not be afraid; it is not intended to hurt you; and if you get tired of yourself, there are books; or if you do not read, maybe you sing—there are musical instruments, and you can choose amongst them. Now I grant you I am not a waiting-maid, having had no education in that line; still, if I may advise, wash your face, and dress your hair, and be beautiful as you can, for by and by he will come"—

"Who will come?" she asked, rising to her knees, and clasping her hands.

The sight was more than enough for him. He fled incontinently, saying: "I will be back in the morning." As he went he snatched up the indispensable lamp; outside, he locked the door; then rowed away, repeating, "Oh, the blood of doves and the tears of women!"

Left thus alone, the unfortunate girl lay on the floor a long time, sobbing, and gradually finding the virtue there is in tears—especially tears of repentance. Afterwhile, with the return of reason—meaning power to think—the silence of the place became noticeable. Listening closely, she could detect no sign of life—nothing indicative of a street, or a house adjoining, or a neighbor, or that there was any outdoors about her at all. The noise of an insect, the note of a bird, a sough of wind, the gurgle of water, would have relieved her from the sense of having in some way fallen off the earth, and been caught by a far away uninhabited planet. That would certainly have been hard; but worse—the idea of being doomed to stay there took possession of her, and becoming intolerable, she walked from room to room, and even tried to take interest in the things around. Will it ever be that a woman can pass a mirror without being arrested by it? Before the tall copper plate she finally stopped. At first, the figure she saw startled her. The air of general discomfiture—hair loose, features tear-stained, eyes red and swollen, garments disarranged—made it look like a stranger. The notion exaggerated itself, and further on she found a positive comfort in the society of the image, which not only looked somebody else, but more and more somebody else who was lost like herself, and, being in the same miserable condition, would be happy to exchange sympathy for sympathy.

Now the spectacle of a person in distress is never pleasant; wherefore permission is begged to dismiss the passage of that night in the cistern briefly as possible. From the couch to the mirror; fearing now, then despairing; one moment calling for help, listening next, her distracted fancy caught by an imaginary sound; too much fevered to care for refreshments; so overwhelmed by the awful sense of being hopelessly and forever lost, she could neither sleep nor control herself mentally. Thus tortured, there were no minutes or hours to her, only a time, that being a peculiarity of the strange planet her habitat. To be sure, she explored her prison intent upon escape, but was as often beaten back by walls without window, loophole or skylight—walls in which there was but one door, fastened outside.

The day following was to the captive in nothing different from the night—a time divisionless, and filled with fear, suspense, and horrible imaginings—a monotony unbroken by a sound. If she could have heard a bell, though ever so faint, or a voice, to whomsoever addressed, it would yet prove her in an inhabited world—nay, could she but have heard a cricket singing!

In the morning the keeper kept his appointment. He came alone and without business except to renew the oil in the lamps. After a careful survey of the palace, as he called it, probably in sarcasm, and as he was about to leave, he offered, if she wanted anything, to bring it upon his return. Was there ever prisoner not in want of liberty? The proposal did but reopen the scene of the evening previous; and he fled from it, repeating as before, "Oh, the blood of doves and the tears of women!"

In the evening he found her more tractable; so at least he thought; and she was in fact quieter from exhaustion. None the less he again fled to escape the entreaties with which she beset him.

She took to the couch the second night. The need of nature was too strong for both grief and fear, and she slept. Of course she knew not of the hunt going on, or of the difficulties in the way of finding her; and in this ignorance the sensation of being lost gradually yielded to the more poignant idea of desertion. Where was Sergius? Would there ever be a fitter opportunity for display of the superhuman intelligence with which, up to this time, she had invested her father, the Prince of India? The stars could tell him everything; so, if now they were silent respecting her, it could only be because he had not consulted them. Situations such as she was in are right quarters of the moon for unreasonable fantasies; and she fell asleep oppressed by a conviction that all the friendly planets, even Jupiter, for whose appearance she had so often watched with the delight of a lover, were hastening to their Houses to tell him where she was, but for some reason he ignored them.

Still later, she fell into a defiant sullenness, one of the many aspects of despair.

In this mood, while lying on the couch, she heard the sound of oars, and almost immediately after felt the floor jar. She sat up, wondering what had brought the keeper back so soon. Steps then approached the door; but the lock there proving troublesome, suggested one unaccustomed to it; whereupon she remembered the rude advice to wash her face and dress her hair, for by and by somebody was coming.

"Now," she thought, "I shall learn who brought me here, and why."

A hope returned to her.

"Oh, it may be my father has at last found me!"

She arose—a volume of joy gathered in her heart ready to burst into expression—when the door was pushed open, and Demedes entered.

We know the figure he thus introduced to her. With averted face he reinserted the key in the lock. She saw the key, heavy enough in emergency for an aggressive weapon—she saw a gloved hand turn it, and heard the bolt plunge obediently into its socket—and the flicker of hope went out. She sunk upon the couch again, sullenly observant.

The visitor—at first unrecognized by her—behaved as if at home, and confident of an agreeable reception. Having made the door safe on the outside, he next secured it inside, by taking the key out. Still averting his face, he went to the mirror, shook the great cloak from his shoulders, and coolly surveyed himself, turning this way and that. He rearranged his cape, took off the cap, and, putting the plumes in better relation, restored it to his head—thrust his gloves on one side under a swordless belt, and the ponderous key under the same belt but on the other side, where it had for company a straight dagger of threatening proportions.

Lael kept watch on these movements, doubtful if the stranger were aware of her presence. Uncertainty on that score was presently removed. Turning from the mirror, he advanced slowly toward her. When under the circlet, just at the point where the light was most favorable for an exhibition of himself, he stopped, doffed the cap, and said to her:

"The daughter of the Prince of India cannot have forgotten me."

Now if, from something said in this chronicle, the reader has been led to exalt the little Jewess into a Bradamante, it were just to undeceive him. She was a woman in promise, of fair intellect subordinate to a pure heart. Any great thing said or done by her would be certain to have its origin in her affections. The circumstances in which she would be other than simple and unaffected are inconceivable. In the beautiful armor, Demedes was handsome, particularly as there was no other man near to force a comparison of stature; yet she did not see any of his braveries—she saw his face alone, and with what feeling may be inferred from the fact that she now knew who brought her where she was, and the purpose of the bringing.

Instead of replying, she shrank visibly further and further from him, until she was an apt reminder of a hare cornered by a hound, or a dove at last overtaken by a hawk.

The suffering she had undergone was discernible in her appearance, for she had not taken the advice of the keeper; in a word, she was at the moment shockingly unlike the lissome, happy, radiant creature whom we saw set out for a promenade two days before. Her posture was crouching; the hair was falling all ways; both hands pressed hard upon her bosom; and the eyes were in fixed gaze, staring at him as at death. She was in the last extremity of fear, and he could not but see it.

"Do not be afraid," he said, hurriedly, and in a tone of pity. "You were never safer than you are here—I swear it, O Princess!"

Observing no change in her or indication of reply, he continued: "I see your fear, and it may be I am its object. Let me come and sit by you, and I will explain everything—where you are—why you were brought here—and by whom.... Or give me a place at your feet.... I will not speak for myself, except as I love you—nay, I will speak for love."

Still not a word from her—only a sullenness in which he fancied there was a threat.... A threat? What could she do? To him, nothing; he was in shirt of steel; but to herself much.... And he thought of suicide, and then of—madness.

"Tell me, O Princess, if you have received any disrespect since you entered this palace? There is but one person from whom it could have proceeded. I know him; and if, against his solemn oath, he has dared an unseemly look or word—if he has touched you profanely—you may choose the dog's death he shall die, and I will give it him. For that I wear this dagger. See!"

In this he was sincere; yet he shall be a student very recently come to lessons in human nature who fails to perceive the reason of his sincerity; possibly she saw it; we speak with uncertainty, for she still kept silent. Again he cast about to make her speak. Reproach, abuse, rage, tears in torrents, fury in any form were preferable to that look, so like an animal's conscious of its last moment.

"Must I talk to you from this distance? I can, as you see, but it is cruel; and if you fear me"—he smiled, as if the idea were amusing. "Oh! if you still fear me, what is there to prevent my compelling the favors I beg?"

The menace was of no more effect than entreaty. Paralysis of spirit from fright was new to him; yet the resources of his wit were without end. Going to the table, he looked it over carefully.

"What!" he cried, turning to her with well-dissembled astonishment. "Hast thou eaten nothing? Two days, and not a crumb of bread in thy pretty throat?—not a drop of wine? This shall not go on—no, by all the goodness there is in Heaven!"

On a plate he then placed a biscuit and a goblet filled with red wine of the clearest sparkle, and taking them to her, knelt at her feet.

"I will tell you truly, Princess—I built this palace for you, and brought you here under urgency of love. God deny me forever, if I once dreamed of starving you! Eat and drink, if only to give me ease of conscience."

He offered the plate to her.

She arose, her face, if possible, whiter than before.

"Do not come near me—keep off!" Her voice was sharp and high. "Keep off!... Or take me to my father's house. This palace is yours—you have the key. Oh, be merciful!"

Madness was very near her.

"I will obey you in all things but one," he said, and returned the plate to the table, content with having brought her to speech. "In all things but one," he repeated peremptorily, standing under the circlet. "I will not take you to your father's house. I brought you here to teach you what I would never have a chance to teach you there—that you are the idol for whom I have dared every earthly risk, and imperilled my soul.... Sit down and rest yourself. I will not come near you to-night, nor ever without your consent.... Yes, that is well. And now you are seated, and have shown a little faith in my word—for which I thank you and kiss your hand—hear me further and be reasonable.... You shall love me."

Into this declaration he flung all the passion of his nature.

"No, no! Draw not away believing yourself in peril. You shall love me, but not as a scourged victim. I am not a brute. I may be won too lightly, by a voice, by bright eyes, by graces of person, by faithfulness where faithfulness is owing, by a soul created for love and aglow with it as a star with light; but I am not of those who kill the beloved, and justify the deed, pleading coldness, scorn, preference for another. Be reasonable, I say, O Princess, and hear how I will conquer you.... Are not the better years of life ours? Why should I struggle or make haste, or be impatient? Are you not where I have chosen to put you?—where I can visit you day and night to assure

myself of your health and spirits?—all in the world, yet out of its sight?...
You may not know what a physician Time is. I do. He has a medicine for
almost every ailment of the mind, every distemper of the soul. He may not
set my lady's broken finger, but he will knit it so, when sound again, the
hurt shall be forgotten. He drops a month—in extreme cases, a year or
years—on a grief, or a bereavement, and it becomes as if it had never been.
So he lets the sun in on prejudices and hates, and they wither, and where
they were, we go and gather the fruits and flowers of admiration, respect—
ay, Princess, of love. Now, in this cause, I have chosen Time for my best
friend; he and I will come together, and stay"—

The conclusion of the speech must be left to the reader, for with the last
word some weighty solid crashed against the raft until it trembled
throughout. Demedes stopped. Involuntarily his hand sought the dagger;
and the action was a confession of surprise. An interval of quiet ensued;
then came a trial of the lock—at first, gentle—another, with energy—a
third one rattled the strong leaf in its frame.

"The villain! I will teach him—No, it cannot be—he would not dare—and
besides I have the boat."

As Demedes thus acquitted the keeper, he cast a serious glance around him,
evidently in thought of defence.

Again the raft was shaken, as if by feet moving rapidly under a heavy
burden. Crash!—and the door was splintered. Once more—crash!—and
door and framework shot in—a thunderbolt had not wrought the wreck
more completely.

Justice now to the Greek. Though a genius all bad, he was manly. Retiring
to a position in front of Lael, he waited, dagger in hand. And he had not
breathed twice, before Nilo thrust his magnificent person through the
breach, and advanced under the circlet.

Returning now. Had the King been in toils, and hard pressed, he would not
have committed himself to the flood and darkness of the cistern in the
manner narrated; at least the probabilities are he would have preferred
battle in the court, and light, though of the city on fire, by which to
conquer or die. But his blood was up, and he was in pursuit, not at bay; to
the genuine fighting man, moreover, a taste of victory is as a taste of blood
to tigers. He was not in humor to bother himself with practical
considerations such as—If I come upon the hiding-place of the Greek,
how, being deaf and dumb, am I to know it? Of what use are eyes in a
hollow rayless as this? Whether he considered the obvious personal dangers
of the adventure—drowning, for instance—is another matter.

The water was cold, and his teeth chattered; for it will be recollected he was astride the poles of the sedan, lashed together. That his body was half submerged was a circumstance he little heeded, since it was rather helpful than otherwise to the hand strokes with which he propelled himself. Nor need it be supposed he moved slowly. The speed attainable by such primitive means in still water is wonderful.

Going straight from the lower platform of the stair, he was presently in total darkness. With a row of columns on either hand, he managed to keep direction; and how constantly and eagerly he employed the one available sense left him may be imagined. His project was to push on until stayed by a boundary wall—then he would take another course, and so on to the end. The enemy, by his theory, was in a boat or floating house. Hopeful, determined, inspirited by the prospect of combat, he made haste as best he could. At last, looking over his left shoulder, he beheld a ruddy illumination, and changed direction thither. Presently he swept into the radius of a stationary light, broken, of course, by intervening pillars and the shadows they cast; then, at his right, a hand lamp in front of what had the appearance of a house rising out of the water, startled him.

Was it a signal?

The King approached warily, until satisfied no ambush was intended—until, in short, the palace of the Greek was before him.

It was his then to surprise; so he drove the ends of the poles against the landing with force sufficient, as we have seen, to interrupt Demedes explaining how he meant to compel the love of Lael.

With all his nicety of contrivance, the Greek had at the last moment forgotten to extinguish the lamp or take it into the house with him. The King recognized it and the boat, yet circumspectly drew his humble craft up out of the water. He next tried the lock, and then the door; finally he used the poles as a ram.

Taking stand under the circlet, there was scant room between it and the blue handkerchief on his head; while the figure he presented, nude to the waist, his black skin glistening with water, his trousers clinging to his limbs, his nostrils dilating, his eyes jets of flame, his cruel white teeth exposed— this figure the dullest fancy can evoke—and it must have appeared to the guilty Greek a very genius of vengeance.

Withal, however, the armor and the dagger brought Demedes up to a certain equality; and, as he showed no flinching, the promise of combat was excellent. It happened, however, that while the two silently regarded each other, Lael recognized the King, and unable to control herself, gave a cry of joy, and started to him. Instinctively Demedes extended a hand to hold her back; the giant saw the opening; two steps so nearly simultaneous the movement was like a leap—and he had the wrist of the other's armed hand in his grip. Words can convey no idea of the outburst attending the assault—it was the hoarse inarticulate falsetto of a dumb man signalizing a triumph. If the reader can think of a tiger standing over him, its breath on his cheek, its roar in his ears, something approximate to the effect is possible.

The Greek's cap fell off, and the dagger rattled to the floor. His countenance knit with sudden pain—the terrible grip was crushing the bones—yet he did not submit. With the free hand, he snatched the key from his belt, and swung it to strike—the blow was intercepted—the key wrenched away. Then Demedes' spirit forsook him—mortal terror showed in his face turned gray as ashes, and in his eyes, enlarged yet ready to burst from their sockets. He had not the gladiator's resignation under judgment of death.

"Save me, O Princess, save me!... He is killing me.... My God—see—hear—he is crushing my bones!... Save me!"

Lael was then behind the King, on her knees, thanking Heaven for rescue. She heard the imploration, and, woman-like, sight of the awful agony extinguished the memory of her wrongs.

"Spare him, Nilo, for my sake, spare him!" she cried.

It was not alone her wrongs that were forgotten—she forgot that the avenger could not hear.

Had he heard, it is doubtful if he had obeyed; for we again remark he was fighting less for her than for his master—or rather for her in his master's interest. And besides, it was the moment of victory, when, of all moments, the difference between the man born and reared under Christian influences and the savage is most impressible.

While she was entreating him, he repeated the indescribable howl, and catching Demedes bore him to the door and out of it. At the edge of the landing, he twisted his fingers in the long locks of the screaming wretch, whose boasted philosophy was of so little worth to him now that he never thought of it—then he plunged him in the water, and held him under until—enough, dear reader!

Lael did not go out. The inevitable was in the negro's face. Retreating to the couch, she there covered her ears with her hands, trying to escape the prayers the doomed man persisted to the last in addressing her.

By and by Nilo returned alone.

He took the cloak from the floor, wrapped her in it, and signed her to go with him; but the distresses she had endured, together with the horrors of the scene just finished, left her half fainting. In his arms she was a child. Almost before she knew it, he had placed her in the boat. With a cord found in the house, he tied the poles behind the vessel, and set out to find the stairs, the tell-tale lamp twinkling at the bow.

Safely arrived there, the good fellow carried his fair charge up the steps to the court—descending again, he brought the poles—going back once more, he drew the boat on the lower platform. Then to hasten to the street door, unbar it, and admit Sergius were scarce a minute's work.

The monk's amazement and delight at beholding Lael, and hers at sight of him, require no labored telling. At that meeting, conventionalities were not observed. He carried her into the passage, and gave her the keeper's chair; after which, reminded of the programme so carefully laid out by him, he returned with Nilo to the court, where the illumination in the sky still dropped its relucent flush. Turning the King face to him he asked:

"Where is the keeper?"

The King walked to the sedan, opened the door, and dragging the dead man forth, flung him sprawling on the pavement.

Sergius stood speechless, seeing what the victor had not—arrests, official inquests, and the dread machinery of the law started, with results not in foresight except by Heaven. Before he had fairly recovered, Nilo had the sedan out and the poles fixed to it, and in the most cheerful, matter-of-fact manner signed him to take up the forward ends.

"Where is the Greek?" the monk asked.

That also the King managed to answer.

"In the cistern—drowned!" exclaimed Sergius, converting the reply into words.

The King drew himself up proudly.

"O Heavens! What will become of us?"

The exclamation signified a curtain rising upon a scene of prosecution against which the Christian covered his face with his hands.... Again Nilo brought him back to present duty.... In a short time Lael was in the chair, and they bearing her off.

Sergius set out first for Uel's house. The time was near morning; but for the conflagration the indications of dawn might have been seen in the east. He was not long in getting to understand the awfulness of the calamity the city had suffered, and that, with thousands of others, the dwellings of Uel and the Prince of India were heaps of ashes on which the gale was expending its undiminished strength.

What was to be done with Lael?

This Sergius answered by leading the way to the town residence of the Princess Irene. There the little Jewess was received, while he took boat and hurried to Therapia.

The Princess came down, and under her roof, Lael found sympathy, rest, and safety. In due time also Uel's last testament reached her, with the purse of jewels left by the Prince of India, and she then assumed guardianship of the bereaved girl.

BOOK V
MIRZA

CHAPTER I
A COLD WIND FROM ADRIANOPLE

It is now the middle of February, 1451. Constantine has been Emperor a trifle over three years, and proven himself a just man and a conscientious ruler. How great he is remains for demonstration, since nothing has occurred to him—nothing properly a trial of his higher qualities.

In one respect the situation of the Emperor was peculiar. The highway from Gallipoli to Adrianople, passing the ancient capital on the south, belonged to the Turks, and they used it for every purpose—military, commercial, governmental—used it as undisputedly within their domain, leaving Constantine territorially surrounded, and with but one neighbor, the Sultan Amurath.

Age had transformed the great Moslem; from dreams of conquest, he had descended to dreams of peace in shaded halls and rose-sprent gardens, with singers, story-tellers, and philosophers for companions, and women, cousins of the houris, to carpet the way to Paradise; but for George Castriot, [Footnote: Iskander-beg—Scanderbeg. *Vide* GIBBON's *Roman Empire.*] he had abandoned the cimeter. Keeping terms of amity with such a neighbor was easy—the Emperor had merely to be himself peaceful. Moreover, when John Palaeologus died, the succession was disputed by Demetrius, a brother to Constantine. Amurath was chosen arbitrator, and he decided in favor of the latter, placing him under a bond of gratitude.

Thus secure in his foreign relations, the Emperor, on taking the throne, addressed himself to finding a consort; of his efforts in that quest the reader is already informed, leaving it to be remarked that the Georgian Princess at last selected for him by Phranza died while journeying to Constantinople. This, however, was business of the Emperor's own inauguration, and in point of seriousness could not stand comparison with another affair imposed upon him by inheritance—keeping the religious factions domiciled in the capital from tearing each other to pieces. The latter called for qualities he does not seem to have possessed. He permitted the sectaries to bombard each other with sermons, bulletins and excommunications which, on the ground of scandal to religion, he should have promptly suppressed; his failure to do so led to its inevitable result— the sectaries presently dominated him.

Now, however, the easy administration of the hitherto fortunate Emperor is to vanish; two additional matters of the gravest import are thrust upon him simultaneously, one domestic, the other foreign; and as both of them become turning points in our story, it is advisable to attend to them here.

When the reins of government fell from the hands of Amurath, they were caught up by Mahommed; in other words, Mahommed is Sultan, and the old regime, with its friendly policies and stately courtesies, is at an end, imposing the necessity for a recast of the relations between the Empires. What shall they be? Such is the foreign question.

Obviously, the subject being of vital interest to the Greek, it was for him to take the initiative in bringing about the definitions desired. With keen appreciation of the danger of the situation he addressed himself to the task. Replying to a request presented through the ambassador resident at Adrianople, Mahommed gave him solemn assurances of his disposition to observe every existing treaty. The response seems to have made him over-confident. Into the gilded council chamber at Blacherne he drew his personal friends and official advisers, and heard them with patience and dignity. At the close of a series of deliberative sessions which had almost the continuity of one session, two measures met his approval. Of these, the first was so extraordinary it is impossible not to attribute its suggestion to Phranza, who, to the immeasurable grief and disgust of our friend the venerable Dean, was now returned, and in the exercise of his high office of Grand Chamberlain.

Allusion has been already made to the religious faith of the mother of Mahommed. [Footnote: "For it was thought that his (Amurath's) eldest son Mahomet, after the death of his father, would have embraced the Christian Religion, being in his childhood instructed therein, as was supposed, by his mother, the daughter of the Prince of Servia, a Christian."—KNOLLES' *Turk. Hist.*, 239, Vol. I.

"He (Mahommed) also entered into league with Constantinus Palaeologus, the Emperor of Constantinople, and the other Princes of Grecia; as also with the Despot of Servia, his Grandfather by the mother's side, as some will have it; howbeit some others write that the Despot his daughter, Amurath his wife (the Despot's daughter, Amurath's wife) was but his Mother-in-law, whom he, under colour of Friendship, sent back again unto her Father, after the death of Amurath, still allowing her a Princely Dowery."—*Ibid.* 230.

On this very interesting point both Von Hammer and Gibbon are somewhat obscure; the final argument, however, is from Phranza: "After the taking of Constantinople, she (the Princess) fled to Mahomet II." (GIBBON'S *Rom. Emp.*, Note 52, 12.) The action is significant of a mother. Mothers-in-law are not usually so doting.] The daughter of a Servian prince, she is supposed to have been a Christian. After the interment of Amurath, she had been returned to her native land. Her age was about fifty. Clothed with full powers, the Grand Chamberlain was despatched to Adrianople to propose a marriage between His Majesty, the Emperor, and the Sultana mother. The fears and uncertainties besetting the Greek must have been overwhelming.

The veteran diplomat was at the same time entrusted with another affair which one would naturally think called for much less delicacy in negotiation. There was in Constantinople then a refugee named Orchan, of whose history little is known beyond the fact that he was a grandson of Sultan Solyman. Sometime presumably in the reign of John Palaeologus, the Prince appeared in the Greek capital as a pretender to the Sultanate; and his claim must have had color of right, at least, since he became the subject of a treaty between Amurath and his Byzantine contemporary, the former binding himself to pay the latter an annual stipend in aspers in consideration of the detention of the fugitive.

With respect to this mysterious person, the time was favorable, in the opinion of the council, for demanding an increase of the stipend. Instructions concerning the project were accordingly delivered to Lord Phranza.

The High Commissioner was received with flattering distinction at Adrianople. He of course presented himself first to the Grand Vizier, Kalil Pacha, of whom the reader may take note, since, aside from his reappearances in these pages, he is a genuine historic character. To further acquaintance with him, it may be added that he was truly a veteran in public affairs, a member of the great family to which the vizierat descended almost in birthright, and a friend to the Greeks, most likely from long association with Amurath, although he has suffered severe aspersion on their account. Kalil advised Phranza to drop the stipend. His master, he said, was not afraid of Orchan, if the latter took the field as an open claimant, short work would be made of him. The warning was disregarded. Phranza submitted his proposals to Mahommed directly, and was surprised by his gentleness and suavity. There was no scene whatever. On the contrary, the marriage overture was forwarded to the Sultana with every indication of approval, nor was the demand touching the stipend rejected; it was simply deferred. Phranza lingered at the Turkish capital, pleased with the attentions shown him, and still more with the character of the Sultan.

In the judgment of the Envoy the youthful monarch was the incarnation of peace. What time he was not mourning the loss of his royal father, he was studying designs for a palace, probably the Watch Tower of the World (*Jehan Numa*), which he subsequently built in Adrianople.

Well for the trusting master in Blacherne, well for Christianity in the East, could the credulous Phranza have looked in upon the amiable young potentate during one of the nights of his residence in the Moslem capital! He would have found him in a chamber of impenetrable privacy, listening while the Prince of India proved the calculations of a horoscope decisive of the favorable time for beginning war with the Byzantines.

"Now, my Lord," he could have heard the Prince say, when the last of the many tables had been refooted for the tenth time—"now we are ready for the ultimate. We are agreed, if I mistake not"—this was not merely a complimentary form of speech, for Mahommed, it should be borne in mind, was himself deeply versed in the intricate and subtle science of planetary prediction—"we are agreed that as thou art to essay the war as its beginner, we should have the most favorable Ascendant, determinable by the Lord, and the Planet or Planets therein or in conjunction or aspect with the Lord; we are also agreed that the Lord of the Seventh House is the Emperor of Constantinople; we are also agreed that to have thee overcome thy adversary, the Emperor, it is better to have the Ascendant in the House of one of the Superior Planets, Saturn, Jupiter or Mars"—

"Jupiter would be good, O Prince," said Mahommed, intensely interested, "yet I prefer Mars."

"My Lord is right again." The Seer hesitated slightly, then explained with a deferential nod and smile: "I was near saying my Lord is always right. Though some of the adepts have preferred Scorpio for the Ascendant, because it is a fixed sign, Mars pleases me best; wherefore toward him have I directed all my observations, seeking a time when he shall certainly be better fortified than the Lord of the Seventh House, as well as elevated above him in our figure of the Heavens."

Mahommed leaned far over toward the Prince, and said imperiously, his eyes singularly bright: "And the ultimate—the time, the time, O Prince! Hast thou found it? Allah forbid it be too soon!—There is so much to be done—so much of preparation."

The Prince smiled while answering:

"My Lord is seeing a field of glory—his by reservation of destiny—and I do not wonder at his impatience to go reaping in it; but" (he became serious) "it is never to be forgotten—no, not even by the most exalted of men—that the Planets march by order of Allah alone." ... Then taking the last of the calculations from the table at his right hand, he continued: "The Ascendant permits my Lord to begin the war next year."

Mahommed heard with hands clinched till the nails seemed burrowing in the flesh of the palms.

"The day, O Prince!—the day—the hour!" he exclaimed.

Looking at the calculation, the Prince appeared to reply from it: "At four o'clock, March twenty-sixth"—

"And the year?"

"Fourteen hundred and fifty-two."

"*Four o'clock, March twenty-sixth, fourteen hundred and fifty-two,*" Mahommed repeated slowly, as if writing and verifying each word. Then he cried with fervor: "There is no God but God!"

Twice he crossed the floor; after which, unwilling probably to submit himself at that moment to observation by any man, he returned to the Prince:

"Thou hast leave to retire; but keep within call. In this mighty business who is worthier to be the first help of my hands than the Messenger of the Stars?"

The Prince saluted and withdrew.

At length Phranza wearied of waiting, and being summoned home left the two affairs in charge of an ambassador instructed to forego no opportunity which might offer to press them to conclusions. Afterwhile Mahommed went into Asia to suppress an insurrection in Caramania. The Greek followed him from town to camp, until, tiring of the importunity, the Sultan one day summoned him to his tent.

"Tell my excellent friend, the Lord of Constantinople, thy master, that the Sultana Maria declines his offer of marriage."

"Well, my Lord," said the ambassador, touched by the brevity of the communication, "did not the great lady deign an explanation?"

"She declined—that is all."

The ambassador hurried a courier to Constantinople with the answer. For the first time he ventured to express a doubt of the Turk's sincerity.

He would have been a wiser man and infinitely more useful to his sovereign, could he have heard Mahommed again in colloquy with the Prince of India.

"How long am I to endure this dog of a *Gabour?*" [Footnote: Mahommed always wrote and spoke of Byzantines as *Romans*, except when in passion; then he called them *Gabours*.] asked the Sultan, angrily. "It was not enough to waylay me in my palace; he pursued me into the field; now he imbitters my bread, now at my bedside he drives sleep from me, now he begrudges me time for prayer. How long, I say?"

The Prince answered quietly: "Until March twenty-sixth, fourteen hundred and fifty-two."

"But if I put him to sleep, O Prince?"

"His master will send another in his place."

"Ah, but the interval! Will it not be so many days of rest?—so many nights of unbroken sleep?"

"Has my Lord finished his census yet? Are his arsenals full? Has he his ships, and sailors, and soldiers? Has he money according to the estimate?"

"No."

"My Lord has said he must have cannon. Has he found an artificer to his mind?"

Mahommed frowned.

"I will give my Lord a suggestion. Does it suit him to reply now to the proposal of marriage, keeping the matter of the stipend open, he may give half relief and still hold the Emperor, who stands more in need of bezants than of a consort."

"Prince," said Mahommed, quickly, "as you go out send my secretary in."

"Despatch a messenger for the ambassador of my brother of Constantinople. I will see him immediately."

This to the secretary.

And presently the ambassador had the matter for report above recited. In the report he might have said with truth—a person styling himself *Prince of India* has risen to be Grand Vizier in fact, leaving the title to Kalil.

These negotiations, lamentably barren of good results, were stretched through half the year. But it is necessary to leave them for the time, that we may return and see if the Emperor had better success in the management of the domestic problem referred to as an inheritance.

CHAPTER II
A FIRE FROM THE HEGUMEN'S TOMB

The great fire burned its way broadly over two hills of the city, stopping at the wall of the garden on the eastern front of Blacherne. How it originated, how many houses were destroyed, how many of the people perished in the flames and in the battle waged to extinguish them, were subjects of unavailing inquiry through many days.

For relief of the homeless, Constantine opened his private coffers. He also assumed personal direction of the removal of the debris cumbering the unsightly blackened districts, and, animated by his example, the whole population engaged zealously in the melancholy work. When Galata, laying her jealousies aside, contributed money and sent companies of laborers over to the assistance of her neighbor, it actually seemed as if the long-forgotten age of Christian brotherhood was to be renewed. But, alas! This unity, bred of so much suffering, so delightful as a rest from factious alarms, so suggestive of angelic society and heavenly conditions in general, disappeared—not slowly, but almost in a twinkling.

It was afternoon of the second day after the fire. Having been on horseback since early morning, the Emperor, in need of repose, had returned to his palace; but met at the portal by an urgent request for audience from the Princess Irene, he received her forthwith. The reader can surmise the business she brought for consideration, and also the amazement with which her royal kinsman heard of the discovery and rescue of Lael. For a spell his self-possession forsook him. In anticipation of the popular excitement likely to be aroused by the news, he summoned his councillors, and after consultation, appointed a commission to investigate the incident, first sending a guard to take possession of the cistern.

Like their master, the commissioners had never heard of the first profanation of the ancient reservoir; as a crime, consequently, this repetition was to them original in all its aspects, and they addressed themselves to the inquiry incredulously; but after listening to Sergius, and to the details the little Jewess was able to give them, the occurrence forced itself on their comprehension as more than a crime at law—it took on the proportions and color of a conspiracy against society and religion. Then its relative consequences presented themselves. Who were concerned in it?

The name of Demedes startled them by suddenly opening a wide horizon of conjecture. Some were primarily disposed to welcome the intelligence for the opportunity it offered His Majesty to crush the Academy of

Epicurus, but a second thought cooled their ardor; insomuch that they began drawing back in alarm. The Brotherhood of the St. James' was powerful, and it would certainly resent any humiliation their venerable Hegumen might sustain through the ignominious exposure of his son.

In great uncertainty, and not a little confusion, the commissionate body hied from the Princess Irene to the cistern. While careful to hide it from his associates, each of them went with a scarce admitted hope that there would be a failure of the confirmations at least with respect to the misguided Demedes; and not to lose sight of Nilo, in whom they already discerned a serviceable scapegoat, they required him to go with them.

The revelations call for a passing notice. In the court the body of the keeper was found upon the pavement. The countenance looked the terror of which the man died, and as a spectacle grimly prepared the beholders for the disclosures which were to follow.

There was need of resolution to make the dismal ferriage from the lower platform in the cistern, but it was done, Nilo at the oars. When the visitors stepped on the landing of the "palace," their wonder was unbounded. When they passed through the battered doorway, and standing under the circlet, in which the lights were dead, gazed about them, they knew not which was most astonishing, the courage of the majestic black or the audacity of the projector of the villanous scheme. But where was he? We may be sure there was no delay in the demand for him. While the fishing tongs were being brought, the apartments were inspected, and a list of their contents made. Then the party collected at the edge of the landing. The secret hope was faint within them, for the confirmations so far were positive, and the terrible negro, not in the least abashed, was showing them where his enemy went down. They gave him the tongs, and at the first plunge he grappled the body, and commenced raising it. They crowded closer around him, awe-struck yet silently praying: Holy Mother, grant it be any but the Hegumen's son! A white hand, the fingers gay with rings, appeared above the water. The fisherman took hold of it, and with a triumphant smile, drew the corpse out, and laid it face up for better viewing. The garments were still bright, the gilded mail sparkled bravely. One stooped with the light, and said immediately:

"It is he—Demedes!"

Then the commissioners looked at each other—there was no need of speech—a fortunate thing, for at that instant there was nothing of which they were more afraid.

Avoidance of the dreaded complications was now impossible—so at least it seemed to them. Up in the keeper's room, whither they hurriedly adjourned, it was resolved to despatch a messenger to His Majesty with an informal statement of the discoveries, and a request for orders. The unwillingness to assume responsibility was natural.

Constantine acted promptly, and with sharp discernment of the opportunity afforded the mischief-makers. The offence was to the city, and it should see the contempt in which the conspirators held it, the danger escaped, and the provocation to the Most Righteous; if then there were seditions, his conscience was acquit. He sent Phranza to break the news to the Hegumen, and went in person to the Monastery, arriving barely in time to receive the blessings of his reverend friend, who, overcome by the shock, died in his arms. Returning sadly to Blacherne, he ordered the corpses of the guilty men to be exposed for two days before the door of the keeper's house, and the cistern thrown open for visitation by all who desired to inspect the Palace of Darkness, as he appropriately termed the floating tenement constructed with such wicked intents. He also issued a proclamation for the suppression of the Epicurean Academy, and appointed a day of Thanksgiving to God for the early exposure of the conspiracy. Nilo he sent to a cell in the Cynegion, ostensibly for future trial, but really to secure him from danger; in his heart he admired the King's spirit, and hoped a day would come when he could safely and suitably reward him.

On the part of the people the commotion which ensued was extraordinary. They left the fire to its smouldering, and in steady currents marched past the ghastly exhibits prepared for them in the street, looked at them, shuddered, crossed themselves, and went their ways apparently thankful for the swiftness of the judgment which had befallen; nor was there one heard to criticise the Emperor's course. The malefactors were dropped, like unclean clods, into the earth at night, without ceremony or a mourner in attendance. Thus far all well.

At length the day of thanksgiving arrived. By general agreement, there was not a sign of dissatisfaction to be seen. The most timorous of the commissioners rested easy. Sancta Sophia was the place appointed for the services, and Constantine had published his intention to be present. He had donned the Basilean robes; his litter was at the door of the palace; his guard of horse and foot was formed, when the officer on duty at the gate down by the Port of Blacherne arrived with a startling report.

"Your Majesty," he said, unusually regardless of the ancient salutation, "there is a great tumult in the city."

The imperial countenance became stern.

"This is a day of thanks to God for a great mercy; who dares profane it by tumult?"

"I must speak from hearsay," the officer answered.... "The funeral of the Hegumen of the St. James took place at daylight this morning"—

"Yes," said Constantine, sighing at the sad reminder, "I had intended to assist the Brotherhood. But proceed."

"The Brothers, with large delegations from the other Monasteries, were assembled at the tomb, when Gennadius appeared, and began to preach, and he wrought upon his hearers until they pushed the coffin into the vault, and dispersed through the streets, stirring up the people."

At this the Emperor yielded to his indignation.

"Now, by the trials and sufferings of the Most Christian Mother, are we beasts insensible to destruction? Or idiots exempt from the penalties of sin and impiety? And he—that genius of unrest—that master of foment—God o' Mercy, what has he laid hold of to lead so many better men to betray their vows and the beads at their belts? Tell me—speak—my patience is nearly gone."

For an instant, be it said, the much tried Sovereign beheld a strong hand move within reach, as offering itself for acceptance. No doubt he saw it as it was intended, the symbol and suggestion of a policy. Pity he did not take it! For then how much of mischance had been averted from himself— Constantinople might not have been lost to the Christian world—the Greek Church had saved its integrity by recognizing the union with the Latins consummated at the Council of Florence—Christianity had not been flung back for centuries in the East, its birthplace.

"Your Majesty," the officer returned, "I can report what I heard, leaving its truth to investigation.... In his speech by the tomb Gennadius admitted the awfulness of the crime attempted by Demedes, and the justice of the punishment the young man suffered, its swiftness proving it to have been directed by Heaven; but he declared its conception was due to the Academy of Epicurus, and that there remained nothing deserving study and penance except the continued toleration without which the ungodly institution had passed quickly, as plagues fly over cities purified against them. The crime, he said, was ended. Let the dead bury the dead. But who were they responsible for grace to the Academy? And he answered himself, my Lord, by naming the Church and the State."

"Ah! He attacked the Church then?"

"No, my Lord, he excused it by saying it had been debauched by an *azymite* Patriarch, and while that servant of prostitution and heresy controlled it, wickedness would be protected and go on increasing."

"And the State—how dealt he with the State?"

"The Church he described as Samson; the Patriarch, as an uncomely Delilah who had speciously shorn it of its strength and beauty; the State, as a political prompter and coadjutor of the Delilah; and Rome, a false God seeking to promote worship unto itself through the debased Church and State."

"God o' Mercy!" Constantine exclaimed, involuntarily signing to the sword-bearer at his back; but recovering himself, he asked with forced moderation: "To the purpose of it all—the object. What did he propose to the Brothers?"

"He called them lovers of God in the livery of Christ, and implored them to gird up their loins, and stand for the religion of the Fathers, lest it perish entirely."

"Did he tell them what to do?"

"Yes, my Lord."

A wistful, eager look appeared on the royal face, and behind it an expectation that now there would be something to justify arrest and exile at least—something politically treasonable.

"He referred next to the thanksgiving services appointed to-day in Sancta Sophia, and declared it an opportunity from Heaven, sent them and all the faithful in the city, to begin a crusade for reform; not by resort to sword and spear, for they were weapons of hell, but by refusing to assist the Patriarch with their presence. A vision had come to him in the night, he said—an angel of the Lord with the Madonna of Blacherne—advising him of the Divine will. Under his further urgency—and my Lord knows his power of speech—the Brothers listening, the St. James' and all present from the other Orders, broke up and took to the streets, where they are now, exhorting the people not to go to the Church, and there is reason to believe they will"—

"Enough," said the Emperor, with sudden resolution. "The good Gregory shall not pray God singly and alone."

Turning to Phranza, he ordered him to summon the court for the occasion. "Let not one stay away," he continued; "and they shall put on their best robes and whole regalia; for, going in state myself, I have need of their utmost splendor. It is my will, further, that the army be drawn from their quarters to the Church, men, music, and flags, and the navies from their ships. And give greeting to the Patriarch, and notify him, lest he make haste. Aside from these preparations, I desire the grumblers be left to pursue their course unmolested. The sincere and holy amongst them will presently have return of clear light."

This counter project was entered upon energetically.

Shortly after noon the military bore down to the old Church, braying the streets with horns, drums and cymbals, and when they were at order in the immense auditorium, their banners hanging unfurled from the galleries, the Emperor entered, with his court; in a word, the brave, honest, white-haired Patriarch had company multitudinous and noble as he could desire. None the less, however, Gennadius had his way also—*the people took no part in the ceremony.*

After the celebration, Constantine, in his chambers up in Blacherne, meditated upon the day and its outcome. Phranza was his sole attendant.

"My dear friend," the Emperor began, breaking a long silence, and much disquieted, "was not my predecessor, the first Constantine, beset with religious dissensions?"

"If we may credit history, my Lord, he certainly was."

"How did he manage them?"

"He called a Council."

"A Council truly—was that all?"

"I do not recollect anything more."

"It was this way, I think. He first settled the faith, and then provided against dispute."

"How, my Lord?"

"Well, there was one Arius, a Libyan, Presbyter of a little church in Alexandria called Baucalis, preacher of the Unity of God"—

"I remember him now."

"Of the Unity of God as opposed to the Trinity. Him the first Constantine sent to prison for life, did he not?"

Thereupon Phranza understood the subject of his master's meditation; but being of a timid soul, emasculated by much practice of diplomacy, usually a tedious, waiting occupation, he hastened to reply: "Even so, my Lord. Yet he could afford to be heroic. He had consolidated the Church, and was holding the world in the hollow of his hand."

Constantine allowed a sigh to escape him, and lapsed into silence; when next he spoke, it was to say slowly:

"Alas, my dear friend! The people were not there"—meaning at Sancta Sophia. "I fear, I fear"—

"What, my Lord?"

Another sigh deeper than the first one: "I fear I am not a statesman, but only a soldier, with nothing to give God and my Empire except a sword and one poor life."

These details will help the reader to a fair understanding of the domestic involvements which overtook the Emperor about the time Mahommed ascended the Turkish throne, and they are to be considered in addition to the negotiations in progress with the Sultan. And as it is important to give an idea of their speeding, we remark further, that from the afternoon of the solemnity in Sancta Sophia the discussion then forced upon him went from bad to worse, until he was seriously deprived both of popular sympathy and the support of the organized religious orders. The success of the solemnity in point of display, and the measures resorted to, were not merely offensive to Gennadius and his ally, the Duke Notaras; they construed them as a challenge to a trial of strength, and so vigorously did they avail themselves of their advantages that, before the Emperor was aware of it, there were two distinct parties in the city, one headed by Gennadius, the other by himself and Gregory the Patriarch.

Month by month the bitterness intensified; month by month the imperial party fell away until there was little of it left outside the court and the army and navy, and even they were subjected to incessant inroads—until, finally, it came to pass that the Emperor was doubtful whom to trust. Thereupon, of course, the season for energetic repressive measures vanished, never to return.

Personalities, abuse, denunciation, lying, and sometimes downright blows took the place of debate in the struggle. One day religion was an exciting cause; next day, politics. Throughout it all, however, Gennadius was obviously the master-spirit. His methods were consummately adapted to the genius of the Byzantines. By confining himself strictly to the Church wrangle, he avoided furnishing the Emperor pretexts for legal prosecution; at the same time he wrought with such cunning that in the monasteries the very High Residence of Blacherne was spoken of as a den of *azymites*, while Sancta Sophia was abandoned to the Patriarch. To be seen in the purlieus of the latter was a signal for vulgar anathemas and social ostracism. His habits meantime were of a sort to make him a popular idol. He grew, if possible, more severely penitential; he fasted and flagellated himself; he slept on the stony floor before his crucifix; he seldom issued from his cell, and when visited there, was always surprised at prayers, the burden of which was forgiveness for signing the detested Articles of Union with the Latins. The physical suffering he endured was not without solace; he had heavenly visions and was attended by angels. If in his solitude he fainted, the Holy Virgin of Blacherne ministered to him, and brought him back to life and labor. First an ascetic, then a Prophet—such was his progression.

And Constantine was a witness to the imposture, and smarted under it; still he held there was nothing for him but to temporize, for if he ordered the seizure and banishment of the all-powerful hypocrite, he could trust no one with the order. The time was dark as a starless night to the high-spirited but too amiable monarch, and he watched and waited, or rather watched and drifted, extending confidence to but two counsellors, Phranza and the Princess Irene. Even in their company he was not always comfortable, for, strange to say, the advice of the woman was invariably heroic, and that of the man invariably weak and accommodating.

From this sketch the tendencies of the government can be right plainly estimated, leaving the suspicion of a difference between the first Constantine and the last to grow as the evils grew.

CHAPTER III
MIRZA DOES AN ERRAND FOR MAHOMMED

Vegetation along the Bosphorus was just issuing from what may be called its budded state. In the gardens and protected spots on the European side white and yellow winged butterflies now and then appeared without lighting, for as yet there was nothing attractive enough to keep them. Like some great men of whom we occasionally hear, they were in the world before their time. In other words the month of May was about a week old, and there was a bright day to recommend it—bright, only a little too much tinctured with March and April to be all enjoyable. The earth was still spongy, the water cold, the air crisp, and the sun deceitful.

About ten o'clock in the morning Constantinopolitans lounging on the sea-wall were surprised by explosive sounds from down the Marmora. Afterwhile they located them, so to speak, on a galley off St. Stephano. At stated intervals, pale blue smoke would burst from the vessel, followed by a hurry-skurry of gulls in the vicinity, and then the roar, muffled by distance. The age of artillery had not yet arrived; nevertheless, cannon were quite well known to fame. Enterprising traders from the West had sailed into the Golden Horn with samples of the new arm on their decks; they were of such rude construction as to be unfit for service other than saluting. [Footnote: Cannon were first made of hooped iron, widest at the mouth. The process of casting them was just coming in.] So, now, while the idlers on the wall were not alarmed, they were curious to make out who the extravagant fellows were, and waited for the flag to tell them.

The stranger passed swiftly, firing as it went; and as the canvas was new and the hull freshly painted in white, it rode the waves to appearances a very beautiful "thing of life;" but the flag told nothing of its nationality. There were stripes on it diagonally set, green, yellow, and red, the yellow in the middle.

"The owners are not Genoese"—such was the judgment on the wall.

"No, nor Venetian, for that is not a lion in the yellow."

"What, then, is it?"

Pursued thus, the galley, at length rounding Point Serail (Demetrius), turned into the harbor. When opposite the tower of Galata, a last salute was fired from her deck; then the two cities caught up the interest, and being able to make out decisively that the sign in the yellow field of the flag was but a coat-of-arms, they said emphatically:

"It is not a national ship—only a great Lord;" and thereupon the question became self-inciting:

"Who is he?"

Hardly had the anchor taken hold in the muddy bed of the harbor in front of the port of Blacherne, before a small boat put off from the strange ship, manned by sailors clad in flowing white trousers, short sleeveless jackets, and red turbans of a style remarkable for amplitude. An officer, probably the sailing-master, went with them, and he, too, was heavily turbaned. A gaping crowd on the landing received the visitor when he stepped ashore and asked to see the captain of the guard. To that dignitary he delivered a despatch handsomely enveloped in yellow silk, saying, in imperfect Greek:

"My Lord, just arrived, prays you to read the enclosure, and send it forward by suitable hand. He trusts to your knowledge of what the proprieties require. He will await the reply on his galley."

The sailing-master saluted profoundly, resumed seat in his boat, and started back to the ship, leaving the captain of the guard to open the envelope and read the communication, which was substantially as follows:

"From the galley, St. Agostino, May 5, Year of our Blessed Saviour, 1451.

"The undersigned is a Christian Noble of Italy, more particularly from his strong Castle Corti on the eastern coast of Italy, near the ancient city of Brindisi. He offers lealty to His Most Christian Majesty, the Emperor of Constantinople, Defender of the Faith according to the crucified Son of God (to whom be honor and praise forevermore), and humbly represents that he is a well-knighted soldier by profession, having won his spurs in battle, and taken the accolade from the hand of Calixtus the Third, Bishop of Rome, and, yet more worthily, His Holiness the Pope: that the time being peaceful in his country, except as it was rent by baronial feuds and forays not to his taste, he left it in search of employment and honors abroad; that he made the pilgrimage to the Holy Sepulchre first, and secured there a number of precious relics, which he is solicitous of presenting to His Imperial Majesty; that from long association with the Moslems, whom Heaven, in its wisdom impenetrable to the understanding of men, permits to profane the Holy Land with their presence and wicked guardianship, he acquired a speaking knowledge of the Arabic and Turkish languages; that he engaged in warfare against those enemies of God, having the powerful sanction therefor of His Holiness aforesaid, by whose direction he occupied himself chiefly with chastising the Berber pirates of Tripoli, from whom he took prisoners, putting them at his oars, where some of them now are. With the august city of Byzantium he has been acquainted many years through report, and, if its fame be truly published, he desires to reside in it, possibly to the end of his days. Wherefore he presumes to address this his respectful petition, praying its submission to His Most Christian Majesty, that he may be assured if the proposal be agreeable to the royal pleasure, and in the meantime have quiet anchorage for his galley.

UGO, COUNT CORTI."

In the eyes of the captain of the guard the paper was singular, but explicit; moreover, the request seemed superfluous, considering the laxity prevalent with respect to the coming and going of persons of all nativities and callings. To be sure, trade was not as it used to be, and, thanks to the enterprise and cunning of the Galatanese across the harbor, the revenues from importations were sadly curtailed; still the old city had its markets, and the world was welcome to them. The argument, however, which silenced the custodian's doubt was, that of the few who rode to the gates in their own galleys and kept them there ready to depart if their reception were in the least chilling, how many signed themselves as did this one? Italian counts were famous fighters, and generally had audiences wherever they knocked. So he concluded to send the enclosure up to the Palace without the intermediation of the High Admiral, a course which would at least save time.

While the affair is thus pending, we may return to Count Corti, and say an essential word or two of him.

The cannon, it is to be remarked, was not the only novelty of the galley. Over the stern, where the aplustre cast its shadow in ordinary crafts, there was a pavilion-like structure, high-raised, flat-roofed, and with small round windows in the sides. Quite likely the progressive ship-builders at Palos and Genoa would have termed the new feature a cabin. It was beyond cavil an improvement; and on this occasion the proprietor utilized it as he well might. Since the first gun off St. Stephano, he had held the roof, finding it the best position to get and enjoy a view of the capital, or rather of the walls and crowned eminences they had so long and all-sufficiently defended. A chair had been considerately brought up and put at his service, but in witness of the charm the spectacle had for him from the beginning, he did not once resort to it.

If only to save ourselves description of the man, and rescue him from a charge of intrusion into the body of our story, we think it better to take the reader into confidence at once, and inform him that Count Corti is in fact our former acquaintance Mirza, the Emir of the Hajj. The difference between his situation now, and when we first had sight of him on his horse under the yellow flag in the valley of Zaribah is remarkable; yet he is the same in one particular at least—he was in armor then, and he is still in armor—that is, he affects the same visorless casque, with its cape of fine rings buckled under the chin, the same shirt and overalls of pliable mail, the same shoes of transverse iron scales working into each other telescopically when the feet are in movement, the same golden spurs, and a surcoat in every particular like the Emir's, except it is brick-dust red instead of green. And this constancy in armor should not be accounted a vanity; it was a habit acquired in the school of arms which graduated him, and which he persisted in partly for the inurement, and partly as a mark of respect for Mahommed, with whom the gleam and clink of steel well fashioned and gracefully worn was a passion, out of which he evolved a suite rivalling those kinsmen of the Buccleuch who—

"—quitted not their harness bright, Neither by day nor yet by night."

Returning once again. It was hoped when Mirza was first introduced that every one who might chance to spend an evening over these pages would perceive the possibilities he prefigured, and adopt him as a favorite; wherefore the interest may be more pressing to know what he, an Islamite supposably without guile, a Janissary of rank, lately so high in his master's confidence, is doing here, offering lealty to the Most Christian Emperor, and denouncing the followers of the Prophet as enemies of God. The appearances are certainly against him.

The explanation due, if only for coherence in our narrative, would be clearer did the reader review the part of the last conversation in the White Castle between the Prince of India and Mahommed, in which the latter is paternally advised to study the Greek capital, and keep himself informed of events within its walls. Yet, inasmuch as there is a current in reading which one once fairly into is loath to be pushed out of, we may be forgiven for quoting a material passage or two.... "There is much for my Lord to do"— the Prince says, speaking to his noble eleve. "It is for him to think and act as if Constantinople were his capital temporarily in possession of another.... It is for him to learn the city within and without; its streets and edifices; its hills and walls; its strong and weak places; its inhabitants, commerce, foreign relations; the character of its ruler, his resources and policies; its daily events; its cliques, clubs, and religious factions; especially is it for him to foment the differences Latin and Greek already a fire which has long been eating out to air in an inflammable house.".... Mahommed, it will be recollected, acceded to the counsel, and in discussing the selection of a person suitable for the secret agency, the Prince said: ... "He who undertakes it should enter Constantinople and live there above suspicion. He must be crafty, intelligent, courtly in manner, accomplished in arms, of high rank, and with means to carry his state bravely; for not only ought he to be conspicuous in the Hippodrome; he should be welcome in the salons and palaces; along with other facilities, he must be provided to buy service in the Emperor's bedroom and council chamber—nay, at his elbow. Mature of judgment, it is of prime importance that he possess my Lord's confidence unalterably."... And when the ambitious Turk demanded: "The man, Prince, the man!"—the wily tutor responded: "My Lord has already named him."—"I?"—"Only to-night my Lord spoke of him as a marvel."—"Mirza?"... The Jew then proceeded: "Despatch him to Italy; let him appear in Constantinople, embarked from a galley, habited like an Italian, and with a suitable Italian title. He speaks Italian already, is fixed in his religion, and in knightly honor. Not all the gifts at the despot's disposal, nor the blandishments of society can shake his allegiance—he worships my Lord."...

Mahommed demurred to the proposal, saying: "So has Mirza become a part of me, I am scarcely myself without him."

Now he who has allowed himself to become interested in the bright young Emir, and pauses to digest these excerpts, will be aware of a grave concern for him. He foresees the outcome of the devotion to Mahommed dwelt upon so strongly by the Prince of India. An order to undertake the secret service will be accepted certainly as it is given. The very assurance that it will be accepted begets solicitude in the affair. Did Mahommed decide affirmatively? What were the instructions given? Having thus settled the coherences, we move on with the narrative.

It will be remembered, further, that close after the departure of the Princess Irene from the old Castle, Mahommed followed her to Therapia, and, as an Arab story-teller, was favored with an extended private audience in which he extolled himself to her at great length, and actually assumed the role of a lover. What is yet more romantic, he came away a lover in fact.

The circumstance is not to be lightly dismissed, for it was of immeasurable effect upon the fortunes of the Emir, and—if we can be excused for connecting an interest so stupendous with one so comparatively trifling—the fate of Constantinople. Theretofore the Turk's ambition had been the sole motive of his designs against that city, and, though vigorous, driving, and possibly enough of itself to have pushed him on, there might yet have been some delay in the achievement. Ambition derived from genius is cautious in its first movements, counts the cost, ponders the marches to be made and the means to be employed, and is at times paralyzed by the simple contemplation of failure; in other words, dread of loss of glory is not seldom more powerful than the hope of glory. After the visit to Therapia, however, love reenforced ambition; or rather the two passions possessed Mahommed, and together they murdered his sleep. He became impatient and irritable; the days were too short, the months too long. Constantinople absorbed him. He thought of nothing else waking, and dreamed of nothing else. Well for him his faith in astrology, for by it the Prince of India was able to hold him to methodic preparation.

There were times when he was tempted to seize the Princess, and carry her off. Her palace was undefended, and he had but to raid it at night. Why not? There were two reasons, either of them sufficient: first, the stern old Sultan, his father, was a just man, and friendly to the Emperor Constantine; but still stronger, and probably the deterrent in fact, he actually loved the Princess with a genuine romantic sentiment, her happiness an equal motive—loved her for herself—a thing perfectly consistent, for in the Oriental idea there is always One the Highest.

Now, it was very lover-like in Mahommed, his giving himself up to thought of the Princess while gliding down the Bosphorus, after leaving his safeguard on her gate. He closed his eyes against the mellow light on the water, and, silently admitting her the perfection of womanhood, held her image before him until it was indelible in memory—face, figure, manner, even her dress and ornaments—until his longing for her became a positive hunger of soul.

As if to give us an illustration of the mal-apropos in coincidence, his august father had selected a bride for him, and he was on the road to Adrianople to celebrate the nuptials when he stopped at the White Castle. The maiden chosen was of a noble Turkish family, but harem born and bred. She might be charming, a very queen in the Seraglio; but, alas! the kinswoman of the Christian Emperor had furnished a glimpse of attractions which the fiancee to whom he was going could never attain—attractions of mind and manner more lasting than those of mere person; and as he finished the comparison, he beat his breast, and cried out: "Ah, the partiality of the Most Merciful! To clothe this Greek with all the perfections, and deny her to me!"

Withal, there was a method in Mahommed's passion. Setting his face sternly against violating his own safeguard by abducting the Princess, he fell into revision of her conversation; and then a light broke in upon him—a light and a road to his object.

He recalled with particularity her reply to the message delivered to her, supposably from himself, containing his avowal that he loved her the more because she was a Christian, and singled out of it these words: ... "A wife I might become, not from temptation of gain or power, or in surrender to love—I speak not in derision of the passion, since, like the admitted virtues, it is from God—nay, Sheik, in illustration of what may otherwise be of uncertain meaning to him, tell Prince Mahommed I might become his wife could I, by so doing, save or help the religion I profess."

This he took to pieces.... "'She might become a wife.' Good!... 'She might become my wife'—on condition.... What condition?" ... He beat his breast again, this time with a laugh.

The rowers looked at him in wonder. What cared he for them? He had discovered a way to make her his.... "Constantinople is the Greek Church," he muttered, with flashing eyes. "I will take the city for my own glory—to her then the glory of saving the Church! On to Constantinople!"

And from that moment the fate of the venerable metropolis may be said to have been finally sealed.

Within an hour after his return to the White Castle, he summoned Mirza, and surprised him by the exuberance of his joy. He threw his arm over the Emir's shoulder, and walked with him, laughing and talking, like a man in wine. His nature was of the kind which, for the escape of feeling, required action as well as words. At length he sobered down.

"Here, Mirza," he said. "Stand here before me.... Thou lovest me, I believe?"

Mirza answered upon his knee: "My Lord has said it."

"I believe thee.... Rise and take pen and paper, and write, standing here before me." [Footnote: A Turkish calligraphist works on his feet as frequently as on a chair, using a pen made of reed and India ink reduced to fluid.]

From a table near by the materials were brought, and the Emir, again upon his knees, wrote as his master dictated.

The paper need not be given in full. Enough that it covered with uncommon literalness—for the Conqueror's memory was prodigious—the suggestions of the Prince of India already quoted respecting the duties of the agent in Constantinople. While writing, the Emir was variously moved; one instant, his countenance was deeply flushed, and in the next very pale; sometimes his hand trembled. Mahommed meantime kept close watch upon him, and now he asked:

"What ails thee?"

"My Lord's will is my will," was the answer—"yet"—

"Out—speak out."

"My Lord is sending me from him, and I dread losing my place at his right hand."

Mahommed laughed heartily.

"Lay the fear betime," he then said, gravely. "Where thou goest, though out of reach of my right hand, there will my thought be. Hear—nay, at my knee."

He laid the hand spoken of on Mirza's shoulder, and stooped towards him. "Ah, my Saladin, thou wert never in love, I take it? Well—I am. Look not up now, lest—lest thou think my bearded cheek hath changed to a girl's."

Mirza did not look up, yet he knew his master was blushing.

"Where thou goest, I would give everything but the sword of Othman to be every hour of the day, for she abideth there.... I see a ring on thy hand—the ruby ring I gave thee the day thou didst unhorse the uncircumcised deputy of Hunyades. Give it back to me. 'Tis well. See, I place it on the third finger of my left hand. They say whoever looketh at her is thenceforth her lover. I caution thee, and so long as this ruby keepeth color unchanged, I shall know thou art keeping honor bright with me—that thou lovest her, because thou canst not help it, yet for my sake, and because I love her.... Look up now, my falcon—look up, and pledge me."

"I pledge my Lord," Mirza answered.

"Now I will tell thee. She is that kinswoman of the *Gabour* Emperor Constantine whom we saw here the day of our arrival. Or didst thou see her? I have forgotten."

"I did not, my Lord."

"Well, thou wilt know her at sight; for in grace and beauty I think she must be a daughter of the houri this moment giving immortal drink to the beloved of Allah, even the Prophet."

Mahommed changed his tone.

"The paper and the pen."

And taking them he signed the instructions, and the signature was the same as that on the safeguard on the gate at Therapia.

"There—keep it well; for when thou gettest to Constantinople, thou wilt become a Christian." He laughed again. "Mirza—the Mirza Mahommed swore by, and appointed keeper of his heart's secret—he a Christian! This will shift the sin of the apostasy to me."

Mirza took the paper.

"I have not chosen to write of the other matter. In what should it be written, if at all, except in my blood—so close is it to me?... These are the things I expect of thee. Art thou listening? She shall be to thee as thine eye. Advise me of her health, and where she goes; with whom she consorts;

what she does and says; save her from harm: does one speak ill of her, kill him, only do it in my name—and forget not, O my Saladin!—as thou hopest a garden and a couch in Paradise—forget not that in Constantinople, when I come, I am to receive her from thy hand peerless in all things as I left her to-day.... Thou hast my will all told. I will send money to thy room to-night, and thou wilt leave to-night, lest, being seen making ready in the morning, some idiot pursue thee with his wonder.... As thou art to be my other self, be it royally. Kings never account to themselves.... Thou wantest now nothing but this signet."

From his breast he drew a large ring, its emerald setting graven with the signature at the bottom of the instructions, and gave it to him.

"Is there a Pacha or a Begler-bey, Governor of a city or a province, property of my father, who refuseth thy demand after showing him this, report him, and *Shintan* will be more tolerable unto him than I, when I have my own. It is all said. Go now.... We will speak of rewards when next we meet.... Or stay! Thou art to communicate by way of this Castle, and for that I will despatch a man to thee in Constantinople. Remember—for every word thou sendest me of the city, I look for two of her.... Here is my hand." Mirza kissed it, and departed.

CHAPTER IV
THE EMIR IN ITALY

We know now who Count Corti is, and the objects of his coming to Constantinople—that he is a secret agent of Mahommed—that, summed up in the fewest words, his business is to keep the city in observation, and furnish reports which will be useful to his master in the preparation the latter is making for its conquest. We also know he is charged with very peculiar duties respecting the Princess Irene.

The most casual consideration of these revelations will make it apparent, in the next place, that hereafter the Emir must be designated by his Italian appellative in full or abbreviated. Before forsaking the old name, there is lively need of information, whether as he now stands on the deck of his galley, waiting the permissions prayed by him of the Emperor Constantine, he is, aside from title, the same Mirza lately so honored by Mahommed.

From the time the ship hove in sight of the city, he had kept his place on the cabin. The sailors, looking up to him occasionally, supposed him bound by the view, so motionless he stood, so steadfastly he gazed. Yet in fact his countenance was not expressive of admiration or rapture. A man with sound vision may have a mountain just before him and not see it; he may be in the vortex of a battle deaf to its voices; a thought or a feeling can occupy him in the crisis of his life to the exclusion of every sense. If perchance it be so with the Emir now, he must have undergone a change which only a powerful cause could have brought about. He had been so content with his condition, so proud of his fame already won, so happy in keeping prepared for the opportunities plainly in his sight, so satisfied with his place in his master's confidence, so delighted when that master laid a hand upon his shoulder and called him familiarly, now his Saladin, and now his falcon.

Faithfully, as bidden, Mirza sallied from the White Castle the night of his appointment to the agency in Constantinople. He spoke to no one of his intention, for he well knew secrecy was the soul of the enterprise. For the same reason, he bought of a dervish travelling with the Lord Mahommed's suite a complete outfit, including the man's donkey and donkey furniture. At break of day he was beyond the hills of the Bosphorus, resolved to skirt the eastern shore of the Marmora and Hellespont, from which the Greek population had been almost entirely driven by the Turks, and at the Dardanelles take ship for Italy direct as possible—a long route and trying—yet there was in it the total disappearance from the eyes of acquaintance needful to success in his venture. His disguise insured him from interruption on the road, dervishes being sacred characters in the estimation of the Faithful, and generally too poor to excite cupidity. A gray-frocked man, hooded, coarsely sandalled, and with a blackened gourd at his girdle for the alms he might receive from the devout, no Islamite meeting him would ever suspect a large treasure in the ragged bundle on the back of the patient animal plodding behind him like a tired dog.

The Dardanelles was a great stopping-place for merchants and tradesmen, Greek, Venetian, Genoese. There Mirza provided himself with an Italian suit, adopted the Italian tongue, and became Italian. He borrowed a chart of the coast of Italy from a sailor, to determine the port at which it would be advisable for him to land.

While settling this point, the conversation had with the Prince of India in the latter's tent at Zaribah arose to mind, and he recalled with particularity all that singular person said with reference to the accent observable in his speech. He also went over the description he himself had given the Prince of the house or castle from which he had been taken in childhood. A woman had borne him outdoors, under a blue sky, along a margin of white sand, an orchard on one hand, the sea on the other. He remembered the report of the waves breaking on the shore, the olive-green color of the trees in the orchard, and the battlemented gate of the castle; whereupon the Prince said the description reminded him of the eastern shore of Italy in the region of Brindisi.

It was a vague remark certainly; but now it made a deeper impression on the Emir than at the moment of its utterance and pointed his attention to Brindisi. The going to Italy, he argued, was really to get a warrant for the character he was to assume in Constantinople; that is, to obtain some knowledge of the country, its geography, political divisions, cities, rulers, and present conditions generally, without which the slightest cross-examination by any of the well-informed personages about the Emperor would shatter his pretensions in an instant. Then it was he fell into a most unusual mood.

Since the hour the turbaned rovers captured him he had not been assailed by a desire to see or seek his country and family. Who was his father? Was his mother living? Probably nothing could better define the profundity of the system underlying the organization of the Janissaries than that he had never asked those questions with a genuine care to have them solved. What a suppression of the most ordinary instincts of nature! How could it have been accomplished so completely? As a circumstance, its tendency is to confirm the theory that men are creatures of education and association.... Was his mother living? Did she remember him? Had she wept for him?

What sort of being was she? If living, how old would she be? And he actually attempted a calculation. Calling himself twenty-six she might not be over forty-five. That was not enough to dim her eyes or more than slightly silver her hair; and as respects her heart, are not the affections of a mother flowers for culling by Death alone?

Such reflections never fail effect. A tenderness of spirit is the first token of their presence; then memory and imagination begin striving; the latter to bring the beloved object back, and the former to surround it with sweetest circumstances. They wrought with Mirza as with everybody else. The yearning they excited in him was a surprise; presently he determined to act on the Prince of India's suggestion, and betake himself to the eastern coast of Italy.

The story of the sack of a castle was of a kind to have wide circulation; at the same time this one was recent enough to be still in the memory of persons living. Finding the place of its occurrence was the difficulty. If in the vicinity of Brindisi—well, he would go and ask. The yearning spoken of did not come alone; it had for companion, Conscience, as yet in the background.

There were vessels bound for Venice. One was taking in water, after which it would sail for Otranto. It seemed a fleet craft, with a fair crew, and a complement of stout rowers. Otranto was south of Brindisi a little way, and the castle he wanted to hear of might have been situated between those cities. Who could tell? Besides, as an Italian nobleman, to answer inquiry in Constantinople, he would have to locate himself somewhere, and possibly the coast in question might accommodate him with both a location and a title. The result was he took passage to Otranto.

While there he kept his role of traveller, but was studious, and picked up a great fund of information bearing upon the part awaiting him. He lived and dressed well, and affected religious circles. It was the day when Italy was given over to the nobles—the day of robbers, fighting, intrigues and usurpations—of free lances and bold banditti—of government by the strong hand, of right determinable by might, of ensanguined Guelphs and Ghibellines. Of these the Emir kept clear.

By chance he fell in with an old man of secondary rank in the city much given to learning, an habitue of a library belonging to one of the monasteries. It came out ere long that the venerable person was familiar with the coast from Otranto to Brindisi, and beyond far as Polignano.

"It was in my sturdier days," the veteran said, with a dismal glance at his shrunken hands. "The people along the shore were much harried by Moslem pirates. Landing from their galleys, the depredators burned habitations, slew the men, and carried off such women as they thought would fetch a price. They even assaulted castles. At last we were driven to the employment of a defensive guard cooperative on land and water. I was a captain. Our fights with the rovers were frequent and fierce. Neither side showed quarter."

The reminiscence stimulated Mirza to inquiry. He asked the old man if he could mention a castle thus attacked.

"Yes, there was one belonging to Count Corti, a few leagues beyond Brindisi. The Count defended himself, but was slain."

"Had he a family?"

"A wife and a boy child."

"What became of them?"

"By good chance the Countess was in Brindisi attending a fete; she escaped, of course. The boy, two or three years of age, was made prisoner, and never heard of afterwards."

A premonition seized Mirza.

"Is the Countess living?"

"Yes. She never entirely recovered from the shock, but built a house near the site of the castle, and clearing a room in the ruins, turned it into a chapel. Every morning and evening she goes there, and prays for the soul of her husband, and the return of her lost boy."

"How long is it since the poor lady was so bereft?"

The narrator reflected, and replied: "Twenty-two or three years."

"May the castle be found?"

"Yes."

"Have you been to it?"

"Many times."

"How was it named?"

"After the Count—*Il Castillo di Corti.*"

"Tell me something of its site."

"It is down close by the sea. A stone wall separates its front enclosure from the beach. Sometimes the foam of the waves is dashed upon the wall. Through a covered gate one looks out, and all is water. Standing on the tower, all landward is orchard and orchard—olive and almond trees intermixed. A great estate it was and is. The Countess, it is understood, has a will executed; if the boy does not return before her death, the Church is to be her legatee."

There was more of the conversation, covering a history of the Corti family, honorable as it was old—the men famous warriors, the women famous beauties.

Mirza dreamed through the night of the Countess, and awoke with a vague consciousness that the wife of the Pacha, the grace of whose care had been about him in childhood—a good woman, gentle and tender—was after all but a representative of the mother who had given him birth, just as on her part every mother is mercifully representative of God. Under strong feeling he took boat for Brindisi.

There he had no trouble in confirming the statements of his Otranto acquaintance. The Countess was still living, and the coast road northwardly would bring him to the ruins of her castle. The journey did not exceed five leagues.

What he might find at the castle, how long he would stay, what do, were so uncertain—indeed everything in the connection was so dependent upon conditions impossible of foresight, that he resolved to set out on foot. To this course he was the more inclined by the mildness of the weather, and the reputation of the region for freshness and beauty.

About noon he was fairly on the road. Persons whom he met—and they were not all of the peasant class—seeing a traveller jaunty in plumed cap, light blue camail, pointed buskins, and close-fitting hose the color of the camail, sword at his side, and javelin in hand, stayed to observe him long as he was in sight, never dreaming they were permitted to behold a favorite of one of the bloody Mahounds of the East.

Over hill and down shallow vales: through stone-fenced lanes; now in the shade of old trees; now along a seashore partially overflowed by languid waves, he went, lighter in step than heart, for he was in the mood by no means uncommon, when the spirit is prophesying evil unto itself. He was sensible of the feeling, and for shame would catch the javelin in the middle and whirl it about him defensively until it sung like a spinning-wheel; at times he stopped and, with his fingers in his mouth, whistled to a small bird as if it were a hunting hawk high in air.

Once, seeing a herd of goats around a house thatched and half-hidden in vines, he asked for milk. A woman brought it to him, with a slice of brown bread; and while he ate and drank, she stared at him in respectful admiration; and when he paid her in gold, she said, courtesying low: "A glad life to my Lord! I will pray the Madonna to make the wish good." Poor creature! She had no idea she was blessing one in whose faith the Prophet was nearer God than God's own Son.

At length the road made an abrupt turn to the right, bringing him to a long stretch of sandy beach. Nearly as he could judge, it was time for the castle to appear, and he was anxious to make it before sundown. Yet in the angle of the wood he saw a wayside box of stone sheltering an image of the Virgin, with the Holy Child in its arms. Besides being sculptured better than usual, the figures were covered with flowers in wreath and bouquet. A dressed slab in front of the structure, evidently for the accommodation of worshippers, invited him to rest, and he took the seat, and looking up at the mother, she appeared to be looking at him. He continued his gaze, and presently the face lost its stony appearance—stranger still, it smiled. It was illusion, of course, but he arose startled, and moved on with quickened step. The impression went with him. Why the smile? He did not believe in images: much less did he believe in the Virgin, except as she was the subject of a goodly story. And absorbed in the thought, he plodded on, leaving the sun to go down unnoticed.

Thereupon the shadows thickened in the woods at his left hand, while the sound of the incoming waves at his right increased as silence laid its velvet finger with a stronger compress on all other pulsations. Here and there a star peeped timidly through the purpling sky—now it was dusk—a little later, it would be night—and yet no castle!

He pushed on more vigorously; not that he was afraid—fear and the falcon of Mahommed had never made acquaintance—but he began to think of a bed in the woods, and worse yet, he wanted the fast-going daylight to help him decide if the castle when he came to it were indeed the castle of his fathers. He had believed all along, if he could see the pile once, his memory would revive and help him to recognition.

At last night fell, and there was darkness trebled on the land, and on the sea darkness, except where ghostly lines of light stretched themselves along the restless water. Should he go on?...

Then he heard a bell—one soft tone near by and silvery clear. He halted. Was it of the earth? A hush deeper of the sound—and he was wondering if another illusion were not upon him, when again the bell!

"Oh!" he muttered, "a trick of the monks in Otranto! Some soul is passing."

He pressed forward, guided by the tolling. Suddenly the trees fell away, and the road brought him to a stone wall heavily coped. On further, a blackened mass arose in dim relief against the sky, with heavy merlons on its top.

"It is the embattled gate!" he exclaimed, to himself—"the embattled gate!—and here the beach!—and, O Allah! the waves there are making the reports they used to!"

The bell now tolled with awful distinctness, filling him with unwonted chills—tolled, as if to discourage his memory in its struggle to lift itself out of a lapse apparently intended to be final as the grave—tolled solemnly, as if his were the soul being rung into the next life. A rush of forebodings threatened him with paralysis of will, and it was only by a strong exertion he overcame it, and brought himself back to the situation, and the question, What next?

Now Mirza was not a man to forego a purpose lightly. Emotional, but not superstitious, he tried the sword, if it were loose in the scabbard, and then, advancing the point of his javelin, entered the darkened gallery of the gate. Just as he emerged from it on the inner side, the bell tolled.

"A Moslem doth not well," he thought, silently repeating a saying of the *jadis*, "to accept a Christian call to prayer; but," he answered in self-excuse, "I am not going to prayer—I am seeking"—he stopped, for very oddly, the face of the Virgin in the stone box back in the angle of the road presented itself to him, and still more oddly, he felt firmer of purpose seeing again the smile on the face. Then he finished the sentence aloud—"my mother *who is a Christian.*"

There was a jar in the conclusion, and he went back to find it, and having found it, he was surprised. Up to that moment, he had not thought of his mother a Christian. How came the words in his mouth now? Who prompted them? And while he was hastily pondering the effect upon her of the discovery that he himself was an Islamite, the image in the box reoccurred to him, this time with the child in its arms; and thereupon the mystery seemed to clear itself at once. "Mother and mother!" he said. "What if my coming were the answer of one of them to the other's prayer?"

The idea affected him; his spirit softened; the heat of tears sprang to his eyelids; and the effort he made to rise above the unmanliness engaged him so he failed to see the other severer and more lasting struggle inevitable if the Countess were indeed the being to whom he owed the highest earthly obligations—the struggle between natural affection and honor, as the latter lay coiled up in the ties binding him to Mahommed.

The condition, be it remarked, is ours; for from that last appearance of the image by the wayside—from that instant, marking a new era in his life—often as the night and its incidents recurred to him, he had never a doubt of his relationship to the Countess. Indeed, not only was she thenceforward his mother, but all the ground within the gate was his by natal right, and the castle was the very castle from which he had been carried away, over the body of his heroic father—*he was the Count Corti!*

These observations will bring the reader to see more distinctly the Emir's state after passing the gate. Of the surroundings, he beheld nothing but shadows more or less dense and voluminous; the mournful murmuring of the wind told him they belonged to trees and shrubbery in clumps. The road he was on, although blurred, was serviceable as a guide, and he pursued it until brought to a building so masked by night the details were invisible. Following its upper line, relieved against the gray sky, he made out a broken front and one tower massively battlemented. A pavement split the road in two; crossing it, he came to an opening, choked with timbers and bars of iron; surmisably the front portal at present in disuse. He needed no explanation of its condition. Fire and battle were familiars of his.

The bell tolled on. The sound, so passing sweet elsewhere, seemed to issue from the yawning portal, leaving him to fancy the interior a lumber of floors, galleries, and roofs in charred tumble down.

Mirza turned away presently, and took the left branch of the road; since he could not get into the castle, he would go around it; and in doing so, he borrowed from the distance traversed a conception of its immensity, as well as of the importance the countship must have enjoyed in its palmy days.

At length he gained the rear of the great pile. The wood there was more open, and he was pleased with the sight of lights apparently gleaming through windows, from which he inferred a hamlet pitched on a broken site. Then he heard singing; and listening, never had human voices seemed to him so impressively solemn. Were they coming or going?

Ere long a number of candles, very tall, and screened from the wind by small lanterns of transparent paper, appeared on the summit of an ascent; next moment the bearers of the candles were in view—boys bareheaded and white frocked. As they began to descend the height, a bevy of friars succeeded them, their round faces and tonsured crowns glistening in ruddy contrast with their black habits. A choir of four singers, three men and one woman, followed the monks. Then a linkman in half armor strode across the summit, lighting the way for a figure, also in black, which at once claimed Mirza's gaze.

As he stared at the figure, the account given him by the old captain in Otranto flashed upon his memory. The widow of the murdered count had cleared a room in the castle, and fitted it up as a chapel, and every morning and evening she went thither to pray for the soul of her husband and the return of her lost boy.

The words were alive with suggestions; but suggestions imply uncertainty; wherefore they are not a reason for the absolute conviction with which the Emir now said to himself:

"It is she—the Countess—my mother!"

There must be in every heart a store of prevision of which we are not aware—occasions bring it out with such sudden and bewildering effect.

Everything—hymn, tolling bell, lights, boys, friars, procession—was accessory to that veiled, slow-marching figure. And in habiliment, movement, air, with what telling force it impersonated sorrow! On the other hand, how deep and consuming the sorrow itself must be!

She—he beheld only her—descended the height without looking up or around—a little stooped, yet tall and of dignified carriage—not old nor yet young—a noble woman worthy reverence.

While he was making these comments, the procession reached the foot of the ascent; then the boys and friars came between, and hid her from his view.

"O Allah! and thou his Prophet!" he exclaimed. "Am I not to see her face? Is she not to know me?"

Curiously the question had not presented itself before; neither when he resolved to come, nor while on the way. To say truth, he had been all the while intent on the one partial object—to see her. He had not anticipated the awakening the sight might have upon his feelings.

"Am I not to discover myself to her? Is she never to know me?" he repeated.

The lights in the hands of the boys were beginning to gleam along a beaten road a short distance in front of the agitated Emir conducting to the castle. He divined at once that the Countess was coming to the chapel for the usual evening service, and that, by advancing to the side of the road, he could get a near view of her as she passed. He started forward impulsively, but after a few steps stopped, trembling like a child imagining a ghost.

Now our conception of the man forbids us thinking him overcome by a trifle, whether of the air or in the flesh. A change so extreme must have been the work of a revelation of quick and powerful consequence—and it was, although the first mention may excite a smile. In the gleam of mental lightning—we venture on the term for want of another more descriptive— he had been reminded of the business which brought him to Italy.

Let us pause here, and see what the reminder means; if only because the debonair Mirza, with whom we have been well pleased, is now to become another person in name and character, commanding our sympathies as before, but for a very different reason.

This was what the lightning gave him to see, and not darkly: If he discovered himself to the Countess, he must expose his history from the night the rovers carried him away. True, the tale might be given generally, leaving its romance to thrill the motherly heart, and exalt him the more; for to whom are heroes always the greatest heroes? Unhappily steps in confession are like links in a chain, one leads to another.... Could he, a Christian born, tell her he was an apostate? Or if he told her, would it not be one more grief to the many she was already breaking under—one, the most unendurable? And as to himself, how could he more certainly provoke a forfeiture of her love?... She would ask—if but to thank God for mercies—to what joyful accident his return was owing? And then? Alas! with her kiss on his brow, could he stand silent? More grievous yet, could he deceive her? If nothing is so murderous of self-respect as falsehood, a new life begun with a lie needs no prophet to predict its end. No, he must answer the truth. This conviction was the ghost which set him trembling. An admission that he was a Moslem would wound her, yet the hope of his conversion would remain—nay, the labor in making the hope good might even renew her interest in life; but to tell her he was in Italy to assist in the overthrow of a Christian Emperor for the exaltation of an infidel—God help him! Was ever such a monster as he would then become in her eyes?... The consequences of that disclosure, moreover, were not to the Countess and himself merely. With a sweep of wing one's fancy is alone capable of, he was borne back to the White Castle, and beheld Mahommed. When before did a Prince, contemplating an achievement which was to ring the world, give trust with such absoluteness of faith? Poor Mirza! The sea rolled indefinitely wide between the White Castle and this one of his fathers; across it, nevertheless, he again heard the words: "As thou art to be my other self, be it royally. Kings never account to themselves." If they made betrayal horrible in thought, what would the fact be?...

Finally, last but not least of the reflections the lightning laid bare, the Emir had been bred a soldier, and he loved war for itself and for the glory it offered unlike every other glory. Was he to bid them both a long farewell?

Poor Mirza! A few paragraphs back allusion was made to a struggle before him between natural affection on one hand and honor on the other. Perhaps it was obscurely stated; if so, here it is amended, and stripped of conditions. He has found his mother. She is coming down the road—there, behind the dancing lights, behind the friars, she is coming to pray for him. Should he fly her recognition or betray his confiding master? Room there may be to say the alternatives were a judgment upon him, but who will deny him pity? ... There is often a suffering, sometimes an agony, in indecision more wearing than disease, deadlier than sword-cuts.

The mournful pageant was now where its lights brought out parts of the face of the smoke-stained building. With a loud clang a door was thrown open, and a friar, in the black vestments usual in masses for the dead, came out to receive the Countess. The interior behind him was dully illuminated. A few minutes more, and the opportunity to see her face would be lost. Still the Emir stood irresolute. Judge the fierceness of the conflict in his breast!

At last he moved forward. The acolytes, with their great candles of yellow wax, were going by as he gained the edge of the road. They looked at him wonderingly. The friars, in Dominican cassocks, stared at him also. Then the choir took its turn. The linkman at sight of him stopped an instant, then marched on. The Emir really beheld none of them; his eyes and thoughts were in waiting; and now—how his heart beat!—how wistfully he gazed!— the Countess was before him, not three yards away.

Her garments, as said, were all black. A thick veil enveloped her head; upon her breast her crossed hands shone ivory white. Two or three times the right hand, in signing the cross, uncovered a ring upon the left—the wedding ring probably. Her bearing was of a person not so old as persecuted by an engrossing anguish. She did not once raise her face.

The Emir's heart was full of prayer.

"O Allah! It is my mother! If I may not speak to her, or kiss her feet—if I may not call her mother—if I may not say, mother, mother, behold, I am thy son come back—still, as thou art the Most Merciful! let me see her face, and suffer her to see mine—once, O Allah! once, if nevermore!"

But the face remained covered—and so she passed, but in passing she prayed. Though the voice was low, lie heard these words: "Oh, sweet Mother! By the Blessed Son of thy love and passion, remember mine, I beseech thee. Be with him, and bring him to me quickly. Miserable woman that I am!"

The world, and she with it, swam in the tears he no longer tried to stay. Stretching his arms toward her, he fell upon his knees, then upon his face; and that the face was in the dust, he never minded. When he looked up, she was gone on, the last of the procession. And he knew she had not seen him.

He followed after. Everybody stood aside to let her enter the door first. The friar received her; she went in, and directly the linkman stood alone outside.

"Stay!" said the linkman, peremptorily. "Who art thou?"

Thus rudely challenged, the Emir awoke from his daze—awoke with all his faculties clear.

"A gentleman of Otranto," he replied.

"What is thy pleasure?"

"Admit me to the chapel."

"Thou art a stranger, and the service is private. Or hast thou been invited?"

"No."

"Thou canst not enter."

Again the world dropped into darkness before Mirza; but this time it was from anger. The linkman never suspected his peril. Fortunately for him, the voice of the female chorister issued from the doorway in tremulous melody. Mirza listened, and became tranquillized. The voice sank next into a sweet unearthly pleading, and completely subdued, he began arguing with himself.... She had not seen him while he was in the dust at her side, and now this repulse at the door—how were they to be taken except as expressions of the will of Heaven?... There was plenty of time—better go away, and return—perhaps to-morrow. He was not prepared to prove his identity, if it were questioned.... There would be a scene, and he shrank from it.... Yes, better retire now.... And he turned to go. Not six steps away, the Countess reappeared to his excited mind, exactly as she had passed praying for him—reappeared—

... "like the painting of a sorrow."

A revulsion of feeling seized him—he halted. Oh, the years she had mourned for him! Her love was deep as the sea! Tears again—and without thought of what he did—all aimlessly—he returned to the door.

"This castle was sacked and burned by pirates, was it not?" he asked the linkman.

"Yes."

"They slew the Count Corti?"

"Yes."

"And carried off his son?"

"Yes."

"Had he other children?"

"No."

"What was the name of the boy?"

"Ugo."

"Well—in thy ear now—thou didst not well in shutting me out—*I am that Ugo.*"

Thereupon the Emir walked resolutely away.

A cry, shrill and broken, overtook him, issuing apparently from the door of the chapel—a second time he heard it, more a moan than a shriek—and thinking the linkman had given the alarm, he quickened his pace to a run, and was soon out on the beach.

The breath of the sea was pleasant and assuring, and falling into a walk, he turned his face toward Brindisi. But the cry pursued him. He imagined the scene in the chapel—the distress of the Countess—the breaking up of the service—the hurry of question—a consultation, and possibly search for him. Every person in the procession but the Countess had seen him; so the only open point in the affair was the one of directest interest to her: Was it her son?

Undoubtedly the suffering lady would not rest until investigation was exhausted. Failing to find the stranger about the castle, horsemen might be sent out on the road. There is terrible energy in mother-love. These reflections stimulated the Emir to haste. Sometimes he even ran; only at the shrine of the Virgin and Child in the angle of the road did he halt. There he cast himself upon the friendly slab to recover breath.

All this of course indicated a preference for Mahommed. And now he came to a decision. He would proceed with the duty assigned him by the young master; then, at the end, he would come back, and assert himself in his native land.

He sat on the slab an hour or more. At intervals the outcry, which he doubted not was his mother's, rang in his ears, and every time he heard it, conscience attacked him with its whip of countless stings. Why subject her to more misery? For what other outcome could there be to the ceaseless contention of fears and hopes now hers? Oh, if she had only seen him when he was so near her in the road! That she did not, was the will of Allah, and the fatalistic Mohammedan teaching brought him a measure of comfort. In further sooth, he had found a location and a title. Thenceforward, and not fictitiously, he was the *Count Corti*; and so entitling himself, he determined to make Brindisi, and take ship for Genoa or Venice in the morning before a messenger could arrive from the castle.

As he arose from the slab, a bird in housel for the night flew out of the box. Its small cheep reminded him of the smile he had fancied on the face of the Madonna, and how, a little later, the smile had, with such timely suggestion of approval, woven itself into his thought of the Countess. He looked up at the face again; but the night was over it like a veil, and he went nearer, and laid his hand softly on the Child. That which followed was not a miracle; only a consequence of the wisdom which permits the enshrinement of a saintly woman and Holy Child as witnesses of the Divine Goodness to humanity. He raised himself higher in the box, and pushing aside a heap of faded floral offerings, kissed the foot of the taller image, saying: "Thus would I have done to my mother." And when he had climbed down, and was in the road, it seemed some one answered him: "Go thy way! God and Allah are the same." We may now urge the narrative. From Brindisi the Emir sailed to Venice. Two weeks in "the glorious city in the sea" informed him of it thoroughly. While there, he found, on the "ways" of an Adriatic builder, the galley in which we have seen him at anchor in the Golden Horn. Leaving an order for the employment of a sailing-master and crew when the vessel was complete, he departed next for Rome. At Padua he procured the harness of a man-at-arms of the period, and recruited a company of *condottieri*—mercenary soldiers of every nationality. With all his sacerdotal authority, Nicholas V., the Holy Father, was sorely tried in keeping his States. The freebooters who unctuously kissed his hand to-day, did not scruple, if opportunity favored, to plunder one of his towns tomorrow. It befell that Count Corti—so the Emir styled himself—found a Papal castle beleaguered by marauders, whom he dispersed, slaying their chief with his own hand. Nicholas, in public audience, asked him to name the reward he preferred.

"Knighthood at thy hands, first of all things," was the reply.

The Holy Father took a sword from one of his officers, and gave him the *accolade*.

"What next, my son?"

"I am tired fighting men who ought to be Christians. Give me, I pray, thy commission to make war upon the Barbary pirates who infest the seas."

This was granted him.

"What next?"

"Nothing, Holy Father, but thy blessing, and a certificate in good form, and under seal, of these favors thou hast done me."

The certificate and the blessing were also granted.

The Count then dismissed his lances, and, hastening to Naples, embarked for Venice. There he supplied himself with suits of the finest Milanese armor he could obtain, and a wardrobe consisting of costumes such as were in vogue with the gay gallants along the Grand Canal. Crossing to Tripoli, he boarded a Moorish merchantman, and made prisoners of the crew and rowers. The prize he gave to his Christian sailors, and sent them home. Summoning his prisoners on deck, he addressed them in Arabic, offering them high pay if they would serve him, and they gratefully accepted his terms.

The Count then directed his prow to what is now Aleppo, with the purpose of procuring Arab horses; and having purchased five of the purest blood, he made sail for Constantinople.

We shall now, for a time, permit the title *Emir* to lapse. The knight we have seen on the deck of the new arrival in the Golden Horn viewing with melancholy interest the cities on either side of the fairest harbor on earth, is in easy English speech, *Count Corti*, the Italian.

Thus far the Count had been successful in his extraordinary mission, yet he was not happy. He had made three discoveries during his journey—his mother, his country, his religion. Ordinarily these relations—if we may so call them—furnish men their greatest sum of contentment; sadly for him, however, he had made a fourth finding, of itself sufficient to dash all the others—in briefest term, he was not in condition to acknowledge either of them. Unable to still the cry heard while retiring from his father's ruined castle, he surrendered himself more and more to the wisdom brought away from the box of the Madonna and Child in the angle of the road to Brindisi—*God and Allah are the same*. Conscience and a growing sense of misappropriated life were making Count Corti a very different person from the light-hearted Emir of Mahommed.

CHAPTER V
THE PRINCESS IRENE IN TOWN

An oblong room divided in the middle crosswise by two fluted pillars of pink-stained marble, light, delicately capped, and very graceful—between the pillars a segmental arch—between the walls and the pillars square ties;—the wall above the pillars elaborately scrolled;—three curtains of woollen stuff uniformly Tyrian dyed filling the open places—the central curtain drawn to the pillars, and held there by silken ropes richly tasselled—the side curtains dropped;—a skylight for each division of the room, and under each skylight an ample brazier dispensing a comfortable degree of warmth;—floor laid in pink and saffron tiles;—chairs with and without arms, some upholstered, all quaintly carved—to each chair a rug harmoniously colored;—massive tables of carven wood, the tops of burnished copper inlaid with blocks of jasper, mostly red and yellow—on the tables murrhine pitchers vase-shaped, with crystal drinking goblets about them;—the skylights conical and of clear glass;—the walls panelled, a picture in every panel, and the raised margins and the whole space outside done in arabesque of studied involution;—doors opposite each other and bare;—such was the reception-room in the town-house of the Princess Irene arranged for the winter.

On an armless chair in one of the divisions of the beautiful room, the Princess sat, slightly bending over a piece of embroidery stretched upon a frame. What with the accessories about her—the chair, a small table at her right covered with the bright materials in use, the slanted frame, and a flexible lion's skin under her feet—she was a picture once seen never forgotten. The wonderful setting of the head and neck upon the Phidian shoulders was admirably complemented by the long arms, bare, round, and of the whiteness of an almond kernel freshly broken, the hands, blue-veined and dimpled, and the fingers, tapering, pliant, nimble, rapid, each seemingly possessed of a separate intelligence.

To the left of the Princess, a little removed, Lael half reclined against a heap of cushions, pale, languid, and not wholly recovered from the effects of the abduction by Demedes, the terrible doom which had overtaken her father, and the disappearance of the Prince of India, the latter unaccountable except upon the hypothesis of death in the great fire. The dying prayer of the son of Jahdai had not failed with the Princess Irene. Receiving the unfortunate girl from Sergius the day after the rescue from the cistern, she accepted the guardianship, and from that hour watched and tended her with maternal solicitude.

The other division of the room was occupied by attendants. They were visible through the opening left by the drawn curtain; yet it is not to be supposed they were under surveillance; on the contrary, their presence in the house was purely voluntary. They read, sang, accepted tasks in embroidery from their mistress, accompanied her abroad, loved her—in a word, their service was in every respect compatible with high rank, and in return they derived a certain education from her. For by universal acknowledgment she was queen and arbiter in the social world of Byzantium; in manner the mirror, in taste and fashion its very form. Indeed, she was the subject of but one objection—her persistent protest against the encumbrance of a veil.

With all her grave meditation, she never lectured her attendants, knowing probably that sermons in example are more impressive than sermons in words. In illustration of the freedom they enjoyed in her presence and hearing, one of them, behind the curtain, touched a stringed instrument—a cithern—and followed the prelude with a song of Anacreontic vein.

THE GOLDEN NOON.

If my life were but a day—
    One morn, one night,
With a golden noon for play,
    And I, of right,
Could say what I would do
With it—what would I do?

Penance to me—e'en the stake,
    And late or soon!—
Yet would Love remain to make
    That golden noon
Delightful—I would do—
Ah, Love, what would I do?

And when the singer ceased there was a merry round of applause.

The ripple thus awakened had scarcely subsided, when the ancient Lysander opened one of the doors, and, after ringing the tiled floor with the butt of his javelin, and bowing statelywise, announced Sergius. Taking a nod from the Princess, he withdrew to give the visitor place.

Sergius went first to Irene, and silently kissed her hand; then, leaving her to resume work, he drew a chair to Lael's side.

Under his respectful manner there was an ease which only an assurance of welcome could have brought him. This is not to be taken in the sense of familiarity; if he ever indulged that vulgarism—something quite out of character with him—it was not in his intercourse with the Princess. She did not require formality; she simply received courtesy from everybody, even the Emperor, as a natural tribute. At the same time, Sergius was nearer in her regard than any other person, for special reasons.

We have seen the sympathetic understanding between the two in the matter of religion. We have seen, also, why she viewed him as a protege. Never had one presented himself to her so gentle and unconventional never one knowing so little of the world. With life all before him, with its ways to learn, she saw he required an adviser through a period of tutelage, and assumed the relation partly through a sense of duty, partly from reverent recollection of Father Hilarion. These were arguments sound in themselves; but two others had recently offered.

In the first place she was aware of the love which had arisen between the monk and Lael. She had not striven to spy it out. Like children, they had affected no disguise of their feeling; and while disallowing the passion a place in her own breast, she did not deprecate or seek to smother it in others. Far from that, in these, her wards, so to speak, it was with her an affair of permissive interest. They were so lovable, it seemed an order of nature they should love each other.

Next, the world was dealing harshly with Sergius; and though he strove manfully to hide the fact, she saw he was suffering. He deserved well, she thought, for his rescue of Lael, and for the opportunity given the Emperor to break up the impiety founded by Demedes. Unhappily her opinion was not subscribed in certain quarters. The powerful Brotherhood of the St. James' amongst others was in an extreme state of exasperation with him. They insisted he could have achieved the rescue without the death of the Greek. They went so far as to accuse him of a double murder—of the son first, then of the father. A terrible indictment! And they were bold and open-mouthed. Out of respect for the Emperor, who was equally outspoken in commendation of Sergius, they had not proceeded to the point of expulsion. The young man was still of the Brotherhood; nevertheless he did not venture to exercise any of the privileges of a member. His cell was vacant. The five services of the day were held in the chapel without him. In short, the Brotherhood were in wait for an opportunity to visit him with their vengeance. In hope of a favorable turn in the situation, he wore the habit of the Order, but it was his only outward sign of fraternity. Without employment, miserable, he found lodgment in the residence of the Patriarch, and what time he was not studying, he haunted the old churches of the city, Sancta Sophia in especial, and spent many hours a dreaming voyager on the Bosphorus.

The glad look which shone in the eyes of the invalid when Sergius took seat by her was very noticeable; and when she reached him her hand, the kiss he left upon it was of itself a declaration of tender feeling.

"I hope my little friend is better, to-day," he said, gravely.

"Yes, much better. The Princess says I may go out soon—the first real spring day."

"That is good news. I wish I could hurry the spring. I have everything ready to take you on the water—a perfect boat, and two master rowers. Yesterday they carried me to the Black Sea and back, stopping for a lunch of bread and figs at the foot of the Giants' Mountain. They boast they can repeat the trip often as there are days in the week."

"Did you stop at the White Castle?" she asked, with a smile.

"No. Our noble Princess was not with me; and in her absence, I feared the Governor might forget to be polite as formerly."

The gracious lady, listening, bent lower over the frame before her. She knew so much more of the Governor than Lael did! But Lael then inquired:

"Where have you been to-day?"

"Well, my little friend, let me see if I can interest you.... This morning I awoke betimes, and set myself to study. Oh, those chapters of John—the fourteenth, fifteenth and sixteenth. There is no need of religious knowledge beyond them. Of the many things they make clear, this is the clearest—the joys of eternal life lie in the saying of the Lord, 'I am the Way, and the Truth, and the Life; no man cometh unto the Father but by Me.' ... After my hours of study, I went to see an old church over in the low garden grounds beyond the aqueduct. Before I could get through the doorway, a flock of goats had to pass out. I will tell His Serenity what I beheld. Better the wreck be cleaned from the face of the earth than desecrated. Holy ground once, holy ground forever."

"Where is the Church?" the Princess inquired.

"In the low grounds between the aqueduct, and the gates of St. Romain and Adrianople."

"It belongs to one of the Brotherhoods. They have farming right in the soil."

"I am sorry to hear it."

As she turned to her work again, he went on with his account of himself.

"I had then two hours and more till noon, and was at loss what to do. Finally I decided to go to the Port of Blacherne—a long walk, but not too long, considering my motive.... Princess, have you heard of the Italian newly arrived?"

"What of him, pray?"

"He is the talk of the city, and if the half told of him be true, we must needs wonder. He travels in his own ship. Merchants have that habit, but he is not a merchant. Kings do so, but he is not a king. He came in saluting with a gun, in style becoming a great admiral; but if he is an admiral, his nationality is a secret. He also flies an unknown flag. They report him further as standing much on his deck in a suit of armor glistening like silver. And what is he? Mouth speaketh unto mouth, with no one to answer. They go then to his ship, pronouncing it the most perfect thing of the kind ever seen in the harbor. Those who have rowed around it say the sailors are not white men, but dark-faced creatures in turbans and black beards, un-Christian and ugly-looking. Fishermen and fruiterers have been permitted on deck—nobody else—and they, returning alive, say the rowers, of whom they caught glimpses, are blacker than the sailors. They also overheard strange noises below—voices not human."

The countenance of the Princess during this recital gradually changed; she seemed disposed to laugh at the exaggerations of the populace.

"So much for town-talk," Sergius continued. "To get sight of the ship, and of the mysterious magnate, I walked across the city to the Port of Blacherne, and was well rewarded. I found the ship drawn in to the quay, and the work of unloading her in progress. Parties of porters were attacking heaps of the cargo already on the landing. Where they were taking the goods I could not learn. I saw five horses lifted out of the hold, and led ashore over a bridge dropped from the vessel's side. Such horses I never before beheld. Two were grays, two bays, and one chestnut-colored. They looked at the sun with wide-open unwinking eyes; they inhaled the air as it were something to drink; their coats shone like silk; their manes were soft like the hair of children; their tails flared out in the breeze like flags; and everybody exclaimed: 'Arabs, Arabs!' There was a groom for each horse—tall men, lean, dust-hued, turbaned, and in black gowns. At sight of the animals, an old Persian who, from his appearance, might have been grandfather of the grooms, begged permission—I could not understand the tongue he used—put his arms around the necks of the animals, and kissed them between the eyes, his own full of tears the while. I suppose they reminded him of his own country.... Then two officers from the palace, representatives doubtless of the Emperor, rode out of the gate in armor, and immediately the stranger issued from his cabin, and came ashore. I confess I lost interest in the horses, although he went to them and scanned them over, lifting their feet and tapping their hoofs with the handle of a dagger. By that time the two officers were dismounted; and approaching with great ceremony, they notified him they had been sent by His Majesty to receive and conduct him to assigned quarters. He replied to them in excellent Greek, acknowledging His Majesty's graciousness, and the pleasure he would have in their escort. From the cabin, two of his men brought a complete equipment, and placed it on the chestnut steed. The furniture was all sheen of satin and gold. Another attendant brought his sword and shield; and after the sword was buckled around him, and the shield at his back, he took hold of the saddle with both hands, and swung himself into the seat with an ease remarkably in contrast with the action of his Greek conductors, who, in mounting, were compelled to make use of their stirrups. The cavalcade then passed the gate into the city."

"You saw him closely?" Lael asked.

"To get to his horse, he passed near me as I am to you, my little friend."

"What did he wear?"

"Oh, he was in armor. A cap of blue steel, with a silver spike on the crown—neck and shoulders covered with a hood of mail—body in a shirt of mail, a bead of silver in each link—limbs to the knees in mail. From the knees down there were splints of steel inlaid with silver; his shoes were of steel, and on the heels long golden spurs. The hood was clasped under the chin, leaving the face exposed—a handsome face, eyes black and bright, complexion olive, though slightly bloodless, expression pleasant."

"How old is he?"

"Twenty-six or seven. Altogether he reminded me of what I have heard of the warriors who used to go crusading."

"What following had he?"

This was from the Princess.

"I can only speak of what I saw—of the keepers of the horses, and of the other men, whom, in my unfamiliarity with military fashions, I will call equerry, armorer, and squire or page. What accounting is to be made of the ship's company, I leave, O Princess, to your better knowledge."

"My inquiry was of his personal suite."

"Then I cannot give you a better answer; but if I may say so much, the most unusual thing observable in his followers was, they were all Orientals—not one of them had a Christian appearance."

"Well"—and the Princess laid her needle down for the first time—"I see how easily a misunderstanding of the stranger may get abroad. Let me tell what I know of him.... Directly he arrived, he despatched a letter to His Majesty, giving an account of himself. He is a soldier by profession, and a Christian; has spent much time in the Holy Land, where he acquired several Eastern languages; obtained permission from the Pontiff Nicholas to make war on the African pirates; manned his galley with captives; and, not wishing to return to his native land and engage in the baronial wars which prevail there at present, he offered his services to His Majesty. He is an Italian nobleman, entitled *Count Corti,* and submitted to His Majesty a certificate, under the hand and seal of the Holy Father, showing that the Holy Father knighted him, and authorized his crusade against the infidels. The preference for a following composed of Orientals is singular; but after all, it is only a matter of taste. The day may come, dear Sergius, when the Christian world will disapprove his method of getting title to servants; but it is not here now.... If further discussion of the Count takes place in your presence, you are at liberty to tell what I tell you. At Blacherne yesterday I had the particulars, together with the other circumstance, that the Emperor gladly accepted the Italian's overture, and assigned him quarters in the Palace of Julian, with leave to moor his galley in the port there. Few noble foreigners have sought our Empire bringing better recommendations."

The fair lady then took up her needle, and was resuming work, when Lysander entered, and, after thumping the floor, announced: "Three o'clock."

The Princess silently arose, and passed out of the room; at the same time there was a commotion behind the curtain, and presently the other apartment was vacated. Sergius lingered a moment.

"Tell me now of yourself," Lael said, giving him her hand.

He kissed the hand fondly, and replied: "The clouds still hang low and dark over me; but my faith is not shaken; they will blow away; and in the meantime, dear little friend, the world is not all cheerless—you love me."

"Yes, I love you," she said, with childish simplicity.

"The Brotherhood has elected a new Hegumen," he continued.

"A good man, I hope."

"The violence with which he denounced me was the chief argument in his favor. But God is good. The Emperor, the Patriarch, and the Princess Irene remain steadfast. Against them the Hegumen will be slow in proceeding to my expulsion. I am not afraid. I will go on doing what I think right. Time and patience are good angels to the unjustly accused. But that any one should hold it a crime to have rescued you—O little friend, dear soul! See the live coal which does not cease burning!"

"And Nilo?"

"He wants nothing in the way of comforts."

"I will go see the poor man the first thing when I get out."

"His cell in the Cynegion is well furnished. The officer in charge has orders direct from the Emperor to see that he suffers no harm. I saw him day before yesterday. He does not know why he is a prisoner, but behaves quietly. I took him a supply of tools, and he passes the time making things in use in his country, mostly implements of war and hunting. The walls of his cell are hung with bows, arrows and lances of such curious form that there is always quite a throng to see them. He actually divides honor with Tamerlane, the king of the lions."

"It should be a very noble lion, for that."

Sergius, seeing her humor, went on: "You say truly, little friend. He has in hand a net of strong thread and thousands of meshes already. 'What is it for?' I asked. In his pantomimic way he gave me to understand: 'In my country we hunt lions with it.' 'How?' said I. And he showed me two balls of lead, one in each corner of the net. Taking the balls in his hands: 'Now we are in front of the game—now it springs at us—up they go this way.' He gave the balls a peculiar toss which sent them up and forward on separating lines. The woven threads spread out in the air like a yellow mist, and I could see the result—the brute caught in the meshes, and entangled. Then the brave fellow proceeded with his pantomime. He threw himself to one side out of the way of the leap—drew a sword, and stabbed and stabbed— and the triumph in his face told me plainly enough. 'There—he is dead!' Just now he is engaged on another work scarcely less interesting to him. A dealer in ivory sent him an elephant's tusk, and he is covering it with the story of a campaign. You see the warriors setting out on the march—in another picture they are in battle—a cloud of arrows in flight—shields on arm—bows bent—and a forest of spears. From the large end he is working down toward the point. The finish will be a victory, and a return with captives and plunder immeasurable.... He is well cared for; yet he keeps asking me about his master the Prince of India. Where is he? When will he come? When he turns to that subject I do not need words from him. His soul gets into his eyes. I tell him the Prince is dead. He shakes his head: 'No, no!' and sweeping a circle in the air, he brings his hands to his breast, as to say: 'No, he is travelling—he will come back for me.'"

Sergius had become so intent upon the description that he lost sight of his hearer; but now a sob recalled him. Bending lower over the hand, he caressed it more assiduously than ever, afraid to look into her face. When at length the sobbing ceased, he arose and said, shamefacedly:

"O dear little friend, you forgive me, do you not?"

From his manner one would have thought he had committed an offence far out of the pale of condonement.

"Poor Sergius," she said. "It is for me to think of you, not you of me." He tried to look cheerful.

"It was stupid in me. I will be more careful. Your pardon is a sweet gift to take away.... The Princess is going to Sancta Sophia, and she may want me. To-morrow—until to-morrow—good-by."

This time he stooped, and kissed her on the forehead; next moment she was alone.

CHAPTER VI
COUNT CORTI IN SANCTA SOPHIA

The Palace of Julian arose the chief embellishment of a large square enclosure on the sea front southeast of the landmark at present called the Burnt Column, and, like other imperial properties of the kind, it was an aggregation of buildings irregular in form and style, and more or less ornate and imposing. A garden stretched around it. The founder, wanting private harborage for his galleys and swarm of lesser boats, dug a basin just inside the city wall, and flooded it with pure Marmoran water; then, for ingress and egress at his sovereign will, he slashed the wall, and of the breach made the *Port of Julian*. [Footnote: Only a shallow depression in the ground, faintly perpetuating the outlines of the harbor, now marks the site of this royal residence.]

Count Corti found the Palace well preserved in and out. He had not purposed hiding himself, yet it was desirable to keep his followers apart much as possible; and for that a situation more to his wish could scarcely have been chosen in the capital.

Issuing from the front door, a minute's walk through a section of the garden brought him to a stairway defended on both sides with massive balustrading. The flight ended in a spacious paved landing; whence, looking back and up, he could see two immense columnar pedestals surmounted by statues, while forward extended the basin, a sheet of water on which, white and light as a gull, his galley rested. He had but to call the watchman on its deck, and a small boat would come to him in a trice. He congratulated himself upon the lodgement.

The portion of the Palace assigned him was in the south end; and, although he enlisted a number of skilful upholsterers, a week and more was industriously taken with interior arrangements for himself, and in providing for the comfort and well-being of his horses; for it is to be said in passing, he had caught enough of the spirit of the nomadic Turk to rate the courser which was to bear him possibly through foughten fields amongst the first in his affections. In this preparation, keeping the scheme to which his master had devoted him ever present, he required no teaching to point out the policy of giving his establishment an air of permanence as well as splendor.

Occupied as he was, he had nevertheless snatched time to look in upon the Hippodrome, and walk once around the Bucoleon and Sancta Sophia. From a high pavilion overhanging his quarters, he had surveyed the stretches of city in the west and southwest, sensible of a lively desire to become intimately acquainted with the bizarre panorama of hills behind hills, so wonderfully house and church crowned.

To say truth, however, the Count was anxious to hear from the Sultan before beginning a career. The man who was to be sent to him might appear any hour, making it advisable to keep close home. He had a report of the journey to Italy, and of succeeding events, including his arrival at Constantinople, ready draughted, and was impatient to forward it. A word of approval from Mahommed would be to him like a new spirit given. He counted upon it as a cure for his melancholia.

Viewing the galley one day, he looked across the basin to where the guard of the Port was being changed, and was struck with the foreign air of the officer of the relief. This, it happened, was singularly pertinent to a problem which had been disturbing his active mind—how he could most safely keep in communication with Mahommed, or, more particularly, how the Sultan's messenger could come with the most freedom and go with the least hindrance. A solution now presented itself. If the Emperor intrusted the guardianship of the gate to one foreigner, why not to another? In other words, why not have the duty committed to himself and his people? Not improbably the charge might be proposed to him; he would wait awhile, and see; if, however, he had to formally request it, could anything be more plausibly suggestive than the relation between the captaincy of that Port and residence in the Palace of Julian? The idea was too natural to be refused; if granted, he was master of the situation. It would be like holding the keys of the city. He could send out and admit as need demanded; and then, if flight became imperative, behold a line of retreat! Here was his galley—yonder the way out.

While he pondered the matter, a servant brought him notice of an officer from Blacherne in waiting. Responding immediately, he found our ancient friend the Dean in the reception room, bringing the announcement that His Majesty the Emperor had appointed audience for him next day at noon; or, if the hour was not entirely convenient, would the Count be pleased to designate another? His Majesty was aware of the attention needful to a satisfactory settlement in strange quarters, and had not interrupted him earlier; for which he prayed pardon.

The Count accepted the time set; after which he conducted his visitor through his apartments, omitting none of them; from the kitchen he even carried him to the stable, whence he had the horses brought one by one. Hospitality and confidence could go no further, and he was amply rewarded. The important functionary was pleased with all he saw, and with nothing more than Corti himself. There could not be a doubt of the friendliness of the report he would take back to Blacherne. In short, the

Count's training in a court dominated by suspicion to a greater degree even than the court in Constantinople was drawn upon most successfully. A glass of wine at parting redolent with the perfume of the richest Italian vintage fixed the new-comer's standing in the Dean's heart. If there had been the least insufficiency in the emblazoned certificate of the Holy Father, here was a swift witness in confirmation.

The day was destined to be eventful to the Count. While he was entertaining the Dean, the men on the deck of the galley, unused to Byzantine customs, were startled by a cry, long, swelling, then mournfully decadent. Glancing in the direction from which it came, they saw a black boat sweeping through the water-way of the Port. A man of dubious complexion, tall and lithe, his scant garments originally white, now stiff with dirt of many hues, a ragged red head-cloth illy confining his coarse black hair, stood in the bow shouting, and holding up a wooden tray covered with fish. The sentinel to whom he thus offered the stock shook his head, but allowed him to pass. At the galley's side there was an interchange of stares between the sailors and the fishermen—such the tenants of the black craft were—leaving it doubtful which side was most astonished. Straightway the fellow in the bow opened conversation, trying several tongues, till finally he essayed the Arabic.

"Who are you?"

"Sailors."

"Where from?"

"Tripoli."

"Children of the Prophet?"

"We believe in Allah and the Last Day, and observe prayer, and pay the appointed alms, and dread none but Allah; we are among the rightly guided." [Footnote: Koran, IX. 18.]

"Blessed be Allah! May his name be exalted here and everywhere!" the fisherman returned; adding immediately: "Whom serve you?"

"A *Scherif* from Italy."

"How is he called?"

"The Count."

"Where is he?"

"In the Palace yonder."

"A Christian?"

"A Christian with an Eastern tongue; and he knows the hours of prayer, and observes them."

"Does he reside here?"

"He is Lord of the Palace."

"When did he arrive?"

"Since the moon fulled."

"Does he want fish?"

The men on the ship laughed.

"Go ask him."

"That is his landing there?"

"Yes."

"All men who live down by the sea eat fish—when they can get them," the dealer said, solemnly. Turning then to his rowers, he bade them: "Forward to the landing."

There he stepped out, dextrously balanced the tray on his head, ascended the stairs, and in front of the great house went persistently from door to door until he came to that of the Count.

"Fish?" he asked the man who answered his knock.

"I will see."

The doorkeeper returned shortly, and said, "No."

"Are you a Moslem?" the fisherman inquired.

"Yes. Blessed be Allah for the right understanding!"

"So am I. Now let me see the master. I want to furnish him with fish for the season."

"He is engaged."

"I will wait for him. Tell him my catch is this morning's—red mullets and choice cuts from a royal sword-fish that leaped ten feet in the air with the spear in his back."

Thereupon he deposited the tray, and took seat by it, much as to say, Time is of no consequence to me. Ere long the Count appeared with the Dean. He glanced at the tray, then at the fisherman—to the latter he gave a second look.

"What beautiful fish!" he said, to the Dean.

"Yes, yes—there are no fish pastures like those of our Bosphorus."

"How do you call this kind?"

"Mullets—red mullets. The old Romans used to fatten them in tanks."

"I thought I had seen their like on our Italian coasts. How do you prepare them for the table?"

"We fry them, Count, in olive oil—pure oil."

All this time Corti was studying the fisherman.

"What meal, pray, will fashion allow them to me dished?" he went on.

"For breakfast especially; though when you come to dine with His Majesty do not be surprised to see them early in course."

"Pardon the detention, my Lord—I will make trial of these in the morning." Then to the fisherman the Count said, carelessly: "Keep thy place until I return."

Corti saw the Dean out of the eastern gate of the enclosure, and returned.

"What, still here!" he said, to the dealer. "Well, go with the doorkeeper to the kitchen. The cook will take what he needs for to-morrow." Speaking to the doorkeeper then: "Bring the man to me. I am fond of fishing, and should like to talk with him about his methods. Sometime he may be willing to take me with him."

By and by the monger was shown into the Count's room, where there was a table, with books and writing material—a corner room full lighted by windows in the south and east. When they were alone, the two gazed at each other.

"Ali, son of Abed-din!" said the Count. "Is it thou?"

"O Emir! All of me that is not fish is the Ali thou hast named."

"God is great!" the first exclaimed.

"Blessed be God!" the other answered.

They were acquaintances of long standing.

Then Ali took the red rag from his head, and from its folds produced a strip of fine parchment with writing on it impervious to water. "Behold, Emir! It is for thee."

The Count received the scrip and read:

"This is he I promised to send. He has money for thee. Thou mayst trust him. Tell me this time of thyself first; then of her; but always after of her first. My soul is scorching with impatience."

There was no date to the screed nor was it signed; yet the Count put it to his forehead and lips. He knew the writing as he knew his own hand.

"O Ali!" he said, his eyes aglow. "Hereafter thou shalt be Ali the Faithful, son of Abed-din the Faithful."

Ali replied with a rueful look: "It is well. What a time I have had waiting for you! Much I fear my bones will never void the damps blown into them by the winter winds, and I perched on the cross-sticks of a floating *dallyan*.... I have money for you, O Emir! and the keeping it has given me care more than enough to turn another man older than his mother. I will bring it to-morrow; after which I shall say twenty prayers to the Prophet—blessed be his name!—where now I say one."

"No, not to-morrow, Ali, but the day after when thou bringest me another supply of fish. There is danger in coming too often—and for that, thou must go now. Staying too long is dangerous as coming too often.... But tell me of our master. Is he indeed the Sultan of Sultans he promised to be? Is he well? Where is he? What is he doing?"

"Not so fast, O Emir, not so fast, I pray you! Better a double mouthful of stale porpoise fat, with a fin bone in it, than so many questions at once."

"Oh, but I have been so long in the slow-moving Christian world without news!"

"Verily, O Emir, Padishah Mahommed will be greatest of the *Gabour* eaters since Padishah Othman—that to your first. He is well. His bones have reached their utmost limit, but his soul keeps growing—that to your second. He holds himself at Adrianople. Men say he is building mosques. I say he is building cannon to shoot bullets big as his father's tomb; when they are fired, the faithful at Medina will hear the noise, and think it thunder—that to your third. And as to his doing—getting ready for war, meaning business for everybody, from the Shiek-ul-Islam to the thieving tax-farmers of Bagdad—to the Kislar-Jinn of Abad-on with them. He has the census finished, and now the Pachas go listing the able-bodied, of whom they have half a million, with as many more behind. They say the young master means to make a *sandjak* of unbelieving Europe."

"Enough, Ali!—the rest next time."

The Count went to the table, and from a secret drawer brought a package wrapped in leather, and sealed carefully.

"This for our Lord—exalted be his name! How wilt thou take it?"

Ali laughed.

"In my tray to the boat, but the fish are fresh, and there are flowers of worse odor in Cashmere. So, O Emir, for this once. Next time, and thereafter, I will have a hiding-place ready."

"Now, Ali, farewell. Thy name shall be sweet in our master's ears as a girl-song to the moon of Ramazan. I will see to it."

Ali took the package, and hid it in the bosom of his dirty shirt. When he passed out of the front door, it lay undistinguishable under the fish and fish meat; and he whispered to the Count in going: "I have an order from the Governor of the White Castle for my unsold stock. God is great!"

Corti, left alone, flung himself on a chair. He had word from Mahommed—that upon which he counted so certainly as a charm in counteraction of the depression taking possession of his spirit. There it was in his hand, a declaration of confidence unheard of in an Oriental despot. Yet the effect was wanting. Even as he sat thinking the despondency deepened. He groped for the reason in vain. He strove for cheer in the big war of which Ali had spoken—in the roar of cannon, like thunder in Medina—in Europe a Sultanic *sandjak*. He could only smile at the exaggeration. In fact, his trouble was the one common to every fine nature in a false position. His business was to deceive and betray—whom? The degradation was casting its shadow before. Heaven help when the eclipse should be full!

For relief he read the screed again: "Tell me this time of thyself first; then of *her*." ... Ah, yes, the kinswoman of the Emperor! He must devise a way to her acquaintance, and speedily. And casting about for it, he became restless, and finally resolved to go out into the city. He sent for the chestnut Arab, and putting on the steel cap and golden spurs had from the Holy Father was soon in the saddle.

It was about three o'clock afternoon, with a wind tempered to mildness by a bright sun. The streets were thronged, while the balconies and overhanging windows had their groups on the lookout for entertainment and gossip. As may be fancied the knightly rider and gallant barb, followed by a dark-skinned, turbaned servant in Moorish costume, attracted attention. Neither master nor man appeared to give heed to the eager looks and sometimes over-loud questions with which they were pursued.

Turning northward presently, the Count caught sight of the dome of Sancta Sophia. It seemed to him a vast, upturned silver bowl glistening in the sky, and he drew rein involuntarily, wondering how it could be upheld; then he was taken with a wish to go in, and study the problem. Having heard from Mahommed, he was lord of his time, and here was noble diversion.

In front of the venerable edifice, he gave his horse to the dark-faced servant, and entered the outer court unattended.

A company, mixed apparently of every variety of persons, soldiers, civilians, monks, and women, held the pavement in scattered groups; and while he halted a moment to survey the exterior of the building, cold and grimly plain from cornice to base, he became himself an object of remark to them. About the same time a train of monastics, bareheaded, and in long gray gowns, turned in from the street, chanting monotonously, and in most intensely nasal tones. The Count, attracted by their pale faces, hollow eyes and unkept beards, waited for them to cross the court. Unkept their beards certainly were, but not white. This was the beginning of the observation he afterward despatched to Mahommed: Only the walls of Byzantium remain for her defence; the Church has absorbed her young men; the sword is discarded for the rosary. Nor could he help remarking that whereas the *frati* of Italy were fat, rubicund, and jolly, these seemed in search of death through the severest penitential methods. His thought recurring to the house again, he remembered having heard how every hour of every day from five o'clock in the morning to midnight was filled with religious service of some kind in Sancta Sophia.

A few stone steps the full length of the court led up to five great doors of bronze standing wide open; and as the train took one of the latter and began to disappear, he chose another, and walked fast in order to witness the entry. Brought thus into the immense vestibule, he stopped, and at once forgot the gray brethren. Look where he might, at the walls, and now up to the ceiling, every inch of space wore the mellowed brightness of mosaic wrought in cubes of glass exquisitely graduated in color. What could he do but stand and gaze at the Christ in the act of judging the world? Such a cartoon had never entered his imagination. The train was gone when he awoke ready to proceed.

There were then nine doors also of bronze conducting from the vestibule. The central and larger one was nearest him. Pushed lightly, it swung open on noiseless hinges; a step or two, and he stood in the nave or auditorium of the Holy House.

The reader will doubtless remember how Duke Vlodomir, the grandson of Olga, the Russian, coming to Constantinople to receive a bride, entered Sancta Sophia the first time, and from being transfixed by what he saw and heard, fell down a convert to Christianity. Not unlike was the effect upon Corti. In a sense he, too, was an unbeliever semi-barbaric in education. Many were the hours he had spent with Mahommed while the latter, indulging his taste, built palaces and mosques on paper, striving for vastness and original splendor. But what was the Prince's utmost achievement in comparison with this interior? Had it been an ocean grotto, another Caprian cave, bursting with all imaginable revelations of light and color, he could not have been more deeply impressed. Without architectural knowledge; acquainted with few of the devices employed in edificial construction, and still less with the mysterious power of combination peculiar to genius groping for effects in form, dimensions, and arrangement of stone on stone with beautiful and sublime intent; yet he had a soul to be intensely moved by such effects when actually set before his eyes. He walked forward slowly four or five steps from the door, looking with excited vision—not at details or to detect the composition of any of the world of objects constituting the view, or with a thought of height, breadth, depth, or value—the marbles of the floor rich in multiformity and hues, and reflective as motionless water, the historic pillars, the varied arches, the extending galleries, the cornices, friezes, balustrades, crosses of gold, mosaics, the windows and interlacing rays of light, brilliance here, shadows yonder—the apse in the east, and the altar built up in it starry with burning candles and glittering with prismatic gleams shot from precious stones and metals in every conceivable form of grace—lamps, cups, vases, candlesticks, cloths, banners, crucifixes, canopies, chairs, Madonnas, Child Christs and Christs Crucified—and over all, over lesser domes, over arches apparently swinging in the air, broad, high, near yet far away, the dome of Sancta Sophia, defiant of imitation, like unto itself alone, a younger sky within the elder—these, while he took those few steps, merged and ran together in a unity which set his senses to reeling, and made question and thought alike impossible.

How long the Count stood thus lost to himself in the glory and greatness of the place, he never knew. The awakening was brought about by a strain of choral music, which, pouring from the vicinity of the altar somewhere, flooded the nave, vast as it was, from floor to dome. No voice more fitting could be imagined; and it seemed addressing itself to him especially. He trembled, and began to think.

First there came to him a comparison in which the Kaaba was a relative. He recalled the day he fell dying at the corner under the Black Stone. He saw the draped heap funereally dismal in the midst of the cloisters. How bare and poor it seemed to him now! He remembered the visages and howling of the demoniac wretches struggling to kiss the stone, though with his own kiss he had just planted it with death. How different the worship here! ... This, he thought next, was his mother's religion. And what more natural than that he should see that mother descending to the chapel in her widow's weeds to pray for him? Tears filled his eyes. His heart arose chokingly in his throat. Why should not her religion be his? It was the first time he had put the question to himself directly; and he went further with it. What though Allah of the Islamite and Jehovah of the Hebrew were the same?—What though the Koran and the Bible proceeded from the same inspiration?—What though Mahomet and Christ were alike Sons of God? There were differences in the worship, differences in the personality of the worshippers. Why, except to allow every man a choice according to his ideas of the proper and best in form and companionship? And the spirit swelled within him as he asked, Who are my brethren? They who stole me from my father's house, who slew my father, who robbed my mother of the lights of life, and left her to the darkness of mourning and the bitterness of ungratified hope—were not they the brethren of my brethren?

At that moment an old man appeared before the altar with assistants in rich canonicals. One placed on the elder's head what seemed a crown all a mass of flaming jewels; another laid upon him a cloak of cloth of gold; a third slipped a ring over one of his fingers; whereupon the venerable celebrant drew nearer the altar, and, after a prayer, took up a chalice and raised it as if in honor to an image of Christ on a cross in the agonies of crucifixion. Then suddenly the choir poured its triumphal thunder abroad until the floor, and galleries, and pendant lamps seemed to vibrate. The assistants and worshippers sank upon their knees, and ere he was aware the Count was in the same attitude of devotion.

The posture consisted perfectly with policy, his mission considered. Soon or late he would have to adopt every form and observance of Christian worship. In this performance, however, there was no premeditation, no calculation. In his exaltation of soul he fancied he heard a voice passing with the tempestuous jubilation of the singers: "On thy knees, O apostate! On thy knees! God is here!"

But his was a combative nature; and coming to himself, and not understanding clearly the cause of his prostration, he presently arose. Of the worshippers in sight, he alone was then standing, and the sonorous music ringing on, he was beginning to doubt the propriety of his action, when a number of women, unobserved before, issued from a shaded corner at the right of the apse, fell into processional order, and advanced slowly toward him.

One moved by herself in front. A reflection of her form upon the polished floor lent uncertainty to her stature, and gave her an appearance of walking on water. Those following were plainly her attendants. They were all veiled; while a white mantle fell from her left shoulder, its ends lost in the folds of the train of her gown, leaving the head, face, and neck bare. Her manner, noticeable in the distance even, was dignified without hauteur, simple, serious, free of affectation. She was not thinking of herself.... Nearer—he heard no foot-fall. Now and then she glided through slanting rays of soft, white light cast from upper windows, and they seemed to derive ethereality from her.... Nearer—and he could see the marvellous pose of the head, and the action of the figure, never incarnation more graceful.... Yet nearer—he beheld her face, in complexion a child's, in expression a woman's. The eyes were downcast, the lips moved. She might have been the theme of the music sweeping around her in acclamatory waves, drowning the part she was carrying in suppressed murmur. He gazed steadfastly at the countenance. The light upon the forehead was an increasing radiance, like a star's refined by passage through the atmospheres of infinite space. A man insensitive to beauty in woman never was, never will be. Vows cannot alter nature; neither can monkish garbs nor years; and it is knowledge of this which makes every woman willing to last sacrifices for the gift; it is power to her, vulgarizing accessories like wealth, coronets and thrones. With this confession in mind, words are not needed to inform the reader of the thrills which assailed the Count while the marvel approached.

The service was over as to her, and she was evidently seeking to retire by the main door; but as he stood in front of it, she came within two or three steps before noticing him. Then she stopped suddenly, astonished by the figure in shining armor. A flush overspread her face; smiling at her alarm, she spoke: "I pray pardon, Sir Knight, for disturbing thy devotions."

"And I, fair lady, am grateful to Heaven that it placed me in thy way to the door unintentionally."

He stepped aside, and she passed on and out.

The interior of the church, but a minute before so overwhelmingly magnificent and impressive, became commonplace and dull. The singing rolled on unheard. His eyes fixed on the door through which she went; his sensations were as if awakening from a dream in which he had seen a heavenly visitant, and been permitted to speak to it.

The spell ceased with the music; then, with swift returning sense, he remembered Mahommed's saying: "Thou wilt know her at sight."

And he knew her—the *Her* of the screed brought only that day by Ali.

Nor less distinctly did he recall every incident of the parting with Mahommed, every word, every injunction—the return of the ruby ring, even then doubtless upon the imperious master's third finger, a subject of hourly study—the further speech, "They say whoever looketh at her is thenceforward her lover"—and the final charge, with its particulars, concluding: "Forget not that in Constantinople, when I come, I am to receive her from thy hand peerless in all things as I left her."

His shoes of steel were strangely heavy when he regained his horse at the edge of the court. For the first time in years, he climbed into the saddle using the stirrup like a man reft of youth. He would love the woman—he could not help it. Did not every man love her at sight?

The idea colored everything as he rode slowly back to his quarters.

Dismounting at the door, it plied him with the repetition, *Every man loves her at sight.*

He thought of training himself to hate her, but none the less through the hours of the night he heard the refrain, *Every man loves her at sight.*

In a clearer condition, his very inability to shut her out of mind, despite his thousand efforts of will, would have taught him that another judgment was upon him.

HE LOVED HER.

CHAPTER VII
COUNT CORTI TO MAHOMMED

At noon the days are a little more yellow, and the shadows a trifle longer, while at evening the snows on the far mountains give the air a coolness gently admonitory of the changing season; with these exceptions there is scarcely a difference between the September to which we now come and the closing stages of June.

Count Corti is fully settled in his position. Withal, however, he is very miserable. A new light has been let in upon his being. He finds it a severe trial to serve a Mahommedan, knowing himself a Christian born, and still more difficult trying to be a Turk, knowing himself an Italian. The stings grow sharper as experience makes it plainer that he is nefariously helping those whom he ought to regard enemies destroy an Emperor and people who never gave him offence. Worst of all, most crushing to spirit, is his passion for the Princess Irene while under obligations to Mahommed prohibitory of every hope, dream, and self-promise ordinarily the sweetest incidents of love.

The person with a mental ailment curable by prompt decision, who yet goes about debating what to do, will ere long find his will power so weakened as to leave him a confirmed wreck. Count Corti seemed likely to become an instance in point. The months since his visit to the paternal castle in Italy, really the beginning of the conflicts tossing him now here, now there, were full of warnings he could but hear; still he continued his course.

His reports to Mahommed were frequent, and as they are of importance to our story, we think it advisable to quote from some of them.

The following is from his first communication after the visit to Sancta Sophia:

"I cast myself at your feet, O my Lord, praying Allah to keep you in health, and strengthen the wise designs which occupy you incessantly.... You bade me always speak first of the kinswoman of the Emperor. Yesterday I rode to the Church supreme in the veneration of the Greeks, erected, it is said, by the Emperor Justinian. Its vastness amazed me, and, knowing my Lord's love for such creations, I declare, were there no other incentive to the conquest of this unbelieving city than the reduction of Sancta Sophia to the religious usages of Islam, its possession would alone justify my Lord's best effort, regardless of life and treasure. The riches accumulated in it through the ages are incalculable; nevertheless its splendors, dazzling as the sun, varied as a rainbow, sunk out of sight when the Princess Irene passed me so near that I had a perfect view of her. Her face is composed of the light of unnumbered stars. The union of all the graces in her person is so far above words that Hafiz, my Lord's prince of poets, would have been dumb before her, or, if he had spoken, it would have been to say, She is the Song of Songs impossible to verse. She spoke to me as she moved by, and her voice was the voice of Love. Yet she had the dignity of a Queen governing the world through a conqueror such as my Lord is to be. Then, the door having closed upon her, I was ready to declare, as I now do, were there no other incentive to the conquest of this unbelieving city than the possession of the womanly perfections belonging to her, she would justify war to the exhaustion of the universe. O my Lord, thou only art worthy of her! And how infinite will be my happiness, if the Prophet through his powerful intercessions with the Most Merciful, permits me to be the servant instrumental in bringing her safely to thy arms!" This report concluded:

"By appointment of His Majesty, the Emperor, I had audience with him yesterday at his High Residence, the Palace of Blacherne. The Court was in full attendance, and, after my presentation to His Majesty, I was introduced to its members. The ceremony was in charge of the Grand Chamberlain, that Phranza with whom my Lord is acquainted. Much I feared lest he should recognize me. Fortunately he is dull and philosophical, and too much given to study of things abstract and far away to be mindful of those close under his nose. Duke Notaras was there also. He conversed with me about Italy. Fortunately I knew more about the *Gabour* country than he—its nobles, cities, manners, and present conditions. He thanked me for information, and when he had my account of the affair which brought me the invaluable certificate of the Bishop of Rome he gave over sounding me. I have more reason to be watchful of him than all the rest of the court; *so has the Emperor*. Phranza is a man to be spared. Notaras is a man to be bowstrung.... I flatter myself the Emperor is my friend. In another month I shall be intrenched in his confidence. He is brave, but weak. An excellent general without lieutenants, without soldiers, and too generous and trustful for a politician, too religious for a statesman. His time is occupied entirely with priests and priestly ceremonies. My Lord will appreciate the resort which enabled me to encamp myself in his trust. Of the five Arab horses I brought with me from Aleppo, I gave him one—a gray, superior to the best he has in his stables. He and his courtiers descended in a body to look at the barb and admire it."

From the third report:

"A dinner at the High Residence. There were present officers of the army and navy, members of the Court, the Patriarch, a number of the Clergy—

Hegumen, as they are called—and the Princess Irene, with a large suite of highborn ladies married and unmarried. His Majesty was the Sun of the occasion, the Princess was the Moon. He sat on a raised seat at one side of the table; she opposite him; the company according to rank, on their right and left. I had eyes for the Moon only, thinking how soon my Lord would be her source of light, and that her loveliness, made up of every loveliness else in the world, would then be the fitting complement of my Lord's glory.... His Majesty did me the honor to lead me to her, and she did me the higher honor of permitting me to kiss her hand. In further thought of what she was to my Lord, I was about making her a salaam, but remembered myself—Italians are not given to that mode of salutation, while the Greeks reserve it for the Emperor, or Basileus as he is sometimes called.... She condescended to talk with me. Her graces of mind are like those of her person—adorable.... I was very deferent, and yielded the choice of topics. She chose two—religion and arms. Had she been a man, she would have been a soldier; being a woman, she is a religious devotee. There is nothing of which she is more desirous than the restoration of the Holy Sepulchre to the Christian powers. She asked me if it were true the Holy Father commissioned me to make war on the Tripolitan pirates, and when I said yes, she replied with a fervor truly engaging: 'The practice of arms would be the noblest of occupations if it were given solely to crusading.' ... She then adverted to the Holy Father. I infer from her speaking of the Bishop of Rome as the Holy Father that she inclines to the party which believes the Bishop rightfully the head of the Church. How did he look? Was he a learned man? Did he set a becoming example to his Clergy? Was he liberal and tolerant? If great calamity were to threaten Christianity in the East, would he lend it material help?... My Lord will have a time winning the Princess over to the Right Understanding; but in the fields of Love who ever repented him of his labor? When my Lord was a boy, he once amused himself training a raven and a bird of paradise to talk. The raven at length came to say, 'O Allah, Allah!' The other bird was beyond teaching, yet my Lord loved it the best, and excused his partiality: 'Oh, its feathers are so brilliant!'"

Again:

"A few days ago, I rode out of the Golden Gate, and turning to the right, pursued along the great moat to the Gate St. Romain. The wall, or rather the walls, of the city were on my right hand, and it is an imposing work. The moat is in places so cumbered I doubt if it can be everywhere flooded.... I bought some snow-water of a peddler, and examined the Gate in and out. Its central position makes it a key of first importance. Thence I journeyed on surveying the road and adjacent country up far as the

Adrianople gate.... I hope my Lord will find the enclosed map of my reconnoissance satisfactory. It is at least reliable."

Again:

"His Majesty indulged us with a hawking party. We rode to the Belgrade forest from which Constantinople is chiefly though not entirely supplied with water.... My Lord's Flower of Flowers, the Princess, was of the company. I offered her my chestnut courser, but she preferred a jennet. Remembering your instructions, O my Lord, I kept close to her bridle. She rides wonderfully well; yet if she had fallen, how many prayers to the Prophet, what amount of alms to the poor, would have availed me with my Lord?... Riding is a lost art with the Greeks, if the ever possessed it. The falcon killed a heron beyond a hill which none of them, except the Emperor, dared cross in their saddles. Some day I will show them how we of my Lord's loving ride.... The Princess came safely home."

Again:

"O my Lord in duty always!... I paid the usual daily visit to the Princess, and kissed her hand upon my admission and departing. She has this quality above other women—she is always the same. The planets differ from her in that they are sometimes overcast by clouds.... From her house, I rode to the imperial arsenal, situated in the ground story of the Hippodrome, northern side. [Footnote: Professor E A Grosvenor.] It is well stored with implements of offence and defence—mangonels, balistas, arbalists, rams—cranes for repairing breaches—lances, javelins, swords, axes, shields, scutums, pavises, armor—timber for ships—cressets for night work—ironmonger machines—arquebuses, but of antique patterns—quarrels and arrows in countless sheaves—bows of every style. In brief, as my Lord's soul is dauntless, as he is an eagle, which does not abandon the firmament scared by the gleam of a huntsman's helmet in the valley, he can bear to hear that the Emperor keeps prepared for the emergencies of war. Indeed, were His Majesty as watchful in other respects, he would be dangerous. Who are to serve all these stores? His native soldiers are not enough to make a bodyguard for my Lord. Only the walls of Byzantium remain for her defence. The Church has swallowed the young men; the sword is discarded for the rosary. Unless the warriors of the West succor her, she will be an easy prey."

Again:

"My Lord enjoined me to be royal.... I have just returned from a sail up the Bosphorus to the Black Sea in my galley. The decks were crowded with guests. Under a silken pavilion pitched on the roof of my cabin, there was a throne for the Princess Irene, and she shone as the central jewel in a kingly crown.... We cast anchor in the bay of Therapia, and went ashore to her palace and gardens. On the outside face of one of the gate-columns, she showed me a brass plate. I recognized my Lord's signature and safeguard, and came near saluting them with a *rik'rath*, but restraining myself, asked her innocently, 'What it was?' O my Lord, verily I congratulate you! She blushed, and cast down her eyes, and her voice trembled while she answered: 'They say the Prince Mahommed nailed it there.' 'What Prince Mahommed?' 'He who is now Sultan of the Turks.' 'He has been here, then? Did you see him?' 'I saw an Arab story-teller.' Her face was the hue of a scarlet poppy, and I feared to go further than ask concerning the plate: 'What does it mean?' And she returned: 'The Turks never go by without prostrating themselves before it. They say it is notice to them that I, and my house and grounds, are sacred from their intrusion.' And then I said: 'Amongst peoples of the East and the Desert, down far as the Barbary coast, the Sultan Mahommed has high fame for chivalry. His bounties to those once fortunate enough to excite his regard are inexhaustible.' She would have had me speak further of you, but out of caution, I was driven to declare I knew nothing beyond the hearsay of the Islamites among whom I had been here and there cast.... My Lord will not require me to describe the palace by Therapia. He has seen it.... The Princess remained there. I was at sore loss, not knowing how I could continue to make report of her to my Lord, until, to my relief she invited me to visit her."

Again:

"I am glad to say, for my Lord's sake, that the October winds, sweeping down from the Black Sea, have compelled his Princess to return to her house in the city, where she will abide till the summer comes again. I saw her to-day. The country life has retouched her cheeks with a just-sufficient stain of red roses; her lips are scarlet, as if she had been mincing fresh-blown bloom of pomegranates; her eyes are clear as a crooning baby's; her neck is downy—round as a white dove's; in her movements afoot, she reminds me of the swaying of a lily-stalk brushed softly by butterflies and humming-birds, attracted to its open cup of paradisean wax. Oh, if I could but tell her of my Lord!"...

This report was lengthy, and included the account of an episode more personal to the Sultanic emissary than any before given his master. It was dated October. The subjoined extracts may prove interesting.

... "Everybody in the East has heard of the Hippodrome, whither I went one day last week, and again yesterday. It was the mighty edifice in which Byzantine vanity aired itself through hundreds of years. But little of it is now left standing. At the north end of an area probably seventy paces wide, and four hundred long, is a defaced structure with a ground floor containing the arsenal, and on that, boxes filled with seats. A lesser building rises above the boxes which is said to have been a palace called the *Kathisma*, from which the Emperor looked down upon the various amusements of the people, such as chariot racing, and battles between the Blue and Green factions. Around the area from the *Kathisma* lie hills of brick and marble—enough to build the Palace as yet hid in my Lord's dreams, and a mosque to becomingly house our Mohammedan religion. In the midst, marking a line central of the race-course, are three relics—a square pillar quite a hundred feet high, bare now, but covered once with plates of brass—an obelisk from Egypt—and a twisted bronze column, representing three writhing serpents, their heads in air. [Footnote: The Hippodrome was the popular pleasure resort in Constantinople. Besides accommodating one hundred thousand spectators, it was the most complete building for the purposes of its erection ever known. The world—including old Rome—had been robbed of statuary for the adornment of this extravaganza. Its enormous level posed in great part upon a substructure of arches on arches, which still exist. The opinion is quite general that it was destroyed by the Turks, and that much of its material went to construct the Mosque Sulymanie. The latter averment is doubtless correct; but it is only justice to say that the Crusaders, so called Christians, who encamped in Constantinople in 1204 were the real vandals. For pastime, merely, they plied their battle-axes on the carvings, inscriptions, and vast collection of statuary in marble and bronze found by them on the spinet, and elsewhere in the edifice. When they departed, the Hippodrome was an irreparable ruin—a convenient and lawful quarry.]... The present Emperor does not honor the ruin with his presence; but the people come, and sitting in the boxes under the KATHISMA, and standing on the heaps near by, find diversion watching the officers and soldiers exercising their horses along the area.... My Lord must know, in the next place, that there is in the city a son of the Orchan who terms himself lawful heir of Solyman of blessed memory—the Orchan pretender to my Lord's throne, whom the Greeks have been keeping in mock confinement—the Orchan who is the subject of the present Emperor's demand on my Lord for an increase of the stipend heretofore paid for the impostor's support. The son of the pretender, being a Turk, affects the martial practices prevalent with us, and enjoys notoriety for accomplishments as a horseman, and in the tourney play djerid. He is even accredited with an intention of one day taking the field against my Lord—this when his father, the old Orchan, dies.... When I entered the Hippodrome one day last week, Orchan the younger occupied the arena before the Kathisma. The boxes were well filled with spectators. Some officers of my acquaintance were present, mounted like myself, and they accosted me politely, and eulogized the performance. Afterwhile I joined in their commendation, but ventured to say I had seen better exercise during my sojourn among the infidels in the Holy Land. They asked me if I had any skill. 'I cannot call it skill,' I said; 'but my instruction was from a noble master, the Sheik of the Jordan.' Nothing would rest them then but a trial. At length I assented on condition that the Turk would engage me in a tourney or a combat without quarter—bow, cimeter, spear—on horseback and in Moslem armor. They were astonished, but agreed to carry the challenge.... Now, O my Lord, do not condemn me. My residence here has extended into months, without an incident to break the peace. Your pleasure is still my rule. I keep the custom of going about on horseback and in armor. Once only—at His Majesty's dinner—I appeared in a Venetian suit—a red mantle and hose, one leg black, the other yellow—red-feathered cap, shoes with the long points chained to my knees. Was there not danger of being mistaken for a strutting bird of show? If my hand is cunning with weapons, should not the Greeks be taught it? How better recommend myself to His Majesty of Blacherne? Then, what an opportunity to rid my Lord of future annoyance! Old Orchan cannot live much longer, while this cheeping chicken is young.... The son of the pretender, being told I was an Italian, replied he would try a tourney with me; if I proved worthy, he would consider the combat.... Yesterday was the time for the meeting. There was a multitude out as witnesses, the Emperor amongst others. He did not resort to the *Kathisma,* but kept his saddle, with a bodyguard of horsemen at his back. His mount was my gray Arab.... We began with volting, demi-volting, jumping, wheeling in retreat, throwing the horse. Orchan was a fumbler.... We took to bows next, twelve arrows each. At full speed he put two bolts in the target, and I twelve, all in the white ring.... Then spear against cimeter. I offered him choice, and he took the spear. In the first career, the blunted head of his weapon fell to the ground shorn off close behind the ferrule. The spectators cheered and laughed, and growing angry, Orchan shouted it was an accident, and challenged me to combat. I accepted, but His Majesty interposed—we might conclude with the spear and sword in tourney again.... My antagonist, charged with malicious intent, resolved to kill me. I avoided his shaft, and as his horse bolted past on my left, I pushed him with my shield, and knocked him from the saddle. They picked him up bleeding nose and ears. His Majesty invited me to accompany him to Blacherne.... I left the Hippodrome sorry not to have been permitted to fight the vain fool; yet my repute in Constantinople is now undoubtedly good—I am a soldier to be cultivated."

Again:

"His Majesty has placed me formally in charge of the gate in front of my quarters. Communication with my Lord is now at all times easy. *The keys of the city are in effect mine.* Nevertheless I shall continue to patronize Ali. His fish are the freshest brought to market."

Again:

"O my Lord, the Princess Irene is well and keeps the morning colors in her cheeks for you. Yet I found her quite distraught. There was unwelcome news at the Palace from His Majesty's ambassador at Adrianople. The Sultan had at last answered the demand for increase of the Orchan stipend—not only was the increase refused, but the stipend itself was withdrawn, and a peremptory order to that effect sent to the province whence the fund has been all along collected.... I made a calculation, with conclusion that my report of the tourney with young Orchan reached my Lord's hand, and I now am patting myself on the back, happy to believe it had something to do with my Lord's decision. The imposition deserved to have its head blown off. Orchan is a dotard. His son's ears are still impaired. In the fall the ground caught him crown first. He will never ride again. The pretension is over.... I rode from the Princess' house directly to Blacherne. The Grand Council was in session: yet the Prefect of the Palace admitted me.... O my Lord, this Constantine is a man, a warrior, an Emperor, surrounded by old women afraid of their shadows. The subject of discussion when I went in was the news from Adrianople. His Majesty was of opinion that your decision, coupled with the order discontinuing the stipend, was sign of a hostile intent. He was in favor of preparing for war. Phranza thought diplomacy not yet spent. Notaras asked what preparations His Majesty had in mind. His Majesty replied, buying cannon and powder, stocking the magazines with provisions for a siege, increasing the navy, repairing the walls, clearing out the moat. He would also send an embassy to the Bishop of Rome, and through him appeal to the Christian powers of Europe for assistance in men and money. Notaras rejoined instantly: 'Rather than a Papal Legate in Constantinople, he would prefer a turbaned Turk.' The Council broke up in confusion.... Verily, O my Lord, I pitied the Emperor. So much courage, so much weakness! His capital and the slender remnant of his empire are lost unless the *Gabours* of Venice and Italy come to his aid. Will they? The Holy Father, using the opportunity, will try once more to bring the Eastern Church to its knees, and failing, will leave it to its fate. If my Lord knocked at these gates to-morrow, Notaras would open one of them, and I another.... Yet the Emperor will fight. He has the soul of a hero."

Again:

"The Princess Irene is inconsolable. Intensely Greek, and patriotic, and not a little versed in politics, she sees nothing cheering in the situation of the Empire. The vigils of night in her oratory are leaving their traces on her face. Her eyes are worn with weeping. I find it impossible not to sympathize with so much beauty tempered by so many virtues. When the worst has befallen, perhaps my Lord will know how to comfort her."

Finally:

"It is a week since I last wrote my Lord. Ali has been sick but keeps in good humor, and says he will be well when Christian winds cease blowing from Constantinople. He prays you to come and stop them.... The diplomatic mishaps of the Emperor have quickened the religious feuds of his subjects. The Latins everywhere quote the speech of Notaras in the Council: 'Rather than a Papal Legate in Constantinople, I prefer a turbaned Turk'—and denounce it as treason to God and the State. It certainly represents the true feeling of the Greek clergy; yet they are chary in defending the Duke.... The Princess is somewhat recovered, although perceptibly paler than is her wont. She is longing for the return of spring, and promises herself health and happiness in the palace at Therapia.... To-morrow, she informs me, there is to be a special grand service in Sancta Sophia. The Brotherhoods here and elsewhere will be present. I will be there also. She hopes peace and rest from doctrinal disputes will follow. We will see."

The extracts above given will help the reader to an idea of life in Constantinople; more especially they portray the peculiar service rendered by Corti during the months they cover.

There are two points in them deserving special notice: The warmth of description indulged with respect to the Princess Irene and the betrayal of the Emperor. It must not be supposed the Count was unaware of his perfidy. He did his writing after night, when the city and his own household were asleep; and the time was chosen, not merely for greater security from discovery, but that no eye might see the remorse he suffered. How often he broke off in the composition to pray for strength to rescue his honor, and save himself from the inflictions of conscience! There were caverns in the mountains and islands off in the mid-seas: why not fly to them? Alas! He was now in a bondage which made him weak as water. It was possible to desert Mahommed, but not the Princess. The dangers thickening around the city were to her as well. Telling her of them were useless; she would never abandon the old Capital; and it was the perpetually recurring comparison of her strength with his own weakness which wrought him his sharpest pangs. Writing of her in poetic strain was easy, for he loved her above every earthly consideration: but when he thought of the intent with which he wrote—that he was serving the love of another, and basely scheming to deliver her to him—there was no refuge in flight; recollection would go with him to the ends of the earth—better death. Not yet—not yet—he would argue. Heaven might send him a happy chance. So the weeks melted into months, and he kept the weary way hoping against reason, conspiring, betraying, demoralizing, sinking into despair.

CHAPTER VIII
OUR LORD'S CREED

Proceeding now to the special service mentioned in the extract from the last report of Count Corti to Mahommed.

The nave of Sancta Sophia was in possession of a multitude composed of all the Brotherhoods of the city, interspersed with visiting delegations from the monasteries of the Islands and many of the hermitic colonies settled in the mountains along the Asiatic shore of the Marmora. In the galleries were many women; amongst them, on the right-hand side, the Princess Irene. Her chair rested on a carpeted box a little removed from the immense pilaster, and raised thus nearly to a level with the top of the balustrade directly before her, she could easily overlook the floor below, including the apse. From her position everybody appeared dwarfed; yet she could see each figure quite well in the light of the forty arched windows above the galleries.

On the floor the chancel, or space devoted to the altar, was separated from the body of the nave by a railing of Corinthian brass, inside which, at the left, she beheld the Emperor, in Basilean regalia, seated on a throne—a very stately and imposing figure. Opposite him was the chair of the Patriarch. Between the altar and the railing arose a baldacchino, the canopy of white silk, the four supporting columns of shining silver. Under the canopy, suspended by a cord, hung the vessel of gold containing the Blessed Sacraments; and to the initiated it was a sufficient publication of the object of the assemblage.

Outside the railing, facing the altar, stood the multitude. To get an idea of its appearance, the reader has merely to remember the description of the bands marching into the garden of Blacherne the night of the *Pannychides*. There were the same gowns black and gray; the same tonsured heads, and heads shock-haired; the same hoods and glistening rosaries; the same gloomy, bearded faces; the same banners, oriflammes, and ecclesiastical gonfalons, each with its community under it in a distinctive group. Back further towards the entrances from the vestibule was a promiscuous host of soldiers and civilians; having no part in the service, they were there as spectators.

The ceremony was under the personal conduct of the Patriarch. Silence being complete, the choir, invisible from the body of the nave, began its magnificent rendition of the *Sanctus*—"Holy, holy, holy, Lord God of Sabaoth. Blessed is He who cometh in the name of the Lord. Hosanna in the highest"—and during the singing, His Serenity was clothed for the rite. Over his cassock, the deacons placed the surplice of white linen, and over that again a stole stiff with gold embroidery. He then walked slowly to the altar, and prayed; and when he had himself communicated, he was led to the baldacchino, where he blessed the Body and the Blood, and mixed them together in chalices, ready for delivery to the company of servers kneeling about him. The Emperor, who, in common with the communicants within and without the railing, had been on his knees, arose now and took position before the altar in a prayerful attitude; whereupon the Patriarch brought him a chalice on a small paten, and he put it to his lips, while the choir rang the dome with triumphal symphony.

His Serenity next returned to the baldacchino, and commenced giving the cups to the servers; at the same time the gate leading from the chancel to the nave was thrown open. Nor rustle of garment, nor stir of foot was heard.

Then a black-gowned figure arose amidst a group not far from the gate, and said, in a hoarse voice, muffled by the flaps of the hood covering his head and face:

"We are here, O Serenity, by thy invitation—here to partake of the Holy Eucharist—and I see thou art about sending it to us. Now not a few present believe there is no grace in leavened bread, and others hold it impiety to partake thereof. Wherefore tell us"—

The Patriarch looked once at the speaker; then, delivering the chalice, signed the servers to follow him; next instant, he stood in the open gateway, and with raised hands, cried out:

"Holy things to the holy!"

Repeating the ancient formula, he stepped aside to allow the cup-bearers to pass into the nave; but they stood still, for there came a skurry of sound not possible of location, so did it at the same moment seem to be from the dome descending and from the floor going up to the dome. It was the multitude rising from their knees.

Now the Patriarch, though feeble in body, was stout of soul and ready-witted, as they usually are whose lives pass in combat and fierce debate. Regarding the risen audience calmly, he betook himself to his chair, and spoke to his assistants, who brought a plain chasuble, and put it on him, covering the golden stole completely. When he again appeared in the spaceway of the open gate, as he presently did, every cleric and every layman in the church to whom he was visible understood he took the interruption as a sacrilege from which he sought by the change of attire to save himself.

"Whoso disturbs the Sacrament in celebration has need of cause for that he does; for great is his offence whatever the cause."

The Patriarch's look and manner were void of provocation, except as one, himself rudely disposed, might discover it in the humility somewhat too studied.

"I heard my Brother—it would be an untruth to say I did not—and to go acquit of deceit, I will answer him, God helping me. Let me say first, while we have some differences in our faith, there are many things about which we are agreed, the things in agreement outnumbering those in difference; and of them not the least is the Real Presence once the Sacraments are consecrated. Take heed, O Brethren! Do any of you deny the Real Presence in the bread and wine of communion?"

No man made answer.

"It is as I said—not one. Look you, then, if I or you—if any of us be tempted to anger or passionate speech, and this house, long dedicated to the worship of God, and its traditions of holiness too numerous for memory, and therefore of record only in the Books of Heaven, fail the restraints due them, lo, Christ is here—Christ in Real Presence—Christ our Lord in Body and Blood!"

The old man stood aside, pointing to the vessel under the baldacchino, and there were sighs and sobs. Some shouted: "Blessed be the Son of God!"

The sensation over, the Patriarch continued:

"O my Brother, take thou answer now. The bread is leavened. Is it therefore less grace-giving?"

"No, no!" But the response was drowned by an affirmative yell so strong there could be no doubt of the majority. The minority, however, was obstinate, and ere long the groups disrupted, and it seemed every man became a disputant. Now nothing serves anger like vain striving to be heard. The Patriarch in deep concern stood in the gateway, exclaiming: "Have a care, O Brethren, have a care! For now is Christ here!" And as the babble kept increasing, the Emperor came to him.

"They are like to carry it to blows, O Serenity."

"Fear not, my son, God is here, and He is separating the wheat from the chaff."

"But the blood shed will be on my conscience, and the *Panagia*"—

The aged Prelate was inflexible. "Nay, nay, not yet! They are Greeks. Let them have it out. The day is young; and how often is shame the miraculous parent of repentance."

Constantine returned to his throne, and remained there standing.

Meantime the tumult went on until, with shouting and gesticulating, and running about, it seemed the assemblage was getting mad with drink. Whether the contention was of one or many things, who may say? Well as could be ascertained, one party, taking cue from the Patriarch, denounced the interruption of the most sacred rite; the other anathematized the attempt to impose leavened bread upon orthodox communicants as a scheme of the devil and his arch-legate, the Bishop of Rome. Men of the same opinions argued blindly with each other; while genuine opposition was conducted with glaring eyes, swollen veins, clinched hands, and voices high up in the leger lines of hate and defiance. The timorous and disinclined were caught and held forcibly. In a word, the scene was purely Byzantine, incredible of any other people.

The excitement afterwhile extended to the galleries, where, but that the women were almost universally of the Greek faction, the same passion would have prevailed; as it was, the gentle creatures screamed *azymite, azymite* in amazing disregard of the proprieties. The Princess Irene, at first pained and mortified, kept her seat until appearances became threatening; then she scanned the vast pit long and anxiously; finally her wandering eyes fell upon the tall figure of Sergius drawn out of the mass, but facing it from a position near the gate of the brazen railing. Immediately she settled back in her chair.

To justify the emotion now possessing her, the reader must return to the day the monk first presented himself at her palace near Therapia. He must read again the confession, extorted from her by the second perusal of Father Hilarion's letter, and be reminded of her education in the venerated Father's religious ideas, by which her whole soul was adherent to his conceptions of the Primitive Church of the Apostles. Nor less must the reader suffer himself to be reminded of the consequences to her—of the judgment of heresy upon her by both Latins and Greeks—of her disposition to protest against the very madness now enacting before her—of her longing, Oh, that I were a man!—of the fantasy that Heaven had sent Sergius to her with the voice, learning, zeal, courage, and passion of truth to enable her to challenge a hearing anywhere-of the persistence with which she had since cared for and defended him, and watched him in his studies, and shared them with him. Nor must the later incident, the giving him a copy of the creed she had formulated—the Creed of Nine Words— be omitted in the consideration.

Now indeed the reader can comprehend the Princess, and the emotions with which she beheld the scene at her feet. The Patriarch's dramatic warning of the Real Presence found in her a ready second; for keeping strictly to Father Hilarion's distinction between a right Creed and a form or ceremony for pious observance, the former essential to salvation, the latter merely helpful to continence in the Creed, it was with her as if Christ in glorified person stood there under the baldacchino. What wonder if, from indignation at the madness of the assembly, the insensate howling, the blasphemous rage, she passed to exaltation of spirit, and fancied the time good for a reproclamation of the Primitive Church?

Suddenly a sharper, fiercer explosion of rage arose from the floor, and a rush ensued—the factions had come to blows!

Then the Patriarch yielded, and at a sign from the Emperor the choir sang the *Sanctus* anew. High and long sustained, the sublime anthem rolled above the battle and its brutalism. The thousands heard it, and halting, faced toward the apse, wondering what could be coming. It even reached into the vortex of combat, and turned all the unengaged there into peacemakers.

Another surprise still more effective succeeded. Boys with lighted candles, followed by bearers of smoking censers, bareheaded and in white, marched slowly from behind the altar toward the open gate, outside which they parted right and left, and stopped fronting the multitude. A broad banner hung to a cross-stick of gold, heavy with fringing of gold, the top of the staff overhung with fresh flowers in wreaths and garlands, the lower corners stayed by many streaming white ribbons in the hands of as many holy men in white woollen chasubles extending to the bare feet, appeared from the same retreat, carried by two brethren known to every one as janitors of the sacred chapel on the hill-front of Blacherne.

The Emperor, the Patriarch, the servers of the chalices, the whole body of assistants inside the railing, fell upon their knees while the banner was borne through the gate, and planted on the floor there. Its face was frayed and dim with age, yet the figure of the woman upon it was plain to sight, except as the faint gray smoke from the censers veiled it in a vanishing cloud.

Then there was an outburst of many voices:

"The *Panagia!* The *Panagia!*"

The feeling this time was reactionary.

"O Blessed Madonna!—Guardian of Constantinople!—Mother of God!—Christ is here!—Hosannas to the Son and to the Immaculate Mother!" With these, and other like exclamations, the mass precipitated itself forward, and, crowding near the historic symbol, flung themselves on the floor before it, grovelling and contrite, if not conquered.

The movement of the candle and censer bearers outside the gate forced Sergius nearer it; so when the *Panagia* was brought to a rest, he, being much taller than its guardians, became an object of general observation, and wishing to escape it if possible, he took off his high hat; whereupon his hair, parted in the middle, dropped down his neck and back fair and shining in the down-beating light.

This drew attention the more. Did any of the prostrate raise their eyes to the Madonna on the banner, they must needs turn to him next; and presently the superstitious souls, in the mood for miracles, began whispering to each other:

"See—it is the Son—it is the Lord himself!"

And of a truth the likeness was startling; although in saying this, the reader must remember the difference heretofore remarked between the Greek and Latin ideals.

About that time Sergius looked up to the Princess, whose face shone out of the shadows of the gallery with a positive radiance, and he was electrified seeing her rise from her chair, and wave a hand to him.

He understood her. The hour long talked of, long prepared for, was at last come—the hour of speech. The blood surged to his heart, leaving him pallid as a dead man. He stooped lower, covered his eyes with his hands, and prayed the wordless prayer of one who hastily commits himself to God; and in the darkness behind his hands there was an illumination, and in the midst of it a sentence in letters each a lambent flame—the Creed of Father Hilarion and the Princess Irene—our Lord's Creed:

"I BELIEVE IN GOD, AND JESUS CHRIST, HIS SON."

This was his theme!

With no thought of self, no consciousness but of duty to be done, trusting in God, he stood up, pushed gently through the kneeling boys and guardians of the *Panagia*, and took position where all eyes could look at the Blessed Mother slightly above him, and then to himself, in such seeming the very Son. It might have been awe, it might have been astonishment, it might have been presentiment; at all events, the moaning, sobbing, praying, tossing of arms, beating of breasts, with the other outward signs of remorse, grief and contrition grotesque and pitiful alike subsided, and the Church, apse, nave and gallery, grew silent—as if a wave had rushed in, and washed the life out of it.

"Men and brethren," he began, "I know not whence this courage to do comes, unless it be from Heaven, nor at whose word I speak, if not that Jesus of Nazareth, worker of miracles which God did by him anciently, yet now here in Real Presence of Body and Blood, hearing what we say, seeing what we do."

"Art thou not He?" asked a hermit, half risen in front of him, his wrap of undressed goatskin fallen away from his naked shoulders.

"No; his servant only am I, even as thou art—his servant who would not have forsaken him at Gethsemane, who would have given him drink on the Cross, who would have watched at the door of his tomb until laid to sleep by the Delivering Angel—his servant not afraid of Death, which, being also his servant, will not pass me by for the work I now do, if the work be not by his word."

The voice in this delivery was tremulous, and the manner so humble as to take from the answer every trace of boastfulness. His face, when he raised it, and looked out over the audience, was beautiful. The spectacle offered him in return was thousands of people on their knees, gazing at him undetermined whether to resent an intrusion or welcome a messenger with glad tidings.

"Men and brethren," he continued, more firmly, casting the old Scriptural address to the farthest auditor, "now are you in the anguish of remorse; but who told you that you had offended to such a degree? See you not the Spirit, sometimes called the Comforter, in you? Be at ease, for unto us are repentance and pardon. There were who beat our dear Lord, and spit upon him, and tore his beard; who laid him on a cross, and nailed him to it with nails in his hands and feet; one wounded him in the side with a spear; yet what did he, the Holy One and the Just? Oh! if he forgave them glorying in their offences, will he be less merciful to us repentant?"

Raising his head a little higher, the preacher proceeded, with increased assurance:

"Let me speak freely unto you; for how can a man repent wholly, if the cause of his sin be not laid bare that he may see and hate it?

"Now before our dear Lord departed out of the world, he left sayings, simple even to children, instructing such as would be saved unto everlasting life what they must do to be saved. Those sayings I call our Lord's Creed, by him delivered unto his disciples, from whom we have them: 'Verily, verily, I say unto you, he that heareth my word, and believeth on him that sent me, hath everlasting life.' So we have the First Article—belief in God. Again: 'Verily, verily, I say unto you, he that believeth on me hath everlasting life.' Behold the Second Article—belief in Christ.

"Now, for that the Son, and he who sent him, are at least in purpose one, belief in either of them is declared sufficient; nevertheless it may be simpler, if not safer, for us to cast the Two Articles together in a single phrase; we have then a Creed which we may affirm was made and left behind him by our Lord himself:

I BELIEVE IN GOD, AND JESUS CHRIST, HIS SON.

And when we sound it, lo! two conditions in all; and he who embraces them, more is not required of him; he is already passed from death unto life—everlasting life.

"This, brethren, is the citadel of our Christian faith; wherefore, to strengthen it. What was the mission of Jesus Christ our Lord to the world? Hear every one! What was the mission of our Lord Jesus Christ? Why was he sent of God, and born into the world? Hearing the question, take heed of the answer: He was sent of God for the salvation of men. You have ears, hear; minds, think; nor shall one of you, the richest in understanding of the Scriptures, in walk nearest the Sinless Example, ever find another mission for him which is not an arraignment of the love of his Father.

"Then, if it be true, as we all say, not one denying it, that our Lord brought to his mission the perfected wisdom of his Father, how could he have departed from the world leaving the way of salvation unmarked and unlighted? Or, sent expressly to show us the way, himself the appointed guide, what welcome can we suppose he would have had from his Father in Heaven, if he had given the duty over to the angels? Or, knowing the deceitfulness of the human heart, and its weakness and liability to temptation, whence the necessity for his coming to us, what if he had given the duty over to men, so much lower than the angels, and then gone away? Rather than such a thought of him, let us believe, if the way had been along the land, he would have planted it with inscribed hills; if over the seas, he would have sown the seas with pillars of direction above the waves; if through the air, he would have made it a path effulgent with suns numerous as the stars. 'I am the Way,' he said—meaning the way lies through me; and you may come to me in the place I go to prepare for you, if only you believe in God and me. Men and brethren, our Lord was true to his mission, and wise in the wisdom of his Father."

At this the hermit in front of the preacher, uttering a shill cry, spread his arms abroad, and quivered from head to foot. Many of those near sprang forward to catch him.

"No, leave him alone," cried Sergius, "leave him alone. The cross he took was heavy of itself; but upon the cross you heaped conditions without sanction, making a burden of which he was like to die. At last he sees how easy it is to go to his Master; that he has only to believe in God and the Master. Leave him with the truth; it was sent to save, not to kill."

The excitement over, Sergius resumed:

"I come now, brethren, to the cause of your affliction. I will show it to you; that is to say, I will show you why you are divided amongst yourselves, and resort to cruelty one unto another; as if murder would help either side of the quarrel. I will show your disputes do not come from anything said or done by our Lord, whose almost last prayer was that all who believed in him might be made perfect in one.

"It is well known to you that our Lord did not found a Church during his life on earth, but gave authority for it to his Apostles. It is known to you also that what his Apostles founded was but a community: for such is the description: 'And all that believed were together, and had all things common; and sold their possessions and goods, and parted them to all men, as every man had need.' [Footnote: Acts ii. 44, 45.] And again: 'And the multitude of them that believed were of one heart and of one soul: neither said any of them that ought of the things which he possessed was his own; but they had all things common.' 'Neither was there any among them that lacked: for as many as were possessors of lands or houses sold them, and brought the prices of the things that were sold, and laid them down at the apostles' feet: and distribution was made unto every man according as he had need.' [Footnote: Acts iv. 32, 34, 35.] But in time this community became known as the Church; and there was nothing of it except our Lord's Creed, in definition of the Faith, and two ordinances for the Church—Baptism for the remission of sins, that the baptized might receive the Comforter, and the Sacraments, that believers, often as they partook of the Body and Blood of Christ, might be reminded of him.

"Lo, now! In the space of three generations this Church, based upon this simple Creed, became a power from Alexandria to Lodinum; and though kings banded to tread it out; though day and night the smell of the blood of the righteous spilt by them was an offence to God; though there was no ingenuity more amongst men except to devise methods for the torture of the steadfast—still the Church grew; and if you dig deep enough for the reasons of its triumphant resistance, these are they: there was Divine Life in the Creed, and the Community was perfect in one; insomuch that the brethren quarrelled not among themselves; neither was there jealousy, envy or rivalry among them; neither did they dispute about immaterial things, such as which was the right mode of baptism, or whether the bread should be leavened or unleavened, or whence the Holy Ghost proceeded, whether from the Father or from the Father and Son together; neither did the elders preach for a price, nor forsake a poor flock for a rich one that their salaries might be increased, nor engage in building costly tabernacles for the sweets of vanity in tall spires; neither did any study the Scriptures seeking a text, or a form, or an observance, on which to go out and draw from the life of the old Community that they might set up a new one; and in their houses of God there were never places for the men and yet other separate places for the women of the congregation; neither did a supplicant for the mercy of God look first at the garments of the neighbor next him lest the mercy might lose a virtue because of a patch or a tatter. The Creed was too plain for quibble or dispute; and there was no ambition in the Church except who should best glorify Christ by living most obedient to his commands. Thence came the perfection of unity in faith and works; and all went well with the Primitive Church of the Apostles; and the Creed was like unto the white horse seen by the seer of the final visions, and the Church was like him who sat upon the horse, with a bow in his hand, unto whom a crown was given; and he went forth conquering and to conquer."

Here the audience was stirred uncontrollably; many fell forward upon their faces; others wept, and the nave resounded with rejoicing. In one quarter alone there was a hasty drawing together of men with frowning brows, and that was where the gonfalon of the Brotherhood of the St. James' was planted. The Hegumen, in the midst of the group, talked excitedly, though in a low tone.

"I will not ask, brethren," Sergius said, in continuance, "if this account of the Primitive Church be true; you all do know it true; yet I will ask if one of you holds that the offending of which you would repent—the anger, and bitter words, and the blows—was moved by anything in our Lord's Creed, let him arise, before the Presence is withdrawn, and say that he thinks. These, lending their ears, will hear him, and so will God. What, will not one arise?

"It is not necessary that I remind you to what your silence commits you. Rather suffer me to ask next, which of you will arise and declare, our Lord his witness, that the Church of his present adherence is the same Church the Apostles founded? You have minds, think; tongues, speak."

There was not so much as a rustle on the floor.

"It was well, brethren, that you kept silence; for, if one had said his Church was the same Church the Apostles founded, how could he have absolved himself of the fact that there are nowhere two parties each claiming to be of the only true Church? Or did he assert both claimants to be of the same Church, and it the only true one, then why the refusal to partake of the Sacraments? Why a division amongst them at all? Have you not heard the aforetime saying, 'Every kingdom divided against itself is brought to desolation'?

"Men and brethren, let no man go hence thinking his Church, whichever it be, is the Church of the Apostles. If he look for the community which was the law of the old brotherhood, his search will be vain. If he look for the unity, offspring of our Lord's last prayer, lo! jealousies, hates, revilements, blows instead. No, your Creed is of men, not Christ, and the semblance of Christ in it is a delusion and a snare." At this the gonfalon of the St. James' was suddenly lifted up, and borne forward to within a few feet of the gate, and the Hegumen, standing in front of it, cried out:

"Serenity, the preacher is a heretic! I denounce"—

He could get no further; the multitude sprang to foot howling. The Princess Irene, and the women in the galleries, also arose, she pale and trembling. Peril to Sergius had not occurred to her when she gave him the signal to speak. The calmness and resignation with which he looked at his accuser reminded her of his Master before Pilate, and taking seat again, she prayed for him, and the cause he was pleading.

At length, the Patriarch, waving his hand, said:

"Brethren, it may be Sergius, to whom we have been listening, has his impulse of speech from the Spirit, even as he has declared. Let us be patient and hear him."

Turning to Sergius, he bade him proceed.

"The three hundred Bishops and Presbyters from whom you have your Creeds, [Footnote: *Encyclopedia Brit.*, VI. 560.] O men and brethren"—so the preacher continued—"took the Two Articles from our Lord's Creed, and then they added others. Thus, which of you can find a text of our Lord treating of his procession from the substance of God? Again, in what passage has our Lord required belief in the personage of the Holy Ghost as an article of faith essential to salvation? [Footnote: Four Creeds are at present used in the Roman Catholic Church; viz., the Apostles' Creed, the Nicene, the Athanasian, that of Pius IV—ADD. and AR., *Catholic Dictionary*, 232.] 'I am the Way,' said our Lord. 'No,' say the three hundred, 'we are the way; and would you be saved, you must believe in us not less than in God and his Son.'"

The auditors a moment before so fierce, even the Hegumen, gazed at the preacher in a kind of awe; and there was no lessening of effect when his manner underwent a change, his head slightly drooping and his voice plaintive.

"The Spirit by whose support and urgency I have dared address you, brethren, admonishes me that my task is nearly finished."

He took hold of the corner of the *Panagia;* so all in view were more than ever impressed with his likeness to their ideal of the Blessed Master.

"The urgency seemed to me on account of your offence to the Real Presence so graciously in our midst; for truly when we are in the depths of penitence it is our nature to listen more kindly to what is imparted for our good; wherefore, as you have minds, I beg you to think. If our Lord did indeed leave a Creed containing the all in all for our salvation, what meant he if not that it should stand in saving purity until he came again in the glory of his going? And if he so intended, and yet uninspired men have added other Articles to the simple faith he asked of us, making it so much the harder for us to go to him in the place he has prepared for us, are they not usurpers? And are not the Articles which they have imposed to be passed by us as stratagems dangerous to our souls?

"Again. The excellence of our Lord's Creed by which it may be always known when in question, its wisdom superior to the devices of men, is that it permits us to differ about matters outside of the faith without weakening our relations to the Blessed Master or imperilling our lot in his promises. Such matters, for example, as works, which are but evidences of faith and forms of worship, and the administration of the two ordinances of the Church, and God and his origin, and whether Heaven be here or there, or like unto this or that. For truly our Lord knew us, and that it was our nature to deal in subtleties and speculate of things not intended we should know during this life; the thought of our minds being restless and always running, like the waters of a river on their way to the sea.

"Again, brethren. If the Church of the Apostles brought peace to its members, so that they dwelt together, no one of them lacking or in need, do not your experiences of to-day teach you wherein your Churches, being those built upon the Creed of the three hundred Bishops, are unlike it? Moreover, see you not if now you have several Churches, some amongst you, the carping and ambitious, will go out and in turn set up new Confessions of Faith, and at length so fill the earth with rival Churches that religion will become a burden to the poor and a byword with fools who delight in saying there is no God? In a village, how much better one House of God, with one elder for its service, and always open, than five or ten, each with a preacher for a price, and closed from Sabbath to Sabbath? For that there must be discipline to keep the faithful together, and to carry on the holy war against sin and its strongholds and captains, how much better one Church in the strength of unity than a hundred diversely named and divided against themselves?

"The Revelator, even that John who while in the Spirit was bidden. 'Write the things which thou hast seen, and the things which are, and the things which shall be hereafter,' wrote, and at the end of his book set a warning: 'If any man shall add unto these things, God shall add unto him the plagues that are written in this book.' I cannot see, brethren, wherein that crime is greater than the addition of Articles to our Lord's Creed; nor do I know any who have more reason to be afraid of those threatened plagues than the priest or preacher who from pride or ambition, or dread of losing his place or living, shall wilfully stand in the way of a return to the Church of the Apostles and its unity. Forasmuch as I also know what penitential life is, and how your minds engage themselves in the solitude of your cells, I give you whereof to think. Men and brethren, peace unto you all!"

The hermit knelt to the preacher, and kissed his hand, sobbing the while; the auditors stared at each other doubtfully; but the Hegumen's time was come. Advancing to the gate, he said:

"This man, O Serenity, is ours by right of fraternity. In thy hearing he hath defamed the Creed which is the rock the Fathers chose for the foundation of our most holy Church. He hath even essayed to make a Creed of his own, and present it for our acceptance—thy acceptance, O Serenity, and that of His Majesty, the only Christian Emperor, as well as ours. And for those things, and because never before in the history of our ancient and most notable Brotherhood hath there been an instance of heresy so much as in thought, we demand the custody of this apostate for trial and judgment. Give him to us to do with."

The Patriarch clasped his hands, and, shaking like a man struck with palsy, turned his eyes upward as if asking counsel of Heaven. His doubt and hesitation were obvious; and neighbor heard his neighbor's heart beat; so did silence once more possess itself of the great auditorium. The Princess Irene arose white with fear, and strove to catch the Emperor's attention; but he, too, was in the bonds waiting on the Patriarch.

Then from his place behind the Hegumen, Sergius spoke:

"Let not your heart be troubled, O Serenity. Give me to my Brotherhood. If I am wrong, I deserve to die; but if I have spoken as the Spirit directed me, God is powerful to save. I am not afraid of the trial."

The Patriarch gazed at him, his withered cheeks glistening with tears; still he hesitated.

"Suffer me, O Serenity!"—thus Sergius again—"I would that thy conscience may never be disquieted on my account; and now I ask not that thou give me to my Brotherhood—I will go with them freely and of my own accord." Speaking then to the Hegumen, he said: "No more, I pray. See, I am ready to be taken as thou wilt."

The Hegumen gave him in charge of the brethren; and at his signal, the gonfalon was raised and carried through the concourse, and out of one of the doors, followed closely by the Brotherhood.

At the moment of starting, Sergius lifted his hands, and shouted so as to be heard above the confusion: "Bear witness, O Serenity—and thou, O Emperor! That no man may judge me an apostate, hear my confession: I believe in God, and Jesus Christ, his Son."

Many of those present remained and partook of the Sacraments; far the greater number hurried away, and it was not long until the house was vacated.

CHAPTER IX
COUNT CORTI TO MAHOMMED

Extract:

"God is God, and Mahomet is his Prophet! May they keep my Lord in health, and help him to all his heart's desires! ... It is now three days since my eyes were gladdened by the presence of the Princess Irene; yet I have been duteously regular in my calls at her house. To my inquiries, her domestic has returned the same answer: 'The Princess is in her chapel praying. She is sadly disturbed in mind, and excuses herself to every one.' Knowing this information will excite my Lord's apprehension, I beg him to accept the explanation of her ailments which I think most probable.... My Lord will gratify me by graciously referring to the account of the special meeting in Sancta Sophia which I had the honor to forward the evening of the day of its occurrence. The conjecture there advanced that the celebration of the Sacrament in highest form was a stratagem of the Patriarch's looking to a reconciliation of the factions, has been confirmed; and more—it has proved a failure. Its effect has inflamed the fanaticism of the Greek party as never before. Notaras, moved doubtless by Gennadius, induced them to suspect His Majesty and the Patriarch of conniving at the wonderful sermon of the monk Sergius; and, as the best rebuke in their power, the Brotherhood of the St. James' erected a Tribunal of Judgment in their monastery last night, and placed the preacher on trial. He defended himself, and drove them to admit his points; that their Church is not the Primitive Church of the Apostles, and that their Creed is an unwarranted enlargement of the two Articles of Faith left by Jesus Christ for the salvation of the world. Yet they pronounced him an apostate and a heretic of incendiary purpose, and condemned him to the old lion in the Cynegion, Tamerlane, famous these many years as a man-eater.... My Lord should also know of the rumor in the city which attributes the Creed of Nine Words— 'I believe in God, and Jesus Christ, his Son'—to the Princess Irene; and her action would seem to justify the story. Directly the meeting in Sancta Sophia was over, she hastened to the Palace, and entreated His Majesty to save the monk from his brethren. My Lord may well think the Emperor disposed to grant her prayer; his feeling for her is warmer than friendship. The gossips say he at one time proposed marriage to her. At all events, being a tender-hearted man—too tender indeed for his high position—it is easy imagining how such unparalleled beauty in tearful distress must have moved him. Unhappily the political situation holds him as in a vice. The Church is almost solidly against him; while of the Brotherhoods this one of the St. James' has been his only stanch adherent. What shall the poor man do? If he saves the preacher, he is himself lost. It appears now she has been brought to understand he cannot interfere. Thrown thus upon the mercy of Heaven, she has buried herself in her oratory. Oh, the full Moon of full Moons! And alas! that she should ever be overcast by a cloud, though it be not heavier than the just-risen morning mist. My Lord—or Allah must come quickly!

* * * * *

"O my Lord! In duty again and always!... Ali did not come yesterday. I suppose the high winds were too unfriendly. So the despatch of that date remained on my hands; and I now open it, and include a supplement.... This morning as usual I rode to the Princess' door. The servant gave me the same report—his mistress was not receiving. It befalls therefore that my Lord must take refuge in his work or in dreams of her—and may I lay a suggestion at his feet, I advise the latter, for truly, if the world is a garden, she is its Queen of Roses.... For the sake of the love my Lord bears the Princess, and the love I bear my Lord, I did not sleep last night, being haunted with thinking how I could be of service to her. What is the use of strength and skill in arms if I cannot turn them to account in her behalf as my Lord would have me?... On my way to the Princess', I was told that the monk, who is the occasion of her sorrow, his sentence being on her conscience, is to be turned in with the lion to-morrow. As I rode away from her house in desperate strait, not having it in power to tell my Lord anything of her, it occurred to me to go see the Cynegion, where the judgment is to be publicly executed. What if the Most Merciful should offer me an opportunity to do the unhappy Princess something helpful? If I shrank from the lion, when killing it would save her a grief, my Lord would never forgive me ... . Here is a description of the Cynegion: The northwest wall of the city drops from the height of Blacherne into a valley next the harbor or Golden Horn, near which it meets the wall coming from the east. Right in the angle formed by the intersection of the walls there is a gate, low, very strong, and always closely guarded. Passing the gate, I found myself in an enclosed field, the city wall on the east, wooded hills south, and the harbor north. How far the enclosure extends up the shore of the harbor, I cannot say exactly—possibly a half or three quarters of a mile. The surface is level and grassy. Roads wind in and out of clumps of selected shrubbery, with here and there an oak tree. Kiosk-looking houses, generally red painted, are frequent, some with roofs, some without. Upon examination I discovered the houses were for the keeping of animals and birds. In one there was an exhibition of fish and reptiles. But much the largest structure, called the Gallery, is situated nearly in the centre of the enclosure; and it astonished me with an interior in general arrangement like a Greek theatre, except it is entirely circular and without a stage division. There is an arena, like a sanded floor, apparently fifty paces in diameter, bounded by a brick wall eighteen or twenty feet in height, and from the top of the wall seats rise one above another for the accommodation of common people; while for the Emperor I noticed a covered stand over on the eastern side. The wall of the arena is broken at regular intervals by doors heavily barred, leading into chambers anciently dens for ferocious animals, but at present prisons for criminals of desperate character. There are also a number of gates, one under the grand stand, the others forming northern, southern and eastern entrances. From this, I am sure my Lord can, if he cares to, draught the Cynegion, literally the Menagerie, comprehending the whole enclosure, and the arena in the middle of it, where the monk will to-morrow expiate his heresy. Formerly combats in the nature of wagers of battle were appointed for the place, and beasts were pitted against each other; but now the only bloody amusement permitted in it is when a criminal or an offender against God is given to the lion. On such occasions, they tell me, the open seats and grand stands are crowded to their utmost capacities.... If the description is tedious, I hope my Lord's pardon, for besides wishing to give him an idea of the scene of the execution to-morrow, I thought to serve him in the day he is looking forward to with so much interest, when the locality will have to be considered with a view to military approach. In furtherance of the latter object, I beg to put my Lord in possession of the accompanying diagram of the Cynegion, observing particularly its relation to the city; by attaching it to the drawings heretofore sent him, he will be enabled to make a complete map of the country adjacent to the landward wall.... Ali has just come in. As I supposed, he was detained by the high winds. His mullets are perfection. With them he brings a young sword-fish yet alive. I look at the mess, and grieve that I cannot send a portion to my Lord for his breakfast. However, a few days now, and he will come to his own; the sea with its fish, and the land and all that belongs to it. The child of destiny can afford to wait."

CHAPTER X
SERGIUS TO THE LION

About ten o'clock the day after the date of Count Corti's last despatch—ten of the morning—a woman appeared on the landing in front of Port St. Peter, and applied to a boatman for passage to the Cynegion.

She was thickly veiled, and wore an every-day overcloak of brown stuff closely buttoned from her throat down. Her hands were gloved, and her feet coarsely shod. In a word, her appearance was that of a female of the middle class, poor but respectable.

The landing was thronged at the time. It seemed everybody wanted to get to the menagerie at once. Boatmen were not lacking. Their craft, of all known models, lay in solid block yards out, waiting turns to get in; and while they waited, the lusty, half-naked fellows flirted their oars, quarrelled with each other in good nature, Greek-like, and yelled volleys at the slow bargain makers whose turns had arrived.

Twice the woman asked if she could have a seat.

"How many of you are there?" she was asked in reply.

"I am alone."

"You want the boat alone?"

"Yes."

"Well, that can't be. I have seats for several—and wife and four babies at home told me to make the most I could out of them. It has been some time since one has tried to look old Tamerlane in the eye, thinking to scare him out of his dinner. The game used to be common; it's not so now."

"But I will pay you for all the seats."

"Full five?"

"Yes."

"In advance?"

"Yes."

"Jump in, then—and get out your money—fifty-five noumias—while I push through these howling water-dogs."

By the time the boat was clear of the pack, truly enough the passenger was with the fare in hand.

"Look," she said, "here is a bezant."

At sight of the gold piece, the man's countenance darkened, and he stopped rowing.

"I can't change that. You might as well have no money at all."

"Friend," she returned, "row me swiftly to the first gate of the Cynegion, and the piece is yours."

"By my blessed patron! I'll make you think you are on a bird, and that these oars are wings. Sit in the middle—that will do. Now!"

The fellow was stout, skilful, and in earnest. In a trice he was under headway, going at racing speed. The boats in the harbor were moving in two currents, one up, the other down; and it was noticeable those in the first were laden with passengers, those of the latter empty. Evidently the interest was at the further end of the line, and the day a holiday to the two cities, Byzantium and Galata. Yet of the attractions on the water and the shores, the woman took no heed; she said never a word after the start; but sat with head bowed, and her face buried in her hands. Occasionally, if the boatman had not been so intent on earning the gold piece, he might have heard her sob. For some reason, the day was not a holiday to her.

"We are nearly there," he at length said.

Without lifting the veil, she glanced at a low wall on the left-hand shore, then at a landing, shaky from age and neglect, in front of a gate in the wall; and seeing it densely blockaded, she spoke:

"Please put me ashore here. I have no time to lose."

The bank was soft and steep.

"You cannot make it."

"I can if you will give me your oar for a step."

"I will."

In a few minutes she was on land. Pausing then to toss the gold piece to the boatman, she heard his thanks, and started hastily for the gate. Within the Cynegion, she fell in with some persons walking rapidly, and talking of the coming event as if it were a comedy.

"He is a Russian, you say?"

"Yes, and what is strange, he is the very man who got the Prince of India's negro"—

"The giant?"

"Yes—who got him to drown that fine young fellow Demedes."

"Where is the negro now?"

"In a cell here."

"Why didn't they give him to the lion?"

"Oh, he had a friend—the Princess Irene."

"What is to be done with him?"

"Afterwhile, when the affair of the cistern is forgotten, he will be given a purse, and set free."

"Pity! For what sport to have seen him in front of the old Tartar!"

"Yes, he's a fighter." In the midst of this conversation, the party came in sight of the central building, externally a series of arches supporting a deep cornice handsomely balustraded, and called the Gallery.

"Here we are!—But see the people on the top! I was afraid we would be too late. Let us hurry."

"Which gate?"

"The western—it's the nearest."

"Can't we get in under the grand stand?"

"No, it's guarded."

These loquacious persons turned off to make the western gate; but the woman in brown kept on, and ere long was brought to the grand stand on the north. An arched tunnel, amply wide, ran under it, with a gate at the further end admitting directly to the arena. A soldier of the foreign legion held the mouth of the tunnel.

"Good friend," she began, in a low, beseeching tone, "is the heretic who is to suffer here yet?"

"He was brought out last night."

"Poor man! I am a friend of his"—her voice trembled—"may I see him?"

"My orders are to admit no one—and I do not know which cell he is in."

The supplicant, sobbing and wringing her hands, stood awhile silent. Then a roar, very deep and hoarse, apparently from the arena, startled her and she trembled.

"Tamerlane!" said the soldier.

"O God!" she exclaimed. "Is the lion turned in already?"

"Not yet. He is in his den. They have not fed him for three days."

She stayed her agitation, and asked: "What are your orders?"

"Not to admit any one."

"To the cells?"

"The cells, and the arena also."

"Oh, I see! You can let me stand at the gate yonder?"

"Well—yes. But if you are the monk's friend, why do you want to see him die?"

She made no reply, but took from a pocket a bezant, and contrived to throw its yellow gleam in the sentinel's eyes.

"Is the gate locked?"

"No, it is barred on this side."

"Does it open into the arena?"

"Yes."

"I do not ask you to violate your orders," she continued, calmly; "only let me go to the gate, and see the man when he is brought out."

She offered him the money, and he took it, saying: "Very well. I can see no harm in that. Go."

The gate in question was open barred, and permitted a view of nearly the whole circular interior. The spectacle presented was so startling she caught one of the bars for support. Throwing back the veil, she looked, breathing sighs which were almost gasps. The arena was clear, and thickly strewn with wet sand. There were the walls shutting it in, like a pit, and on top of them, on the ascending seats back to the last one—was it a cloud she beheld? A second glance, and she recognized the body of spectators, men, women and children, compacted against the sky. How many of them there were! Thousands and thousands! She clasped her hands, and prayed.

Twelve o'clock was the hour for the expiation.

Waiting so wearily there at the gate—praying, sighing, weeping by turns—the woman was soon forgotten by the sentinel. She had bought his pity. In his eyes she was only a lover of the doomed monk. An hour passed thus. If the soldier's theory were correct, if she were indeed a poor love-lorn creature come to steal a last look at the unfortunate, she eked small comfort from her study of the cloud of humanity on the benches. Their jollity, their frequent laughter and hand-clapping reached her in her retreat. "Merciful God!" she kept crying. "Are these beings indeed in thy likeness?"

In a moment of wandering thought, she gave attention to the fastenings of the gate, and observed the ends of the bar across it rested in double iron sockets on the side toward her; to pass it, she had only to raise the bar clear of the socket and push.

Afterwhile the door of a chamber nearly opposite her opened, and a man stood in the aperture. He was very tall, gigantic even; and apparently surprised by what he beheld, he stepped out to look at the benches, whereat the light fell upon him and she saw he was black. His appearance called for a roar of groans, and he retired, closing the door behind him. Then there was an answering roar from a cell near by at her left. The occupants of the benches applauded long and merrily, crying, "Tamerlane! Tamerlane!" The woman shrank back terrified.

A little later another man entered the arena, from the western gate. Going to the centre he looked carefully around him; as if content with the inspection, he went next to a cell and knocked. Two persons responded by coming out of the door; one an armed guardsman, the other a monk. The latter wore a hat of clerical style, and a black gown dropping to his bare feet, its sleeves of immoderate length completely muffling his hands. Instantly the concourse on the benches arose. There was no shouting—one might have supposed them all suddenly seized with shuddering sympathy. But directly a word began passing from mouth to mouth; at first, it was scarcely more than a murmur; soon it was a byname on every tongue:

"The heretic! The heretic!"

The monk was Sergius.

His guard conducted him to the centre of the field, and, taking off his hat, left him there. In going he let his gauntlet fall. Sergius picked it up, and gave it to him; then calm, resigned, fearless, he turned to the east, rested his hands on his breast palm to palm, closed his eyes, and raised his face. He may have had a hope of rescue in reserve; certain it is, they who saw him, taller of his long gown, his hair on his shoulders and down his back, his head upturned, the sunlight a radiant imprint on his forehead, and wanting only a nimbus to be the Christ in apparition, ceased jeering him; it seemed to them that in a moment, without effort, he had withdrawn his thoughts from this world, and surrendered himself. They could see his lips move; but what they supposed his last prayer was only a quiet recitation: "I believe in God, and Jesus Christ, his Son."

The guard withdrawn, three sharp mots of a trumpet rang out from the stand. A door at the left of the tunnel gate was then slowly raised; whereupon a lion stalked out of the darkened depths, and stopped on the edge of the den thus exposed, winking to accustom his eyes to the day-splendor. He lingered there very leisurely, turning his ponderous head from right to left and up and down, like a prisoner questioning if he were indeed at liberty. Having viewed the sky and the benches, and filled his deep chest with ample draughts of fresh air, suddenly Tamerlane noticed the monk. The head rose higher, the ears erected, and, snuffing like a hound, he fretted his shaggy mane; his yellow eyes changed to coals alive, and he growled and lashed his sides with his tail. A majestic figure was he now. "What is it?" he appeared asking himself. "Prey or combat?" Still in a maze, he stepped out into the arena, and shrinking close to the sand, inched forward creeping toward the object of his wonder.

The spectators had opportunity to measure him, and drink their fill of terror. The monk was a goodly specimen of manhood, young, tall, strong; but a fig for his chances once this enemy struck him or set its teeth in his flesh! An ox could not stand the momentum of that bulk of bone and brawn. It were vain telling how many—not all of them women and children—furtively studied the height of the wall enclosing the pit to make sure of their own safety upon the seats.

Sergius meantime remained in prayer and recitation; he was prepared for the attack, but as a non-resistant; if indeed he thought of battle, he was not merely unarmed—the sleeves of his gown deprived him of the use of his hands. From the man to the lion, from the lion to the man, the multitude turned shivering, unable nevertheless to look away.

Presently the lion stopped, whined, and behaved uneasily. Was he afraid? Such was the appearance when he began trotting around at the base of the wall, halting before the gates, and seeking an escape. Under the urgency, whatever it was, from the trot he broke into a gallop, without so much as a glance at the monk.

A murmur descended from the benches. It was the people recovering from their horror, and impatient. Ere long they became positive in expression; in dread doubtless of losing the catastrophe of the show, they yelled at the cowardly beast.

In the height of this tempest, the gate of the tunnel under the grand stand opened quickly, and was as quickly shut. Death brings no deeper hush than fell upon the assemblage then. A woman was crossing the sand toward the monk! Round sped the lion, forward she went! Two victims! Well worth the monster's hunger through the three days to be so banqueted on the fourth!

There are no laws of behavior for such situations. Impulse and instinct rush in and take possession. While the thousands held their breath, they were all quickened to know who the intruder was.

She was robed in white, was bareheaded and barefooted. The dress, the action, the seraphic face were not infrequent on the water, and especially in the churches; recognition was instantaneous, and through the eager crowded ranks the whisper flew:

"God o' Mercy! It is the Princess—the Princess Irene!"

Strong men covered their eyes, women fainted.

The grand stand had been given up to the St. James', and they and their intimates filled it from the top seat to the bottom; and now directly the identity became assured, toward them, or rather to the Hegumen conspicuous in their midst, innumerable arms were outstretched, seconding the cry: "Save her! Save her! Let the lion be killed!"

Easier said than done. Crediting the Brotherhood with lingering sparks of humanity, the game was beyond their interference. The brute was lord. Who dared go in and confront him?

About this time, the black man, of whom we have spoken, looked out of his cell again. To him the pleading arms were turned. He saw the monk, the Princess, and the lion making its furious circuit—saw them and retreated, but a moment after reappeared, attired in the savageries which were his delight. In the waist-belt he had a short sword, and over his left shoulder a roll like a fisherman's net. And now he did not retreat.

The Princess reached Sergius safely, and placing a hand on his arm, brought him back, as it were, to life and the situation.

"Fly, little mother—by the way you came—fly!" he cried, in mighty anguish. "O God! it is too late—too late."

Wringing his hands, he gave way to tears.

"No, I will not fly. Did I not bring you to this? Let death come to us both. Better the quick work of the lion than the slow torture of conscience. I will not fly! We will die together. I too believe in God and Jesus Christ his Son."

She reached up, and rested her hand upon his shoulder. The repetition of the Creed, and her companionship restored his courage, and smiling, despite the tears on his cheeks, he said:

"Very well, little mother. The army of the martyrs will receive us, and the dear Lord is at his mansion door to let us in."

The lion now ceased galloping. Stopping over in the west quarter of the field, he turned his big burning eyes on the two thus resigning themselves, and crouching, put himself in motion toward them; his mane all on end; his jaws agape, their white armature whiter of the crimson tongue lolling adrip below the lips. He had given up escape, and, his curiosity sated, was bent upon his prey. The charge of cowardice had been premature. The near thunder of his roaring was exultant and awful.

There was great ease of heart to the people when Nilo—for he it was—taking position between the devoted pair and their enemy, shook the net from his shoulder, and proceeded to give an example of his practice with lions in the jungles of Kash-Cush.

Keeping the brute steadily eye to eye, he managed so that while retaining the leaden balls tied to its disengaged corners one in each hand, the net was presently in an extended roll on the ground before him. Leaning forward then, his hands bent inwardly knuckle to knuckle at his breast, his right foot advanced, the left behind the right ready to carry him by a step left aside, he waited the attack—to the beholders, a figure in shining ebony, giantesque in proportions, Phidian in grace.

Tamerlane stopped. What new wonder was this? And while making the study, he settled flat on the sand, and sunk his roaring into uneasy whines and growls.

By this time every one looking on understood Nilo's intent—that he meant to bide the lion's leap, and catch and entangle him in the net. What nerve and nicety of calculation—what certainty of eye—what knowledge of the savage nature dealt with—what mastery of self, limb and soul were required for the feat!

Just at this crisis there was a tumult in the grand stand. Those who turned that way saw a man in glistening armor pushing through the brethren there in most unceremonious sort. In haste to reach the front, he stepped from bench to bench, knocking the gowned Churchmen right and left as if they were but so many lay figures. On the edge of the wall, he tossed his sword and shield into the arena, and next instant leaped after them. Before astonishment was spent, before the dull of faculties could comprehend the intruder, before minds could be made up to so much as yell, he had fitted the shield to his arm, snatched up the sword, and run to the point of danger. There, with quick understanding of the negro's strategy, he took place behind him, but in front of the Princess and the monk. His agility, cumbered though he was, his amazing spirit, together with the thought that the fair woman had yet another champion over whom the lion must go ere reaching her, wrought the whole multitude into ecstasy. They sprang upon the benches, and their shouting was impossible of interpretation except as an indication of a complete revulsion of feeling. In fact, many who but a little before had cheered the lion or cursed him for cowardice now prayed aloud for his victims.

The noise was not without effect on the veteran Tamerlane. He surveyed the benches haughtily once, then set forward again, intent on Nilo.

The movement, in its sinuous, flexile gliding, resembled somewhat a serpent's crawl. And now he neither roared nor growled. The lolling tongue dragged the sand; the beating of the tail was like pounding with a flail; the mane all erect trebly enlarged the head; and the eyes were like live coals in a burning bush. The people hushed. Nilo stood firm; thunder could as easily have diverted a statue; and behind him, not less steadfast and watchful, Count Corti kept guard. Thirty feet away—twenty-five—twenty—then the great beast stopped, collected himself, and with an indescribable roar launched clear of the ground. Up, at the same instant, and forward on divergent lines, went the leaden balls; the netting they dragged after them had the appearance of yellow spray blown suddenly in the air. When the monster touched the sand again, he was completely enveloped.

The struggle which ensued—the gnashing of teeth, the bellowing, the rolling and blind tossing and pitching, the labor with the mighty limbs, the snapping of the net, the burrowing into the sand, the further and more inextricable entanglement of the enraged brute may be left to imagination. Almost before the spectators realized the altered condition, Nilo was stabbing him with the short sword.

The well-directed steel at length accomplished the work, and the pride of the Cynegion lay still in the bloody tangle—then the benches found voice.

Amidst the uproar Count Corti went to Nilo.

"Who art thou?" he asked, in admiration.

The King smiled, and signified his inability to hear or speak. Whereupon the Count led him to the Princess.

"Take heart, fair saint," he said. "The lion is dead, and thou art safe."

She scarcely heard him.

He dropped upon his knee.

"The lion is dead, O Princess, and here is the hand which slew him—here thy rescuer."

She looked her gratitude to Nilo—speak she could not.

"And thou, too," the Count continued, to the monk, "must have thanks for him."

Sergius replied: "I give thee thanks, Nilo—and thou, noble Italian—I am only a little less obliged to thee—thou wast ready with thy sword."

He paused, glanced at the grand stand, and went on: "It is plain to me, Count Corti, that thou thinkest my trial happily ended. The beast is dead truly; but yonder are some not less thirsty for blood. It is for them to say what I must further endure. I am still the heretic they adjudged me. Do thou therefore banish me from thy generous mind; then thou canst give it entirely to her who is most in need of it. Remove the Princess—find a chair for her, and leave me to God."

"What further can they do?" asked the Count. "Heaven hath decided the trial in thy favor. Have they another lion?"

The propriety of the monk's suggestion was obvious; it was not becoming for the Princess to remain in the public eye; besides, under reaction of spirit, she was suffering.

"Have they another lion?" the Count repeated.

Anxious as he was to assist the Princess, he was not less anxious, if there was further combat, to take part in it. The Count was essentially a fighting man. The open door of Nilo's cell speedily attracted his attention.

"Help me, sir monk. Yonder is a refuge for the Princess. Let us place her in safety. I will return, and stay with thee. If the reverend Christians, thy brethren in the grand stand, are not content, by Allah"—he checked himself—"their cruelty would turn the stomach of a Mohammedan."

A few minutes, and she was comfortably housed in the cell.

"Now, go to thy place; I will send for a chair, and rejoin thee."

At the tunnel gate, the Count was met by a number of the St. James', and he forgot his errand.

"We have come," said one of them to Sergius, "to renew thy arrest."

"Be it so," Sergius replied; "lead on."

But Count Corti strode forward.

"By whose authority is this arrest renewed?" he demanded.

"Our Hegumen hath so ordered."

"It shall not be—no, by the Mother of your Christ, it shall not be unless you bring me the written word of His Majesty making it lawful."

"The Hegumen"—

"I have said it, and I carry a sword"—the Count struck the hilt of the weapon with his mailed hand, so the clang was heard on the benches. "I have said it, and my sword says it. Go, tell thy Hegumen."

Then Sergius spoke:

"I pray you interfere not. The Heavenly Father who saved me this once is powerful to save me often."

"Have done, sir monk," the Count returned, with increasing earnestness. "Did I not hear thee say the same in thy holy Sancta Sophia, in such wise that these deserved to cast themselves at thy feet? Instead, lo! the lion there. And for the truth, which is the soul of the world as God is its Maker—the Truth and the Maker being the same—it is not interest in thee alone which moves me. She, thy patroness yonder, is my motive as well. There are who will say she followed thee hither being thy lover; but thou knowest better, and so do I. She came bidden by conscience, and except thou live, there will be no ease of conscience for her—never. Wherefore, sir monk, hold thy peace. Thou shalt no more go hence of thine own will than these shall take thee against it.... Return, ye men of blood—return to him who sent you, and tell him my sword vouches my word, being so accustomed all these years I have been a man. Bring they the written word of His Majesty, I will give way. Let them send to him."

The brethren stared at the Count. Had he not been willing to meet old Tamerlane with that same sword? They turned about, and were near the tunnel gate going to report, when it was thrown open with great force, and the Emperor Constantine appeared on horseback, the horse bloody with spurring and necked with foam. Riding to the Count he drew rein.

"Sir Count, where is my kinswoman?"

Corti kissed his hand.

"She is safe, Your Majesty—she is in the cell yonder."

The Emperor's eye fell upon the carcass of the lion.

"Thou didst it, Count?"

"No—this man did it."

The Emperor gazed at Nilo, thus designated, and taking a golden chain of fine workmanship from his neck, he threw it over the black King's. At the door of the cell, he dismounted; within, he kissed the Princess on the forehead.

"A chair will be here directly."

"And Sergius?" she asked.

"The Brotherhood must forego their claim now. Heaven has signified its will."

He thereupon entered into explanation. The necessity upon him was sore and trying, else he had never surrendered Sergius to the Brotherhood. He expected the Hegumen would subject him to discipline—imprisonment or penance. He had even signed the order placing the lion at service, supposing they meant merely a trial of the monk's constancy. Withal the proceeding was so offensive he had refused to witness it. An officer came to the palace with intelligence which led him to believe the worst was really intended. To stop it summarily, he had ordered a horse and a guard. Another officer reported the Princess in the arena with Sergius and the lion. With that His Majesty had come at speed. And he was grateful to God for the issue.

In a short time the sedan was brought, and the Princess borne to her house.

Summoning the Brotherhood from the grand stand, the Emperor forbade their pursuing Sergius further; the punishment had already been too severe. The Hegumen protested. Constantine arose in genuine majesty, and denouncing all clerical usurpations, he declared that for the future he would be governed by his own judgment in whatever concerned the lives of his subjects and the welfare of his empire. The declaration was heard by the people on the benches.

By his order, Sergius was conducted to Blacherne, and next day installed a janitor of the imperial Chapel; thus ending his connection with the Brotherhood of the St. James'.

"Your Majesty," said Count Corti, at the conclusion of the scene in the arena, "I pray a favor."

Constantine, by this time apprised of the Count's gallantry, bade him speak.

"Give me the keeping of this negro."

"If you mean his release from prison, Sir Count, take him. He can have no more suitable guardian. But it is to be remembered he came to the city with one calling himself the Prince of India, and if at any time that mysterious person reappears, the man is to be given back to his master."

The Count regarded Nilo curiously—he was merely recalling the Prince.

"Your Majesty is most gracious. I accept the condition."

The captain of the guard, coming to the tunnel under the grand stand, was addressed by the sentinel there.

"See—here are a dress, a pair of shoes, and a veil. I found them by the gate there."

"How came they there?"

"A woman asked me to let her stand by the gate, and see the heretic when they brought him out, and I gave her permission. She wore these things."

"The Princess Irene!" exclaimed the officer. "Very well. Send them to me, and I will have her pleasure taken concerning them."

The Cynegion speedily returned to its customary state. But the expiation remained in the public mind a date to which all manner of events in city life was referred; none of them, however, of such consequence as the loss to the Emperor of the allegiance of the St. James'. Thenceforth the Brotherhoods were united against him.

BOOK VI
CONSTANTINE

CHAPTER I
THE SWORD OF SOLOMON

The current of our story takes us once more to the White Castle at the mouth of the Sweet Waters of Asia.

It is the twenty-fifth of March, 1452. The weather, for some days cloudy and tending to the tempestuous, changed at noon, permitting the sun to show himself in a field of spotless blue. At the edge of the mountainous steep above Roumeli Hissar, the day-giver lingered in his going down, as loath to leave the life concentrated in the famous narrows in front of the old Castle.

On the land, there was an army in waiting; therefore the city of tents and brushwood booths extending from the shore back to the hills, and the smoke pervading the perspective in every direction.

On the water, swinging to each other, crowding all the shallows of the delta of the little river, reaching out into the sweep of the Bosphorus, boats open and boats roofed—scows, barges, galleys oared and galleys with masts—ships—a vast conglomerate raft.

About the camp, and to and fro on the raft, men went and came, like ants in storing time. Two things, besides the locality, identified them—their turbans, and the crescent and star in the red field of the flags they displayed.

History, it would appear, takes pleasure in repetition. Full a thousand years before this, a greater army had encamped on the banks of the same Sweet Waters. Then it was of Persians; now it is of Turks; and curiously there are no soldiers to be seen, but only working men, while the flotilla is composed of carrying vessels; here boats laden with stone; there boats with lime; yonder boats piled high with timber.

At length the sun, drawing the last ravelling of light after it, disappeared. About that time, the sea gate in front of the Palace of Julian down at Constantinople opened, and a boat passed out into the Marmora. Five men plied the oars. Two sat near the stern. These latter were Count Corti and Ali, son of Abed-din the Faithful.

Two hours prior, Ali, with a fresh catch of fish, entered the gate, and finding no purchaser in the galley, pushed on to the landing, and thence to the Palace.

"O Emir," he said, when admitted to the Count, "the Light of the World, our Lord Mahommed is arrived."

The intelligence seemed to strike the Count with a sudden ague.

"Where is he?" he asked, his voice hollow as from a closed helmet. Ere the other could answer, he added a saving clause: "May the love of Allah be to him a staff of life!"

"He is at the White Castle with Mollahs, Pachas, and engineers a host.... What a way they were in, rushing here and there, like squealing swine, and hunting quarters, if but a crib to lie in and blow! Shintan take them, beards, boots, and turbans! So have they lived on fat things, slept on divans of down under hangings of silk, breathed perfumed airs in crowded harems, Heaven knows if now they are even fit to stop an arrow. They thought the old Castle of Bajazet-Ilderim another Jehan-Numa. By the delights of Paradise, O Emir—ha, ha, ha!—it was good to see how little the Light of the World cared for them! At the Castle, he took in with him for household the ancient *Gabour* Ortachi-Khalil and a Prince of India, whom he calls his Messenger of the Stars; the rest were left to shift for themselves till their tents arrive. Halting the Incomparables, [Footnote: Janissaries.] out beyond Roumeli-Hissar, he summoned the Three Tails, [Footnote: Pachas.] nearly dead from fatigue, having been in the saddle since morning, and rode off with them fast as his Arab could gallop across the country, and down the long hill behind Therapia, drawing rein at the gate before the Palace of the Princess Irene."

"The Palace of the Princess Irene," the Count repeated. "What did he there?"

"He dismounted, looked at the brass plate on the gate-post, went in, and asked if she were at home. Being told she was yet in the city, he said: 'A message for her to be delivered to-night. Here is a purse to pay for going. Tell her Aboo-Obeidah, the Singing Sheik'—only the Prophet knows of such a Sheik—'has been here, bidden by Sultan Mahommed to see if her house had been respected, and inquire if she has yet her health and happiness.' With that, he called for his horse, and went through the garden and up to the top of the promontory; then he returned to Hissar faster than he went to Therapia; and when, to take boat for the White Castle, he walked down the height, two of the Three Tails had to be lifted from their saddles, so nearly dead were they."

Here Ali stopped to laugh.

"Pardon me, O Emir," he resumed, "if I say last what I should have said first, it being the marrow of the bone I bring you.... Before sitting to his pilaf, our Lord Mahommed sent me here. 'Thou knowest to get in and out of the unbelieving city,' he said. 'Go privily to the Emir Mirza, and bid him come to me to-night.'"

"What now, Ali?"

"My Lord was too wise to tell me."

"It is a great honor, Ali. I shall get ready immediately."

When the night was deep enough to veil the departure, the Count seated himself in the fisher's boat, a great cloak covering his armor. Half a mile below the Sweet Waters the party was halted.

"What is this, Ali?"

"The Lord Mahommed's galleys of war are down from the Black Sea. These are their outlyers."

At the side of one of the vessels, the Count showed the Sultan's signet, and there was no further interruption.

A few words now with respect to Corti.

He had become a Christian. Next, the bewilderment into which the first sight of the Princess Irene had thrown him instead of passing off had deepened into hopeless love.

And farther—Constantine, a genuine knight himself; in fact more knight than statesman; delighting in arms, armor, hounds, horses, and martial exercises, including tournaments, hawking, and hunting, found one abiding regret on his throne—he could have a favorite but never a comrade. The denial only stimulated the desire, until finally he concluded to bring the Italian to Court for observation and trial, his advancement to depend upon the fitness, tact, and capacity he might develop.

One day an order was placed in the Count's hand, directing him to find quarters at Blacherne. The Count saw the honor intended, and discerned that acceptance would place him in better position to get information for Mahommed, but what would the advantage avail if he were hindered in forwarding his budget promptly?

No, the mastership of the gate was of most importance; besides which the seclusion of the Julian residence was so favorable to the part he was playing; literally he had no one there to make him afraid.

Upon receipt of the order he called for his horse, and rode to Blacherne, where his argument of the necessity of keeping the Moslem crew of his galley apart brought about a compromise. His Majesty would require the Count's presence during the day, but permit him the nights at Julian. He was also allowed to retain command of the gate.

A few months then found him in Constantine's confidence, the imperial favorite. Yet more surprising as a coincidence, he actually became to the Emperor what he had been to Mahommed. He fenced and jousted with him, instructed him in riding, trained him to sword and bow. Every day during certain hours he had his new master's life at mercy. With a thrust of sword, stroke of battle-axe, or flash of an arrow, it was in his power to rid Mahommed of an opponent concerning whom he wrote: "O my Lord, I think you are his better, yet if ever you meet him in personal encounter, have a care."

But the unexpected now happened to the Count. He came to have an affection for this second lord which seriously interfered with his obligations to the first one. Its coming about was simple. Association with the Greek forced a comparison with the Turk. The latter's passion was a tide before which the better gifts of God to rulers—mercy, justice, discrimination, recognition of truth, loyalty, services—were as willows in the sweep of a wave. Constantine, on the other hand, was thoughtful, just, merciful, tender-hearted, indisposed to offend or to fancy provocation intended. The difference between a man with and a man without conscience—between a king all whose actuations are dominated by religion and a king void of both conscience and religion—slowly but surely, we say, the difference became apparent to the Count, and had its inevitable consequences.

Such was the Count's new footing in Blacherne.

The changes wrought in his feeling were forwarded more than he was aware by the standing accorded him in the reception-room of the Princess Irene.

After the affair at the Cynegion he had the delicacy not to push himself upon the attention of the noble lady. In preference he sent a servant every morning to inquire after her health. Ere long he was the recipient of an invitation to come in person; after which his visits increased in frequency. Going to Blacherne, and coming from it, he stopped at her house, and with every interview it seemed his passion for her intensified.

Now it were not creditable to the young Princess' discernment to say she was blind to his feeling; yet she was careful to conceal the discovery from him, and still more careful not to encourage his hope. She placed the favor shown him to the account of gratitude; at the same time she admired him, and was deeply interested in the religious sentiment he was beginning to manifest.

In the Count's first audience after the rescue from the lion, she explained how she came to be drawn to the Cynegion. This led to detail of her relations with Sergius, concluding with the declaration: "I gave him the signal to speak in Sancta Sophia, and felt I could not live if he died the death, sent to it by me."

"Princess," the Count replied, "I heard the monk's sermon in Sancta Sophia, but did not know of your giving the signal. Has any one impugned your motive in going to the Cynegion? Give me his name. My sword says you did well."

"Count Corti, the Lord has taken care of His own."

"As you say, Princess Irene. Hear me before addressing yourself to something else.... I remember the words of the Creed—or if I have them wrong correct me: 'I believe in God, and Jesus Christ, his Son.'"

"It is word for word."

"Am I to understand you gave him the form?"

"The idea is Father Hilarion's."

"And the Two Articles. Are they indeed sayings of Jesus Christ?"

"Even so."

"Give me the book containing them."

Taking a New Testament from the table, she gave it to him.

"You will find the sayings easily. On the margins opposite them there are markings illuminated in gold."

"Thanks, O Princess, most humbly. I will return the book."

"No, Count, it is yours."

An expression she did not understand darkened his face.

"Are you a Christian?" she asked.

He flushed deeply, and bowed while answering:

"My mother is a Christian."

That night Count Corti searched the book, and found that the strength of faith underlying his mother's prayers for his return to her, and the Princess' determination to die with the monk, were but Christian lights.

"Princess Irene," he said one day, "I have studied the book you gave me; and knowing now who Christ is, I am ready to accept your Creed. Tell me how I may know myself a believer?"

A lamp in the hollow of an alabaster vase glows through the transparency; so her countenance responded to the joy behind it.

"Render obedience to His commands—do His will, O Count—then wilt thou be a believer in Christ, and know it."

The darkness she had observed fall once before on his face obscured it again, and he arose and went out in silence.

Brave he certainly was, and strong. Who could strike like him? He loved opposition for the delight there was in overcoming it; yet in his chamber that night he was never so weak. He resorted to the book, but could not read. It seemed to accuse him. "Thou Islamite—thou son of Mahomet, though born of a Christian, whom servest thou? Judas, what dost thou in this city? Hypocrite—traitor—which is thy master, Mahomet or Christ?"

He fell upon his knees, tore at his beard, buried his head in his arms. He essayed prayer to Christ.

"Jesus—Mother of Jesus—O my mother!" he cried in agony.

The hour he was accustomed to give to Mahommed came round. He drew out the writing materials. "The Princess"—thus he began a sentence, but stopped—something caught hold of his heart—the speaking face of the beloved woman appeared to him—her eyes were reproachful—her lips moved—she spoke: "Count Corti, I am she whom thou lovest; but what dost thou? Is it not enough to betray my kinsman? Thy courage—what makest thou of it but wickedness? ... Write of me to thy master. Come every day, and contrive that I speak, then tell him of it. Am I sick? Tell him of it. Do I hold to this or that? Tell him. Am I shaken by visions of ruin to my country? Tell him of them. What is thy love if not the servant for hire of his love? Traitor—panderer!"

The Count pushed the table from him, and sprang to foot writhing. To shut out the word abhorrent above all other words, he clapped his hands tight over his ears—in vain.

"Panderer!"—he heard with his soul—"Panderer! When thou hast delivered me to Mahommed, what is he to give thee? How much?"

Thus shame, like a wild dog, bayed at him. For relief he ran out into the garden. And it was only the beginning of misery. Such the introduction or first chapter, what of the catastrophe? He could not sleep for shame.

In the morning he ordered his horse, but had not courage to go to Blacherne. How could he look at the kindly face of the master he was betraying? He thought of the Princess. Could he endure her salutation? She whom he was under compact to deliver to Mahommed? A paroxysm of despair seized him.

He rode to the Gate St. Romain, and out of it into the country. Gallop, gallop—the steed was good—his best Arab, fleet and tireless. Noon overtook him—few things else could—still he galloped. The earth turned into a green ribbon under the flying hoofs, and there was relief in the speed. The air, whisked through, was soothing. At length he came to a wood, wild and interminable, Belgrade, though he knew it not, and dismounting by a stream, he spent the day there. If now and then the steed turned its eyes upon him, attracted by his sighs, groans and prayer, there was at least no accusation in them. The solitude was restful; and returning after nightfall, he entered the city through the sortie under the Palace of Blacherne known as the Cercoporta.

It is well pain of spirit has its intermissions; otherwise long life could not be; and if sleep bring them, so much the better.

Next day betimes, the Count was at Blacherne.

"I pray grace, O my Lord!" he said, speaking to the question in the Emperor's look. "Yesterday I had to ride. This confinement in the city deadens me. I rode all day."

The good, easy master sighed: "Would I had been with you, Count."

Thus he dismissed the truancy. But with the Princess it was a lengthy chapter. If the Emperor was never so gracious, she seemed never so charming. He wrote to Mahommed in the evening, and walked the garden the residue of the night.

So weeks and months passed, and March came—even the night of the twenty-fifth, with its order from the Sultan to the White Castle—an interval of indecision, shame, and self-indictment. How many plans of relief he formed who can say? Suicide he put by, a very last resort. There was also a temptation to cut loose from Mahommed, and go boldly over to the Emperor. That would be a truly Christian enlistment for the approaching war; and aside from conformity to his present sympathies, it would give him a right to wear the Princess' favor on his helmet. But a fear shook the resort out of mind. Mahommed, whether successful or defeated, would demand an explanation of him, possibly an accounting. He knew the Sultan. Of all the schemes presented, the most plausible was flight. There was the gate, and he its keeper, and beyond the gate, the sunny Italian shore, and his father's castle. The seas and sailing between were as green landscapes to a weary prisoner, and he saw in them only the joy of going and freedom to do. Welcome, and to God the praise! More than once he locked his portables of greatest value in the cabin of the galley. But alas! He was in bonds. Life in Constantinople now comprehended two of the ultimate excellencies to him, Princess Irene and Christ—and their joinder in the argument he took to be no offence.

From one to another of these projects he passed, and they but served to hide the flight of time. He was drifting—ahead, and not far, he heard the thunder of coming events—yet he drifted.

In this condition, the most envied man in Constantinople and the most wretched, the Sultan's order was delivered to him by Ali.

The time for decision was come. Tired—ashamed—angry with himself, he determined to force the end.

The Count arrived at the Castle, was immediately admitted to the Sultan; indeed, had he been less resolute, his master's promptitude would have been a circumstance of disturbing significance.

Observation satisfied him Mahommed was in the field; for with all his Epicureanism in times of peace, when a campaign was in progress the Conqueror resolved himself into a soldierly example of indifference to luxury. In other words, with respect to furnishment, the interior of the old Castle presented its every day ruggedness.

One lamp fixed to the wall near the door of the audience chamber struggled with the murk of a narrow passage, giving to view an assistant chamberlain, an armed sentinel, and two jauntily attired pages in waiting. Surrendering his sword to the chamberlain, the Count halted before the door, while being announced; at the same time, he noticed a man come out of a neighboring apartment clad in black velvet from head to foot, followed closely by a servant. It was the Prince of India.

The mysterious person advanced slowly, his eyes fixed on the floor, his velvet-shod feet giving out no sound. His air indicated deep reflection. In previous encounters with him, the Count had been pleased; now his sensations were of repugnance mixed with doubt and suspicion. He had not time to account for the change. It may have had origin in the higher prescience sometimes an endowment of the spirit by which we stand advised of a friend or an enemy; most likely, however, it was a consequence of the curious tales abroad in Constantinople; for at the recognition up sprang the history of the Prince's connection with Lael, and her abandonment by him, the more extraordinary from the evidences of his attachment to her. Up sprang also the opinion of universal prevalence in the city that he had perished in the great fire. What did it all mean? What kind of man was he?

The servant carried a package wrapped in gold-embroidered green silk.

Coming near, the Prince raised his eyes—stopped—smiled—and said:

"Count Corti—or Mirza the Emir—which have I the honor of meeting?"

In spite of the offence he felt, Corti blushed, such a flood of light did the salutation let in upon the falsity of his position. Far from losing presence of mind, he perceived at once how intimately the Prince stood in the councils of the Sultan.

"The Lord Mahommed must be heard before I can answer," he returned, calmly.

In an instant the Prince became cordial.

"That was well answered," he said. "I am pleased to have my judgment of you confirmed. Your mission has been a trying one, but you have conducted it like a master. The Lord Mahommed has thanked me many times that I suggested you for it. He is impatient to see you. We will go in together."

Mahommed, in armor, was standing by a table on which were a bare cimeter, a lamp brightly burning, and two large unrolled maps. In one of the latter, the Count recognized Constantinople and its environs cast together from his own surveys.

Retired a few steps were the two Viziers, Kalil Pacha and his rival, Saganos Pacha, the Mollah Kourani, and the Sheik Akschem-sed-din. The preaching of the Mollah had powerfully contributed to arousing the fanatical spirit of the Sultan's Mohammedan subjects. The four were standing in the attitude usual to Turkish officials in presence of a superior, their heads bowed, their hands upon their stomachs. In speaking, if they raised their eyes from the floor it was to shoot a furtive glance, then drop them again.

"This is the grand design of the work by which you will be governed," Mahommed said to the counsellors, laying the finger points of his right hand upon the map unknown to the Count, and speaking earnestly. "You will take it, and make copies tonight; for if the stars fail not, I will send the masons and their workmen to the other shore in the morning."

The advisers saluted—it would be difficult to say which of them with the greatest unction.

Looking sharply at Kalil, the master asked: "You say you superintended the running of the lines in person?"

Kalil saluted separately, and returned: "My Lord may depend upon the survey."

"Very well. I wait now only the indication of Heaven that the time is ripe for the movement. Is the Prince of India coming?"

"I am here, my Lord."

Mahommed turned as the Prince spoke, and let his eyes rest a moment upon Count Corti, without a sign of recognition.

"Come forward, Prince," he said. "What is the message you bring me?"

"My Lord," the Prince replied, after prostration, "in the Hebrew Scriptures there is a saying in proof of the influence the planets have in the affairs of men: 'Then fought the kings of Canaan in Taanach by the waters of Megiddo; they fought from heaven; the stars in their courses fought against Sisera.' Now art thou truly Sultan of Sultans. To-morrow—the twenty-sixth of March—will be memorable amongst days, for then thou mayst begin the war with the perfidious Greek. From four o'clock in the morning the stars which fought against Sisera will fight for Mahommed. Let those who love him salute and rejoice."

The counsellors, dropping on their knees, fell forward, their faces on their hands. The Prince of India did the same. Count Corti alone remained standing, and Mahommed again observed him.

"Hear you," the latter said, to his officers. "Go assemble the masons and their workmen, the masters of boats, and the chiefs charged with duties. At four o'clock in the morning I will move against Europe. The stars have said it, and their permission is my law. Rise!"

As his associates were moving backward with repeated genuflections, the Prince of India spoke:

"O most favored of men! Let them stay a moment."

At a sign from the Sultan they halted; thereupon the Prince of India beckoned Syama to come, and taking the package from his hands, he laid it on the table.

"For my Lord Mahommed," he said.

"What is it?" Mahommed demanded.

"A sign of conquest.... My Lord knows King Solomon ruled the world in his day, its soul of wisdom. At his death dominion did not depart from him. The secret ministers in the earth, the air and the waters, obedient to Allah, became his slaves. My Lord knows of whom I speak. Who can resist them? ... In the tomb of Hiram, King of Tyre, the friend of King Solomon, I found a sarcophagus. It was covered with a model in marble of the Temple of the Hebrew Almighty God. Removing the lid, lo! the mummy of Hiram, a crown upon its head, and at its feet the sword of Solomon, a present without price. I brought it away, resolved to give it to him whom the stars should elect for the overthrow of the superstitions devised by Jesus, the bastard son of Joseph the carpenter of Nazareth.... Undo the wrappings, Lord Mahommed."

The Sultan obeyed, and laying the last fold of the cloth aside, drew back staring, and with uplifted hands.

"Kalil—Kourani—Akschem-sed-din—all of you, come look. Tell me what it is—it blinds me."

The sword of Solomon lay before them; its curved blade a gleam of splendor, its scabbard a mass of brilliants, its hilt a ruby so pure we may say it retained in its heart the life of a flame.

"Take it in hand, Lord Mahommed," said the Prince of India.

The young Sultan lifted the sword, and as he did so down a groove in its back a stream of pearls started and ran, ringing musically, and would not rest while he kept the blade in motion. He was speechless from wonder.

"Now may my Lord march upon Constantinople, for the stars and every secret minister of Solomon will fight for him."

So saying, the Prince knelt before the Sultan, and laid his lips on the instep of his foot, adding: "Oh, my Lord! with that symbol in hand, march, and surely as Tabor is among the mountains and Carmel by the sea, so surely Christ will give place to Mahomet in Sancta Sophia. March at four o'clock."

And the counsellors left kisses on the same instep, and departed.

Thence through the night the noises of preparation kept the space between the hills of the narrows alive with echoes. At the hour permitted by the stars—four o'clock—a cloud of boats cast loose from the Asiatic shore, and with six thousand laborers, handmen to a thousand master masons, crossed at racing speed to Europe. "God is God, and Mahomet is his Prophet," they shouted. The vessels of burden, those with lime, those with stone, those with wood, followed as they were called, and unloading, hauled out, to give place to others.

Before sun up the lines of the triangular fort whose walls near Roumeli-Hissar are yet intact, prospectively a landmark enduring as the Pyramids, were defined and swarming with laborers. The three Pachas, Kalil, Sarudje, and Saganos, superintended each a side of the work, and over them all, active and fiercely zealous, moved Mahommed, the sword of Solomon in his hand.

And there was no lack of material for the structure extensive as it was. Asia furnished its quota, and Christian towns and churches on the Bosphorus were remorselessly levelled for the stones in them; wherefore the outer faces of the curtains and towers are yet speckled with marbles in block, capital and column.

Thus Mahommed, taking his first step in the war so long a fervid dream, made sure of his base of operations.

On the twenty-eighth of August, the work completed, from his camp on the old Asometon promontory he reconnoitred the country up to the ditch of Constantinople, and on the first of September betook himself to Adrianople.

CHAPTER II
MAHOMMED AND COUNT CORTI MAKE A WAGER

Upon the retirement of the Prince of India and the counsellors, Mahommed took seat by the table, and played with the sword of Solomon, making the pearls travel up and down the groove in the blade, listening to their low ringing, and searching for inscriptions. This went on until Count Corti began to think himself forgotten. At length the Sultan, looking under the guard, uttered an exclamation—looked again—and cried out:

"O Allah! It is true!—May I be forgiven for doubting him!—Come, Mirza, come see if my eyes deceive me. Here at my side!"

The Count mastered his surprise, and was presently leaning over the Sultan's shoulder.

"You remember, Mirza, we set out together studying Hebrew. Against your will I carried you along with me until you knew the alphabet, and could read a little. You preferred Italian, and when I brought the learned men, and submitted to them that Hebrew was one of a family of tongues more or less alike, and would have sent you with them to the Sidonian coast for inscriptions, you refused. Do you remember?"

"My Lord, those were the happiest days of my life."

Mahommed laughed. "I kept you three days on bread and water, and let you off then because I could not do without you.... But for the matter now. Under this guard—look—are not the brilliants set in the form of letters?"

Corti examined closely.

"Yes, yes; there are letters—I see them plainly—a name."

"Spell it."

"S-O-L-O-M-O-N."

"Then I have not deceived myself," Mahommed exclaimed. "Nor less has the Prince of India deceived me." He grew more serious. "A marvellous man! I cannot make him out. The more I do with him the more incomprehensible he becomes. The long past is familiar to him as the present to me. He is continually digging up things ages old, and amazing me with them. Several times I have asked him when he was born, and he has always made the same reply: 'I will tell when you are Lord of

Constantinople.' ... How he hates Christ and the Christians! ... This is indeed the sword of Solomon—and he found it in the tomb of Hiram, and gives it to me as the elect of the stars now. Ponder it, O Mirza! Now at the mid of the night in which I whistle up my dogs of war to loose them on the *Gabour*—How, Mirza—what ails you? Why that change of countenance? Is he not a dog of an unbeliever? On your knees before me—I have more to tell you than to ask. No, spurs are troublesome. To the door and bid the keeper there bring a stool—and look lest the lock have an ear hanging to it. Old Kalil, going out, though bowing, and lip-handing me, never took his eyes off you."

The stool brought, Corti was about to sit.

"Take off your cap"—Mahommed spoke sternly—"for as you are not the Mirza I sent away, I want to see your face while we talk. Sit here, in the full of the light."

The Count seated, placed his hooded cap on the floor. He was perfectly collected. Mahommed fingered the ruby hilt while searching the eyes which as calmly searched his.

"How brave you are!" the Sultan began, but stopped. "Poor Mirza!" he began again, his countenance softened. One would have said some tender recollection was melting the shell of his heart. "Poor Mirza! I loved you better than I loved my father, better than I loved my brothers, well as I loved my mother—with a love surpassing all I ever knew but one, and of that we will presently speak. If honor has a soul, it lives in you, and the breath you draw is its wine, purer than the first expressage of grapes from the Prophet's garden down by Medina. Your eyes look truth, your tongue drips it as a broken honey-comb drips honey. You are truth as God is God."

He was speaking sincerely.

"Fool—fool—that I let you go!—and I would not—no, by the rose-door of Paradise and the golden stairs to the House of Allah, I would not had I loved my full moon of full moons less. She was parted from me; and with whose eyes could I see her so well as with yours, O my falcon? Who else would report to me so truly her words? Love makes men and lions mad; it possessed me; and I should have died of it but for your ministering. Wherefore, O Mirza"—

The Count had been growing restive; now he spoke. "My Lord is about committing himself to some pledge. He were wise, did he hear me first."

"Perhaps so," the Sultan rejoined, uncertainly, but added immediately: "I will hear you."

"It is true, as my Lord said, I am not the Mirza he despatched to Italy. The changes I have undergone are material; and in recounting them I anticipate his anger. He sees before him the most wretched of men to whom death would be mercy."

"Is it so bad? You were happy when you went away. Was not the mission to your content?"

"My Lord's memory is a crystal cup from which nothing escapes—a cup without a leak. He must recall how I prayed to stay with him."

"Yes, yes."

"My dread was prophetic."

"Tell me of the changes."

"I will—and truly as there is but one God, and he the father of life and maker of things. First, then, the affection which at my going was my Lord's, and which gave me to see him as the Light of the World, and the perfection of glory in promise, is now divided."

"You mean there is another Light of the World? Be it so, and still you leave me flattered. How far you had to travel before finding the other! Who is he?"

"The Emperor of the Greeks."

"Constantine? Are his gifts so many and rich? The next."

"I am a Christian."

"Indeed? Perhaps you can tell me the difference between God and Allah. Yesterday Kourani said they were the same."

"Nay, my Lord, the difference is between Christ and Mahomet."

"The mother of the one was a Jewess, the mother of the other an Arab—I see. Go on."

The Count did not flinch. "My Lord, great as is your love of the Princess Irene"—Mahommed half raised his hands, his brows knit, his eyes filled with fire, but the Count continued composedly—"mine is greater."

The Sultan recovered himself.

"The proof, the proof!" he said, his voice a little raised. "My love of her is consuming me, but I see you alive."

"My Lord's demand is reasonable. I came here to make the avowal, and die. Would my Lord so much?"

"You would die for the Princess?"

"My Lord has said it."

"Is there not something else in the urgency?"

"Yes—honor."

The Count's astonishment was unspeakable. He expected an outburst of wrath unappeasable, a summons for an executioner; instead, Mahommed's eyes became humid, and resting his elbow on the table, and his face on the thumb and forefinger, he said, gazing sorrowfully:

"Ahmed was my little brother. His mother published before my father's death, that my mother was a slave. She was working for her child already, and I had him smothered in a bath. Cruel? God forgive me! It was my duty to provide for the peace of my people. I had a right to take care of myself; yet will I never be forgiven. Kismet!... I have had many men slain since. I travel, going to mighty events beckoned by destiny. The ordinary cheap soul cannot understand how necessary it is that my path should be smooth and clear; for sometime I may want to run; and he will amuse or avenge himself by stamping me in history a monster without a soul. Kismet! ... But you, my poor Mirza, you should know me better. You are my brother without guile. I am not afraid to love you. I do love you. Let us see.... Your letters from Constantinople—I have them all—told me so much more than you intended, I could not suspect your fidelity. They prepared me for everything you have confessed. Hear how in my mind I disposed of them point by point.... 'Mirza,' I said, 'pities the *Gabour* Emperor; in the end he will love him. Loving a hundred men is less miraculous in a man than loving one. He will make comparisons. Why not? The *Gabour* appeals to him through his weakness, I through my strength. I would rather be feared than pitied. Moreover, the *Gabour's* day runs to its close, and as it closes, mine opens. Pity never justified treason.' ... And I said, too, on reading the despatch detailing your adventures in Italy: 'Poor Mirza! now has he discovered he is an Italian, stolen when a child, and having found his father's castle and his mother, a noble woman, he will become a Christian, for so would I in his place.' Did I stop there? The wife of the Pacha who received you from your abductors is in Broussa. I sent to her asking if she had a keepsake or memento which would help prove your family and country. See what she returned to me."

From under a cloth at the further end of the table, Mahommed drew a box, and opening it, produced a collar of lace fastened with a cameo pin. On the pin there was a graven figure.

"Tell me, Mirza, if you recognize the engraving." The Count took the cameo, looked at it, and replied, with a shaking voice:

"The arms of the Corti! God be praised!"

"And here—what are these, and what the name on them?"

Mahommed gave him a pair of red morocco half-boots for a child, on which, near the tops, a name was worked in silk.

"It is mine, my Lord—my name—'Ugo.'"

He cast himself before the Sultan, and embraced his knees, saying, in snatches as best he could:

"I do not know what my Lord intends—whether he means I am to die or live—if it be death, I pray him to complete his mercy by sending these proofs to my mother"—

"Poor Mirza, arise! I prefer to have your face before me."

Directly the Count was reseated, Mahommed continued:

"And you, too, love the Princess Irene? You say you love her more than I? And you thought I could not endure hearing you tell it? That I would summon black Hassan with his bowstring? With all your opportunities, your seeing and hearing her, as the days multiplied from tens to hundreds, is it for me to teach you she will come to no man except as a sacrifice? What great thing have you to offer her? While I—well, by this sword of Solomon, to-morrow morning I set out to say to her: 'For thy love, O my full Moon of full Moons, for thy love thou shalt have the redemption of thy Church.'... And besides, did I not foresee your passion? Courtiers stoop low and take pains to win favor; but no courtier, not even a professional, intending merely to please me, could have written of her as you did; and by that sign, O Mirza, I knew you were in the extremity of passion. Offended? Not so, not so! I sent you to take care of her—fight for her—die, if her need were so great. Of whom might I expect such service but a lover? Did I not, the night of our parting, foretell what would happen?" He paused gazing at the ruby of the ring on his finger.

"See, Mirza! There has not been a waking hour since you left me but I have looked at this jewel; and it has kept color faithfully. Often as I beheld it, I said: 'Mirza loves her because he cannot help it; yet he is keeping honor with me. Mirza is truth, as God is God. From his hand will I receive her in Constantinople'"—

"O my Lord"—

"Peace, peace! The night wanes, and you have to return. Of what was I speaking? Oh, yes"—

"But hear me, my Lord. At the risk of your displeasure I must speak."

"What is it?"

"In her presence my heart is always like to burst, yet, as I am to be judged in the last great day, I have kept faith with my Lord. Once she thanked me—it was after I offered myself to the lion—O Heaven! how nearly I lost my honor! Oh, the agony of that silence! The anguish of that remembrance! I have kept the faith, my Lord. But day by day now the will to keep it grows weaker. All that holds me steadfast is my position in Constantinople. What am I there?"

The Count buried his face in his hands, and through the links in his surcoat the tremor which shook his body was apparent.

Mahommed waited.

"What am I there? Having come to see the goodness of the Emperor, I must run daily to betray him. I am a Christian; yet as Judas sold his Master, I am under compact to sell my religion. I love a noble woman, yet am pledged to keep her safely, and deliver her to another. O my Lord, my Lord! This cannot go on. Shame is a vulture, and it is tearing me—my heart bleeds in its beak. Release me, or give me to death. If you love me, release me."

"Poor Mirza!"

"My Lord, I am not afraid."

Mahommed struck the table violently, and his eyes glittered. "That ever one should think I loved a coward! Yet more intolerable, that he whom I have called brother should know me so little! Can it be, O Mirza, can it be, you tell me these things imagining them new to me? ... Let me have done. What we are saying would have become us ten years ago, not now. It is unmanly. I had a purpose in sending for you.... Your mission in Constantinople ends in the morning at four o'clock. In other words, O Mirza, the condition passes from preparation for war with the *Gabour* to war. Observe now. You are a fighting man—a knight of skill and courage. In the rencounters to which I am going—the sorties, the assaults, the duels single and in force, the exchanges with all arms, bow, arbalist, guns small and great, the mines and countermines—you cannot stay out. You must fight. Is it not so?"

Corti's head arose, his countenance brightened.

"My Lord, I fear I run forward of your words—forgive me."

"Yes, give ear.... The question now is, whom will you fight—me or the *Gabour*?"

"O my Lord"—

"Be quiet, I say. The issue is not whether you love me less. I prefer you give him your best service."

"How, my Lord?"

"I am not speaking in contempt, but with full knowledge of your superiority with weapons—of the many of mine who must go down before you. And that you may not be under restraint of conscience or arm-tied in the melee, I not only conclude your mission, but release you from every obligation to me."

"Every obligation!"

"I know my words, Emir, yet I will leave nothing uncertain.... You will go back to the city free of every obligation to me—arm-free, mind-free. Be a Christian, if you like. Send me no more despatches advisory of the Emperor"—

"And the Princess Irene, my Lord?"

Mahommed smiled at the Count's eagerness.

"Have patience, Mirza.... Of the moneys had from me, and the properties heretofore mine in trust, goods, horses, arms, armor, the galley and its crew, I give them to you without an accounting. You cannot deliver them to me or dispose of them, except with an explanation which would weaken your standing in Blacherne, if not undo you utterly. You have earned them."

Corti's face reddened.

"With all my Lord's generosity, I cannot accept this favor. Honor"—

"Silence, Emir, and hear me. I have never been careless of your honor. When you set out for Italy, preparatory to the mission at Constantinople, you owed me duty, and there was no shame in the performance; but now— so have the changes wrought—that which was honorable to Mirza the Emir is scandalous to Count Corti. After four o'clock you will owe me no duty; neither will you be in my service. From that hour Mirza, my falcon, will cease to be. He will have vanished. Or if ever I know him more, it will be as Count Corti, Christian, stranger, and enemy."

"Enemy—my Lord's enemy? Never!"

The Count protested with extended arms.

"Yes, circumstances will govern. And now the Princess Irene."

Mahommed paused; then, summoning his might of will, and giving it expression in a look, he laid a forcible hand on the listener's shoulder.

"Of her now.... I have devised a promotion for you, Emir. After to-night we will be rivals."

Corti was speechless—he could only stare.

"By the rose-door of Paradise—the only oath fit for a lover—or, as more becoming a knight, by this sword of Solomon, Emir, I mean the rivalry to be becoming and just. I have an advantage of you. With women rank and riches are as candles to moths. On the other side your advantage is double; you are a Christian, and may be in her eyes day after day. And not to leave you in mean condition, I give you the moneys and property now in your possession; not as a payment—God forbid!—but for pride's sake—my pride. Mahommed the Sultan may not dispute with a knight who has only a sword."

"I have estates in Italy."

"They might as well be in the moon. I shall enclose Constantinople before you could arrange with the Jews, and have money enough to buy a feather for your cap. If this were less true, comes then the argument: How can you dispose of the properties in hand, and quiet the gossips in the *Gabour's* palace? 'Where are your horses?' they will ask. What answer have you? 'Where your galley?' Answer. 'Where your Mohammedan crew?' Answer."

The Count yielded the debate, saying: "I cannot comprehend my Lord. Such thing was never heard of before."

"Must men be restrained because the thing they wish to do was never heard of before? Shall I not build a mosque with five minarets because other builders stopped with three? ... To the sum of it all now. Christian or Moslem, are you willing to refer our rivalry for the young woman to God?"

"My wonder grows with listening to my Lord."

"Nay, this surprises you because it is new. I have had it in mind for months. It did not come to me easily. It demanded self-denial—something I am unused to.... Here it is—I am willing to call Heaven in, and let it decide whether she shall be mine or yours—this lily of Paradise whom all men love at sight. Dare you as much?"

The soldier spirit arose in the Count.

"Now or then, here or there, as my Lord may appoint. I am ready. He has but to name his champion."

"I protest. The duel would be unequal. As well match a heron and a hawk. There is a better way of making our appeal. Listen.... The walls of Constantinople have never succumbed to attack. Hosts have dashed against them, and fled or been lost. It may be so with me; but I will march, and in my turn assault them, and thou defending with thy best might. If I am beaten, if I retire, be the cause of failure this or that, we—you and I, O Mirza—will call it a judgment of Heaven, and the Princess shall be yours; but if I success and enter the city, it shall be a judgment no less, and then"—Mahommed's eyes were full of fire—"then"—

"What then, my Lord?"

"Thou shalt see to her safety in the last struggle, and conduct her to Sancta Sophia, and there deliver her to me as ordered by God."

Corti was never so agitated. He turned pale and red—he trembled visibly.

Mahommed asked mockingly: "Is it Mirza I am treating with, or Count Corti? Are Christians so unwilling to trust God?"

"But, my Lord, it is a wager you offer me."

"Call it so."

"And its conditions imply slavery for the Princess. Change them, my Lord—allow her to be consulted and have her will, be the judgment this or that."

Mahommed clinched his hands.

"Am I a brute? Did ever woman lay her head on my breast perforce?"

The Count replied, firmly:

"Such a condition would be against us both alike."

The Sultan struggled with himself a moment.

"Be it so," he rejoined. "The wager is my proposal, and I will go through with it. Take the condition, Emir. If I win, she shall come to me of her free will or not at all."

"A wife, my Lord?"

"In my love first, and in my household first—my Sultana."

The animation which then came to the Count was wonderful. He kissed Mahommed's hand.

"Now has my Lord outdone himself in generosity. I accept. In no other mode could the issue be made so absolutely a determination of Heaven."

Mahommed arose.

"We are agreed.—The interview is finished.—Ali is waiting for you."

He replaced the cover on the box containing the collar and the half-boots.

"I will send these to the Countess your mother; for hereafter you are to be to me Ugo, Count Corti.... My falcon hath cast its jess and hood. Mirza is no more. Farewell Mirza."

Corti was deeply moved. Prostrating himself, he arose, and replied:

"I go hence more my Lord's lover than ever. Death to the stranger who in my presence takes his name in vain."

As he was retiring, Mahommed spoke again:

"A word, Count.... In what we are going to, the comfort and safety of the Princess Irene may require you to communicate with me. You have ready wit for such emergencies. Leave me a suggestion."

Corti reflected an instant.

"The signal must proceed from me," he said. "My Lord will pitch his tent in sight"—

"By Solomon, and this his sword, yes! Every *Gabour* who dares look over the wall shall see it while there is a hill abiding."

The Count bowed.

"I know my Lord, and give him this—God helping me, I will make myself notorious to the besiegers as he will be to the besieged. If at any time he sees my banderole, or if it be reported to him, let him look if my shield be black; if so, he shall come himself with a shield the color of mine, and place himself in my view. My Lord knows I make my own arrows. If I shoot one black feathered, he must pick it up. The ferrule will be of hollow lead covering a bit of scrip."

"Once more, Count Corti, the issue is with God. Good night."

Traversing the passage outside the door, the Count met the Prince of India.

"An hour ago I would have entitled you Emir: but now"—the Prince smiled while speaking—"I have stayed to thank Count Corti for his kindness to my black friend Nilo."

"Your servant?"

"My friend and ally—Nilo the King.... If the Count desires to add to the obligation, he will send the royal person to me with Ali when he returns to-night."

"I will send him."

"Thanks, Count Corti."

The latter lingered, gazing into the large eyes and ruddy face, expecting at least an inquiry after Lael. He received merely a bow, and the words: "We will meet again."

Night was yet over the city, when Ali, having landed the Count, drew out of the gate with Nilo. The gladness of the King at being restored to his master can be easily fancied.

CHAPTER III
THE BLOODY HARVEST

In June, a few days after the completion of the enormous work begun by Mahommed on the Asometon promontory, out of a gate attached to the High Residence of Blacherne, familiarly known as the Caligaria, there issued a small troop of horsemen of the imperial military establishment.

The leader of this party—ten in all—was Count Corti. Quite a body of spectators witnessed the exit, and in their eyes he was the most gallant knight they had ever seen. They cheered him as, turning to the right after issuance from the gate, he plunged at a lively trot into the ravine at the foot of the wall, practically an immense natural fosse. "God and our Lady of Blacherne," they shouted, and continued shouting while he was in sight, notwithstanding he did not so much as shake the banderole on his lance in reply.

Of the Count's appearance this morning it is unnecessary to say more than that he was in the suit of light armor habitual to him, and as an indication of serious intent, bore, besides the lance, a hammer or battle-axe fixed to his saddle-bow, a curved sword considerably longer, though not so broad as a cimeter, a bow and quiver of arrows at his back, and a small shield or buckler over the quiver. The favorite chestnut Arab served him for mount, its head and neck clothed in flexible mail. The nine men following were equipped like himself in every particular, except that their heads were protected by close-fitting conical caps, and instead of armor on their legs, they wore flowing red trousers.

Of them it may be further remarked, their mode of riding, due to their short stirrups, was indicative of folk akin to the Bedouin of the Desert.

Upon returning from the last interview with Mahommed in the White Castle, the Count had subjected the crew of his galley to rigorous trial of fitness for land service. Nine of them he found excellent riders after their fashion, and selecting them as the most promising, he proceeded to instruct them in the use of the arms they were now bearing. His object in this small organization was a support to rush in after him rather than a battle front. That is, in a charge he was to be the lance's point, and they the broadening of the lance's blade; while he was engaged, intent on the foe before him, eight of them were to guard him right and left, and, as the exigencies of combat might demand, open and close in fan-like movement. The ninth man was a fighter in their rear. In the simple manoeuvring of this order of battle he had practised them diligently through the months. The skill attained was remarkable; and the drilling having been in the Hippodrome, open to the public, the concourse to see it had been encouraging.

In truth, the wager with Mahommed had supplied the Count with energy of body and mind. He studied the chances of the contest, knowing how swiftly it was coming, and believed it possible to defend the city successfully. At all events, he would do his best, and if the judgment were adverse, it should not be through default on his part.

The danger—and he discerned it with painful clearness—was in the religious dissensions of the Greeks; still he fancied the first serious blow struck by the Turks, the first bloodshed, would bring the factions together, if only for the common safety.

It is well worth while here to ascertain the views and feelings of the people whom Count Corti was thus making ready to defend. This may be said of them generally: It seemed impossible to bring them to believe the Sultan really intended war against the city.

"What if he does?" they argued. "Who but a young fool would think of such a thing? If he comes, we will show him the banner of the Blessed Lady from the walls."

If in the argument there was allusion to the tower on the Asometon heights, so tall one could stand on its lead-covered roof, and looking over the intermediate hills, almost see into Constantinople, the careless populace hooted at the exaggeration: "There be royal idiots as well as every-day idiots. Staring at us is one thing, shooting at us is another. Towers with walls thirty feet thick are not movable."

One day a report was wafted through the gates that a gun in the water battery of the new Turkish fort had sunk a passing ship. "What flag was the ship flying?" "The Venetian." "Ah, that settles it," the public cried. "The Sultan wants to keep the Venetians out of the Black Sea. The Turks and the Venetians have always been at war."

A trifle later intelligence came that the Sultan, lingering at Basch-Kegan, supposably because the air along the Bosphorus was better than the air at Adrianople, had effected a treaty by which the Podesta of Galata bound his city to neutrality; still the complacency of the Byzantines was in no wise disturbed. "Score one for the Genoese. It is good to hear of their beating the Venetians."

Occasionally a wanderer—possibly a merchant, more likely a spy—passing the bazaars of Byzantium, entertained the booth-keepers with stories of cannon being cast for the Sultan so big that six men tied together might be fired from them at once. The Greeks only jeered. Some said: "Oh, the

Mahound must be intending a salute for the man in the moon of Ramazan!" Others decided: "Well, he is crazier than we thought him. There are many hills on the road to Adrianople, and at the foot of every hill there is a bridge. To get here he must invent wings for his guns, and even then it will be long before they can be taught to fly."

At times, too, the old city was set agog with rumors from the Asiatic provinces opposite that the Sultan was levying unheard-of armies; he had half a million recruits already, but wanted a million. "Oh, he means to put a lasting quietus on Huniades and his Hungarians. He is sensible in taking so many men."

In compliment to the intelligence of the public, this obliviousness to danger had one fostering circumstance—the gates of the city on land and water stood open day and night.

"See," it was everywhere said, "the Emperor is not alarmed. Who has more at stake than he? He is a soldier, if he is an *azymite*. He keeps ambassadors with the Sultan—what for, if not to be advised?"

And there was a great deal in the argument.

At length the Greek ambassadors were expelled by Mahommed. It was while he lay at Basch-Kegan. They themselves brought the news. This was ominous, yet the public kept its spirits. The churches, notably Sancta Sophia, were more than usually crowded with women; that was all, for the gates not only remained open, but traffic went in and out of them unhindered—out even to the Turkish camp, the Byzantines actually competing with their neighbors of Galata in the furnishment of supplies. Nay, at this very period every morning a troop of the Imperial guard convoyed a wagon from Blacherne out to Basch-Kegan laden with the choicest food and wines; and to the officer receiving them the captain of the convoy invariably delivered himself: "From His Majesty, the Emperor of the Romans and Greeks, to the Lord Mahommed, Sultan of the Turks. Prosperity and long life to the Sultan."

If these were empty compliments, if the relations between the potentates were slippery, if war were hatching, what was the Emperor about?

Six months before the fort opposite the White Castle was begun, Constantine had been warned of Mahommed's projected movement against his capital. The warning was from Kalil Pacha; and whether Kalil was moved by pity, friendship, or avarice is of no moment; certain it is the Emperor acted upon the advice. He summoned a council, and proposed war; but was advised to send a protesting embassy to the enemy. A scornful answer was returned. Seeing the timidity of his cabinet, cast upon himself, he resolved to effect a policy, and accordingly expostulated, prayed, sent presents, offered tribute, and by such means managed to satisfy his advisers; yet all the time he was straining his resources in preparation.

In the outset, he forced himself to face two facts of the gravest import: first, of his people, those of age and thews for fighting were in frocks, burrowing in monasteries; next, the clergy and their affiliates were his enemies, many openly preferring a Turk to an *azymite*. A more discouraging prospect it is difficult to imagine. There was but one hope left him. Europe was full of professional soldiers. Perhaps the Pope had influence to send him a sufficient contingent. Would His Holiness interest himself so far? The brave Emperor despatched an embassy to Rome, promising submission to the Papacy, and praying help in Christ's name.

Meantime his agents dispersed themselves through the Aegean, buying provisions and arms, enginery, and war material of all kinds. This business kept his remnant of a navy occupied. Every few days a vessel would arrive with stores for the magazine under the Hippodrome. By the time the fort at Roumeli Hissar was finished, one of his anxieties was in a measure relieved. The other was more serious. Then the frequency with which he climbed the Tower of Isaac, the hours he passed there gazing wistfully southward down the mirror of the Marmora, became observable. The valorous, knightly heart, groaning under the humiliations of the haughty Turk, weary not less of the incapacity of his own people to perceive their peril, and arise heroically to meet it, found opportunity to meditate while he was pacing the lofty lookout, and struggling to descry the advance of the expected succor.

In this apology the reader who has wondered at the inaction of the Emperor what time the Sultan was perfecting his Asiatic communications is answered. There was nothing for him but a siege. To that alternative the last of the Romans was reduced. He could not promise himself enough of his own subjects to keep the gates, much less take the field.

The country around Constantinople was given to agriculture. During the planting season, and the growing, the Greek husbandmen received neither offence nor alarm from the Turks. But in June, when the emerald of the cornfields was turning to gold, herds of mules and cavalry horses began to ravage the fields, and the watchmen, hastening from their little huts on the hills to drive them out, were set upon by the soldiers and beaten. They complained to the Emperor, and he sent an embassy to the Sultan praying him to save the crops from ruin. In reply, Mahommed ordered the son of Isfendiar, a relative, to destroy the harvest. The peasants resisted, and not unsuccessfully. In the South, and in the fields near Hissar on the north, there were deaths on both sides. Intelligence of the affair coming to Constantine, he summoned Count Corti.

"The long expected has arrived," he said. "Blood has been shed. My people have been attacked and slain in their fields; their bodies lie out unburied. The war cannot be longer deferred. It is true the succors from the Holy Father have not arrived; but they are on the way, and until they come we must defend ourselves. Cold and indifferent my people have certainly been. Now I will make a last effort to arouse them. Go out toward Hissar, and recover the dead. Have the bodies brought in just as they are. I will expose them in the Hippodrome. Perhaps their bruises and blood may have an effect; if not, God help this Christian city. I will give you a force."

"Your Majesty," the Count replied, "such an expedition might provoke an advance upon the city before you are entirely prepared. Permit me to select a party from my own men." "As you choose. A guide will accompany you."

To get to the uplands, so to speak, over which, north of Galata, the road to Hissar stretched, Corti was conducted past the Cynegion and through the districts of Eyoub to the Sweet Waters of Europe, which he crossed by a bridge below the site of the present neglected country palace of the Sultan. Up on the heights he turned left of Pera, and after half an hour's rapid movement was trending northward parallel with the Bosphorus, reaches of which were occasionally visible through cleftings of the mountainous shore. Straw-thatched farmhouses dotted the hills and slopes, and the harvest spread right and left in cheerful prospect.

The adventurer had ample time to think; but did little of it, being too full of self-gratulation at having before him an opportunity to recommend himself to the Emperor, with a possibility of earning distinction creditable in the opinion of the Princess Irene.

At length an exclamation of his guide aroused him to action.

"The Turks, the Turks!"

"Where?"

"See that smoke."

Over a hilltop in his front, the Count beheld the sign of alarm crawling slowly into the sky.

"Here is a village—to our left, but"—

"Have done," said Corti, "and get me to the fire. Is there a nearer way than this?"

"Yes, under the hill yonder."

"Is it broken?"

"It narrows to a path, but is clear."

The Count spoke in Arabic to his followers, and taking the gallop, pushed the guide forward. Shortly a party of terror-stricken peasants ran down toward him.

"Why do you run? What is the matter?" he asked.

"Oh, the Turks, the Turks!"

"What of them? Stand, and tell me."

"We went to work this morning cutting corn, for it is now ripe enough. The Mahounds broke in on us. We were a dozen to their fifty or more. We only escaped, and they set fire to the field. O Christ, and the Most Holy Mother! Let us pass, or we too will be slain!"

"Are they mounted?"

"Some have horses, some are afoot."

"Where are they now?"

"In the field on the hill."

"Well, go to the village fast as you can, and tell the men there to come and pick up their dead. Tell them not to fear, for the Emperor has sent me to take care of them."

With that the Count rode on.

This was the sight presented him when he made the ascent: A wheat field sloping gradually to the northeast; fire creeping across it crackling, smoking, momentarily widening; through the cloud a company of Turkish soldiers halted, mostly horsemen, their arms glinting brightly in the noon sun; blackened objects, unmistakably dead men, lying here and there. Thus the tale of the survivors of the massacre was confirmed.

Corti gave his lance with the banderole on it to the guide. By direction his Berbers drove their lances into the earth that they might leave them standing, drew their swords, and brought their bucklers forward. Then he led them into the field. A few words more, directions probably, and he started toward the enemy, his followers close behind two and two, with a rear-guardsman. He allowed no outcry, but gradually increased the pace.

There were two hundred and more yards to be crossed, level, except the slope, and with only the moving line of fire as an impediment. The crop, short and thin, was no obstacle under the hoofs.

The Turks watched the movement herded, like astonished sheep. They may not have comprehended that they were being charged, or they may have despised the assailants on account of their inferiority in numbers, or they may have relied on the fire as a defensive wall; whatever the reason, they stood passively waiting.

When the Count came to the fire, he gave his horse the spur, and plunging into the smoke and through the flame full speed, appeared on the other side, shouting: "Christ and Our Lady of Blacherne!" His long sword flashed seemingly brighter of the passage just made. Fleckings of flame clung to the horses. What the battle-cry of the Berbers we may not tell. They screamed something un-Christian, echoes of the Desert. Then the enemy stirred; some drew their blades, some strung their bows; the footmen amongst them caught their javelins or half-spears in the middle, and facing to the rear, fled, and kept flying, without once looking over their shoulders.

One man mounted, and in brighter armor than the others, his steel cap surmounted with an immense white turban, a sparkling aigrette pinned to the turban, cimeter in hand, strove to form his companions—but it was too late. "Christ and our Lady of Blacherne!"—and with that Corti was in their midst; and after him, into the lane he opened, his Berbers drove pell-mell, knocking Turks from their saddles, and overthrowing horses—and there was cutting and thrusting, and wounds given, and souls rendered up through darkened eyes.

The killing was all on one side; then as a bowl splinters under a stroke, the Turkish mass flew apart, and went helter-skelter off, each man striving to take care of himself. The Berbers spared none of the overtaken.

Spying the man with the showy armor, the Count made a dash to get to him, and succeeded, for to say truth, he was not an unwilling foeman. A brief combat took place, scarcely more than a blow, and the Turk was disarmed and at mercy.

"Son of Isfendiar," said Corti, "the slaying these poor people with only their harvest knives for weapons was murder. Why should I spare your life?"

"I was ordered to punish them."

"By whom?"

"My Lord the Sultan."

"Do your master no shame. I know and honor him."

"Yesterday they slew our Moslems."

"They but defended their own.... You deserve death, but I have a message for the Lord Mahommed. Swear by the bones of the Prophet to deliver it, and I will spare you."

"If you know my master, as you say, he is quick and fierce of temper, and if I must die, the stroke may be preferable at your hand. Give me the message first."

"Well, come with me."

The two remained together until the flight and pursuit were ended; then, the fire reduced to patches for want of stalks to feed it, the Count led the way back to the point at which he entered the field. Taking his lance from the guide, he passed it to the prisoner.

"This is what I would have you do," he said. "The lance is mine. Carry it to your master, the Lord Mahommed, and say to him, Ugo, Count Corti, salute him, and prays him to look at the banderole, and fix it in his memory. He will understand the message, and be grateful for it. Now will you swear?"

The banderole was a small flag of yellow silk, with a red moon in the centre, and on the face of the moon a white cross. Glancing at it, the son of Isfendiar replied:

"Take off the cross, and you show me a miniature standard of the *Silihdars*, my Lord's guard of the Palace." Then looking the Count full in the face, he added: "Under other conditions I should salute you Mirza, Emir of the Hajj."

"I have given you my name and title. Answer."

"I will deliver the lance and message to my Lord—I swear it by the bones of the Prophet."

Scarcely had the Turk disappeared in the direction of Hissar, when a crowd of peasants, men and women, were seen coming timorously from the direction of the village. The Count rode to meet them, and as they were provided with all manner of litters, by his direction the dead Greeks were collected, and soon, with piteous lamentations, a funeral cortege was on the road moving slowly to Constantinople. Anticipating a speedy reappearance of the Turks, hostilities being now unavoidable, Count Corti despatched messengers everywhere along the Bosphorus, warning the farmers and villagers to let their fields go, and seek refuge in the city. So it came about that the escort of the murdered peasants momentarily increased until at the bridge over the Sweet Waters of Europe it became a column composed for the most part of women, children, and old men. Many of the women carried babies. The old men staggered under such goods as they could lay their hands on in haste. The able-bodied straggled far in the rear with herds of goats, sheep, and cattle; the air above the road rang with cries and prayers, and the road itself was sprinkled with tears. In a word, the movement was a flight.

Corti, with his Berbers, lingered in the vicinity of the field of fight watchful of the enemy. In the evening, having forwarded a messenger to the Emperor, he took stand at the bridge; and well enough, for about dusk a horde of Turkish militia swept down from the heights in search of plunder and belated victims. At the first bite of his sword, they took to their heels, and were not again seen.

By midnight the settlements and farmhouses of the up-country were abandoned; almost the entire district from Galata to Fanar on the Black Sea was reduced to ashes. The Greek Emperor had no longer a frontier or a province—all that remained to him was his capital.

Many of the fugitives, under quickening of the demonstration at the bridge, threw their burdens away; so the greater part of them at an early hour after nightfall appeared at the Adrianople gate objects of harrowing appeal, empty-handed, broken down, miserable.

Constantine had the funeral escort met at the gate by torch-bearers, and the sextons of the Blacherne Chapel. Intelligence of the massacre, and that the corpses of the harvesters would be conveyed to the Hippodrome for public exposure, having been proclaimed generally through the city, a vast multitude was also assembled at the gate. The sensation was prodigious.

There were twenty litters, each with a body upon it unwashed and in bloody garments, exactly as brought in. On the right and left of the litters the torchmen took their places. The sextons lit their long candles, and formed in front. Behind trudged the worn, dust-covered, wretched fugitives; and as they failed to realize their rescue, and that they were at last in safety, they did not abate their lamentations. When the innumerable procession passed the gate, and commenced its laborious progress along the narrow streets, seldom, if ever, has anything of the kind more pathetic and funereally impressive been witnessed.

Let be said what may, after all nothing shall stir the human heart like the faces of fellowmen done to death by a common enemy. There was no misjudgment of the power of the appeal in this instance. It is no exaggeration to say Byzantium was out assisting—so did the people throng the thoroughfares, block the street intersections, and look down from the windows and balconies. Afar they heard the chanting of the sextons, monotonous, yet solemnly effective; afar they saw the swaying candles and torches; and an awful silence signalized the approach of the pageant; but when it was up, and the bodies were borne past, especially when the ghastly countenances of the sufferers were under eye plainly visible in the red torchlight, the outburst of grief and rage in every form, groans, curses, prayers, was terrible, and the amazing voice, such by unity of utterance, went with the dead, and followed after them until at last the Hippodrome was reached. There the Emperor, on horseback, and with his court and guards, was waiting, and his presence lent nationality to the mournful spectacle.

Conducting the bearers of the litters to the middle of the oblong area, he bade them lay their burdens down, and summoned the city to the view.

"Let there be no haste," he said, "for, in want of their souls, the bruised bodies of our poor countrymen shall lie here all tomorrow, every gaping wound crying for vengeance. Then on the next day it will be for us to say what we will do—fight, fly, or surrender."

Through the remainder of the night the work of closing the gates and making them secure continued without cessation. The guards were strengthened at each of them, and no one permitted to pass out. Singular to say, a number of eunuchs belonging to the Sultan were caught and held. Some of the enraged Greeks insisted on their death; but the good heart of the Emperor prevailed, and the prisoners were escorted to their master. The embassy which went with them announced the closing of the gates.

"Since neither oaths, nor treaty, nor submission can secure peace, pursue your impious warfare"—thus Constantine despatched to Mahommed. "My trust is in God; if it shall please him to mollify your heart, I shall rejoice in the change; if he delivers the city in your hands, I submit without a murmur to his holy will. But until he shall pronounce between us, it is my duty to live and die in defence of my people." [Footnote: Gibbon]

Mahommed answered with a formal declaration of war.

It remains to say that the bodies of the harvesters were viewed as promised. They lay in a row near the Twisted Serpent, and the people passed them tearfully; in the night they were taken away and buried.

Sadder still, the result did not answer the Emperor's hope. The feeling, mixed of sorrow and rage, was loudly manifested; but it was succeeded by fear, and when the organization of companies was attempted, the exodus was shameful. Thousands fled, leaving about one hundred thousand behind, not to fight, but firm in the faith that Heaven would take care of the city.

After weeks of effort, five thousand Greeks took the arms offered them, and were enrolled.

CHAPTER IV
EUROPE ANSWERS THE CRY FOR HELP

A man in love, though the hero of many battles, shall be afraid in the presence of his beloved, and it shall be easier for him to challenge an enemy than to ask her love in return.

Count Corti's eagerness to face the lion in the gallery of the Cynegion had established his reputation in Constantinople for courage; his recent defence of the harvesters raised it yet higher; now his name was on every tongue.

His habit of going about in armor had in the first days of his coming subjected him to criticism; for the eyes before which he passed belonged for the most part to a generation more given to prospecting for bezants in fields of peace than the pursuit of glory in the ruggeder fields of war. But the custom was now accepted, and at sight of him, mounted and in glistening armor, even the critics smiled, and showered his head with silent good wishes, or if they spoke it was to say to each other: "Oh, that the Blessed Mother would send us more like him!" And the Count knew he had the general favor. We somehow learn such things without their being told us.

Up in the empyrean courtly circles his relations were quite as gratifying. The Emperor made no concealment of his partiality, and again insisted on bringing him to Blacherne.

"Your Majesty," the Count said one day, "I have no further need of my galley and its crew. I beg you to do with them as you think best."

Constantine received the offer gratefully.

"The galley is a godsend. I will order payment for it. Duke Notaras, the Grand Admiral, will agree with you about the price."

"If Your Majesty will permit me to have my way," the Count rejoined, "you will order the vessel into the harbor with the fleet, and if the result of the war is with Your Majesty, the Grand Admiral can arrange for the payment; if otherwise"—he smiled at the alternative—"I think neither Your Majesty nor myself will have occasion for a ship."

The galley was transferred from the Bay of Julian to anchorage in the Golden Horn. That night, speaking of the tender, the Emperor said to Phranza: "Count Corti has cast his lot with us. As I interpret him, he does not mean to survive our defeat. See that he be charged to select a bodyguard to accompany me in action."

"Is he to be Captain of the guard?"

"Yes."

The duty brought the Count to Blacherne. In a few days he had fifty men, including his nine Berbers.

These circumstances made him happy. He found peace of mind also in his release from Mahommed. Not an hour of the day passed without his silently thanking the Sultan for his magnanimity.

But no matter for rejoicing came to him like the privilege of freely attending the Princess Irene.

Not only was her reception-room open to him; whether she went to Blacherne or Sancta Sophia, he appeared in her train. Often when the hour of prayer arrived, she invited him as one of her household to accompany her to the apartment she had set apart for chapel exercises; and at such times he strove to be devout, but in taking her for his pattern of conduct— as yet he hardly knew when to arise or kneel, or cross himself—if his thoughts wandered from the Madonna and Child to her, if sometimes he fell to making comparisons in which the Madonna suffered as lacking beauty—nay, if not infrequently he caught himself worshipping the living woman at the foot of the altar rather than the divinity above it, few there were who would have been in haste to condemn him even in that day. There is nothing modern in the world's love of a lover.

By the treaty with Mahommed he was free to tell the Princess of his passion; and there were moments in which it seemed he must cast himself at her feet and speak; but then he would be seized with a trembling, his tongue would unaccountably refuse its office, and he would quiet himself with the weakling's plea—another time—to-morrow, to-morrow. And always upon the passing of the opportunity, the impulse being laid with so many of its predecessors in the graveyard of broken resolutions—every swain afraid keeps such a graveyard—always he sallied from her door eager for an enemy on whom to vent his vexation. "Ah," he would say, with prolonged emphasis upon the exclamation—"if Mahommed were only at the gate! Is he never coming?"

One day he dismounted at the Princess' door, and was ushered into the reception-room by Lysander. "I bring you good news," he said, in course of the conversation.

"What now?" she asked.

"Every sword counts. I am just from the Port of Blacherne, whither I accompanied the Grand Equerry to assist in receiving one John Grant, who has arrived with a following of Free Lances, mostly my own countrymen."

"Who is John Grant?"

"A German old in Eastern service; more particularly an expert in making and throwing hollow iron balls filled with inflammable liquid. On striking, the balls burst, after which the fire is unquenchable with water."

"Oh! our Greek fire rediscovered!"

"So he declares. His Majesty has ordered him the materials he asks, and that he go to work to-morrow getting a store of his missiles ready. The man declares also, if His Holiness would only proclaim a crusade against the Turks. Constantinople has not space on her walls to hold the volunteers who would hasten to her defence. He says Genoa, Venice, all Italy, is aroused and waiting."

"John Grant is welcome," the Princess returned; "the more so that His Holiness is slow."

Afterward, about the first of December, the Count again dismounted at her door with news.

"What is it now?" she inquired.

"Noble Princess, His Holiness has been heard from."

"At last?"

"A Legate will arrive to-morrow."

"Only a Legate! What is his name?"

"Isidore, Grand Metropolitan of Russia."

"Brings he a following?"

"No soldiers; only a suite of priests high and low."

"I see. He comes to negotiate. Alas!"

"Why alas?"

"Oh, the factions, the factions!" she exclaimed, disconsolately; then, seeing the Count still in wonder, she added: "Know you not that Isidore, familiarly called the Cardinal, was appointed Metropolitan of the Russian Greek Church by the Pope, and, rejected by it, was driven to refuge in Poland? What welcome can we suppose he will receive here?"

"Is he not a Greek?"

"Yes, truly; but being a Latin Churchman, the Brotherhoods hold him an apostate. His first demand will be to celebrate mass in Sancta Sophia. If the world were about shaking itself to pieces, the commotion would be but little greater than the breaking of things we will then hear. Oh, it is an ill wind which blows him to our gates!" Meantime the Hippodrome had been converted into a Campus Martius, where at all hours of the day the newly enlisted men were being drilled in the arms to which they were assigned; now as archers, now as slingers; now with balistas and catapults and arquebuses; now to the small artillery especially constructed for service on the walls. And as trade was at an end in the city, as in fact martial preparation occupied attention to the exclusion of business in the commercial sense, the ancient site was a centre of resort. Thither the Count hastened to work off the disheartenment into which the comments of the Princess had thrown him.

That same week, however, he and the loyal population of Constantinople in general, were cheered by a coming of real importance. Early one morning some vessels of war hove in sight down the Marmora. Their flags proclaimed them Christian. Simultaneously the lookouts at Point Demetrius reported a number of Turkish galleys plying to and fro up the Bosphorus. It was concluded that a naval battle was imminent. The walls in the vicinity of the Point were speedily crowded with spectators. In fact, the anxiety was great enough to draw the Emperor from his High Residence. Not doubting the galleys were bringing him stores, possibly reinforcements, he directed his small fleet in the Golden Horn to be ready to go to their assistance. His conjecture was right; yet more happily the Turks made no attempt upon them. Turning into the harbor, the strangers ran up the flags of Venice and Genoa, and never did they appear so beautiful, seen by Byzantines—never were they more welcome. The decks were crowded with helmed men who responded vigorously to the cheering with which they were saluted.

Constantine in person received the newcomers at the Port of Blacherne. From the wall over the gate the Princess Irene, with an escort of noble ladies, witnessed the landing.

A knight of excellent presence stepped from a boat, and announced himself.

"I am John Justiniani of Genoa," he said, "come with two thousand companions in arms to the succor of the most Christian Emperor Constantine. Guide me to him, I pray."

"The Emperor is here—I am he."

Justiniani kissed the hand extended to him, and returned with fervor:

"Christ and the Mother be praised! Much have I been disquieted lest we should be too late. Your Majesty, command me."

"Duke Notaras," said the Emperor, "assist this noble gentleman and his companions. When they are disembarked, conduct them to me. For the present I will lodge them in my residence." Then he addressed the Genoese: "Duke Notaras, High Admiral of the Empire, will answer your every demand. In God's name, and for the imperilled religion of our Redeeming Lord, I bid you welcome."

It seemed the waving of scarfs and white hands on the wall, and the noisy salutations of the people present, were not agreeable to the Duke; although coldly polite, he impressed Justiniani as an ill second to the stately but courteous Emperor.

At night there was an audience in the Very High Residence, and Justiniani assisted Phranza in the presentation of his companions; and though the banquet which shortly succeeded the audience may not, in the courses served or in its table splendors, have vied with those Alexis resorted to for the dazzlement of the chiefs of the first crusade, it was not entirely wanting in such particulars; for it has often happened, if the chronicles may be trusted, that the expiring light of great countries has lingered longest in their festive halls, just as old families have been known to nurture their pride in sparkling heirlooms, all else having been swept away. The failings on this occasion, if any there were, Constantine more than amended by his engaging demeanor. Soldier not less than Emperor, he knew to win the sympathy and devotion of soldiers. Of his foreign guests that evening many afterwards died hardly distinguishing between him and the Holy Cause which led them to their fate.

The table was long, and without head or foot. On one side, in the middle, the Emperor presided; opposite him sat the Princess Irene; and on their right and left, in gallant interspersion, other ladies, the wives and daughters of senators, nobles, and officials of the court, helped charm the Western chivalry.

And of the guests, the names of a few have been preserved by history, together with the commands to which they were assigned in the siege.

There was Andrew Dinia, under Duke Notaras, a captain of galleys.

There was the Venetian Contarino, intrusted with the defence of the Golden Grate.

There was Maurice Cataneo, a soldier of Genoa, commandant of the walls on the landward side between the Golden Gate and the Gate Selimbria.

There were two brothers, gentlemen of Genoa,

Paul Bochiardi and Antonin Troilus Bochiardi, defendants of the Adrianople Gate.

There was Jerome Minotte, Bayle of Venice, charged with safe keeping the walls between the Adrianople Gate and the Cerco Portas.

There was the artillerist, German John Grant, who, with Theodore Carystos, made sure of the Gate Charsias.

There was Leonardo de Langasco, another Genoese, keeper of the Wood Gate.

There was Gabriel Travisan; with four hundred other Venetians, he maintained the stretch of wall on the harbor front between Point Demetrius and the Port St. Peter.

There was Pedro Guiliani, the Spanish Consul, assigned to the guardianship of the wall on the sea side from Point Demetrius to the Port of Julian.

There also was stout Nicholas Gudelli; with the Emperor's brother, he commanded the force in reserve.

Now these, or the major part of them, may have been Free Lances; yet they did not await the motion of Nicholas, the dilatory Pope, and were faithful, and to-day exemplify the saying:

> "That men may rise on stepping-stones
> Of their dead selves to higher things."

CHAPTER V
COUNT CORTI RECEIVES A FAVOR

"Gracious Princess, the Italian, Count Corti, is at the door. He prays you to hear a request from him."

"Return, Lysander, and bring the Count."

It was early morning, with February in its last days.

The visitor's iron shoes clanked sharply on the marble floor of the reception room, and the absence of everything like ornament in his equipment bespoke preparation for immediate hard service.

"I hope the Mother is keeping you well," she said, presenting her hand to him.

With a fervor somewhat more marked than common, he kissed the white offering, and awaited her bidding.

"My attendants are gone to the chapel, but I will hear you—or will you lend us your presence at the service, and have the audience afterwards?"

"I am in armor, and my steed is at the door, and my men biding at the Adrianople Gate; wherefore, fair Princess, if it be your pleasure, I will present my petition now."

In grave mistrust, she returned:

"God help us, Count! I doubt you have something ill to relate. Since the good Gregory fled into exile to escape his persecutors, but more especially since Cardinal Isidore attempted Latin mass in Sancta Sophia, and the madman Gennadius so frightened the people with his senseless anathemas, [Footnote: The scene here alluded to by the Princess Irene is doubtless the one so vividly described by Gibbon as having taken place in Sancta Sophia, the 12th of December, 1452, being the mass celebrated by Cardinal Isidore in an attempt to reconcile the Latin and Greek factions.

Enumerating the consequences of the same futile effort at compromise, Von Hammer says: "Instead of uniting for the common defence, the Greeks and Latins fled, leaving the churches empty; the priests refused the sacrament to the dying who were not of their faith; the monks and nuns repudiated confessors who acknowledged the *henoticon* (decree ordaining the reunion of the two churches); a spirit of frenzy took possession of the convents; one *religieuse*, to the great scandal of all the faithful, adopted the faith and costume of the Mussulmans, eating meat and adoring the Prophet. Thus Lent passed." (Vol. II., p. 397.)

To the same effect we read in the Universal History of the Catholic Church (Vol. XXII., p. 103): "The religious who affected to surpass others in sanctity of life and purity of faith, following the advice of Gennadius and their spiritual advisers, as well as that of the preachers and laity of their party, condemned the decree of union, and anathematized those who approved or might approve it. The common people, sallying from the monasteries, betook themselves to the taverns; there flourishing glasses of wine, they reviled all who had consented to the union, and drinking in honor of an image of the Mother of God, prayed her to protect and defend the city against Mahomet, as she had formerly defended it against Chosroes and the Kagan. We will have nothing to do with assistance from the Latins or a union with them. Far from us be the worship of the *azymites*."] I have been beset with forebodings until I startle at my own thoughts. It were gentle, did you go to your request at once."

She permitted him to lead her to an armless chair, and, standing before her, he spoke with decision:

"Princess Irene, now that you have resolved finally to remain in the city, and abide the issue of the siege, rightly judging it an affair determinable by God, it is but saying the truth as I see it, that no one is more interested in what betides us from day to day than you; for if Heaven frowns upon our efforts at defence, and there comes an assault, and we are taken, the Conqueror, by a cruel law of war, has at disposal the property both public and private he gains, and every living thing as well. We who fight may die the death he pleases; you—alas, most noble and virtuous lady, my tongue refuses the words that rise to it for utterance!"

The rose tints in her cheeks faded, yet she answered: "I know what you would say, and confess it has appalled me. Sometimes it tempts me to fly while yet I can; then I remember I am a Palaeologus. I remember also my kinsman the Emperor is to be sustained in the trial confronting him. I remember too the other women, high and low, who will stay and share the fortunes of their fighting husbands and brothers. If I have less at stake than they, Count Corti, the demands of honor are more rigorous upon me."

The count's eyes glowed with admiration, but next moment the light in them went out.

"Noble lady," he began, "I hope it will not be judged too great a familiarity to say I have some days been troubled on your account. I have feared you might be too confident of our ability to beat the enemy. It seems my duty to warn you of the real outlook that you may permit us to provide for your safety while opportunities favor."

"For my flight, Count Corti?"

"Nay, Princess Irene, your retirement from the city."

She smiled at the distinction he made, but replied:

"I will hear you, Count."

"It is for you to consider, O Princess—if reports of the Sultan's preparation are true—this assault in one feature at least will be unparalleled. The great guns for which he has been delaying are said to be larger than ever before used against walls. They may destroy our defences at once; they may command all the space within those defences; they may search every hiding-place; the uncertainties they bring with them are not to be disregarded by the bravest soldier, much less the unresisting classes.... In the next place, I think it warrantable from the mass of rumors which has filled the month to believe the city will be assailed by a force much greater than was ever drawn together under her walls. Suffer me to refer to them, O Princess... The Sultan is yet at Adrianople assembling his army. Large bodies of footmen are crossing the Hellespont at Gallipolis and the Bosphorus at Hissar; in the region of Adrianople the country is covered with hordes of horsemen speaking all known tongues and armed with every known weapon—Cossacks from the north, Arabs from the south, Koords and Tartars from the east, Roumanians and Slavs from beyond the Balkans. The roads from the northwest are lined with trains bringing supplies and siege-machinery. The cities along the shores of the Black Sea have yielded to Mahommed; those which defied him are in ruins. An army is devastating Morea. The brother whom His Majesty the Emperor installed ruler there is dead or a wanderer, no man can say in what parts. Assistance cannot be expected from him. Above us, far as the sea, the bays are crowded with ships of all classes; four hundred hostile sail have been counted from the hill-tops. And now that there is no longer a hope of further aid from the Christians of Europe, the effect of the news upon our garrison is dispiriting. Our garrison! Alas, Princess, with the foreigners come to our aid, it is not sufficient to man the walls on the landward side alone."

"The picture is gloomy, Count, but if you have drawn it to shake my purpose, it is not enough. I have put myself in the hands of the Blessed Mother. I shall stay, and be done with as God orders."

Again the Count's face glowed with admiration.

"I thought as much, O Princess," he said warmly; "yet it seemed to me a duty to advise you of the odds against us; and now, the duty done, I pray you hear me as graciously upon another matter.... Last night, seeing the need of information of the enemy, I besought His Majesty to allow me to ride toward Adrianople. He consented, and I set out immediately; but before going, before bidding you adieu, noble Princess and dear lady, I have a prayer to offer you."

He hesitated; then plucking courage from the embarrassment of silence, went on:

"Dear lady, your resolution to stay and face the dangers of the siege and assault fills me with alarm for your safety."

He cast himself upon his knees, and stretched his hands to her.

"Give me permission to protect you. I devote my sword to you, and the skill of my hands—my life, my soul. Let me be your knight."

She arose, but he continued:

"Some day, deeds done for your country and religion may give me courage to speak more boldly of what I feel and hope; but now I dare go no further than ask what you have just heard. Let me be your protector and knight through the perils of the siege at least."

The Princess was pleased with the turn his speech had taken. She thought rapidly. A knight in battle, foremost in the press, her name a conquering cry on his lips were but the constituents of a right womanly ambition. She answered:

"Count Corti, I accept thy offer."

Taking the hand she extended, he kissed it reverently, and said:

"I am happy above other men. Now, O Princess, give me a favor—a glove, a scarf—something I may wear, to prove me thy knight."

She took from her neck a net of knitted silk, pinkish in hue, and large enough for a kerchief or waist sash.

"If I go about this gift," she said, her face deeply suffused, "in a way to provoke a smile hereafter; if in placing it around thy neck with my own hands"—with the words, she bent over him, and dropped the net outside the hood so the ends hung loosely down his breast—"I overstep any rule of modesty, I pray you will not misunderstand me. I am thinking of my country, my kinsman, of religion and God, and the service even unto noble deeds thou mayst do them. Rise, Count Corti. In the ride before thee now, in the perils to come, thou shalt have my prayers."

The Count arose, but afraid to trust himself in further speech, he carried her hand to his lips again, and with a simple farewell, hurried out, and mounting his horse rode at speed for the Adrianople Gate.

Four days after, he reentered the gate, bringing a prisoner, and passing straight to the Very High Residence, made report to the Emperor, Justiniani and Duke Notaras in council.

"I have been greatly concerned for you, Count," said Constantine; "and not merely because a good sword can be poorly spared just now."

The imperial pleasure was unfeigned.

"Your Majesty's grace is full reward for my performance," the Count replied, and rising from the salutation, he began his recital.

"Stay," said the Emperor, "I will have a seat brought that you may be at ease."

Corti declined: "The Arabs have a saying, Your Majesty—'A nest for a setting bird, a saddle for a warrior.' The jaunt has but rested me, and there was barely enough danger in it.... The Turk is an old acquaintance. I have lived with him, and been his guest in house and tent, and as a comrade tempted Providence at his side under countless conditions, until I know his speech and usages, himself scarcely better. My African Berbers are all Mohammedans who have performed the Pilgrimage. One of them is a muezzin by profession; and if he can but catch sight of the sun, he will never miss the five hours of prayer. None of them requires telling the direction to Mecca.... I issued from Your Majesty's great gate about the third hour, and taking the road to Adrianople, journeyed till near midday before meeting a human being. There were farms and farmhouses on my right and left, and the fields had been planted in good season; but the growing grain was wasted; and when I sought the houses to have speech with their tenants they were forsaken. Twice we were driven off by the stench of bodies rotting before the doors."

"Greeks?"

"Greeks, Your Majesty.... There were wild hogs in the thickets which fled at sight of us, and vultures devouring the corpses."

"Were there no other animals, no horses or oxen?" asked Justiniani.

"None, noble Genoese—none seen by us, and the swine were spared, I apprehend, because their meat is prohibited to the children of Islam.... At length Hadifah, whom I have raised to be a Sheik—Your Majesty permitting—and whose eyes discover the small things with which space is crowded as he were a falcon making circles up near the sun—Hadifah saw a man in the reeds hiding; and we pursued the wretch, and caught him, and he too was a Greek; and when his fright allowed him to talk, he told us a band of strange people, the like of whom he had never seen, attacked his hut, burned it, carried off his goats and she buffaloes; and since that hour, five weeks gone, he had been hunting for his wife and three girl-children. God be merciful to them! Of the Turks he could tell nothing except that now, everything of value gone, they too had disappeared. I gave the poor man a measure of oaten cakes, and left him to his misery. God be merciful to him also!"

"Did you not advise him to come to me?"

"Your Majesty, he was a husband and father seeking his family; with all humility, what else is there for him to do?"

"I give your judgment credit, Count. There is nothing else."

"I rode on till night, meeting nobody, friend or foe—on through a wide district, lately inhabited, now a wilderness. The creatures of the Sultan had passed through it, and there was fire in their breath. We discovered a dried-up stream, and by sinking in its bed obtained water for our horses. There, in a hollow, we spent the night.... Next morning, after an hour's ride, we met a train of carts drawn by oxen. The groaning and creaking of the distraught wheels warned me of the encounter before the advance guard of mounted men, quite a thousand strong, were in view. I did not draw rein"—

"What!" cried Justiniani, astonished. "With but a company of nine?"

The Count smiled.

"I crave your pardon, gallant Captain. In my camp the night before, I prepared my Berbers for the meeting."

"By the bones of the saints, Count Corti, thou dost confuse me the more! With such odds against thee, what preparations were at thy command?"

"'There was never amulet like a grain of wit in a purse under thy cap.' Good Captain, the saying is not worse of having proceeded from a Persian. I told my followers we were likely at any moment to be overtaken by a force too strong for us to fight; but instead of running away, we must meet them heartily, as friends enlisted in the same cause; and if they asked whence we were, we must be sure of agreement in our reply. I was to be a Turk; they, Egyptians from west of the Nile. We had come in by the new fortress opposite the White Castle, and were going to the mighty Lord Mahommed in Adrianople. Beyond that, I bade them be silent, leaving the entertainment of words to me."

The Emperor and Justiniani laughed, but Notaras asked: "If thy Berbers are Mohammedans, as thou sayest, Count Corti, how canst thou rely on them against Mohammedans?"

"My Lord the High Admiral may not have heard of the law by which, if one Arab kills another, the relatives of the dead man are bound to kill him, unless there be composition. So I had merely to remind Hadifah and his companions of the Turks we slew in the field near Basch-Kegan."

Corti continued: "After parley with the captain of the advance guard, I was allowed to ride on; and coming to the train, I found the carts freighted with military engines and tools for digging trenches and fortifying camps. There were hundreds of them, and the drivers were a multitude. Indeed, Your Majesty, from head to foot the caravan was miles in reach, its flanks well guarded by groups of horsemen at convenient intervals."

This statement excited the three counsellors.

"After passing the train," the Count was at length permitted to resume, "my way was through bodies of troops continuously—all irregulars. It must have been about three o'clock in the afternoon when I came upon the most surprising sight. Much I doubt if ever the noble Captain Justiniani, with all his experience, can recall anything like it.

"First there was a great company of pioneers with tools for grading the hills and levelling the road; then on a four-wheeled carriage two men stood beating a drum; their sticks looked like the enlarged end of a galley oar. The drum responded to their blows in rumbles like dull thunder from distant clouds. While I sat wondering why they beat it, there came up next sixty oxen yoked in pairs. Your Majesty can in fancy measure the space they covered. On the right and left of each yoke strode drivers with sharpened goads, and their yelling harmonized curiously with the thunder of the drum. The straining of the brutes was pitiful to behold. And while I wondered yet more, a log of bronze was drawn toward me big at one end as the trunk of a great plane tree, and so long that thirty carts chained together as one wagon, were required to support it laid lengthwise; and to steady the piece on its rolling bed, two hundred and fifty stout laborers kept pace with it unremittingly watchful. The movement was tedious, but at last I saw"—

"A cannon!" exclaimed the Genoese.

"Yes, noble Captain, the gun said to be the largest ever cast."

"Didst thou see any of the balls?"

"Other carts followed directly loaded with gray limestones chiselled round; and to my inquiry what the stones were for, I was told they were bullets twelve spans in circumference, and that the charge of powder used would cast them a mile."

The inquisitors gazed at each other mutely, and their thoughts may be gathered from the action of the Emperor. He touched a bell on a table, and to Phranza, who answered the call, he said: "Lord Chamberlain, have two men well skilled in the construction of walls report to me in the morning. There is work for them which they must set about at once. I will furnish the money." [Footnote: Before the siege by the Turks, two monks, Manuel Giagari and Neophytus of Rhodes, were charged with repairing the walls, but they buried the sums intrusted to them for these works; and in the pillage of the city seventy thousand pieces of gold thus advanced by the Emperor were unearthed.—VON HAMMER, Vol. II., p. 417.]

"I have but little more of importance to engage Your Majesty's attention.... Behind the monster cannon, two others somewhat smaller were brought up in the same careful manner. I counted seventeen pieces all brass, the least of them exceeding in workmanship and power the best in the Hippodrome."

"Were there more?" Justiniani asked.

"Many more, brave Captain, but ancient, and unworthy mention.... The day was done when, by sharp riding, I gained the rear of the train. At sunrise on the third day, I set out in return.... I have a prisoner whom this august council may examine with profit. He will, at least, confirm my report."

"Who is he?"

"The captain of the advance guard."

"How came you by him?"

"Your Majesty, I induced him to ride a little way with me, and at a convenient time gave his bridle rein to Hadifah. In his boyhood the Sheik was trained to leading camels, and he assures me it is much easier to lead a horse."

The sally served to lighten the sombre character of the Count's report, and in the midst of the merriment, he was dismissed. The prisoner was then brought in, and put to question; next day the final preparation for the reception of Mahommed was begun.

With a care equal to the importance of the business, Constantine divided the walls into sections, beginning on the landward side of the Golden Gate or Seven Towers, and ending at the Cynegion. Of the harbor front he made one division, with the Grand Gate of Blacherne and the Acropolis or Point Serail for termini; from Point Serail to the Seven Towers he stationed patrols and lookouts, thinking the sea and rocks sufficient to discourage assault in that quarter.

His next care was the designation of commandants of the several divisions. The individuals thus honored have been already mentioned; though it may be well to add how the Papal Legate, Cardinal Isidore, doffing his frock and donning armor, voluntarily accepted chief direction along the harbor—an example of martial gallantry which ought to have shamed the lukewarm Greeks morosely skulking in their cells.

Shrewdly anticipating a concentration of effort against the Gate St. Romain, and its two auxiliary towers, Bagdad and St. Romain, the former on the right hand and the latter on the left, he assigned Justiniani to its defence.

Upon the walls, and in the towers numerously garnishing them, the gallant Emperor next brought up his guns and machines, with profuse supplies of missiles.

Then, after flooding the immense ditch, he held a review in the Hippodrome, whence the several detachments marched to their stations.

Riding with his captains, and viewing the walls, now gay with banners and warlike tricking, Constantine took heart, and told how Amurath, the peerless warrior, had dashed his Janissaries against them, and rued the day.

"Is this boy Mahommed greater than his father?" he asked.

"God knows," Isidore responded, crossing himself breast and forehead.

And well content, the cavalcade repassed the ponderous Gate St. Romain. All that could be done had been done. There was nothing more but to wait.

CHAPTER VI
MAHOMMED AT THE GATE ST. ROMAIN

In the city April seemed to have borrowed from the delays of Mahommed; never month so slow in coming. At last, however, its first day, dulled by a sky all clouds, and with winds from the Balkans.

The inertness of the young Sultan was not from want of will or zeal. It took two months to drag his guns from Adrianople; but with them the army moved, and as it moved it took possession, or rather covered the land. At length, he too arrived, bringing, as it were, the month with him; and then he lost no more time.

About five miles from the walls on the south or landward side, he drew his hordes together in the likeness of a line of battle, and at a trumpet call they advanced in three bodies simultaneously. So a tidal wave, far extending, broken, noisy, terrible, rises out of the deep, and rolls upon a shore of stony cliffs.

Near ten o'clock in the forenoon of the sixth of April the Emperor mounted the roof of the tower of St. Romain, mentioned as at the left of the gate bearing the same name. There were with him Justiniani, the Cardinal Isidore, John Grant, Phranza, Theophilus Palaeologus, Duke Notaras, and a number of inferior persons native and foreign. He had come to see all there was to be seen of the Turks going into position.

The day was spring-like, with just enough breeze to blow the mists away.

The reader must think of the roof as an immense platform accessible by means of a wooden stairway in the interior of the tower, and battlemented on the four sides, the merlons of stone in massive blocks, and of a height to protect a tall man, the embrasures requiring banquettes to make them serviceable. In arrangement somewhat like a ship's battery, there are stoutly framed arbalists and mangonels on the platform, and behind them, with convenient spaces between, arquebuses on tripods, cumbrous catapults, and small cannon on high axles ready for wheeling into position between the merlons. Near each machine its munitions lie in order. Leaning against the walls there are also spears, javelins, and long and cross bows; while over the corner next the gate floats an imperial standard, its white field emblazoned with the immemorial Greek cross in gold. The defenders of the tower are present; and as they are mostly Byzantines, their attitudes betray much more than cold military respect, for they are receiving the Emperor, whom they have been taught to regard worshipfully.

They study him, and take not a little pride in observing that, clad in steel cap-a-pie, he in no wise suffers by comparison with the best of his attendants, not excepting Justiniani, the renowned Genoese captain. Not more to see than be seen, the visor of his helmet is raised; and stealing furtive glances at his countenance, noble by nature, but just now more than ordinarily inspiring, they are better and stronger for what they read in it.

On the right and left the nearest towers obstruct the view of the walls in prolongation; but southward the country spreads before the party a campania rolling and fertile, dotted with trees scattered and in thin groves, and here and there an abandoned house. The tender green of vegetation upon the slopes reminds those long familiar with them that grass is already invading what were lately gardens and cultivated fields. Constantine makes the survey in silence, for he knows how soon even the grass must disappear. Just beyond the flooded ditch at the foot of the first or outward wall is a road, and next beyond the road a cemetery crowded with tombs and tombstones, and brown and white mausolean edifices; indeed, the chronicles run not back to a time when that marginal space was unallotted to the dead. From the far skyline the eyes of the fated Emperor drop to the cemetery, and linger there.

Presently one of his suite calls out: "Hark! What sound is that?"

They all give attention.

"It is thunder."

"No—thunder rolls. This is a beat."

Constantine and Justiniani remembered Count Corti's description of the great drum hauled before the artillery train of the Turks, and the former said calmly:

"They are coming."

Almost as he spoke the sunlight mildly tinting the land in the farness seemed to be troubled, and on the tops of the remote hillocks there appeared to be giants rolling them up, as children roll snow-balls—and the movement was toward the city.

The drum ceased not its beating or coming. Justiniani by virtue of his greater experience, was at length able to say:

"Your Majesty, it is here in front of us; and as this Gate St. Romain marks the centre of your defences, so that drum marks the centre of an advancing line, and regulates the movement from wing to wing."

"It must be so, Captain; for see—there to the left—those are bodies of men."

"And now, Your Majesty, I hear trumpets."

A little later some one cried out:

"Now I hear shouting."

And another: "I see gleams of metal."

Ere long footmen and horsemen were in view, and the Byzantines, brought to the wall by thousands, gazed and listened in nervous wonder; for look where they might over the campania, they saw the enemy closing in upon them, and heard his shouting, and the neighing of horses, the blaring of horns, and the palpitant beating of drums.

"By our Lady of Blacherne," said the Emperor, after a long study of the spectacle, "it is a great multitude, reaching to the sea here on our left, and, from the noise, to the Golden Horn on our right; none the less I am disappointed. I imagined much splendor of harness and shields and banners, but see only blackness and dust. I cannot make out amongst them one Sultanic flag. Tell me, most worthy John Grant—it being reported that thou hast great experience combating with and against these hordes—tell me if this poverty of appearance is usual with them."

The sturdy German, in a jargon difficult to follow, answered: "These at our left are the scum of Asia. They are here because they have nothing; their hope is to better their condition, to return rich, to exchange ragged turbans for crowns, and goatskin jackets for robes of silk. Look, Your Majesty, the tombs in front of us are well kept; to-morrow if there be one left standing, it will have been rifled. Of the lately buried there will not be a ring on a finger or a coin under a tongue. Oh, yes, the ghouls will look better next week! Only give them time to convert the clothes they will strip from the dead into fresh turbans. But when the Janissaries come Your Majesty will not be disappointed. See—their advance guard now—there on the rising ground in front of the gate."

There was a swell of ground to the right of the gate rather than in front of it, and as the party looked thither, a company of horsemen were seen riding slowly but in excellent order, and the sheen of their arms and armor silvered the air about them. Immediately other companies deployed on the right and left of the first one; then the thunderous drum ceased; whereat, from the hordes out on the campania, brought to a sudden standstill, detachments dashed forward at full speed, and dismounting, began digging a trench.

"Be this Sultan like or unlike his father, he is a soldier. He means to cover his army, and at the same time enclose us from sea to harbor. To-morrow, my Lord, only high-flying hawks can communicate with us from the outside."

This, from Justiniani to the Emperor, was scarcely noticed, for behind the deploying Janissaries, there arose an outburst of music in deep volume, the combination of clarions and cymbals so delightful to warriors of the East; at the same instant a yellow flag was displayed. Then old John Grant exclaimed:

"The colors of the *Silihdars!* Mahommed is not far away. Nay, Your Majesty, look—the Sultan himself!"

Through an interval of the guard, a man in chain mail shooting golden sparkles, helmed, and with spear in hand and shield at his back, trotted forth, his steed covered with flowing cloths. Behind him appeared a suite mixed of soldiers and civilians, the former in warlike panoply, the latter in robes and enormous turbans. Down the slope the foremost rider led as if to knock at the gate. On the tower the cannon were loaded, and run into the embrasures.

"Mahommed, saidst thou, John Grant?"

"Mahommed, Your Majesty."

"Then I call him rash; but as we are not ashamed of our gates and walls, let him have his look in peace.... Hear you, men, let him look, and go in peace."

The repetition was in restraint of the eager gunners.

Further remark was cut short by a trumpet sounded at the foot of the tower. An officer peered over the wall, and reported: "Your Majesty, a knight just issued from the gate is riding forth. I take him to be the Italian, Count Corti."

Constantine became a spectator of what ensued.

Ordinarily the roadway from the country was carried over the deep moat in front of the Gate St. Romain by a floor of stout timbers well balustraded at the sides, and resting on brick piers. Of the bridge nothing now remained but a few loose planks side by side ready to be hastily snatched from their places. To pass them afoot was a venture; yet Count Corti, when the Emperor looked at him from the height, was making the crossing mounted, and blowing a trumpet as he went.

"Is the man mad?" asked the Emperor, in deep concern.

"Mad? No, he is challenging the Mahounds to single combat; and, my lords and gentlemen, if he be skilful as he is bold, then, by the Three Kings of Cologne, we will see some pretty work in pattern for the rest of us."

Thus Grant replied.

Corti made the passage safely, and in the road beyond the moat halted, and drove the staff of his banderole firmly in the ground. A broad opening through the cemetery permitted him to see and be seen by the Turks, scarcely a hundred yards away. Standing in his stirrups, he sounded the trumpet again—a clear call ringing with defiance.

Mahommed gave over studying the tower and deep-sunken gate, and presently beckoned to his suite.

"What is the device on yon pennon?" he asked.

"A moon with a cross on its face."

"Say you so?"

Twice the defiance was repeated, and so long the young Sultan, sat still, his countenance unusually grave. He recognized the Count; only he thought of him by the dearer Oriental name, Mirza. He knew also how much more than common ambition there was in the blatant challenge—that it was a reminder of the treaty between them, and, truly interpreted, said, in effect: "Lo, my Lord! she is well, and for fear thou judge me unworthy of her, send thy bravest to try me." And he hesitated—an accident might quench the high soul. Alas, then, for the Princess Irene in the day of final assault! Who would deliver her to him? The hordes, and the machinery, all the mighty preparation, were, in fact, less for conquest and glory than love. Sore the test had there been one in authority to say to him: "She is thine, Lord Mahommed; thine, so thou take her, and leave the city."

A third time the challenge was delivered, and from the walls a taunting cheer descended. Then the son of Isfendiar, recognizing the banderole, and not yet done with chafing over his former defeat, pushed through the throng about Mahommed, and prayed:

"O my Lord, suffer me to punish yon braggart."

Mahommed replied: "Thou hast felt his hand already, but go—I commend thee to thy houris."

He settled in his saddle smiling. The danger was not to the Count.

The arms, armor, weapons, and horse-furniture of the Moslem were identical with the Italian's; and it being for the challenged party to determine with what the duel should be fought, whether with axe, sword, lance or bow, the son of Isfendiar chose the latter, and made ready while advancing. The Count was not slow in imitating him.

Each held his weapon—short for saddle service—in the left hand, the arrow in place, and the shield on the left forearm.

No sooner had they reached the open ground in the cemetery than they commenced moving in circles, careful to keep the enemy on the shield side at a distance of probably twenty paces. The spectators became silent. Besides the skill which masters in such affrays should possess, they were looking for portents of the result.

Three times the foemen encircled each other with shield guard so well kept that neither saw an opening to attack; then the Turk discharged his arrow, intending to lodge it in the shoulder of the other's horse, the buckling attachments of the neck mail being always more or less imperfect. The Count interposed his shield, and shouted in Osmanli: "Out on thee, son of Isfendiar! I am thy antagonist, not my horse. Thou shalt pay for the cowardice."

He then narrowed the circle of his movement, and spurring full speed, compelled the Turk to turn on a pivot so reduced it was almost a halt. The exposure while taking a second shaft from the quiver behind the right shoulder was dangerously increased. "Beware!" the Count cried again, launching his arrow through the face opening of the hood.

The son of Isfendiar might never attain his father's Pachalik. There was not voice left him for a groan. He reeled in his saddle, clutching the empty air, then tumbled to the earth.

The property of the dead man, his steed, arms, and armor, were lawful spoils; but without heeding them, the Count retired to his banderole, and, amidst the shouts of the Greeks on the walls and towers, renewed the challenge. A score of chiefs beset the Sultan for permission to engage the insolent *Gabour.*

To an Arab Sheik, loudest in importunity, he said: "What has happened since yesterday to dissatisfy thee with life?"

The Sheik raised a lance with a flexible shaft twenty feet in length, made of a cane peculiar to the valley of the Jordan, and shaking it stoutly, replied:

"Allah, and the honor of my tribe!"

Perceiving the man's reliance in his weapon, Mahommed returned: "How many times didst thou pray yesterday?"

"Five times, my Lord."

"And to-day?"

"Twice."

"Go, then; but as yon champion hath not a lance to put him on equality with thee, he will be justified in taking to the sword."

The Sheik's steed was of the most precious strain of El-Hejaz; and sitting high in the saddle, a turban of many folds on his head, a striped robe drawn close to the waist, his face thin, coffee-colored, hawk-nosed, and lightning-eyed, he looked a king of the desert. Galloping down on the Christian, he twirled the formidable lance dextrously, until it seemed not more than a stalk of dried papyrus.

The Count beheld in the performance a trick of the *djerid* he had often practised with Mahommed. Uncertain if the man's robe covered armor, he met him with an arrow, and seeing it fall off harmless, tossed the bow on his back, drew sword, and put his horse in forward movement, caracoling right and left to disturb the enemy's aim. Nothing could be more graceful than this action.

Suddenly the Sheik stopped playing, and balancing the lance overhead, point to the foe, rushed with a shrill cry upon him. Corti's friends on the tower held their breath; even the Emperor said: "It is too unequal. God help him!" At the last moment, however—the moment of the thrust—changing his horse to the right, the Count laid himself flat upon its side, under cover of his shield. The thrust, only a little less quick, passed him in the air, and before the Sheik could recover or shorten his weapon, the trained foeman was within its sweep. In a word, the Arab was at mercy. Riding with him side by side, hand on his shoulder, the Count shouted: "Yield thee!"

"Dog of a Christian, never! Do thy worst."

The sword twirled once—a flash—then it descended, severing the lance in front of the owner's grip. The fragment fell to the earth.

"Now yield thee!"

The Sheik drew rein.

"Why dost thou not kill me?"

"I have a message for thy master yonder, the Lord Mahommed."

"Speak it then."

"Tell him he is in range of the cannon on the towers, and only the Emperor's presence there restrains the gunners. There is much need for thee to haste."

"Who art thou?"

"I am an Italian knight who, though thy Lord's enemy, hath reason to love him. Wilt thou go?"

"I will do as thou sayest."

"Alight, then. Thy horse is mine."

"For ransom?"

"No."

The Sheik dismounted grumblingly, and was walking off when the cheering of the Greeks stung him to the soul.

"A chance—O Christian, another chance—to-day—to-morrow!"

"Deliver the message; it shall be as thy Lord may then appoint. Bestir thyself."

The Count led the prize to the banderole, and flinging the reins over it, faced the gleaming line of Janissaries once more, trumpet at mouth. He saw the Sheik salute Mahommed; then the attendants closed around them. "A courteous dog, by the Prophet!" said the Sultan. "In what tongue did he speak?"

"My Lord, he might have been bred under my own tent."

The Sultan's countenance changed.

"Was there not more of his message?"

He was thinking of the Princess Irene.

"Yes, my Lord."

"Repeat it."

"He will fight me again to-day or to-morrow, as my Lord may appoint— and I want my horse. Without him, El-Hejaz will be a widow."

A red spot appeared on Mahommed's forehead.

"Begone!" he cried angrily. "Seest thou not, O fool, that when we take the city we will recover thy horse? Fight thou shalt not, for in that day I shall have need of thee."

Thereupon he bade them open for him, and rode slowly back up the eminence, and when he disappeared Corti was vainly sounding his trumpet.

The two horses were led across the dismantled bridge, and into the gate.

"Heaven hath sent me a good soldier," said the Emperor to the Count, upon descending from the tower.

Then Justiniani asked: "Why didst thou spare thy last antagonist?"

Corti answered truthfully.

"It was well done," the Genoese returned, offering his hand.

"Ay," said Constantine, cordially, "well done. But mount now, and ride with us."

"Your Majesty, a favor first.... A man is in the road dead. Let his body be placed on a bier, and carried to his friends."

"A most Christian request! My Lord Chamberlain, attend to it."

The cavalcade betook itself then to other parts, the better to see the disposition of the Turks; and everywhere on the landward side it was the same—troops in masses, and intrenchments in progress. Closing the inspection at set of sun, the Emperor beheld the sea and the Bosphorus in front of the Golden Horn covered with hundreds of sails.

"The leaguer is perfected," said the Genoese.

"And the issue with God," Constantine replied. "Let us to Hagia St. Sophia."

CHAPTER VII
THE GREAT GUN SPEAKS

The first sufficient gleam of light next morning revealed to the watchmen on the towers an ominous spectacle. Through the night they had heard a medley of noises peculiar to a multitude at work with all their might; now, just out of range of their own guns, they beheld a continuous rampart of fresh earth grotesquely spotted with marbles from the cemetery.

In no previous siege of the Byzantine capital was there reference to such a preliminary step. To the newly enlisted, viewing for the first time an enemy bodily present, it seemed like the world being pared down to the smallest dimensions; while their associate veterans, to whom they naturally turned for comfort, admitted an appreciable respect for the Sultan. Either he had a wise adviser, they said, or he was himself a genius.

Noon—and still the workmen seemed inexhaustible—still the rampart grew in height—still the hordes out on the campania multiplied, and the horizon line west of the Gate St. Romain was lost in the increasing smoke of a vast bivouac.

Nightfall—and still the labor.

About midnight, judging by the sounds, the sentinels fancied the enemy approached nearer the walls; and they were not mistaken. With the advent of the second morning, here and there at intervals, ill-defined mounds of earth were seen so much in advance of the intrenched line that, by a general order, a fire of stones and darts was opened upon them; and straightway bodies of bowmen and slingers rushed forward, and returned the fire, seeking to cover the mound builders. This was battle.

Noon again—and battle.

In the evening—battle.

The advantage of course was with the besieged.

The work on the mounds meanwhile continued, while the campania behind the intrenchment was alive with a creaking of wheels burdened by machinery, and a shouting of ox-drivers; and the veterans on the walls said the enemy was bringing up his balistas and mangonels.

The third morning showed the mounds finished, and crowned with mantelets, behind which, in working order and well manned, every sort of engine known in sieges from Alexander to the Crusaders was in operation. Thenceforward, it is to be observed, the battle was by no means one-sided.

In this opening there was no heat or furore of combat; it was rather the action of novices trying their machines, or, in modern artillery parlance, finding the range. Many minutes often intervened between shots, and as the preliminary object on the part of the besiegers was to destroy the merlons sheltering the warders, did a stone strike either wall near the top, the crash was saluted by cheers.

Now the foreigners defending were professionals who had graduated in all the arts of town and castle taking. These met the successes of their antagonists with derision. "Apprentices," they would say, "nothing but apprentices."... "See those fellows by the big springal there turning the winch the wrong way!" ... "The turbaned sons of Satan! Have they no eyes? I'll give them a lesson. Look!" And if the bolt fell truly, there was loud laughter on the walls.

The captains, moreover, were incessantly encouraging the raw men under them. "Two walls, and a hundred feet of flooded ditch! There will be merry Christmas in the next century before the Mahounds get to us at the rate they are coming. Shoot leisurely, men—leisurely. An infidel for every bolt!"

Now on the outer wall, which was the lower of the two, and naturally first to draw the enemy's ire, and then along the inner, the Emperor went, indifferent to danger or fatigue, and always with words of cheer.

"The stones under our feet are honest," he would say. "The Persian came thinking to batter them down, but after many days he fled; and search as we will, no man can lay a finger on the face of one of them, and say, 'Here Chosroes left a scar.' So Amurath, sometimes called Murad, this young man's father, wasted months, and the souls of his subjects without count; but when he fled not a coping block had been disturbed in its bed. What has been will be again. God is with us."

When the three days were spent, the Greeks under arms began to be accustomed to the usage, and make merry of it, like the veterans.

The fourth day about noon the Emperor, returning from a round of the walls, ascended the Bagdad tower mentioned as overlooking the Gate St. Romain on the right hand; and finding Justiniani on the roof, he said to him: "This fighting, if it may be so called, Captain, is without heart. But two of our people have been killed; not a stone is shaken. To me it seems the Sultan is amusing us while preparing something more serious."

"Your Majesty," the Genoese returned, soberly, "now has Heaven given you the spirit of a soldier and the eyes as well. Old John Grant told me within an hour that the yellow flag on the rising ground before us denotes the Sultan's quarters in the field, and is not to be confounded with his battle flag. It follows, I think, could we get behind the Janissaries dismounted on the further slope of the rise, yet in position to meet a sally, we would discover the royal tent not unwisely pitched, if, as I surmise, this gate is indeed his point of main attack. And besides here are none of the old-time machines as elsewhere along our front; not a catapult, or bricole, or bible— as some, with wicked facetiousness, have named a certain invention for casting huge stones; nor have we yet heard the report of a cannon, or arquebus, or bombard, although we know the enemy has them in numbers. Wherefore, keeping in mind the circumstance of his presence here, the omissions satisfy me the Sultan relies on his great guns, and that, while amusing us, as Your Majesty has said, he is mounting them. To-morrow, or perhaps next day, he will open with them, and then"—

"What then?" Constantine asked.

"The world will have a new lesson in warfare."

The Emperor's countenance, visible under his raised visor, knit hard.

"Dear, dear God!" he said, half to himself. "If this old Christian empire should be lost through folly of mine, who will there be to forgive me if not Thou?"

Then, seeing the Genoese observing him with surprise, he continued:

"It is a simple tale, Captain.... A Dacian, calling himself Urban, asked audience of me one day, and being admitted, said he was an artificer of cannon; that he had plied his art in the foundries of Germany, and from study of powder was convinced of the practicality of applying it to guns of heavier calibre than any in use. He had discovered a composition of metals, he said, which was his secret, and capable, when properly cast, of an immeasurable strain. Would I furnish him the materials, and a place, with appliances for the work such as he would name, I might collect the machines in my arsenal, and burn them or throw them into the sea. I might even level my walls, and in their stead throw up ramparts of common earth, and by mounting his guns upon them secure my capital against the combined powers of the world. He refused to give me details of his processes. I asked him what reward he wanted, and he set it so high I laughed. Thinking to sound him further, I kept him in my service a few days; but becoming weary of his importunities, I dismissed him. I next heard of him at Adrianople. The Sultan Mahommed entertained his propositions, built him a foundry, and tried one of his guns, with results the fame of which is a wonder to the whole East. It was the log of bronze

Count Corti saw on the road—now it is here—and Heaven sent it to me first."

"Your Majesty," returned the Genoese, impressed by the circumstance, and the evident remorse of the Emperor, "Heaven does not hold us accountable for errors of judgment. There is not a monarch in Europe who would have accepted the man's terms, and it remains to be seen if Mahommed, as yet but a callow youth, has not been cheated. But look yonder!"

As he spoke, the Janissaries in front of the gate mounted and rode forward, probably a hundred yards, pursued by a riotous shouting and cracking of whips. Presently a train of buffaloes, yoked and tugging laboriously at something almost too heavy for them, appeared on the swell of earth; and there was a driver for every yoke, and every driver whirled a long stick with a longer lash fixed to it, and howled lustily.

"It is the great gun," said Constantine. "They are putting it in position."

Justiniani spoke to the men standing by the machines: "Make ready bolt and stone."

The balistiers took to their wheels eagerly, and discharged a shower of missiles at the Janissaries and ox-drivers.

"Too short, my men—more range."

The elevation was increased; still the bolts fell short.

"Bring forward the guns!" shouted Justiniani.

The guns were small bell-mouthed barrels of hooped iron, muzzle loading, mounted on high wheels, and each shooting half a dozen balls of lead large as walnuts. They were carefully aimed. The shot whistled and sang viciously.

"Higher, men!" shouted the Genoese, from a merlon. "Give the pieces their utmost range."

The Janissaries replied with a yell. The second volley also failed. Then Justiniani descended from his perch.

"Your Majesty," he said, "to stop the planting of the gun there is nothing for us but a sally."

"We are few, they are many," was the thoughtful reply. "One of us on the wall is worth a score of them in the field. Their gun is an experiment. Let them try it first."

The Genoese replied: "Your Majesty is right."

The Turks toiled on, backing and shifting their belabored trains, until the monster at last threatened the city with its great black Cyclopean eye.

"The Dacian is not a bad engineer," said the Emperor.

"See, he is planting other pieces."

Thus Justiniani; for oxen in trains similar to the first one came up tugging mightily, until by mid-afternoon on each flank of the first monster three other glistening yellow logs lay on their carriages in a like dubious quiet, leaving no doubt that St. Romain was to be overwhelmed, if the new agencies answered expectations.

If there was anxiety here, over the way there was impatience too fierce for control. Urban, the Dacian, in superintendency of the preparation, was naturally disposed to be careful, so much, in his view, depended on the right placement of the guns; but Mahommed, on foot, and whip in hand, was intolerant, and, not scrupling to mix with the workmen, urged them vehemently, now with threats, now with promises of reward.

"Thy beasts are snails! Give me the goad," he cried, snatching one from a driver. Then to Urban: "Bring the powder, and a bullet, for when the sun goes down thou shalt fire the great gun. Demur not. By the sword of Solomon, there shall be no sleep this night in yon *Gabour* city, least of all in the palace they call Blacherne."

The Dacian brought his experts together. The powder in a bag was rammed home; with the help of a stout slab, a stone ball was next rolled into the muzzle, then pushed nakedly down on the bag. Of a truth there was need of measureless strength in the composition of the piece. Finally the vent was primed, and a slow-match applied, after which Urban reported:

"The gun is ready, my Lord."

"Then watch the sun, and—*Bismillah!*—at its going down, fire.... Aim at the gate—this one before us—and if thou hit it or a tower on either hand, I will make thee a *begler-bey*."

The gun-planting continued. Finally the sun paused in cloudy splendor ready to carry the day down with it. The Sultan, from his tent of many annexes Bedouin fashion, walked to where Urban and his assistants stood by the carriage of the larger piece.

"Fire!" he said.

Urban knelt before him.

"Will my Lord please retire?"

"Why should I retire?"

"There is danger."

Mahommed smiled haughtily.

"Is the piece trained on the gate?"

"It is; but I pray"—

"Now if thou wilt not have me believe thee a dog not less than an unbeliever, rise, and do my bidding."

The Dacian, without more ado, put the loose end of the slow-match into a pot of live coals near by, and when it began to spit and sputter, he cast it off. His experts fled. Only Mahommed remained with him; and no feat of daring in battle could have won the young Padishah a name for courage comparable to that the thousands looking on from a safe distance now gave him.

"Will my Lord walk with me a little aside? He can then see the ball going."

Mahommed accepted the suggestion.

"Look now in a line with the gate, my Lord."

The match was at last spent. A flash at the vent—a spreading white cloud—a rending of the air—the rattle of wheels obedient to the recoil of the gun—a sound thunder in volume, but with a crackle sharper than any thunder—and we may almost say that, with a new voice, and an additional terror, war underwent a second birth.

Mahommed's ears endured a wrench, and for a time he heard nothing; but he was too intent following the flight of the ball to mind whether the report of the gun died on the heights of Galata or across the Bosphorus at Scutari. He saw the blackened sphere pass between the towers flanking the gate, and speed on into the city—how far, or with what effect, he could not tell, nor did he care.

Urban fell on his knees.

"Mercy, my Lord, mercy!"

"For what? That thou didst not hit the gate? Rise, man, and see if the gun is safe." And when it was so reported, he called to Kalil, the Vizier, now come up: "Give the man a purse, and not a lean one, for, by Allah! he is bringing Constantinople to me."

And despite the ringing in his ears, he went to his tent confident and happy. On the tower meantime Constantine and the Genoese beheld the smoke leap forth and curtain the gun, and right afterward they heard the huge ball go tearing past them, like an invisible meteor. Their eyes pursued the sound—where the missile fell they could not say—they heard a crash, as if a house midway the city had been struck—then they gazed at each other, and crossed themselves.

"There is nothing for us now but the sally," said the Emperor.

"Nothing," replied Justiniani. "We must disable the guns."

"Let us go and arrange it."

There being no indication of further firing, the two descended from the tower.

The plan of sortie agreed upon was not without ingenuity. The gate under the palace of Blacherne called *Cercoporta* was to be opened in the night. [Footnote: In the basement of the palace of Blacherne there was an underground exit, Cercoporta or gate of the Circus; but Isaac Comnenus had walled it up in order to avoid the accomplishment of a prediction which announced that the Emperor Frederick would enter Constantinople through it.... But before the siege by Mahommed the exit was restored, and it was through it the Turks passed into the city.—VON HAMMER, *Hist. de l'Empire Ottoman.*] Count Corti, with the body-guard mounted, was to pass out by it, and surprise the Janissaries defending the battery. Simultaneously Justiniani should sally by the Gate St. Romain, cross the moat temporarily bridged for the purpose, and, with the footmen composing the force in reserve, throw himself upon the guns.

The scheme was faithfully attempted. The Count, stealing out of the ancient exit in the uncertain light preceding the dawn, gained a position unobserved, and charged the careless Turks. By this time it had become a general report that the net about his neck was a favor of the Princess Irene, and his battle cry confirmed it—*For God and Irene!* Bursting through the half-formed opposition, he passed to the rear of the guns, and planted his banderole at the door of Mahommed's tent. Had his men held together, he might have returned with a royal prisoner.

While attention was thus wholly given the Count, Justiniani overthrew the guns by demolishing the carriages. A better acquaintance with the operation known to moderns as "spiking a piece," would have enabled him to make the blow irreparable. The loss of Janissaries was severe; that of the besieged trifling. The latter, foot and horse, returned by the Gate St. Romain unpursued.

Mahommed, aroused by the tumult, threw on his light armor, and rushed out in time to hear the cry of his assailant, and pluck the banderole from its place. At sight of the moon with the cross on its face, his wrath was uncontrollable. The Aga in command and all his assistants were relentlessly impaled.

There were other sorties in course of the siege, but never another surprise.

CHAPTER VIII
MAHOMMED TRIES HIS GUNS AGAIN

Hardly had the bodies making the sortie retired within the gate when the Janissaries on the eminence were trebly strengthened, and the noises in that quarter, the cracking of whips, the shouting of ox-drivers, the hammering betokened a prodigious activity. The besieged, under delusion that the guns had been destroyed, could not understand the enemy. Not until the second ensuing morning was the mystery solved. The watchmen on the towers, straining to pierce the early light, then beheld the great bronze monster remounted and gaping at them through an embrasure, and other monsters of a like kind on either side of it, fourteen in all, similarly mounted and defended.

The warders on the towers, in high excitement, sent for Justiniani, and he in turn despatched a messenger to the Emperor. Together on the Bagdad tower the two discussed the outlook.

"Your Majesty," said the Genoese, much chagrined, "the apostate Dacian must be master of his art. He has restored the cannon I overthrew."

After a time Constantine replied: "I fear we have underrated the new Sultan. Great as a father may be, it is possible for a son to be greater."

Perceiving the Emperor was again repenting the dismissal of Urban, the Captain held his peace until asked: "What shall we now do?"

"Your Majesty," he returned, "it is apparent our sally was a failure. We slew a number of the infidels, and put their master—may God confound him!—to inconvenience, and nothing more. Now he is on guard, we may not repeat our attempt. My judgment is that we let him try his armament upon our walls. They may withstand his utmost effort."

The patience this required was not put to a long test. There was a sudden clamor of trumpets, and the Janissaries, taking to their saddles, and breaking right and left into divisions, cleared the battery front. Immediately a vast volume of smoke hid the whole ground, followed by a series of explosions. Some balls passing over the defences ploughed into the city; and as definitions of force, the sounds they made in going were awful; yet they were the least of the terrors. Both the towers were hit, and they shook as if an earthquake were wrestling with them. The air whitened with dust and fragments of crushed stone. The men at the machines and culverins cowered to the floor. Constantine and the Genoese gazed at each other until the latter bethought him, and ordered the fire returned. And it was well done, for there is nothing which shall bring men round from fright like action.

Then, before there could be an exchange of opinion between the high parties on the tower, a man in half armor issued from the slowly rising cloud, and walked leisurely forward. Instead of weapons, he carried an armful of stakes, and something which had the appearance of a heavy gavel. After a careful examination of the ground to the gate, he halted and drove a stake, and from that point commenced zigzagging down the slope, marking each angle.

Justiniani drew nearer the Emperor, and said, in a low voice: "With new agencies come new methods. The assault is deferred."

"Nay, Captain, our enemy must attack; otherwise he cannot make the moat passable."

"That, Your Majesty, was the practice. Now he will gain the ditch by a trench."

"With what object?"

"Under cover of the trench, he will fill the ditch."

Constantine viewed the operation with increased gravity. He could see how feasible it was to dig a covered way under fire of the guns, making the approach and the bombardment simultaneous; and he would have replied, but that instant a mob of laborers—so the spades and picks they bore bespoke them—poured from the embrasure of the larger gun, and, distributing themselves at easy working intervals along the staked line, began throwing up the earth on the side next the city. Officers with whips accompanied and stood over them.

The engineer—if we may apply the modern term—was at length under fire of the besieged; still he kept on; only when he exhausted his supply of stakes did he retire, leaving it inferrible that the trench was to run through the opening in the cemetery to the bridge way before the gate.

At noon, the laborers being well sunk in the ground, the cannon again vomited fire and smoke, and with thunderous reports launched their heavy bullets at the towers. Again the ancient piles shook from top to base. Some of the balistiers were thrown down. The Emperor staggered under the shock. One ball struck a few feet below a merlon of the Bagdad, and when the dust blew away, an ugly crack was seen in the exposed face of the wall, extending below the roof.

While the inspection of damages immediately ordered is in progress, we take the liberty of transporting the reader elsewhere, that he may see the effect of this amazing warfare on other parties of interest in the tragedy.

Count Corti was with his guard at the foot of the tower when the first discharge of artillery took place. He heard the loud reports and the blows of the shot which failed not their aim; he heard also the sound of the bullets flying on into the city, and being of a quick imagination, shuddered to think of the havoc they might inflict should they fall in a thickly inhabited district. Then it came to him that the residence of the Princess Irene must be exposed to the danger. Like a Christian and a lover, he, sought to allay the chill he felt by signing the cross repeatedly, and with unction, on brow and breast. The pious performance brought no relief. His dread increased. Finally he sent a man with a message informing the Emperor that he was gone to see what damage the guns had done in the city.

He had not ridden far when he was made aware of the prevalence of an extraordinary excitement. It seemed the entire population had been brought from their houses by the strange thunder, and the appalling flight of meteoric bodies over their roofs. Men and women were running about asking each other what had happened. At the corners he was appealed to:

"Oh, for Christ's sake, stop, and tell us if the world is coming to an end!" Arid in pity lie answered: "Do not be so afraid, good people. It is the Turks. They are trying to scare us by making a great noise. Go back into your houses."

"But the bullets which passed over us. What of them?"

"Where did they strike?"

"On further. God help the sufferers!"

One cry he heard so often it made an impression upon him:

"The *Panagia!* Tell His Majesty, as he is a Christian, to bring the Blessed Madonna from the Chapel."

With each leap of his horse he was now nearing the alighting places of the missiles, and naturally the multiplying signs of terror he observed, together with a growing assurance that the abode of the Princess was in the range of danger, quickened his alarm for her. The white faces of the women he met and passed without a word reminded him the more that she was subject to the same peril, and in thought of her he forgot to sympathize with them.

In Byzantium one might be near a given point yet far away; so did the streets run up and down, and here and there, their eccentricities in width and direction proving how much more accident and whim had to do with them originally than art or science. Knowing this, the Count was not sparing of his horse, and as his blood heated so did his fancy. If the fair Princess were unhurt, it was scarcely possible she had escaped the universal terror. He imagined her the object of tearful attention from her attendants. Or perhaps they had run away, and left her in keeping of the tender Madonna of Blacherne.

At last he reached a quarter where the throng of people compelled him to slacken his gait, then halt and dismount. It was but a few doors from the Princess'. One house—a frame, two stories—appeared the object of interest.

"What has happened?" he asked, addressing a tall man, who stood trembling and praying to a crucifix in his hand.

"God protect us, Sir Knight! See how clear the sky is, but a great stone— some say it was a meteor—struck this house. There is the hole it made. Others say it was a bullet from the Turks.—Save us, O Son of Mary!" and he fell to kissing the crucifix.

"Was anybody hurt?" the Count asked, shaking the devotee.

"Yes—two women and a child were killed.—Save us, O Son of God! Thou hast the power from the Father."

The Count picked his way toward the house till he could get no further, so was it blocked by a mass of women on their knees, crying, praying, and in agony of fright. There, sure enough, was a front beaten in, exposing the wrecked interior. But who was the young woman at the door calmly directing some men bringing out the body of one apparently dead? Her back was to him, but the sunlight was tangled in her uncovered hair, making gold of it. Her figure was tall and slender, and there was a marvellous grace in her action. Who was she? The Count's heart was prophetic. He gave the bridle rein to a man near by, and holding his sword up, pushed through the kneeling mass. He might have been more considerate in going; but he was in haste, and never paused until at the woman's side. "God's mercy, Princess Irene!" he cried, "what dost thou here? Are there not men to take this charge upon them?"

And in his joy at finding her safe, he fell upon his knees, and, without waiting for her to offer the favor, took one of her hands, and carried it to his lips.

"Nay, Count Corti, is it not for me to ask what thou dost here?"

Her face was solemn, and he could hardly determine if the eyes she turned to him were not chiding; yet they were full of humid violet light, and she permitted him to keep the hand while he replied:

"The Turk is for the time having his own way. We cannot get to him.... I came in haste to—to see what his guns have done—or—why should I not say it? Princess, I galloped here fearing thou wert in need of protection and help. I remembered that I was thy accepted knight."

She understood him perfectly, and, withdrawing her hand, returned: "Rise, Count Corti, thou art in the way of these bearing the dead."

He stood aside, and the men passed him with their burden—a woman drenched in blood.

"Is this the last one?" she asked them.

"We could find no other."

"Poor creature! ... Yet God's will be done! ... Bear her to my house, and lay her with the others." Then to the Count she said: "Come with me."

The Princess set out after the men. Immediately the women about raised a loud lamentation; such as were nearest her cried out: "Blessings on you!" and they kissed the hem of her gown, and followed her moaning and weeping. The body was borne into the house, and to the chapel, and all who wished went in. Before the altar, two others were lying lifeless on improvised biers, an elderly woman and a half-grown girl. The Lady in picture above the altar looked down on them, as did the Holy Child in her arms; and there was much comfort to the spectators in the look. Then, when the third victim was decently laid out, Sergius began the service for the dead. The Count stood by the Princess, her attendants in group a little removed from them.

In the midst of the holy ministration, a sound like distant rolling thunder penetrated the chapel. Every one present knew what it was by this time—knew at least it was not thunder—and they cried out, and clasped each other—from their knees many fell grovelling on the floor. Sergius' voice never wavered. Corti would have extended his arms to give the Princess support; but she did not so much as change color; her hands holding a silver triptych remained firm. The deadly bullets were in the air and might alight on the house; yet her mind was too steadfast, her soul too high, her faith too exalted for alarm; and if the Count had been prone to love her for her graces of person, now he was prompted to adore her for her courage.

Outside near by, there was a crash as of a flying solid smiting another dwelling, and, without perceptible interval, an outcry so shrill and unintermitted it required no explanation.

The Princess was the first to speak.

"Proceed, Sergius," she said; nor might one familiar with her voice have perceived any alteration in it from the ordinary; then to the Count again: "Let us go out; there may be others needing my care."

At the door Corti said: "Stay, O Princess—a word, I pray."

She had only to look at his face to discover he was the subject of a fierce conflict of spirit.

"Have pity on me, I conjure you. Honor and duty call me to the gate; the Emperor may be calling me; but how can I go, leaving you in the midst of such peril and horrors?"

"What would you have me do?"

"Fly to a place of safety."

"Where?"

"I will find a place; if not within these walls, then"—

He stopped, and his eyes, bright with passion, fell before hers; for the idea he was about giving his tongue would be a doubly dishonorable coinage, since it included desertion of the beleaguered city, and violation of his compact with Mahommed.

"And then?" she asked.

And love got the better of honor.

"I have a ship in the harbor, O Princess Irene, and a crew devoted to me, and I will place you on its deck, and fly with you. Doubt not my making the sea; there are not Christians and Mohammedans enough to stay me once my anchor is lifted, and my oars out; and on the sea freedom lives, and we will follow the stars to Italy, and find a home."

Again he stopped, his face this time wrung with sudden anguish; then he continued:

"God forgive, and deal with me mercifully! I am mad! ... And thou, O Princess—do thou forgive me also, and my words and weakness. Oh, if not for my sake, then for that which carried me away! Or if thou canst not forget, pity me, pity me, and think of the wretchedness now my portion. I had thy respect, if not thy love; now both are lost—gone after my honor. Oh! I am most miserable—miserable!"

And wringing his hands, he turned his face from her.

"Count Corti," she replied gently, "thou hast saved thyself. Let the affair rest here. I forgive the proposal, and shall never remind thee of it. Love is madness. Return to duty; and for me"—she hesitated—"I hold myself ready for the sacrifice to which I was born. God is fashioning it; in His own time, and in the form He chooses, He will send it to me.... I am not afraid, and be thou not afraid for me. My father was a hero, and he left me his spirit. I too have my duty born within the hour—it is to share the danger of my kinsman's people, to give them my presence, to comfort them all I can. I will show thee what thou seemest not to have credited—that a woman can be brave as any man. I will attend the sick, the wounded, and suffering. To the dying I will carry such consolation as I possess—all of them I can reach—and the dead shall have ministration. My goods and values have long been held for the poor and unfortunate; now to the same service I consecrate myself, my house, my chapel, and altar.... There is my hand in sign of forgiveness, and that I believe thee a true knight. I will go with thee to thy horse."

He bowed his head, and silently struggling for composure, carried the hand to his lips.

"Let us go now," she said.

They went out together.

Another dwelling had been struck; fortunately it was unoccupied.

In the saddle, he stayed to say: "Thy soul, O Princess Irene, is angelic as thy face. Thou hast devoted thyself to the suffering. Am I left out? What word wilt thou give me?"

"Be the true knight thou art, Count Corti, and come to me as before."

He rode away with a revelation; that in womanly purity and goodness there is a power and inspiration beyond the claims of beauty.

The firing continued. Seven times that day the Turks assailed the Gate St. Romain with their guns; and while a few of the stones discharged flew amiss into the city, there were enough to still further terrorize the inhabitants. By night all who could had retreated to vaults, cellars, and such hiding-places as were safe, and took up their abodes in them. In the city but one woman went abroad without fear, and she bore bread and medicines, and dressed wounds, and assuaged sorrows, and as a Madonna in fact divided worship with the Madonna in the chapel up by the High Residence. Whereat Count Corti's love grew apace, though the recollection of the near fall he had kept him humble and circumspect.

The same day, but after the second discharge of the guns, Mahommed entered the part of his tent which, with some freedom, may be termed his office and reception-room, since it was furnished with seats and a large table, the latter set upon a heavily tufted rug, and littered over with maps and writing and drawing materials. Notable amongst the litter was the sword of Solomon. Near it lay a pair of steel gauntlets elegantly gilt. One stout centre-tree, the main support of the roof of camel's hair, appeared gayly dressed with lances, shields, arms, and armor; and against it, strange to say, the companion of a bright red battle-flag, leant the banderole Count Corti had planted before the door the morning of the sally. A sliding flap overhead, managed by cords in the interior, was drawn up, admitting light and air.

The office, it may be added, communicated by gay portieres with four other apartments, each having its separate centre-tree; one occupied by Kalil, the Vizier; one, a bed-chamber, so to speak; one, a stable for the imperial stud; the fourth belonged to no less a person than our ancient and mysterious acquaintance, the Prince of India.

Mahommed was in half-armor; that is, his neck, arms, and body were in chain mail, the lightest and most flexible of the East, exquisitely gold-washed, and as respects fashion exactly like the suit habitually affected by Count Corti. His nether limbs were clad in wide trousers of yellow silk, drawn close at the ankles. Pointed shoes of red leather completed his equipment, unless we may include a whip with heavy handle and long lash. Could Constantine have seen him at the moment, he would have recognized the engineer whose performance in tracing the trench he had witnessed with so much interest in the morning.

The Grand Chamberlain received him with the usual prostration, and in that posture waited his pleasure.

"Bring me water. I am thirsty."

The water was brought.

"The Prince of India now."

Presently the Prince appeared in the costume peculiar to him—a cap and gown of black velvet, loose trousers, and slippers. His hair and beard were longer than when we knew him a denizen of Constantinople, making his figure seem more spare and old; otherwise he was unchanged. He too prostrated himself; yet as he sank upon his knees, he gave the Sultan a quick glance, intended doubtless to discover his temper more than his purpose.

"You may retire."

This to the Chamberlain.

Upon the disappearance of the official, Mahommed addressed the Prince, his countenance flushed, his eyes actually sparkling.

"God is great. All things are possible to him. Who shall say no when he says yes? Who resist when he bids strike? Salute me, and rejoice with me, O Prince. He is on my side. It was he who spoke in the thunder of my guns. Salute me, and rejoice. Constantinople is mine! The towers which have outlasted the ages, the walls which have mocked so many conquerors— behold them tottering to their fall! I will make dust of them. The city which has been a stumbling-block to the true faith shall be converted in a night. Of the churches I will make mosques. Salute me and rejoice! How may a soul contain itself knowing God has chosen it for such mighty things? Rise, O Prince and rejoice with me!"

He caught up the sword of Solomon, and in a kind of ecstasy strode about flourishing it.

The Prince, arisen, replied simply: "I rejoice with my Lord;" and folding his arms across his breast, he waited, knowing he had been summoned for something more serious than to witness an outburst so wild—that directly this froth would disappear, as bubbles vanish from wine just poured. The most absolute of men have their ways—this was one of Mahommed's. And behind his composed countenance the Jew smiled, for, as he read it, the byplay was an acknowledgment of his influence over the chosen of God.

And he was right. Suddenly Mahommed replaced the sword, and standing before him, asked abruptly:

"Tell me, have the stars fixed the day when I may assault the Gabours?"

"They have, my Lord."

"Give it to me."

The Prince returned to his apartment, and came back with a horoscope.

"This is their decision, my Lord."

In his character of Messenger of the Stars, the Prince of India dispensed with every observance implying inferiority.

Without looking at the Signs, or at the planets in their Houses; without noticing the calculations accompanying the chart; glancing merely at the date in the central place, Mahommed frowned, and said:

"The twenty-ninth of May! Fifty-three days! By Allah and Mahomet arid Christ—all in one—if by the compound the oath will derive an extra virtue—what is there to consume so much time? In three days I will have the towers lording this gate they call St. Romain in the ditch, and the ditch filled. In three days, I say."

"Perhaps my Lord is too sanguine—perhaps he does not sufficiently credit the skill and resources of the enemy behind the gate—perhaps there is more to do than he has admitted into his anticipations."

Mahommed darted a look at the speaker.

"Perhaps the stars have been confidential with their messenger, and told him some of the things wanting to be done."

"Yes, my Lord." The calmness of the Prince astonished Mahommed.

"And art thou permitted to be confidential with me?" he asked.

"My Lord must break up this collection of his guns, and plant some of them against the other gates; say two at the Golden Gate, one at the Caligaria, and before the Selimbria and the Adrianople two each. He will have seven left.... Nor must my Lord confine his attack to the landward side; the weakest front of the city is the harbor front, and it must be subjected. He should carry there at least two of his guns."

"Sword of Solomon!" cried Mahommed. "Will the stars show me a road to possession of the harbor? Will they break the chain which defends its entrance? Will they sink or burn the enemy's fleet?"

"No; those are heroisms left for my Lord's endeavor."

"Thou dost taunt me with the impossible."

The Prince smiled.

"Is my Lord less able than the Crusaders? I know he is not too proud to be taught by them. Once, marching upon the Holy City, they laid siege to Nicea, and after a time discovered they could not master it without first mastering Lake Ascanius. Thereupon they hauled their ships three leagues overland, and launched them in the lake." [Footnote: VON HAMMER, *Hist. de l'Emp. Ottoman.*]

Mahommed became thoughtful.

"If my Lord does not distribute the guns; if he confines his attack to St. Romain, the enemy, in the day of assault, can meet him at the breach with his whole garrison. More serious, if the harbor is left to the Greeks, how can he prevent the Genoese in Galata from succoring them? My Lord derives information from those treacherous people in the day; does he know of the intercourse between the towns by boats in the night? If they betray one side, will they be true to the other? My Lord, they are Christians; so are these with whom we are at war."

The Sultan sank into a seat; and satisfied with the impression he had made, the Prince wisely allowed him his thoughts.

"It is enough!" said the former, rising. Then fixing his eye on his confederate, he asked: "What stars told thee these things, O Prince?"

"My Lord, the firmament above is God's, and the sun and planets there are his mercifully to our common use. But we have each of us a firmament of our own. In mine, Reason is the sun, and of its stars I mention two—Experience and Faith. By the light of the three, I succeed; when I refuse them, one or all, I surrender to chance."

Mahommed caught up the sword, and played with its ruby handle, turning it at angles to catch its radiations; at length he said:

"Prince of India, thou hast spoken like a Prophet. Go call Kalil and Saganos."

CHAPTER IX
THE MADONNA TO THE RESCUE

We have given the opening of the siege of Byzantium by Mahommed with dangerous minuteness, the danger of course being from the critic. We have posted the warders on their walls, and over against them set the enemy in an intrenched line covering the whole landward side of the city. We have planted Mahommed's guns, and exhibited their power, making it a certainty that a breach in the wall must be sooner or later accomplished. We have shown the effect of the fire of the guns, not only on the towers abutting the gate which was the main object of attack, but on the non-combatants, the women and children, in their terror seeking safety in cellars, vaults, and accessible underground retreats. We have carefully assembled and grouped those of our characters who have survived to this trying time; and the reader is informed where they are, the side with which their fortunes are cast, their present relations to each other, and the conditions which environ them. In a word, the reader knows their several fates are upon them, and the favors we now most earnestly pray are to be permitted to pass the daily occurrences of the siege, and advance quickly to the end. Even battles can become monotonous in narrative.

The Sultan, we remark, adopted the suggestions of the Prince of India. He distributed his guns, planting some of them in front of the several gates of the city. To control the harbor, he, in modern parlance, erected a battery on a hill by Galata; then in a night, he drew a part of his fleet, including a number of his largest vessels, from Besich-tasch on the Bosphorus over the heights and hollows of Pera, a distance of about two leagues, and dropped them in the Golden Horn. These Constantine attacked. Justiniani led the enterprise, but was repulsed. A stone bullet sunk his ship, and he barely escaped with his life. Most of his companions were drowned; those taken were pitilessly hung. Mahommed next collected great earthen jars—their like may yet be seen in the East—and, after making them air-tight, laid a bridge upon them out toward the single wall defending the harbor front. At the further end of this unique approach he placed a large gun; and so destructive was the bombardment thus opened that fire-ships were sent against the bridge and battery. But the Genoese of Galata betrayed the scheme, and it was baffled. The prisoners captured were hanged in view of the Greeks, and in retaliation Constantine exposed the heads of a hundred and sixty Turks from the wall.

On the landward side Mahommed was not less fortunate. The zigzag trench was completed, and a footing obtained for his men in the moat, whence they strove to undermine the walls.

Of the lives lost during these operations no account was taken, since the hordes were the victims. Their bodies were left as debris in the roadway so expensively constructed. Day after day the towers Bagdad and St. Romain were more and more reduced. Immense sections of them tumbling into the ditch were there utilized. Day after day the exchange of bullets, bolts, stones, and arrows was incessant. The shouting in many tongues, heating of drums, and blowing of horns not seldom continued far into the night.

The Greeks on their side bore up bravely. Old John Grant plied the assailants with his inextinguishable fire. Constantine, in seeming always cheerful, never shirking, visited the walls; at night, he seconded Justiniani in hastening needful repairs. Finally the steady drain upon the stores in magazine began to tell. Provisions became scarce, and the diminution of powder threatened to silence the culverins and arquebuses. Then the Emperor divided his time between the defences and Sancta Sophia— between duty as a military commander, and prayer as a Christian trustful in God. And it was noticeable that the services at which he assisted in the ancient church were according to Latin rites; whereat the malcontents in the monasteries fell into deeper sullenness, and refused the dying the consolation of their presence. Gennadius assumed the authority of the absent Patriarch, and was influential as a prophet. The powerful Brotherhood of the St. James', composed of able-bodied gentry and nobles who should have been militant at the gates, regarded the Emperor as under ban. Notaras and Justiniani quarrelled, and the feud spread to their respective followers.

One day, about the time the Turkish ships dropped, as it were, from the sky into the harbor, when the store of powder was almost exhausted, and famine menaced the city, five galleys were reported in the offing down the Marmora. About the same time the Turkish flotilla was observed making ready for action. The hungry people crowded the wall from the Seven Towers to Point Serail. The Emperor rode thither in haste, while Mahommed betook himself to the shore of the sea. A naval battle ensued under the eyes of the two. [Footnote: The following is a translation of Von Hammer's spirited account of this battle:

"The 15th of April, 1453, the Turkish fleet, of more than four hundred sails, issued from the bay of Phidalia, and directing itself toward the mouth of the Bosphorus on the western side, cast anchor near the two villages to-day Besich-tasch. A few days afterward five vessels appeared in the Marmora, one belonging to the Emperor, and four to the Genoese. During the month of March they had been unable to issue from Scio; but a favorable wind arising, they arrived before Constantinople, all their sails unfurled. A division of the Turkish fleet, more than a hundred and fifty in number, advanced to bar the passage of the Christian squadron and guard the entrance to the harbor. The sky was clear, the sea tranquil, the walls crowded with spectators. The Sultan himself was on the shore to enjoy the spectacle of a combat in which the superiority of his fleet seemed to promise him a certain victory. But the eighteen galleys at the head of the division, manned by inexperienced soldiers, and too low at the sides, were instantly covered with arrows, pots of Greek fire, and a rain of stones launched by the enemy. They were twice repulsed. The Greeks and the Genoese emulated each other in zeal. Flectanelli, captain of the imperial galley, fought like a lion; Cataneo, Novarro, Balaneri, commanding the Genoese, imitated his example. The Turkish ships could not row under the arrows with which the water was covered; they fouled each other, and two took fire. At this sight Mahommed could not contain himself; as if he would arrest the victory of the Greeks, he spurred his horse in the midst of the ships. His officers followed him trying to reach the vessels combating only a stone's throw away. The soldiers, excited by shame or by fear, renewed the attack, but without success, and the five vessels, favored by a rising wind, forced a passage through the opposition, and happily entered the harbor."] The Christian squadron made the Golden Horn, and passed triumphantly behind the chain defending it. They brought supplies of corn and powder. The relief had the appearance of a merciful Providence, and forthwith the fighting was renewed with increased ardor. Kalil the Vizier exhorted Mahommed to abandon the siege.

"What, retire now? Now that the gate St. Romain is in ruins and the ditch filled?" the Sultan cried in rage. "No, my bones to Eyoub, my soul to Eblis first. Allah sent me here to conquer."

Those around attributed his firmness, some to religious zeal, some to ambition; none of them suspected how much the compact with Count Corti had to do with his decision.

To the lasting shame of Christian Europe, the arrival of the five galleys, and the victory they achieved, were all of succor and cheer permitted the heroic Emperor.

But the unequal struggle wore on, and with each set of sun Mahommed's hopes replumed themselves. From much fondling and kissing the sword of Solomon, and swearing by it, the steel communicated itself to his will; while on the side of the besieged, failures, dissensions, watching and labor, disparity in numbers, inferiority in arms, the ravages of death, and the neglect of Christendom, slowly but surely invited despair.

Weeks passed thus. April went out; and now it is the twenty-third of May. On the twenty-ninth—six days off—the stars, so we have seen, will permit an assault.

And on this day the time is verging midnight. Between the sky and the beleaguered town a pall of clouds is hanging thick. At intervals light showers filter through the pall, and the drops fall perpendicularly, for there is no wind. And the earth has its wrap of darkness, only over the seven hills of the old capital it appears to be in double folds oppressively close. Darkness and silence and vacancy, which do not require permission to enter by a gate, have possession of the streets and houses; except that now and then a solitary figure, gliding swiftly, turns a corner, pauses to hear, moves on again, and disappears as if it dropped a curtain behind it. Desertion is the rule. The hush is awful. Where are the people?

To find each other friends go from cellar to cellar. There are vaults and arched passages, crypts under churches and lordly habitations, deep, damp, mouldy, and smelling of rotten air, sheltering families. In many districts all life is underground. Sociality, because it cannot exist under such conditions save amongst rats and reptiles, ceased some time ago. Yet love is not dead—thanks, O Heaven, for the divine impulse!—it has merely taken on new modes of expression; it shows itself in tears, never in laughter; it has quit singing, it moans; and what moments mothers are not on their knees praying, they sit crouched, and clasping their little ones, and listen pale with fear and want. Listening is the universal habit; and the start and exclamation with which in the day the poor creatures recognize the explosive thunder of Mahommed's guns explain the origin of the habit.

At this particular hour of the twenty-third of May there are two notable exceptions to the statement that darkness, silence and vacancy have possession of the streets and houses.

By a combination of streets most favorable for the purpose, a thoroughfare had come into use along which traffic preferably drove its bulky commodities from St. Peter's on the harbor to the Gates St. Romain and Adrianople; its greater distance between terminal points being offset by advantages such as solidity, width and gentler grades. In one of the turns of this very crooked way there is now a murky flush cast by flambeaux sputtering and borne in hand. On either side one may see the fronts of houses without tenants, and in the way itself long lines of men tugging with united effort at some cumbrous body behind them. There is no clamor. The labor is heavy, and the laborers in earnest. Some of them wear round steel caps, but the majority are civilians with here and there a monk, the latter by the Latin cross at his girdle an *azymite*. Now and then the light flashes back from a naked torso streaming with perspiration. One man in armor rides up and down the lines on horseback. He too is in earnest. He speaks low when he has occasion to stop and give a direction, but his face seen in flashes of the light is serious, and knit with purpose. The movement of the lines is slow; at times they come to a dead stand-still. If the halt appears too long the horseman rides back and comes presently to the black hull of a dismantled galley on rollers. The stoppages are to shift the rollers forward. When the shifting is done, he calls out: "Make ready, men!" Whereupon every one in the lines catches hold of a rope, and at his "Now—for love of Christ!" there follows a pull with might, and the hull drags on.

In these later days of the siege there are two persons actively engaged in the defence who are more wrought upon by the untowardness of the situation than any or all their associates—they are the Emperor and Count Corti.

There should be no difficulty in divining the cause of the former's distress. It was too apparent to him that his empire was in desperate straits; that as St. Romain underwent its daily reduction so his remnant of State and power declined. And beholding the dissolution was very like being an enforced witness of his own dying.

But Count Corti with the deepening of the danger only exerted himself the more. He seemed everywhere present—now on the ruins of the towers, now in the moat, now foremost in a countermine, and daily his recklessness increased. His feats with bow and sword amazed his friends. He became a terror to the enemy. He never tired. No one knew when he slept. And as note was taken of him, the question was continually on the lip, What possesses the man? He is a foreigner—this is not his home—he has no kindred here—what can be his motive? And there were who said it was Christian zeal; others surmised it was soldier habit; others again, that for some reason he was disgusted with life; yet others, themselves of sordid natures, said the Emperor affected him, and that he was striving for a great reward in promise. As in the camps of the besiegers none knew the actual reason of Mahommed's persistence, so here the secret of the activity which left the Count without a peer in performance and daring went without explanation.

A few—amongst them the Emperor—were aware of the meaning of the red net about the Italian's neck—it shone so frequently through the smoke and dust of hourly conflict as to have become a subject of general observation—yet in the common opinion he was only the lady's knight; and his battle cry, *For Christ and Irene—Now!* did but confirm the opinion. Time and time again, Mahommed beheld the doughty deeds of his rival, heard his shout, saw the flash of his blade, sometimes near, sometimes afar, but always where the press was thickest. Strange was it that of the two hosts he alone understood the other's inspiration? He had only to look into his own heart, and measure the force of the passion there.

The horseman we see in charge of the removal of the galley-hulk this night of the twenty-third of May is Count Corti. It is wanted at St. Romain. The gate is a hill of stone and mortar, without form; the moat almost level from side to side; and Justiniani has decided upon a barricade behind a new ditch. He will fill the hull with stones, and defend from its deck; and it must be on the ground by break of day.

Precisely as Count Corti was bringing the galley around the turn of the thoroughfare, Constantine was at the altar in Sancta Sophia where preparations for mass were making; that is, the priests were changing their vestments, and the acolytes lighting the tall candles. The Emperor sat in his chair of state just inside the brass railing, unattended except by his sword-bearer. His hands were on his knees, his head bowed low. He was acknowledging a positive need of prayer. The ruin at the gate was palpable; but God reigned, and might be reserving his power for a miraculous demonstration.

The preparation was about finished when, from the entrances of the Church opposite the nave, a shuffling of many feet was heard. The light in that quarter was weak, and some moments passed before the Emperor perceived a small procession advancing, and arose. The garbs were of orthodox Brotherhoods which had been most bitter in their denunciation. None of them had approached the door of the holy house for weeks.

The imperial mind was greatly agitated by the sight. Were the brethren recanting their unpatriotic resolutions? Had Heaven at last given them an understanding of the peril of the city? Had it brought to them a realization of the consequences if it fell under the yoke of the Turk?—That the whole East would then be lost to Christendom, with no date for its return? A miracle!—and to God the glory! And without a thought of himself the devoted man walked to the gate of the railing, and opening it, waited to receive the penitents.

Before him in front of the gate they knelt—in so far they yielded to custom.

"Brethren," he said, "this high altar has not been honored with your presence for many days. As Basileus, I bid you welcome back, and dare urge the welcome in God's holy name. Reason instructs me that your return is for a purpose in some manner connected with the unhappy condition in which our city and empire, not to mention our religion, are plunged. Rise, one of you, and tell me to what your appearance at this solemn hour is due."

A brother in gray, old and stooped, arose, and replied:

"Your Majesty, it cannot be that you are unacquainted with the traditions of ancient origin concerning Constantinople and Hagia Sophia; forgive us, however, if we fear you are not equally well informed of a more recent prophecy, creditably derived, we think, and presume to speak of its terms. 'The infidels'—so the prediction runs—'will enter the city; but the instant they arrive at the column of Constantine the Great, an angel will descend from Heaven, and put a sword in the hands of a man of low estate seated at the foot of the column, and order him to avenge the people of God with it. Overcome by sudden terror, the Turks will then take to flight, and be driven, not only from the city, but to the frontier of Persia.' [Footnote: Von Hammer.] This prediction relieves us, and all who believe in it, from fear of Mahommed and his impious hordes, and we are grateful to Heaven for the Divine intervention. But, Your Majesty, we think to be forgiven, if we desire the honor of the deliverance to be accounted to the Holy Mother who has had our fathers in care for so many ages, and redeemed them miraculously in instances within Your Majesty's knowledge. Wherefore to our purpose.... We have been deputed by the Brotherhoods in Constantinople, united in devotion to the Most Blessed Madonna of Blacherne, to pray your permission to take the *Panagia* from the Church of the Virgin of Hodegetria, where it has been since the week of the Passover, and intrust it to the pious women of the city. To-morrow at noon, Your Majesty consenting, they will assemble at the Acropolis, and with the banner at their head, go in procession along the walls and to every threatened gate, never doubting that at the sight of it the Sultan and his unbaptized hordes will be reft of breath of body or take to flight.... This we pray of Your Majesty, that the Mother of God may in these degenerate days have back the honor and worship accorded her by the Emperors and Greeks of former times."

The old man ceased, and again fell upon his knees, while his associate deputies rang the space with loud *Amens.*

It was well the light was dim, and the Emperor's face in shadow; it was well the posture of the petitioners helped hide him from close study; a feeling mixed of pity, contempt, and unutterable indignation seized him, distorting his features, and shaking his whole person. Recantation and repentance!— Pledge of loyalty!—Offer of service at the gates and on the shattered walls!—Heaven help him! There was no word of apology for their errors and remissness—not a syllable in acknowledgment of his labors and services—and he about to pray God for strength to die if the need were, as became the Emperor of a brave and noble people!

An instant he stood gazing at them—an instant of grief, shame, mortification, indignation, all heightened by a burning sense of personal wrong. Ay, God help him!

"Bear with me a little," he said quietly, and passing the waiting priests, went and knelt upon a step of the altar in position to lay his head upon the upper step. Minutes passed thus. The deputies supposed him praying for the success of the morrow's display; he was in fact praying for self-possession to answer them as his judgment of policy demanded.

At length he arose, and returned to them, and had calmness to say:

"Arise, brethren, and go in peace. The keeper of the Church will deliver the sacred banner to the pious women. Only I insist upon a condition; if any of them are slain by the enemy, whom you and they know to have been bred in denial of womanly virtue, scorning their own mothers and wives, and making merchandise of their daughters—if any of them be slain, I say, then you shall bear witness to those who sent you to me that I am innocent of the blood-guilt. Arise, and go in peace."

They marched out of the Church as they had come in, and he proceeded with the service.

Next day about ten o'clock in the morning there was a lull in the fighting at the Gate St. Romain. It were probably better to say the Turks for some reason rested from their work of bringing stones, tree-trunks, earth in hand carts, and timbers wrenched from houses—everything, in fact, which would serve to substantially fill the moat in that quarter. Then upon the highest heap of what had been the tower of Bagdad Count Corti appeared, a black shield on his arm, his bow in one hand, his banderole in the other.

"Have a care, have a care!" his friends halloed. "They are about firing the great gun."

Corti seemed not to hear, but deliberately planted the banderole, and blowing his trumpet three times, drew an arrow from the quiver at his back. The gun was discharged, the bullet striking below him. When the dust cleared away, he replied with his trumpet. Then the Turks, keeping their distance, set up a cry. Most of the arrows shot at him fell short. Seeing their indisposition to accept his challenge, he took seat upon a stone.

Not long then until a horseman rode out from the line of Janissaries still guarding the eminence, and advanced down the left of the zigzag galloping.

He was in chain mail glistening like gold, but wore flowing yellow trousers, while his feet were buried in shoe-stirrups of the royal metal. Looking over the small round black shield on his left arm, and holding a bow in the right hand, easy in the saddle, calm, confident, the champion slackened speed when within arrow flight, but commenced caracoling immediately. A prolonged hoarse cry arose behind him. Of the Christians, the Count alone recognized the salute of the Janissaries, still an utterance amongst Turkish soldiers, in literal translation: *The Padishah! Live the Padishah!* The warrior was Mahommed himself!

Arising, the Count placed an arrow at the string, and shouted, "*For Christ and Irene—Now!*" With the last word, he loosed the shaft.

Catching the missile lightly on his shield, Mahommed shouted back: "*Allah-il-Allah!*" and sent a shaft in return. The exchange continued some minutes. In truth, the Count was not a little proud of the enemy's performance. If there was any weakness on his part, if his clutch of the notch at the instant of drawing the string was a trifle light, the fault was chargeable to a passing memory. This antagonist had been his pupil. How often in the school field, practising with blunted arrows, the two had joyously mimicked the encounter they were now holding. At last a bolt, clanging dully, dropped from the Sultan's shield, and observing that it was black feathered, he swung from his seat to the ground, and, shifting the horse between him and the foe, secured the missile, and remounted.

"*Allah-il-Allah!*" he cried, slowly backing the charger out of range.

The Count repeated the challenge through his trumpet, and sat upon the stone again; but no other antagonist showing himself, he at length descended from the heap.

In his tent Mahommed examined the bolt; and finding the head was of lead, he cut it open, and extracted a scrip inscribed thus:

"To-day at noon a procession of women will appear on the walls. You may know it by the white banner a monk will bear, with a picture of the Madonna painted on it. *The Princess Irene marches next after the banner.*"

Mahommed asked for the time. It was half after ten o'clock. In a few minutes the door was thronged by mounted officers, who, upon receiving a verbal message from him, sped away fast as they could go.

Thereupon the conflict was reopened. Indeed, it raged more fiercely than at any previous time, the slingers and bowmen being pushed up to the outer edge of the moat, and the machines of every kind plied over their heads. In his ignorance of the miracle expected of the Lady of the Banner, Mahommed had a hope of deterring the extraordinary march.

Nevertheless at the appointed hour, ten o'clock, the Church of the Virgin of Hodegetria was surrounded by nuns and monks; and presently the choir of Sancta Sophia issued from the house, executing a solemn chant; the Emperor followed in Basilean vestments; then the *Panagia* appeared.

At sight of the picture of the Very Holy Virgin painted front view, the eyes upraised, the hands in posture of prayer, the breast covered by a portrait of the Child, the heads encircled by the usual nimbus, the mass knelt, uttering cries of adoration.

The Princess Irene, lightly veiled and attired in black, advanced, and, kissing the fringed corners of the hallowed relic, gathered the white staying ribbons in her hands; thereupon the monk appointed to carry it moved after the choir, and the nuns took places. And there were tears and sighs, but not of fear. The Mother of God would now assume the deliverance of her beloved capital. As it had been to the Avars, and later to the Russians under Askold and Dir, it would be now to Mahommed and his ferocious hordes—all Heaven would arm to punish them. They would not dare look at the picture twice, or if they did—well, there are many modes of death, and it will be for the dear Mother to choose. Thus the women argued. Possibly a perception of the failure in the defence, sharpened by a consciousness of the horrors in store for them if the city fell by assault, turned them to this. There is no relief from despair like faith.

From the little church, the devotees of the Very Holy Virgin took their way on foot to the southeast, chanting as they went, and as they went their number grew. Whence the accessions, none inquired.

They first reached a flight of steps leading to the banquette or footway along the wall near the Golden Gate. The noise of the conflict, the shouting and roar of an uncounted multitude of men in the heat and fury of combat, not to more than mention the evidences of the conflict— arrows, bolts, and stones in overflight and falling in remittent showers— would have dispersed them in ordinary mood; but they were under protection—the Madonna was leading them—to be afraid was to deny her saving grace. And then there was no shrinking on the part of the Princess Irene. Even as she took time and song from the choir, they borrowed of her trust.

At the foot of the steps the singers turned aside to allow the *Panagia* to go first. The moment of miracle was come! What form would the manifestation take? Perhaps the doors and windows of Heaven would open for a rain of fire—perhaps the fighting angels who keep the throne of the Father would appear with swords of lightning—perhaps the Mother and Son would show themselves. Had they not spared and converted the Khagan of the Avars? Whatever the form, it were not becoming to stand between the *Panagia* and the enemy.

The holy man carrying the ensign was trustful as the women, and he ascended the steps without faltering. Gathering the ribbons a little more firmly in her hands, the Princess kept her place. Up—up they were borne—

Mother and Son. Then the white banner was on the height—seen first by the Greeks keeping the wall, and in the places it discovered them, they fell upon their faces, next by the hordes. And they—oh, a miracle, a miracle truly!—they stood still. The bowman drawing his bow, the slinger whirling his sling, the arquebusers taking aim matches in hand, the strong men at the winches of the mangonels, all stopped—an arresting hand fell on them—they might have been changed to pillars of stone, so motionlessly did they stand and look at the white apparition. *Kyrie Eleison*, thrice repeated, then *Christie Eleison*, also thrice repeated, descended to them in the voices of women, shrilled by excitement.

And the banner moved along the wall, not swiftly as if terror had to do with its passing, but slowly, the image turned outwardly, the Princess next it, the ribbons in her hands; after her the choir in full chant; and then the long array of women in ecstasy of faith and triumph; for before they were all ascended, the hordes at the edge of the moat, and those at a distance—or rather such of them as death or wounds would permit—were retreating to their entrenchment. Nor that merely—the arrest which had fallen at the Golden Gate extended along the front of leaguerment from the sea to Blacherne, from Blacherne to the Acropolis.

So it happened that in advance of the display of the picture, without waiting for the *Kyrie Eleison* of the glad procession, the Turks took to their defences; and through the city, from cellar, and vault, and crypt, and darkened passage, the wonderful story flew; and there being none to gainsay or explain it, the miracle was accepted, and the streets actually showed signs of a quick return to their old life. Even the very timid took heart, and went about thanking God and the *Panagia Blachernitissa*.

And here and there the monks passed, sleek and blithe, and complacently twirling the Greek crosses at the whip-ends of their rosaries of polished horn buttons large as walnuts, saying:

"The danger is gone. See what it is to have faith! Had we kept on trusting the *azymites*, whether Roman cardinal or apostate Emperor, a muezzin would ere long, perhaps to-morrow, be calling to prayer from the dome of Hagia Sophia. Blessed be the *Panagia!* To-night let us sleep; and then—then we will dismiss the mercenaries with their Latin tongues."

But there will be skeptics to the last hour of the last day; so is the world made of kinds of men. Constantine and Justiniani did not disarm or lay aside their care. In unpatriotic distrust, they kept post behind the ruins of St. Romain, and saw to it that the labor of planting the hull of the galley for a new wall, strengthened with another ditch of dangerous depth and width, was continued.

And they were wise; for about four o'clock in the afternoon, there was a blowing of horns on the parapet by the monster gun, and five heralds in tunics stiff with gold embroidery, and trousers to correspond—splendid fellows, under turbans like balloons, each with a trumpet of shining silver— set out for the gate, preceding a stately unarmed official.

The heralds halted now and then to execute a flourish. Constantine, recognizing an envoy, sent Justiniani and Count Corti to meet him beyond the moat, and they returned with the Sultan's formal demand for the surrender of the city. The message was threatening and imperious. The Emperor replied offering to pay tribute. Mahommed rejected the proposal, and announced an assault.

The retirement of the hordes at sight of the *Panagia* on the wall was by Mahommed's order. His wilfulness extended to his love—he did not intend the Princess Irene should suffer harm.

CHAPTER X
THE NIGHT BEFORE THE ASSAULT

The artillery of Mahommed had been effective, though not to the same degree, elsewhere than at St. Romain. Jerome the Italian and Leonardo di Langasco the Genoese, defending the port of Blacherne in the lowland, had not been able to save the Xiloporta or Wood Gate on the harbor front harmless; under pounding of the floating battery it lay in the dust, like a battered helmet.

John Grant and Theodore de Carystos looked at the green hills of Eyoub in front of the gate Caligaria or Charsias, assigned to them, through fissures and tumbles-down which made their hearts sore. The Bochiardi brothers, Paul and Antonin, had fared no better in their defence of the gate Adrianople. At the gate Selimbria, Theophilus Palaeologus kept the Imperial flag flying, but the outer faces of the towers there were in the ditch serving the uses of the enemy. Contarino the Venetian, on the roof of the Golden Gate, was separated from the wall reaching northward to Selimbria by a breach wide enough to admit a chariot. Gabriel Trevisan, with his noble four hundred Venetians, kept good his grip on the harbor wall from the Acropolis to the gate of St. Peter's. Through the incapacity or treason of Duke Notaras, the upper portion of the Golden Horn was entirely lost to the Christians. From the Seven Towers to Galata the Ottoman fleet held the wall facing the Marmora as a net of close meshes holds the space of water it is to drag. In a word, the hour for assault had arrived, and from the twenty-fourth to evening of the twenty-eighth of May Mahommed diligently prepared for the event.

The attack he reduced to a bombardment barely sufficient to deter the besiegers from systematic repairs. The reports of his guns were but occasionally heard. At no time, however, was the energy of the man more conspicuous. Previously his orders to chief officers in command along the line had been despatched to them; now he bade them to personal attendance; and, as may be fancied, the scene at his tent was orientally picturesque from sunrise to sunset. Such an abounding of Moslem princes and princes not Moslem, of Pachas, and Beys, and Governors of Castles, of Sheiks, and Captains of hordes without titles; such a medley of costumes, and armor, and strange ensigns; such a forest of tall shafts flying red horse-tails; such a herding of caparisoned steeds; such a company of trumpeters and heralds—had seldom if ever been seen. It seemed the East from the Euphrates and Red Sea to the Caspian, and the West far as the Iron Gates of the Danube, were there in warlike presence. Yet for the most part these selected lions of tribes kept in separate groups and regarded each other askance, having feuds and jealousies amongst themselves; and there was reason for their good behavior—around them, under arms, were fifteen thousand watchful Janissaries, the flower of the Sultan's host, of whom an old chronicler has said, Each one is a giant in stature, and the equal of ten ordinary men.

Throughout those four days but one man had place always at Mahommed's back, his confidant and adviser—not Kalil, it is to be remarked, or Saganos, or the Mollah Kourani, or Akschem-sed-din the Dervish.

"My Lord," the Prince of India had argued when the Sultan resolved to summon his vassal chiefs to personal conference, "all men love splendor; pleasing the eye is an inducement to the intelligent; exciting the astonishment of the vulgar disposes them to submit to superiority in another without wounding their vanity. The Rajahs in my country practise this philosophy with a thorough understanding. Having frequently to hold council with their officials, into the tent or hall of ceremony they bring their utmost riches. The lesson is open to my Lord."

So when his leaders of men were ushered into the audience, the interior of Mahommed's tent was extravagantly furnished, and their prostrations were at the step of a throne. Nevertheless in consenting to the suggestion, the Sultan had insisted upon a condition.

"They shall not mistake me for something else than a warrior—a politician or a diplomatist, for instance—or think the heaviest blow I can deal is with the tongue or a pen. Art thou hearing, Prince?"

"I hear, my Lord."

"So, by the tomb of the Prophet—may his name be exalted!—my household, viziers and all, shall stand at my left; but here on my right I will have my horse in panoply; and he shall bear my mace and champ his golden bit, and be ready to tread on such of the beggars as behave unseemly."

And over the blue and yellow silken rugs of Khorassan, with which the space at the right of the throne was spread, the horse, bitted and house led, had free range, an impressive reminder of the master's business of life.

As they were Christians or Moslems, Mahommed addressed the vassals honored by his summons, and admitted separately to his presence; for the same arguments might not be pleasing to both.

"I give you trust," he would say to the Christian, "and look for brave and loyal service from you.... I shall be present with you, and as an eyewitness judge of your valor, and never had men such incentives. The wealth of ages is in the walls before us, and it shall be yours—money, jewels, goods and people—all yours as you can lay hands on it. I reserve only the houses and churches. Are you poor, you may go away rich; if rich, you may be richer; for what you get will be honorable earnings of your right hand of which none shall dispossess you—and to that treaty I swear.... Rise now, and put your men in readiness. The stars have promised me this city, and their promises are as the breath of the God we both adore."

Very different in style and matter were his utterances to a Moslem.

"What is that hanging from thy belt?"

"It is a sword, my Lord."

"God is God, and there is no other God—*Amin!* And he it was who planted iron in the earth, and showed the miner where it was hid, and taught the armorer to give it form, and harden it, even the blade at thy belt; for God had need of an instrument for the punishment of those who say 'God hath partners.' ... And who are they that say 'God hath partners—a Son and his Mother'? Here have they their stronghold; and here have we been brought to make roads through its walls, and turn their palaces of unbelief into harems. For that thou hast thy sword, and I mine—*Amin!*... It is the will of God that we despoil these *Gabours* of their wealth and their women; for are they not of those of whom it is said: 'In their hearts is a disease, and God hath increased their disease, and for them is ordained a painful punishment, because they have charged the Prophet of God with falsehood'? That they who escape the sharpness of our swords shall be as beggars, and slaves, and homeless wanderers—such is the punishment, and it is the judgment of God—*Amin!* ... That they shall leave all they have behind them—so also hath God willed, and I say it shall be. I swear it. And that they leave behind them is for us who were appointed from the beginning of the world to take it; that also God wills, and I say it shall be. I swear it. *Amin!* ... What if the way be perilous, as I grant it is? Is it not written: 'A soul cannot die except by permission of God, according to a writing of God, definite as to time'? And if a man die, is it not also written: 'Repute not those slain in God's cause to be dead; nay, alive with God, they are provided for'? They are people of the 'right hand,' of whom it is written: 'They shall be brought nigh God in the gardens of delight, upon inwrought couches reclining face to face. Youths ever young shall go unto them round about with goblets and ewers, and a cup of flowing wine; and fruits of the sort which they shall choose, and the flesh of birds of the kind which they shall desire, and damsels with eyes like pearls laid up, we will give them as a reward for that which they have done.' ... But the appointed time is not yet for all of us—nay, it is for the fewest—*Amin!* ... And when the will of God is done, then for such as live, lo! over the walls yonder are gold refined and coined, and gold in vessels, and damsels on silken couches, their cheeks like roses of Damascus, their arms whiter and cooler than lilies, and as pearls laid up are their eyes, and their bodies sweeter than musk on the wings of the south wind in a grove of palms. With the gold we can make gardens of delight; and the damsels set down in the gardens, ours the fault if the promise be not made good as it was spoken by the Prophet—'Paradise shall be brought near unto the pious, to a place not distant from them, so they shall see it!' ... Being of those who shall 'receive their books in the right hand,' more need not be said unto you. I only reserve for myself the houses when you have despoiled them, and the churches. Make ready yourself and your people, and tell them faithfully what I say, and swear to. I will come to you with final orders. Arise!" [Footnote: For the quotations in this speech, see *Selections from the Koran*, by EDWARD WILLIAM LANE.]

From sunrise to sunset of the twenty-seventh Mahommed was in the saddle going with the retinue of a conqueror from chief to chief. From each he drew a detachment to be held in reserve. One hundred thousand men were thus detached.

"See to it," he said finally, "that you direct your main effort against the gate in front of you.... Put the wild men in the advance. The dead will be useful in the ditch.... Have the ladders at hand.... At the sound of my trumpets, charge.... Proclaim for me that he who is first upon the walls shall have choice of a province. I will make him governor. God is God. I am his servant, ordering as he has ordered."

On the twenty-eighth, he sent all the dervishes in camp to preach to the Moslems in arms; and of such effect were their promises of pillage and Paradise that after the hour of the fifth prayer, the multitude, in all quite two hundred and fifty thousand, abandoned themselves to transports of fanaticism. Of their huts and booths they made heaps, and at night set fire to them; and the tents of the Pachas and great officers being illuminated, and the ships perfecting the blockade dressed in lights, the entrenchment from Blacherne to the Seven Towers, and the sea thence to the Acropolis, were in a continued brilliance reaching up to the sky. Even the campania was invaded by the dazzlement of countless bonfires.

And from the walls the besieged, if they looked, beheld the antics of the hordes; if they listened, they heard the noise, in the distance, a prolonged, inarticulate, irregular clamor of voices, near by, a confusion of songs and cries. At times the bray of trumpets and the roll of drums great and small shook the air, and smothered every rival sound. And where the dervishes came, in their passage from group to group, the excitement arose out of bounds, while their dancing lent diablerie to the scene.

Assuredly there was enough in what they beheld to sink the spirit of the besieged, even the boldest of them. The cry *Allah-il-Allah* shouted from the moat was trifling in comparison with what they might have overheard around the bonfires.

"Why do you burn your huts?" asked a prudent officer of his men.

"Because we will not need them more. The city is for us to-morrow. The Padishah has promised and sworn."

"Did he swear it?"

"Ay, by the bones of the Three in the Tomb of the Prophet."

At another fire, the following:

"Yes, I have chosen my palace already. It is on the hill over there in the west."

And again:

"Tell us, O son of Mousa, when we are in the town what will you look for?"

"The things I most want."

"Well, what things?"

"May the Jinn fill thy stomach with green figs for such a question of my mother's son! What things? Two horses out of the Emperor's stable. And thou—what wilt thou put thy hand to first?"

"Oh, I have not made up my mind! I am thinking of a load of gold for my camel—enough to take my father and his three wives to Mecca, and buy water for them from the Zem zem. Praised be Allah!"

"Bah! Gold will be cheap."

"Yes, as bezants; but I have heard of a bucket the unbelieving Greeks use at times for mixing wine and bread in. It is when they eat the body of their God. They say the bucket is so big it takes six fat priests to lift it."

"It is too big. I'll gather the bezants."

"Well," said a third, with a loud Moslem oath, "keep to your gold, whether in pots or coin. For me—for me"—

"Ha, ha!—he don't know."

"Don't I? Thou grinning son of a Hindoo ape."

"What is it, then?"

"The thing which is first in thy mind."

"Name it."

"A string of women."

"Old or young?"

"An *hoo-rey-yeh* is never old."

"What judgment!" sneered the other. "I will take some of the old ones as well."

"What for?"

"For slaves to wait on the young. Was it not said by a wise man, 'Sweet water in the jar is not more precious than peace in the family'?"

Undoubtedly the evil genius of Byzantium in this peril was the Prince of India.

"My Lord," he had said, cynically, "of a truth a man brave in the day can be turned into a quaking coward at night; you have but to present him a danger substantial enough to quicken his imagination. These Greeks have withstood you stoutly; try them now with your power a vision of darkness."

"How, Prince?"

"In view and hearing from the walls let the hordes kindle fires to-night. Multiply the fires, if need be, and keep the thousands in motion about them, making a spectacle such as this generation has not seen; then"—

The singular man stopped to laugh.

Mahommed gazed at him in silent wonder.

"Then," he continued, "so will distorted fancy do its work, that by midnight the city will be on its knees praying to the Mother of God, and every armed man on the walls who has a wife or daughter will think he hears himself called to for protection. Try it, my Lord, and thou mayst whack my flesh into ribbons if by dawn the general fear have not left but a half task for thy sword."

It was as the Jew said.

Attracted by the illumination in the sky, suggestive of something vast and terrible going on outside the walls, and still full of faith in a miraculous deliverance, thousands hastened to see the mercy. What an awakening was in store for them! Enemies seemed to have arisen out of the earth—devils, not men. The world to the horizon's rim appeared oppressed with them. Nor was it possible to misapprehend the meaning of what they beheld.

"To-morrow—to-morrow"—they whispered to each other—"God keep us!" and pouring back into the streets, they became each a preacher of despair. Yet—marvelous to say—the monks sallied from their cells with words of cheer.

"Have faith," they said. "See, we are not afraid. The Blessed Mother has not deserted her children. Believe in her. She is resolved to allow the *azymite* Emperor to exhaust his vanity that in the last hour he and his Latin myrmidons may not deny her the merit of the salvation. Compose yourselves, and fear not. The angel will find the poor man at the column of Constantine."

The ordinary soul beset with fears, and sinking into hopelessness, is always ready to accept a promise of rest. The people listened to the priestly soothsayers. Nay, the too comforting assurance made its way to the defenders at the gates, and hundreds of them deserted their posts; leaving the enemy to creep in from the moat, and, with hooks on long poles, actually pull down some of the new defences.

It scarcely requires telling how these complications added weight to the cares with which the Emperor was already overladen. Through the afternoon he sat by the open window of a room above the Cercoporta, or sunken gate under the southern face of his High Residence, [Footnote: This room is still to be seen. The writer once visited it. Arriving near, his Turkish *cavass* requested him to wait a moment. The man then advanced alone and cautiously, and knocked at the door. There was a conference, and a little delay; after which the *cavass* announced it was safe to go in. The mystery was revealed upon entering. A half dozen steaming tubs were scattered over the paved floor, and by each of them stood a scantily attired woman with a dirty *yashmak* covering her face. The chamber which should have been very sacred if only because there the last of the Byzantine Emperors composedly resigned himself to the inevitable, had become a filthy den devoted to one of the most ignoble of uses. The shame is, of course, to the Greeks of Constantinople.] watching the movements of the Turks. The subtle prophet which sometimes mercifully goes before death had discharged its office with him. He had dismissed his last hope. Beyond peradventure the hardest task to one pondering his fate uprisen and standing before him with all its attending circumstances, is to make peace with himself; which is simply viewing the attractions of this life as birds of plumage in a golden cage, and deliberately opening the door, and letting them loose, knowing they can never return. This the purest and noblest of the imperial Greeks—the evil times in which his race as a ruler was run prevent us from terming him the greatest—had done.

He was in armor, and his sword rested against the cheek of a window. His faithful attendants came in occasionally, and spoke to him in low tones; but for the most part he was alone.

The view of the enemy was fair. He could see their intrenchment, and the tents and ruder quarters behind it. He could see the standards, many of them without meaning to him, the detachments on duty and watchful, the horsemen coming and going, and now and then a column in movement. He could hear the shouting, and he knew the meaning of it all—the final tempest was gathering.

About four o'clock in the afternoon, Phranza entered the room, and going to his master's right hand, was in the act of prostrating himself.

"No, my Lord," said the Emperor, reaching out to stay him, and smiling pleasantly, "let us have done with ceremony. Thou hast been true servant to me—I testify it, God hearing—and now I promote thee. Be as my other self. Speak to me standing. To-morrow is my end of days. In death no man is greater than another. Tell me what thou bringest."

On his knees, the Grand Chamberlain took the steel-gloved hand nearest him, and carried it to his lips.

"Your Majesty, no servant had ever a more considerate and loving master."

An oppressive silence followed. They were both thinking the same thought, and it was too sad for speech.

"The duty Your Majesty charged me with this morning "—thus Phranza upon recovery of his composure—"I attended to."

"And you found it?"

"Even as Your Majesty had warning. The Hegumens of the Brotherhoods"—

"All of them, O Phranza?"

"All of them, Your Majesty—assembled in a cloister of the Pantocrator."

"Gennadius again!"

The Emperor's hands closed, and there was an impatient twitching of his lips.

"Though why should I be astonished? Hark, my friend! I will tell thee what I have as yet spoken to no man else. Thou knowest Kalil the Vizier has been these many years my tributary, and that he hath done me many kindly acts, not always in his master's interest. The night of the day our Christian ships beat the Turks the Grand Vizier sent me an account of a stormy scene in Mahommed's tent, and advised me to beware of Gennadius. Ah, I had fancied myself prepared to drink the cup Heaven hath in store for me, lees and all, without a murmur, but men will be men until their second birth. It is nature! ... Oh, my Phranza, what thinkest thou the false monk is carrying under his hood?"

"Some egg of treason, I doubt not."

"Having driven His Serenity, the pious and venerable Gregory, into exile, he aspires to succeed him."

"The hypocrite!—the impostor!—the perjured!—He, Patriarch!" cried Phranza, with upraised eyes.

"And from whose hands thinkest thou he dreams of deriving the honor?"

"Not Your Majesty's."

The Emperor smiled faintly. "No—he regards Mahommed the Sultan a better patron, if not a better Christian."

"Forbid it Heaven!" and Phranza crossed himself repeatedly.

"Nay, good friend, hear his scheme, then thou mayst call the forbidding powers with undeniable reason....He undertook—so Kalil privily declared—if Mahommed would invest him with the Patriarchate, to deliver Constantinople to him."

"By what means? He has no gate in keeping—he is not even a soldier."

"My poor Phranza! Hast thou yet to learn that perfidy is not a trait of any class? This gowned traitor hath a key to all the gates. Hear him—I will ply the superstition of the Greeks, and draw them from the walls with a prophecy."

Phranza was able to cry out: "Oh! that so brave a prince, so good a master should be at the mercy of—of such a"—

"With all thy learning, I see thou lackest a word. Let it pass, let it pass—I understand thee....But what further hast thou from the meeting?"

Phranza caught the hand again, and laid his forehead upon it while he replied: "To-night the Brotherhoods are to go out, and renew the story of the angel, and the man at the foot of the column of Constantine." The calmness of the Emperor was wonderful. He gazed at the Turks through the window, and, after reflection, said tranquilly:

"I would have saved it—this old empire of our fathers; but my utmost now is to die for it—ay, as if I were blind to its unworthiness. God's will be done, not mine!"

"Talk not of dying—O beloved Lord and master, talk not so! It is not too late for composition. Give me your terms, and I will go with them to"—

"Nay, friend, I have done better—I have made peace with myself.... I shall be no man's slave. There is nothing more for me—nothing except an honorable death. How sweet a grace it is that we can put so much glory in dying! A day of Greek regeneration may come—then there may be some to do me honor—some to find worthy lessons in my life—perchance another Emperor of Byzantium to remember how the last of the Palaeologae accepted the will of God revealed to him in treachery and treason.... But there is one at the door knocking as he were in haste. Let him enter."

An officer of the guard was admitted.

"Your Majesty," he said, after salutation, "the Captain Justiniani, and the Genoese, his friends, are preparing to abandon the gates."

Constantine seized his sword, and arose.

"Tell me about it," he said, simply.

"Justiniani has the new ditch at St. Romain nearly completed, and wanting some cannon, he made request for them of the High Admiral, who refused, saying, 'The foreign cowards must take care of themselves.'"

"Ride, sir, to the noble Captain, and tell him I am at thy heels."

"Is the Duke mad?" Constantine continued, the messenger having departed. "What can he want? He is rich, and hath a family—boys verging on manhood, and of excellent promise. Ah, my dear friend in need, what canst thou see of gain for him from Mahommed?"

"Life, your Majesty—life, and greater riches."

"How? I did not suppose thou thoughtest so ill of men."

"Of some—of some—not all." Then Phranza raised his head, and asked, bitterly: "If five galleys won the harbor, every Moslem sail opposing, why could not twelve or more do better? Does not Mahommed draw his supplies by sea?"

The Emperor looked out of the window again, but not at the Turks.

"Lord Phranza," he said, presently, "thou mayst survive to-morrow's calamity; if so, being as thou art skilful with the pen, write of me in thy day of leisure two things; first, I dared not break with Duke Notaras while Mahommed was striving for my gates—he could and would have seized my throne—the Church, the Brotherhoods, and the people are with him—I am an *azymite*. Say of me next that I have always held the decree of union proclaimed by the Council of Florence binding upon Greek conscience, and had I lived, God helping me roll back this flood of Islam, it should have been enforced.... Hither—look hither, Lord Phranza"—he pointed out of the window—"and thou wilt see an argument of as many divisions as there are infidels beleaguering us why the Church of Christ should have one head; and as to whether the head should be Patriarch or Bishop, is it not enough that we are perishing for want of Western swords?"—He would have fallen into silence again, but roused himself: "So much for the place I would have in the world's memory.... But to the present affair. Reparation is due Justiniani and his associates. Do thou prepare a repast in the great dining hall. Our resources are so reduced I may not speak of it as a banquet; but as thou lovest me do thy best with what we have. For my part, I will ride and summon every noble Greek in arms for Church and State, and the foreign captains. In such cheer, perhaps, we can heal the wounds inflicted by Notaras. We can at least make ready to die with grace."

He went out, and taking horse, rode at speed to the Gate St. Romain, and succeeded in soothing the offended Genoese.

At ten o'clock the banquet was held. The chroniclers say of it that there were speeches, embraces, and a fresh resolution to fight, and endure the worst or conquer. And they chose a battle-cry—*Christ and Holy Church*. At separating, the Emperor, with infinite tenderness, but never more knightly, prayed forgiveness of any he might have wronged or affronted; and the guests came one by one to bid him adieu, and he commended them to God, and the gratitude of Christians in the ages to come, and his hands were drenched with their tears.

From the Very High Residence he visited the gates, and was partially successful in arresting the desertions actually in progress.

Finally, all other duties done, his mind turning once more to God, he rode to Sancta Sophia, heard mass, partook of the Communion, and received absolution according to Latin rite; after which the morrow could hold no surprise for him. And he found comfort repeating his own word: How sweet a grace it is that we can put so much glory in dying.

CHAPTER XI
COUNT CORTI IN DILEMMA

From the repast at Blacherne—festive it was in no sense—Count Corti escorted the Emperor to the door of Sancta Sophia; whence, by permission, and taking with him his nine Berbers, he rode slowly to the residence of the Princess Irene. Slowly, we say, for nowhere in the pent area of Byzantium was there a soul more oppressed.

If he looked up, it was to fancy all the fortunate planets seated in their Houses helping Mahommed's star to a fullest flood of splendor; if he looked down, it was to see the wager—and his soul cried out, Lost! Lost! Though one be rich, or great, or superior in his calling, wherein is the profit of it if he have lost his love?

Besides the anguish of a perception of his rival's better fortune, the Count was bowed by the necessity of deciding certain consequences unforeseen at the time the wager was made. The place of the surrender of the Princess was fixed. Thinking forward now, he could anticipate the scene in the great church—the pack of fugitives, their terror and despair, the hordes raging amongst them. How was he single-handed to save her unharmed in the scramble of the hour? Thoughts of her youth, beauty, and rank, theretofore inspirations out of Heaven, set him to shivering with an ague more like fear than any he had ever known.

Nor was this all. The surrender was by the terms to be to Mahommed himself. The Sultan was to demand her of him. He groaned aloud: "Oh, dear God and Holy Mother, be merciful, and let me die!" For the first time it was given him to see, not alone that he might lose the woman to his soul all the sun is to the world, but her respect as well. By what management was he to make the surrender without exposing the understanding between the conqueror and himself? She would be present—she would see what took place—she would hear what was said. And she would not be frightened. The image of the Madonna above the altar in the nave would not be more calm. The vaguest suspicion of a compact, and she the subject, would put her upon inquiry; then—"Oh, fool—idiot—insensate as my sword-grip!" Thus, between groans, he scourged himself.

It was late, but her home was now a hospital filled with wounded men, and she its sleepless angel. Old Lysander admitted him.

"The Princess Irene is in the chapel."

Thus directed, the Count went thither well knowing the way.

A soldier just dead was the theme of a solemn recital by Sergius. The room was crowded with women in the deepest excitement of fear. Corti understood the cause. Poor creatures! They had need of religious comfort. A thousand ghosts in one view could not have overcome them as did the approach of the morrow.

At the right of the altar, he discovered the Princess in the midst of her attendants, who kept close to her, like young birds to the mother in alarm. She was quiet and self-contained. Apparently she alone heard the words of the reader; and whereas the Count came in a penitent—doubtful—in a maze—unknowing what to do or where to turn, one glance at her face restored him. He resolved to tell her his history, omitting only the character in which he entered her kinsman's service, and the odious compact with Mahommed. Her consent to accompany him to Sancta Sophia must be obtained; for that he was come.

His presence in the chapel awakened a suppressed excitement, and directly the Princess came to him.

"What has happened, Count Corti? Why are you here?"

"To speak with you, O Princess Irene'

"Go with me, then."

She conducted him into a passage, and closed the door behind them.

"The floor of my reception room is overlaid with the sick and suffering—my whole house is given up to them. Speak here; and if the news be bad, dear Count, it were mercy not to permit the unfortunates to hear you."

She was not thinking of herself. He took the hand extended to him, and kissed it—to him it was the hand of more than the most beautiful woman in the world—it was the hand of a saint in white transfiguration.

"Thy imperial kinsman, O Princess, is at the church partaking of the Holy Communion, and receiving absolution."

"At this hour? Why is he there, Count?"

Corti told her of the repast at the palace, and recounted the scene at parting.

"It looks like despair. Can it be the Emperor is making ready to die? Answer, and fear not for me. My life has been a long preparation. He believes the defence is lost—the captains believe so—and thou?"

"O Princess, it is terrible saying, but I too expect the judgment of God in the morning."

The hall was so dimly lighted he could not see her face; but the nerve of sympathy is fine—he felt she trembled. Only a moment—scarcely longer than taking a breath—then she answered:

"Judgment is for us all. It will find me here."

She moved as if to return to the chapel; but he stepped before her, and drawing out a chair standing by the door, said, firmly, yet tenderly:

"You are weary. The labor of helping the unfortunate these many days— the watching and anxiety—have been trying upon you. Sit, I pray, and hear me."

She yielded with a sigh.

"The judgment which would find you here, O Princes, would not be death, but something more terrible, so terrible words burn in thinking of it. I have sworn to defend you: and the oath, and the will to keep it, give me the right to determine where and how the defence shall be made. If there are advantages, I want them, for your sweet sake."

He stopped to master his feeling.

"You have never stood on the deck of a ship in wreck, and seen the sea rush in to overwhelm it," he went on presently: "I have; and I declare to you, O beloved lady, nothing can be so like to-morrow when the hordes break into the city, as that triumph of waters; and as on the deck there was no place of safety for the perishing crew, neither will there be place of safety for man, woman, or child in Byzantium then—least of all for the kinswoman of the Emperor—for her—permit me to say it—whose loveliness and virtue are themes for story-tellers throughout the East. As a prize—whether for ransom or dishonor—richer than the churches and the palaces, and their belongings, be they jewels or gold, or anointed crown, or bone of Saint, or splinter of the True Cross, or shred from the shirt of Christ—to him who loves her, a prize of such excellence that glory, even the glory Mahommed is now dreaming of when he shall have wrenched the keys of the gates from their rightful owner dead in the bloody breach, would pale if set beside it for comparison, and sink out of sight—think you she will not be hunted? Or that the painted Mother above the altar, though it spoke through a miraculous halo, could save her when found? No, no, Princess, not here, not here!... You know I love you; in an unreasoning moment I dared tell you so; and you may think me passion-blind, and that I hung the vow to defend you upon my soul's neck, thinking it light as this favor you were pleased to give me; that love being a braggart, therefore I am a braggart. Let me set myself right in your opinion—your good opinion, O Princess, for it is to me a world of such fair shining I dream of it as of a garden in Paradise.... If you do not know how hardly I have striven in this war, send, I pray, and ask any of the captains, or the most Christian sovereign I have just left making his peace with God. Some of them called me mad, but I pardoned them—they did not know the meaning of my battle-cry—'For Christ and Irene'—that I was venturing life less for Constantinople, less for religion—I almost said, less for Christ—than for you, who are all things in one to me, the fairest on earth, the best in Heaven.... At last, at last I am driven to admit we may fail—that to-morrow, whether I am here or there, at your side or under the trampling, you may be a prisoner at mercy."

At these words, of infinite anguish in utterance, the Princess shuddered, and looked up in silent appeal.

"Attend me now. You have courage above the courage of women; therefore I may speak with plainness.... What will become of you—I give the conclusion of many wrangles with myself—what will become of you depends upon the hands which happen to be laid on you first. O Princess, are you giving me heed? Do you comprehend me?"

"The words concern me more than life, Count."

"I may go on then.... I have hope of saving your life and honor. You have but to do what I advise. If you cannot trust me, further speech were idleness, and I might as well take leave of you. Death in many forms will be abroad to-morrow—nothing so easily found."

"Count Corti," she returned, "if I hesitate pledging myself, it is not because of distrust. I will hear you."

"It is well said, dear lady."

He stopped—a pleasant warmth was in his heart—a perception, like dim light, began breaking through the obscurities in his mind. To this moment, in fact, he had trouble gaining his own consent to the proposal on his tongue; it seemed so like treachery to the noble woman—so like a cunning inveiglement to deliver her to Mahommed under the hated compact. Now suddenly the proposal assumed another appearance—it was the best course—the best had there been no wager, no compact, no obligation but knightly duty to her. As he proceeded, this conviction grew clearer, bringing him ease of conscience and the subtle influence of a master arguing right. He told her his history then, holding nothing back but the two points mentioned. Twice only she interrupted him.

"Your mother, Count Corti—poor lady—how she has suffered! But what happiness there is in store for her!" And again: "How wonderful the escape from the falsehoods of the Prophet! There is no love like Christ's love unless—unless it be a mother's."

At the conclusion, her chin rested in the soft palm of her hand, and the hand, unjewelled, was white as marble just carven, and, like the arm, a wonder of grace. Of what was she thinking?—Of him? Had he at last made an impression upon her? What trifles serve the hope of lovers! At length she asked:

"Then, O Count, thou wert his playmate in childhood?"

A bitter pang struck him—that pensiveness was for Mahommed—yet he answered: "I was nearest him until he took up his father's sword."

"Is he the monster they call him?"

"To his enemies, yes—and to all in the road to his desires, yes—but to his friends there was never such a friend."

"Has he heart to"—

The omission, rather than the question, hurt him—still he returned:

"Yes, once he really loves."

Then she appeared to awake.

"To the narrative now—Forgive my wandering."

The opportunity to return was a relief to him, and he hastened to improve it.

"I thank you for grace, O Princess, and am reminded of the pressure of time. I must to the gate again with the Emperor.... This is my proposal. Instead of biding here to be taken by some rapacious hordesman, go with me to Sancta Sophia, and when the Sultan comes thither—as he certainly will—deliver yourself to him. If, before his arrival, the plunderers force the doors of the holy house, I will stand with you, not, Princess, as Count Corti the Italian, but Mirza the Emir and Janissary, appointed by the Sultan to guard you. My Berbers will help the assumption."

He had spoken clearly, yet she hesitated.

"Ah," he said, "you doubt Mahommed. He will be upon honor. The glory-winners, Princess, are those always most in awe of the judgment of the world."

Yet she sat silent.

"Or is it I who am in your doubt?"

"No, Count. But my household—my attendants—the poor creatures are trembling now—some of them, I was about saying, are of the noblest families in Byzantium, daughters of senators and lords of the court. I cannot desert them—no, Count Corti, not to save myself. The baseness would be on my soul forever. They must share my fortune, or I their fate."

Still she was thinking of others!

More as a worshipper than lover, the Count replied: "I will include them in my attempt to save you. Surely Heaven will help me, for your sake, O Princess."

"And I can plead for them with him. Count Corti, I will go with you."

The animation with which she spoke faded in an instant.

"But thou—O my friend, if thou shouldst fall?"

"Nay, let us be confident. If Heaven does not intend your escape, it would be merciful, O beloved lady, did it place me where no report of your mischance and sorrows can reach me. Looking at the darkest side, should I not come for you, go nevertheless to the Church. Doubt not hearing of the entry of the Turks. Seek Mahommed, if possible, and demand his protection. Tell him, I, Mirza the Emir, counselled you. On the other side, be ready to accompany me. Make preparation to-night—have a chair at hand, and your household assembled—for when I come, time will be scant.... And now, God be with you! I will not say be brave—be trustful."

She extended her hand, and he knelt, and kissed it.

"I will pray for you, Count Corti."

"Heaven will hear you."

He went out, and rejoining the Emperor, rode with him from the Church to Blacherne.

CHAPTER XII
THE ASSAULT

The bonfires of the hordes were extinguished about the time the Christian company said their farewells after the last supper in the Very High Residence, and the hordes themselves appeared to be at rest, leaving Night to reset her stars serenely bright over the city, the sea, and the campania.

To the everlasting honor of that company, be it now said, they could under cover of the darkness have betaken themselves to the ships and escaped; yet they went to their several posts. Having laid their heads upon the breast of the fated Emperor, and pledged him their lives, there is no account of one in craven refuge at the break of day. The Emperor's devotion seems to have been a communicable flame.

This is the more remarkable when it is remembered that in the beginning the walls were relied upon to offset the superiority of the enemy in numbers, while now each knight and man-at-arms knew the vanity of that reliance—knew himself, in other words, one of scant five thousand men— to such diminished roll had the besieged been reduced by wounds, death and desertion—who were to muster on the ruins of the outer wall, or in the breaches of the inner, and strive against two hundred and fifty thousand goaded by influences justly considered the most powerful over ferocious natures—religious fanaticism and the assurance of booty without limit. The silence into which the Turkish host was sunk did not continue a great while. The Greeks on the landward walls became aware of a general murmur, followed shortly by a rumble at times vibrant—so the earth complains of the beating it receives from vast bodies of men and animals in hurried passage.

"The enemy is forming," said John Grant to his associate Carystos, the archer.

Minotle, the Venetian bayle, listening from the shattered gate of Adrianople, gave order: "Arouse the men. The Turks are coming."

Justiniani, putting the finishing touches upon his masked repairs behind what had been the alley or passage between the towers Bagdad and St. Romain, was called to by his lookout: "Come up, Captain—the infidels are stirring—they seem disposed to attack."

"No," the Captain returned, after a brief observation, "they will not attack to-night—they are getting ready."

None the less, without relieving his working parties, he placed his command in station.

At Selimbria and the Golden Gate the Christians stood to arms. So also between the gates. Then a deep hush descended upon the mighty works—mighty despite the slugging they had endured—and the silence was loaded with anxiety.

For such of my readers as have held a night-watch expectant of battle at disadvantage in the morning it will be easy putting themselves in the place of these warders at bay; they can think their thoughts, and hear the heavy beating of their hearts; they will remember how long the hours were, and how the monotony of the waiting gnawed at their spirits until they prayed for action, action. On the other hand, those without the experience will wonder how men can bear up bravely in such conditions—and that is a wonder.

In furtherance of his plan, Mahommed drew in his irregulars, and massed them in the space between the intrenchment and the ditch; and by bringing his machines and small guns nearer the walls, he menaced the whole front of defence with a line amply provided with scaling ladders and mantelets. Behind the line he stationed bodies of horsemen to arrest fugitives, and turn them back to the fight. His reserves occupied the intrenchments. The Janissaries were retained at his quarters opposite St. Romain.

The hordes were clever enough to see what the arrangement portended for them, and they at first complained.

"What, grumble, do they?" Mahommed answered. "Ride, and tell them I say the first choice in the capture belongs to the first over the walls. Theirs the fault if the city be not an empty nest to all who come after them."

The earth in its forward movement overtook the moon just before daybreak; then in the deep hush of expectancy and readiness, the light being sufficient to reveal to the besieged the assault couchant below them, a long-blown flourish was sounded by the Turkish heralds from the embrasure of the great gun.

Other trumpeters took up the signal, and in a space incredibly short it was repeated everywhere along the line of attack. A thunder of drums broke in upon the music. Up rose the hordes, the archers and slingers, and the ladder bearers, and forward, like a bristling wave, they rushed, shouting every man as he pleased. In the same instant the machines and light guns were set in operation. Never had the old walls been assailed by such a tempest of bolts, arrows, stones and bullets—never had their echoes been awakened by an equal explosion of human voices, instruments of martial music, and cannon. The warders were not surprised by the assault so much as by its din and fury; and when directly the missiles struck them, thickening into an uninterrupted pouring rain, they cowered behind the merlons, and such other shelters as they could find.

This did not last long—it was like the shiver and gasp of one plunged suddenly into icy water. The fugitives were rallied, and brought back to their weapons, and to replying in kind; and having no longer to shoot with care, the rabble fusing into a compact target, especially on the outer edge of the ditch, not a shaft, or bolt, or stone, or ball from culverin went amiss. Afterwhile, their blood warming with the work, and the dawn breaking, they could see their advantage of position, and the awful havoc they were playing; then they too knew the delight in killing which more than anything else proves man the most ferocious of brutes.

The movement of the hordes was not a dash wholly without system—such an inference would be a great mistake. There was no pretence of alignment or order—there never is in such attacks—forlorn hopes, receiving the signal, rush on, each individual to his own endeavor; here, nevertheless, the Pachas and Beys directed the assault, permitting no blind waste of effort. They hurled their mobs at none but the weak places—here a breach, there a dismantled gate.

Thousands were pushed headlong into the moat. The ladders then passed down to such of them as had footing were heavy, but they were caught willingly; if too short, were spliced; once planted so as to bring the coping of the wall in reach, they swarmed with eager adventurers, who, holding their shields and pikes overhead, climbed as best they could. Those below cheered their comrades above, and even pushed them up.

"The spoils—think of the spoils—the gold, the women!... *Allah-il-Allah!*... Up, up—it is the way to Paradise!"

Darts and javelins literally cast the climbers in a thickened shade. Sometimes a ponderous stone plunging down cleaned a ladder from top to bottom; sometimes, waiting until the rounds were filled, the besieged applied levers, and swung a score and more off helpless and shrieking. No matter—*Allah-il-Allah!* The living were swift to restore and attempt the fatal ascents.

Every one dead and every one wounded became a serviceable clod; rapidly as the dump and cumber of humanity filled the moat the ladders extended their upward reach; while drum-beat, battle-cry, trumpet's blare, and the roar of cannon answering cannon blent into one steady all-smothering sound.

In the stretches of space between gates, where the walls and towers were intact, the strife of the archers and slingers was to keep the Greeks occupied, lest they should reenforce the defenders hard pressed elsewhere.

During the night the blockading vessels had been warped close into the shore, and, the wall of the seafront being lower than those on the land side, the crews, by means of platforms erected on the decks, engaged the besieged from a better level. There also, though attempts at escalade were frequent, the object was chiefly to hold the garrison in place.

In the harbor, particularly at the Wood Gate, already mentioned as battered out of semblance to itself by the large gun on the floating battery, the Turks exerted themselves to effect a landing; but the Christian fleet interposed, and there was a naval battle of varying fortune.

So, speaking generally, the city was wrapped in assault; and when the sun at last rode up into the clear sky above the Asiatic heights, streets, houses, palaces, churches—the hills, in fact, from the sea to the Tower of Isaac— were shrouded in ominous vapor, through which such of the people as dared go abroad flitted pale and trembling; or if they spoke to each other, it was to ask in husky voices, What have you from the gates?

Passing now to the leading actors in this terrible tragedy. Mahommed retired to his couch early the night previous. He knew his orders were in course of execution by chiefs who, on their part, knew the consequences of failure. The example made of the Admiral in command of the fleet the day the five relieving Christian galleys won the port was fresh in memory. [Footnote: He was stretched on the ground and whipped like a common malefactor.]

"To-morrow, to-morrow," he kept repeating, while his pages took off his armor, and laid the pieces aside. "To-morrow, to-morrow," lingered in his thoughts, when, his limbs stretched out comfortably on the broad bronze cot which served him for couch, sleep crept in as to a tired child, and laid its finger of forgetfulness upon his eyelids. The repetition was as when we run through the verse of a cheerful song, thinking it out silently, and then recite the chorus aloud. Once he awoke, and, sitting up, listened. The mighty host which had its life by his permission was quiet—even the horses in their apartment seemed mindful that the hour was sacred to their master. Falling to sleep again, he muttered: "To-morrow, to-morrow—Irene and glory. I have the promise of the stars."

To Mahommed the morrow was obviously but a holiday which was bringing him the kingly part in a joyous game—a holiday too slow in coming.

About the third hour after midnight he was again awakened. A man stood by his cot imperfectly shading the light of a lamp with his hand.

"Prince of India!" exclaimed Mahommed, rising to a sitting posture.

"It is I, my Lord."

"What time is it?"

The Prince gave him the hour.

"Is it so near the break of day?" Mahommed yawned. "Tell me"—he fixed his eyes darkly on the visitor—"tell me first why thou art here?"

"I will, my Lord, and truly. I wished to see if you could sleep. A common soul could not. It is well the world has no premonitory sense."

"Why so?"

"My Lord has all the qualities of a conqueror."

Mahommed was pleased.

"Yes, I will make a great day of to-morrow. But, Prince of India, what shadows are disturbing thee? Why art thou not asleep?"

"I too have a part in the day, my Lord."

"What part?"

"I will fight, and"—

Mahommed interrupted him with a laugh.

"Thou!" and he looked the stooped figure over from head to foot.

"My Lord has two hands—I have four—I will show them."

Returning to his apartment, the Prince reappeared with Nilo.

"Behold, my Lord!"

The black was in the martial attire of a king of Kash-Cush—feathered coronet, robe of blue and red hanging from shoulder to heel, body under the robe naked to the waist, assegai in the oft-wrapped white sash, skirt to the knees glittering with crescents and buttons of silver, sandals beaded with pearls. On his left arm depended a shield rimmed and embossed with brass; in his right hand he bore a club knotted, and of weight to fell a bull at a blow. Without the slightest abashment, but rather as a superior, the King looked down at the young Sultan.

"I see—I understand—I welcome the four hands of the Prince of India," Mahommed said, vivaciously; then, giving a few moments of admiration to the negro, he turned, and asked:

"Prince, I have a motive for to-morrow—nay, by the cool waters of Paradise, I have many motives. Tell me thine. In thy speech and action I have observed a hate for these Greeks deep as the Shintan's for God. Why? What have they done to thee?"

"They are Christians," the Jew returned, sullenly.

"That is good, Prince, very good—even the Prophet judged it a justification for cleaning the earth of the detestable sect—yet it is not enough. I am not old as thou"—Mahommed lost the curious gleam which shone in the visitor's eyes—"I am not old as thou art; still I know hate like thine must be from a private grievance."

"My Lord is right. To-morrow I will leave the herd to the herd. In the currents of the fight I will hunt but one enemy—Constantine. Judge thou my cause."

Then he told of Lael—of his love for her—of her abduction by Demedes—his supplication for the Emperor's assistance—the refusal.

"She was the child of my soul," he continued, passionately. "My interest in life was going out; she reinspired it. She was the promise of a future for me, as the morning star is of a gladsome day. I dreamed dreams of her, and upon her love builded hopes, like shining castles on high hills. Yet it was not enough that the Greek refused me his power to discover and restore her. She is now in restraint, and set apart to become the wife of a Christian—a Christian priest—may the fiends juggle for his ghost!—To-morrow I will punish the tyrant—I will give him a dog's death, and then seek her. Oh! I will find her—I will find her—and by the light there is in love, I will show him what all of hell there can be in one man's hate!"

For once the cunning of the Prince overreached itself. In the rush of passion he forgot the exquisite sensory gifts of the potentate with whom he was dealing; and Mahommed, observant even while shrinking from the malignant fire in the large eyes, discerned incoherencies in the tale, and that it was but half told; and while he was resolving to push his Messenger of the Stars to a full confession, a distant rumble invaded the tent, accompanied by a trample of feet outside.

"It is here, Prince of India—the day of Destiny. Let us get ready, thou for thy revenge, I for glory and"—Irene was on his tongue, but he suppressed the name. "Call my chamberlain and equerry.... On the table there thou mayst see my arms—a mace my ancestor Ilderim [Footnote: Bajazet.] bore at Nicopolis, and thy sword of Solomon.... God is great, and the Jinn and the Stars on my side, what have we to fear?"

Within half an hour he rode out of the tent.

"Blows the wind to the city or from it?" he asked his chief Aga of Janissaries.

"Toward the city, my Lord."

"Exalted be the name of the Prophet! Set the Flower of the Faithful in order—a column of front wide as the breach in the gate—and bring the heralds. I shall be by the great gun."

Pushing his horse on the parapet, he beheld the space before him, down quite to the moat—every trace of the cemetery had disappeared—dark with hordes assembled and awaiting the signal. Satisfied, happy, he looked then toward the east. None better than he knew the stars appointed to go before the sun—their names were familiar to him—now they were his friends. At last a violet corona infinitely soft glimmered along the hill tops beyond Scutari.

"Stand out now," he cried to the five in their tabards of gold—"stand out now, and as ye hope couches in Paradise, blow—blow the stones out of their beds yonder—God was never so great!"

Then ensued the general advance which has been described, except that here, in front of St. Romain, there was no covering the assailants with slingers and archers. The fill in the ditch was nearly level with the outer bank, from which it may be described as an ascending causeway. This advantage encouraged the idea of pouring the hordesmen *en masse* over the hill composed of the ruins of what had been the towers of the gate.

There was an impulsive dash under incitement of a mighty drumming and trumpeting—a race, every man of the thousands engaged in it making for the causeway—a jam—a mob paralyzed by its numbers. They trampled on each other—they fought, and in the rebound were pitched in heaps down the perpendicular revetment on the right and left of the fill. Of those thus unfortunate the most remained where they fell, alive, perhaps, but none the less an increasing dump of pikes, shields, and crushed bodies; and in the roar above them, cries for help, groans, and prayers were alike unheard and unnoticed.

All this Justiniani had foreseen. Behind loose stones on top of the hill, he had collected culverins, making, in modern phrase, a masked battery, and trained the pieces to sweep the causeway; with them, as a support, he mixed archers and pikemen. On either flank, moreover, he stationed companies similarly armed, extending them to the unbroken wall, so there was not a space in the breach undefended.

The Captain, on watch and expectant, heard the signal.

"To the Emperor at Blacherne," he bade; "and say the storm is about to break. Make haste." Then to his men: "Light the matches, and be ready to throw the stones down."

The hordesmen reached the edge of the ditch; that moment the guns were unmasked, and the Genoese leader shouted:

"Fire, my men!—*Christ and Holy Church!*"

Then from the Christian works it was bullet, bolt, stone, and shaft, making light of flimsy shield and surcoat of hide; still the hordesmen pushed on, a river breasting an obstruction. Now they were on the causeway. Useless facing about—behind them an advancing wall—on both sides the ditch. Useless lying down—that was to be smothered in bloody mire. Forward, forward, or die. What though the causeway was packed with dead and wounded?—though there was no foothold not slippery?—though the smell of hot blood filled every nostril?—though hands thrice strengthened by despair grappled the feet making stepping blocks of face and breast? The living pressed on leaping, stumbling, staggering; their howl, "Gold—spoils—women—slaves," answered from the smoking hill, "*Christ and Holy Church.*"

And now, the causeway crossed, the leading assailants gain the foot of the rough ascent. No time to catch breath—none to look for advantage—none to profit by a glance at the preparation to receive them—up they must go, and up they went. Arrows and javelins pierce them; stones crush them; the culverins spout fire in their faces, and, lifting them off their uncertain footing, hurl them bodily back upon the heads and shields of their comrades. Along the brow of the rocky hill a mound of bodies arises wondrous quick, an obstacle to the warders of the pass who would shoot, and to the hordesmen a barrier.

Slowly the corona on the Scutarian hills deepened into dawn. The Emperor joined Justiniani. Count Corti came with him. There was an affectionate greeting.

"Your Majesty, the day is scarcely full born, yet see how Islam is rueing it."

Constantine, following Justiniani's pointing, peered once through the smoke; then the necessity of the moment caught him, and, taking post between guns, he plied his long lance upon the wretches climbing the rising mound, some without shields, some weaponless, most of them incapable of combat.

With the brightening of day the mound grew in height and width, until at length the Christians sallied out upon it to meet the enemy still pouring on.

An hour thus.

Suddenly, seized with a comprehension of the futility of their effort, the hordesmen turned, and rushed from the hill and the causeway.

The Christians suffered but few casualties; yet they would have gladly rested. Then, from the wall above the breach, whence he had used his bow, Count Corti descended hastily.

"Your Majesty," he said, his countenance kindled with enthusiasm, "the Janissaries are making ready."

Justiniani was prompt. "Come!" he shouted. "Come every one! We must have clear range for the guns. Down with these dead! Down with the living. No time for pity!"

Setting the example, presently the defenders were tossing the bodies of their enemies down the face of the hill.

On his horse, by the great gun, Mahommed had observed the assault, listening while the night yet lingered. Occasionally a courier rode to him with news from this Pacha or that one. He heard without excitement, and returned invariably the same reply:

"Tell him to pour the hordes in."

At last an officer came at speed.

"Oh, my Lord, I salute you. The city is won."

It was clear day then, yet a light not of the morning sparkled in Mahommed's eyes. Stooping in his saddle, he asked: "What sayest thou? Tell me of it, but beware—if thou speakest falsely, neither God nor Prophet shall save thee from impalement to the roots of thy tongue."

"As I have to tell my Lord what I saw with my own eyes, I am not afraid.... My Lord knows that where the palace of Blacherne begins on the south there is an angle in the wall. There, while our people were feigning an assault to amuse the Greeks, they came upon a sunken gate"—

"The Cercoporta—I have heard of it."

"My Lord has the name. Trying it, they found it unfastened and unguarded, and, pushing through a darkened passage, discovered they were in the Palace. Mounting to the upper floor, they attacked the unbelievers. The fighting goes on. From room to room the Christians resist. They are now cut off, and in a little time the quarter will be in our possession."

Mahommed spoke to Kalil: "Take this man, and keep him safely. If he has spoken truly, great shall be his reward; if falsely, better he were not his mother's son." Then to one of his household: "Come hither.... Go to the sunken gate Cercoporta, pass in, and find the chief now fighting in the palace of Blacherne. Tell him I, Mahommed, require that he leave the Palace to such as may follow him, and march and attack the defenders of this gate, St. Romain, in the rear. He shall not stop to plunder. I give him one hour in which to do my bidding. Ride thou now as if a falcon led thee. For Allah and life!"

Next he called his Aga of Janissaries.

"Have the hordes before this gate retired. They have served their turn; they have made the ditch passable, and the *Gabours* are faint with killing them. Observe, and when the road is cleared let go with the Flower of the Faithful. A province to the first through; and this the battle-cry: *Allah-il-Allah!* They will fight under my eye. Minutes are worth kingdoms. Go thou, and let go."

Always in reserve, always the last resort in doubtful battle, always the arm with which the Sultans struck the finishing blow, the Janissaries thus summoned to take up the assault were in discipline, spirit, and splendor of appearance the *elite* corps of the martial world.

Riding to the front, the Aga halted to communicate Mahommed's orders. Down the columns the speech was passed.

The Flower of the Faithful were in three divisions dismounted. Throwing off their clumsy gowns, they stood forth in glittering mail, and shaking their brassy shields in air, shouted the old salute: "*Live the Padishah! Live the Padishah!*"

The road to the gate was cleared; then the Aga galloped back, and when abreast of the yellow flag of the first division, he cried: "*Allah-il-Allah!* Forward!"

And drum and trumpet breaking forth, a division moved down in column of fifties. Slowly at first, but solidly, and with a vast stateliness it moved. So at Pharsalia marched the legion Caesar loved—so in decision of heady fights strode the Old Guard of the world's last Conqueror.

Approaching the ditch, the fresh assailants set up the appointed battle-cry, and quickening the step to double time rushed over the terrible causeway.

Mahommed then descended to the ditch, and remained there mounted, the sword of Solomon in his hand, the mace of Ilderim at his saddle bow; and though hearing him was impossible, the Faithful took fire from his fire—enough that they were under his eye.

The feat attempted by the hordes was then repeated, except now there was order in disorder. The machine, though shaken and disarranged, kept working on, working up. Somehow its weight endured. Slowly, with all its drench and cumber, the hill was surmounted. Again a mound arose in front of the battery—again the sally, and the deadly ply of pikes from the top of the mound.

The Emperor's lance splintered; he fought with a pole-axe; still even he became sensible of a whelming pressure. In the gorge, the smoke, loaded with lime-dust, dragged rather than lifted; no man saw down it to the causeway; yet the ascending din and clamor, possessed of the smiting power of a gust of wind, told of an endless array coming.

There was not time to take account of time; but at last a Turkish shield appeared over the ghastly rampart, glimmering as the moon glimmers through thick vapor. Thrusts in scores were made at it, yet it arose; then a Janissary sprang up on the heap, singing like a muezzin, and shearing off the heads of pikes as reapers shear green rye. He was a giant in stature and strength. Both Genoese and Greeks were disposed to give him way. The Emperor rallied them. Still the Turk held his footing, and other Turks were climbing to his support. Now it looked as if the crisis were come, now as if the breach were lost.

In the last second a cry *For Christ and Irene* rang through the melee, and Count Corti, leaping from a gun, confronted the Turk.

"Ho, Son of Ouloubad! Hassan, Hassan!" [Footnote: One of the Janissaries, Hassan d'Ouloubad, of gigantic stature and prodigious strength, mounted to the assault under cover of his shield, his cimeter in the right hand. He reached the rampart with thirty of his companions. Nineteen of them were cast down, and Hassan himself fell struck by a stone.—VON HAMMER.] he shouted, in the familiar tongue.

"Who calls me?" the giant asked, lowering his shield, and gazing about in surprise.

"I call you—I, Mirza the Emir. Thy time has come. *Christ and Irene. Now!*"

With the word the Count struck the Janissary fairly on the flat cap with his axe, bringing him to his knees. Almost simultaneously a heavy stone descended upon the dazed man from a higher part of the wall, and he rolled backward down the steep.

Constantine and Justiniani, with others, joined the Count, but too late. Of the fifty comrades composing Hassan's file, thirty mounted the rampart. Eighteen of them were slain in the bout. Corti raged like a lion; but up rushed the survivors of the next file—and the next—and the vantage-point was lost. The Genoese, seeing it, said:

"Your Majesty, let us retire."

"Is it time?"

"We must get a ditch between us and this new horde, or we are all dead men."

Then the Emperor shouted: "Back, every one! For love of Christ and Holy Church, back to the galley!"

The guns, machines, store of missiles, and space occupied by the battery were at once abandoned. Constantine and Corti went last, facing the foe, who warily paused to see what they had next to encounter.

The secondary defence to which the Greeks resorted consisted of the hulk brought up, as we have seen, by Count Corti, planted on its keel squarely in rear of the breach, and filled with stones. From the hulk, on right and left, wings of uncemented masonry extended to the main wall in form thus:

[Illustration]

A ditch fronted the line fifteen feet in width and twelve in depth, provided with movable planks for hasty passage. Culverins were on the hulk, with ammunition in store.

Greatly to the relief of the jaded Christians, who, it is easy believing, stood not on the order of going, they beheld the reserves, under Demetrius Palaeologus and Nicholas Giudalli, in readiness behind the refuge.

The Emperor, on the deck, raised the visor of his helmet, and looked up at an Imperial flag drooping in the stagnant air from a stump of the mast. Whatever his thought or feeling, no one could discern on his countenance an unbecoming expression. The fact, of which he must have been aware, that this stand taken ended his empire forever, had not shaken his resolution or confidence. To Demetrius Palaeologus, who had lent a hand helping him up the galley's side, he said: "Thank you, kinsman. God may still be trusted. Open fire."

The Janissaries, astonished at the new and strange defence, would have retreated, but could not; the files ascending behind drove them forward. At the edge of the ditch the foremost of them made a despairing effort to resist the pressure rushing them to their fate—down they went in mass, in their last service no better than the hordesmen—clods they became—clods in bright harness instead of bull-hide and shaggy astrakhan.

From the wings, bolts and stones; from the height of the wall, bolts and stones; from the hulk, grapeshot; and the rattle upon the shields of the Faithful was as the passing of empty chariots over a Pompeiian street. Imprecations, prayers, yells, groans, shrieks, had lodgement only in the ear of the Most Merciful. The open maw of a ravenous monster swallowing the column fast as Mahommed down by the great moat drove it on—such was the new ditch.

Yet another, the final horror. When the ditch was partially filled, the Christians brought jugs of the inflammable liquid contributed to the defence by John Grant; and cast them down on the writhing heap. Straightway the trench became a pocket of flame, or rather an oven from which the smell of roasting human flesh issued along with a choking cloud!

The besieged were exultant, as they well might be—they were more than holding the redoubtable Flower of the Faithful at bay—there was even a merry tone in their battle-cry. About that time a man dismounted from a foaming horse, climbed the rough steps to the deck of the galley, and delivered a message to the Emperor.

"Your Majesty. John Grant, Minotle the bayle, Carystos, Langasco, and Jerome the Italian are slain. Blacherne is in possession of the Turks, and they are marching this way. The hordes are in the streets. I saw them, and heard the bursting of doors, and the screams of women."

Constantine crossed himself three times, and bowed his head.

Justiniani turned the color of ashes, and exclaimed:

"We are undone—undone! All is lost!" And that his voice was hoarse did not prevent the words being overheard. The fire slackened—ceased. Men fighting jubilantly dropped their arms, and took up the cry—"All is lost! The hordes are in, the hordes are in!"

Doubtless Count Corti's thought sped to the fair woman waiting for him in the chapel, yet he kept clear head.

"Your Majesty," he said, "my Berbers are without. I will take them, and hold the Turks in check while you draw assistance from the walls. Or"—he hesitated, "or I will defend your person to the ships. It is not too late."

Indeed, there was ample time for the Emperor's escape. The Berbers were keeping his horse with Corti's. He had but to mount, and ride away. No doubt he was tempted. There is always some sweetness in life, especially to the blameless. He raised his head, and said to Justiniani:

"Captain, my guard will remain here. To keep the galley they have only to keep the fire alive in the ditch. You and I will go out to meet the enemy." ...

Then he addressed himself to Corti: "To horse, Count, and bring Theophilus Palaeologus. He is on the wall between this gate and the gate Selimbria.... Ho, Christian gentlemen," he continued, to the soldiers closing around him, "all is not lost. The Bochiardi at the Adrianople gate have not been heard from. To fly from an unseen foe were shameful, We are still hundreds strong. Let us descend, and form. God cannot"—

That instant Justiniani uttered a loud cry, and dropped the axe he was holding. An arrow had pierced the scales of his gauntlet, and disabled his hand. The pain, doubtless, was great, and he started hastily as if to descend from the deck. Constantine called out:

"Captain, Captain!"

"Give me leave, Your Majesty, to go and have this wound dressed."

"Where, Captain?"

"To my ship."

The Emperor threw his visor up—his face was flushed—in his soul indignation contended with astonishment.

"No, Captain, the wound cannot be serious; and besides, how canst thou get to thy ships?"

Justiniani looked over the bulwark of the vessel. The alley from the gate ran on between houses abutting the towers. A ball from one of Mahommed's largest guns had passed through the right-hand building, leaving a ragged fissure. Thither the Captain now pointed.

"God opened that breach to let the Turks in. I will go out by it."

He stayed no longer, but went down the steps, and in haste little short of a run disappeared through the fissure so like a breach.

The desertion was in view of his Genoese, of whom a few followed him, but not all. Many who had been serving the guns took swords and pikes, and gathering about the Emperor, cried out:

"Give orders, Your Majesty. We will bide with you."

He returned them a look full of gratitude.

"I thank you, gentlemen. Let us go down, and join our shields across the street. To my guard I commit defence of the galley."

Unfastening the purple half-cloak at his back, and taking off his helmet, he called to his sword-bearer: "Here, take thou these, and give me my sword.... Now, gallant gentlemen—now, my brave countrymen—we will put ourselves in the keeping of Heaven. Come!"

They had not all gained the ground, however, when there arose a clamor in their front, and the hordesmen appeared, and blocking up the passage, opened upon them with arrows and stones, while such as had javelins and swords attacked them hand to hand.

The Christians behaved well, but none better than Constantine. He fought with strength, and in good countenance; his blade quickly reddened to the hilt.

"Strike, my countrymen, for city and home. Strike, every one, for *Christ and Holy Church!*"

And answering him: "*Christ and Holy Church!*" they all fought as they had strength, and their swords were also reddened to the hilt. Quarter was not asked; neither was it given. Theirs to hold the ground, and they held it. They laid the hordesmen out over it in scattered heaps which grew, and presently became one long heap the width of the alley; and they too fell, but, as we are willing to believe, unconscious of pain because lapped in the delirium of battle-fever.

Five minutes—ten—fifteen—then through the breach by which Justiniani ingloriously fled Theophilus Palaeologus came with bared brand to vindicate his imperial blood by nobly dying; and with him came Count Corti, Francesco de Toledo, John the Dalmatian, and a score and more Christian gentlemen who well knew the difference between an honorable death and a dishonored life.

Steadily the sun arose. Half the street was in its light, the other half in its shade; yet the struggle endured; nor could any man have said God was not with the Christians. Suddenly a louder shouting arose behind them. They who could, looked to see what it meant, and the bravest stood stone still at sight of the Janissaries swarming on the galley. Over the roasting bodies of their comrades, undeterred by the inextinguishable fire, they had crossed the ditch, and were slaying the imperial body-guard. A moment, and they would be in the alley, and then—

Up rose a wail: "The Janissaries, the Janissaries! *Kyrie Eleison!*" Through the knot of Christians it passed—it reached Constantine in the forefront, and he gave way to the antagonist with whom he was engaged.

"God receive my soul!" he exclaimed; and dropping his sword, he turned about, and rushed back with wide extended arms.

"Friends—countrymen!—Is there no Christian to kill me?"

Then they understood why he had left his helmet off.

While those nearest stared at him, their hearts too full of pity to do him the last favor one can ask of another, from the midst of the hordesmen there came a man of singular unfitness for such a scene—indeed a delicate woman had not been more out of place—for he was small, stooped, withered, very white haired, very pale, and much bearded—a black velvet cap on his head, and a gown of the like about his body, unarmed, and in every respect unmartial. He seemed to glide in amongst the Christians as he had glided through the close press of the Turks; and as the latter had given him way, so now the sword points of the Christians went down—men in the heat of action forgot themselves, and became bystanders—such power was there in the unearthly eyes of the apparition.

"Is there no Christian to kill me?" cried the Emperor again.

The man in velvet stood before him.

"Prince of India!"

"You know me? It is well; for now I know you are not beyond remembering." The voice was shrill and cutting, yet it shrilled and cut the sharper.

"Remember the day I called on you to acknowledge God, and give him his due of worship. Remember the day I prayed you on my knees to lend me your power to save my child, stolen for a purpose by all peoples held unholy. Behold your executioner!"

He stepped back, and raised a hand; and ere one of those standing by could so much as cry to God, Nilo, who, in the absorption of interest in his master, had followed him unnoticed—Nilo, gorgeous in his barbarisms of Kash-Cush, sprang into the master's place. He did not strike; but with infinite cruel cunning of hand—no measurable lapse of time ensuing—drew the assegai across the face of the astonished Emperor. Constantine—never great till that moment of death, but then great forever—fell forward upon his shield, calling in strangled utterance: "God receive my soul!"

The savage set his foot upon the mutilated countenance, crushing it into a pool of blood. An instant, then through the petrified throng, knocking them right and left, Count Corti appeared.

"*For Christ and Irene!*" he shouted, dashing the spiked boss of his shield into Nilo's eyes—down upon the feathered coronal he brought his sword—and the negro fell sprawling upon the Emperor.

Oblivious to the surroundings, Count Corti, on his knees, raised the Emperor's head, slightly turning the face—one look was enough. "His soul is sped!" he said; and while he was tenderly replacing the head, a hand grasped his cap. He sprang to his feet. Woe to the intruder, if an enemy!

The sword which had known no failure was drawn back to thrust—above the advanced foot the shield hung in ready poise—between him and the challenger there was only a margin of air and the briefest interval of time— his breath was drawn, and his eyes gleamed with vengeful murder—but— some power invisible stayed his arm, and into his memory flashed the lightning of recognition.

"Prince of India," he shouted, "never wert thou nearer death!"

"Thou—liest! Death—and—I"—

The words were long drawn between gasps, and the speech was never finished. The tongue thickened, then paralyzed. The features, already distorted with passion, swelled, and blackened horribly. The eyes rolled back—the hands flew up, the fingers apart and rigid—the body rocked— stiffened—then fell, sliding from the Count's shield across the dead Emperor.

The combat meantime had gone on. Corti, with a vague feeling that the Prince's flight of soul was a mystery in keeping with his life, took a second to observe him, and muttered: "Peace to him also!"

Looking about him then, he was made aware that the Christians, attacked in front and rear, were drawing together around the body of Constantine— that their resistance was become the last effort of brave men hopeless except of the fullest possible payment for their lives. This was succeeded by a conviction of duty done on his part, and of every requirement of honor fulfilled; thereupon with a great throb of heart, his mind reverted to the Princess Irene waiting for him in the chapel. He must go to her. But how? And was it not too late?

There are men whose wits are supernaturally quickened by danger. The Count, pushing through the intervening throng, boldly presented himself to the Janissaries, shouting while warding the blows they aimed at him:

"Have done, O madmen! See you not I am your comrade, Mirza the Emir? Have done, I say, and let me pass. I have a message for the Padishah!"

He spoke Turkish, and having been an idol in the barracks—their best swordsman—envied, and at the same time beloved—they knew him, and with acclamations opened their files, and let him pass.

By the fissure which had served Justiniani, he escaped from the terrible alley, and finding his Berbers and his horse, rode with speed for the residence of the Princess Irene.

Not a Christian survived the combat. Greek, Genoese, Italian lay in ghastly composite with hordesmen and mailed Moslems around the Emperor. In dying they had made good their battle-cry—*For Christ and Holy Church!* Let us believe they will yet have their guerdon.

About an hour after the last of them had fallen, when the narrow passage was deserted by the living—the conquerors having moved on in search of their hire—the Prince of India aroused, and shook himself free of the corpses cumbering him. Upon his knees he gazed at the dead—then at the place—then at the sky. He rubbed his hands—made sure he was sound of person—he seemed uncertain, not of life, but of himself. In fact, he was asking, Who am I? And the question had reference to the novel sensations of which he was conscious. What was it coursing through his veins? Wine?—Elixir?—Some new principle which, hidden away amongst the stores of nature, had suddenly evolved for him? The weights of age were gone. In his body—bones, arms, limbs, muscles—he recognized once more the glorious impulses of youth; but his mind—he started—the ideas which had dominated him were beginning to return—and memory! It surged back upon him, and into its wonted chambers, like a wave which, under pressure of a violent wind, has been momentarily driven from a familiar shore. He saw, somewhat faintly at first, the events which had been promontories and lofty peaks cast up out of the level of his long existence. Then THAT DAY and THAT EVENT! How distinctly they reappeared to him! They must be the same—must be—for he beheld the multitude on its way to Calvary, and the Victim tottering under the Cross; he heard the Tribune ask, "Ho, is this the street to Golgotha?" He heard his own answer, "I will guide you;" and he spit upon the fainting Man of Sorrows, and struck him. And then the words—"TARRY THOU TILL I COME!" identified him to himself. He looked at his hands—they were black with what had been some other man's life-blood, but under the stain the skin was smooth—a little water would make them white. And what was that upon his breast? Beard—beard black as a raven's wing! He plucked a lock of hair from his head. It, too, was thick with blood, but it was black. Youth—youth—joyous, bounding, eager, hopeful youth was his once more! He stood up, and there was no creak of rust in the hinges of his joints; he knew he was standing inches higher in the sunlit air; and a cry burst from him—"O God, I give thanks!" The hymn stopped there, for between him and the sky, as if it were ascending transfigured, he beheld the Victim of the Crucifixion; and the eyes, no longer sad, but full of accusing majesty, were looking downward at him, and the lips were in speech: "TARRY THOU TILL I COME!" He covered his face with his hands. Yes, yes, he had his youth back again, but it was with the old mind and nature—youth, that the curse upon him might, in the mortal sense, be eternal! And pulling his black hair with his young hands, wrenching at his black beard, it was given him to see he had undergone his fourteenth transformation, and that between this one and the last there was no lapse of connection. Old age had passed, leaving the conditions and circumstances of its going to the youth which succeeded. The new life in starting picked up and loaded itself with every burden and all the misery of the old. So now while burrowing, as it were, amongst dead men, his head upon the breast of the Emperor whom, treating Nilo as an instrument in his grip, he had slain, he thought most humanly of the effects of the transformation.

First of all, his personal identity was lost, and he was once more a Wanderer without an acquaintance, a friend, or a sympathizer on the earth. To whom could he now address himself with a hope of recognition? His heart went out primarily to Lael—he loved her. Suppose he found her, and offered to take her in his arms; she would repulse him. "Thou art not my father. He was old—thou art young." And Syama, whose bereavements of sense had recommended him for confidant in the event of his witnessing the dreaded circumstance just befallen—if he addressed himself to Syama, the faithful creature would deny him. "No; my master was old—his hair and beard were white—thou art a youth. Go hence." And then Mahommed, to whom he had been so useful in bringing additional empire, and a glory which time would make its own forever—did he seek Mahommed again—"Thou art not the Prince of India, my peerless Messenger of the Stars. He was old—his hair and beard were white—thou art a boy. Ho, guards, take this impostor, and do with him as ye did with Balta-Ogli stretch him on the ground, and beat the breath out of him."

There is nothing comes to us, whether in childhood or age, so crushing as a sense of isolation. Who will deny it had to do with the marshalling of worlds, and the peopling them—with creation?

These reflections did but wait upon the impulse which still further identified him to himself—the impulse to go and keep going—and he cast about for solaces.

"It is the Judgment," he said, with a grim smile; "but my stores remain, and Hiram of Tyre is yet my friend. I have my experience of more than a thousand years, and with it youth again. I cannot make men better, and God refuses my services. Nevertheless I will devise new opportunities. The earth is round, and upon its other side there must be another world. Perhaps I can find some daring spirit equal to the voyage and discovery—some one Heaven may be more willing to favor. But this meeting place of the old continents"—he looked around him, and then to the sky—"with my farewell, I leave it the curse of the most accursed. The desired of nations, it shall be a trouble to them forever."

Then he saw Nilo under a load of corpses, and touched by remembrance of the poor savage's devotion, he uncovered him to get at his heart, which was still beating. Next he threw away his cap and gown, replaced them with a bloody tarbousche and a shaggy Angora mantle, selected a javelin, and sauntered leisurely on into the city. Having seen Constantinople pillaged by Christians, he was curious to see it now sacked by Moslems—there might be a further solace in the comparison.

[Footnote: According to the earliest legends, the Wandering Jew was about thirty years old when he stood in the road to Golgotha, and struck the Saviour, and ordered him to go forward. At the end of every hundred years, the undying man falls into a trance, during which his body returns to the age it was when the curse was pronounced. In all other respects he remains unchanged.]

CHAPTER XIII
MAHOMMED IN SANCTA SOPHIA

Count Corti, we may well believe, did not spare his own steed, or those of his Berbers; and there was a need of haste of which he was not aware upon setting out from St. Romain. The Turks had broken through the resistance of the Christian fleet in the harbor, and were surging into the city by the gate St. Peter (Phanar), which was perilously near the residence of the Princess Irene.

Already the spoil-seekers were making sure of their hire. More than once he dashed by groups of them hurrying along the streets in search of houses most likely to repay plundering. There were instances when he overtook hordesmen already happy in the possession of "strings of slaves;" that is to say, of Greeks, mostly women and children, tied by their hands to ropes, and driven mercilessly on. The wailing and prayers of the unfortunate smote the Count to the heart; he longed to deliver them; but he had given his best efforts to save them in the struggle to save the city, and had failed; now it would be a providence of Heaven could he rescue the woman waiting for him in such faith as was due his word and honor specially plighted to her. As the pillagers showed no disposition to interfere with him, he closed his eyes and ears to their brutalities, and sped forward.

The district in which the Princess dwelt was being overrun when he at last drew rein at her door. With a horrible dread, he alighted, and pushed in unceremoniously. The reception-room was empty. Was he too late? Or was she then in Sancta Sophia? He flew to the chapel, and blessed God and Christ and the Mother, all in a breath. She was before the altar in the midst of her attendants. Sergius stood at her side, and of the company they alone were perfectly self-possessed. A white veil lay fallen over her shoulders; save that, she was in unrelieved black. The pallor of her countenance, caused, doubtless, by weeks of care and unrest, detracted slightly from the marvelous beauty which was hers by nature; but it seemed sorrow and danger only increased the gentle dignity always observable in her speech and manner.

"Princess Irene," he said, hastening forward, and reverently saluting her hand, "if you are still of the mind to seek refuge in Sancta Sophia, I pray you, let us go thither."

"We are ready," she returned. "But tell me of the Emperor."

The Count bent very low.

"Your kinsman is beyond insult and further humiliation. His soul is with God."

Her eyes glistened with tears, and partly to conceal her emotion she turned to the picture above the altar, and said, in a low voice, and brokenly:

"O Holy Mother, have thou his soul in thy tender care, and be with me now, going to what fate I know not."

The young women surrounded her, and on their knees filled the chapel with sobbing and suppressed wails. Striving for composure himself, the Count observed them, and was at once assailed by an embarrassment.

They were twenty and more. Each had a veil over her head; yet from the delicacy of their hands he could imagine their faces, while their rank was all too plainly certified by the elegance of their garments. As a temptation to the savages, their like was not within the walls. How was he to get them safely to the Church, and defend them there? He was used to military problems, and decision was a habit with him; still he was sorely tried— indeed, he was never so perplexed.

The Princess finished her invocation to the Holy Mother.

"Count Corti," she said, "I now place myself and these, my sisters in misfortune, under thy knightly care. Only suffer me to send for one other.—Go, Sergius, and bring Lael."

One other!

"Now God help me!" he cried, involuntarily; and it seemed he was heard.

"Princess," he returned, "the Turks have possession of the streets. On my way I passed them with prisoners whom they were driving, and they appeared to respect a right of property acquired. Perhaps they will be not less observant to me; wherefore bring other veils here—enough to bind these ladies two and two."

As she seemed hesitant, he added: "Pardon me, but in the streets you must all go afoot, to appearances captives just taken."

The veils were speedily produced, and the Princess bound her trembling companions in couples hand to hand; submitting finally to be herself tied to Lael. Then when Sergius was more substantially joined to the ancient Lysander, the household sallied forth.

A keener realization of the situation seized the gentler portion of the procession once they were in the street, and they there gave way to tears, sobs, and loud appeals to the Saints and Angels of Mercy.

The Count rode in front; four of his Berbers moved on each side; Sheik Hadifah guarded the rear; and altogether a more disconsolate company of captives it were hard imagining. A rope passing from the first couple to the last was the only want required to perfect the resemblance to the actual slave droves at the moment on nearly every thoroughfare in Constantinople.

The weeping cortege passed bands of pillagers repeatedly.

Once what may be termed a string in fact was met going in the opposite direction; women and children, and men and women were lashed together, like animals, and their lamentations were piteous. If they fell or faltered, they were beaten. It seemed barbarity could go no further.

Once the Count was halted. A man of rank, with a following at his heels, congratulated him in Turkish:

"O friend, thou hast a goodly capture."

The stranger came nearer.

"I will give you twenty gold pieces for this one," pointing to the Princess Irene, who, fortunately, could not understand him—"and fifteen for this one."

"Go thy way, and quickly," said Corti, sternly.

"Dost thou threaten me?"

"By the Prophet, yes—with my sword, and the Padishah."

"The Padishah! Oh, ho!" and the man turned pale. "God is great—I give him praise."

At last the Count alighted before the main entrance of the Church. By friendly chance, also—probably because the site was far down toward the sea, in a district not yet reached by the hordesmen—the space in front of the vestibule was clear of all but incoming fugitives; and he had but to knock at the door, and give the name of the Princess Irene to gain admission.

In the vestibule the party were relieved of their bonds; after which they passed into the body of the building, where they embraced each other, and gave praise aloud for what they considered a final deliverance from death and danger; in their transports, they kissed the marbles of the floor again and again.

While this affecting scene was going on, Corti surveyed the interior. The freest pen cannot do more than give the view with a clearness to barely stimulate the reader's imagination.

It was about eleven o'clock. The smoke of battle which had overlain the hills of the city was dissipated; so the sun, nearing high noon, poured its full of splendor across the vast nave in rays slanted from south to north, and a fine, almost impalpable dust hanging from the dome in the still air, each ray shone through it in vivid, half-prismatic relief against the shadowy parts of the structure. Such pillars in the galleries as stood in the paths of the sunbeams seemed effulgent, like emeralds and rubies. His eyes, however, refused everything except the congregation of people.

"O Heaven!" he exclaimed. "What is to become of these poor souls!"

Byzantium, it must be recalled, had had its triumphal days, when Greeks drew together, like Jews on certain of their holy occasions; undoubtedly the assemblages then were more numerous, but never had there been one so marked by circumstances. This was the funeral day of the Empire!

Let the reader try to recompose the congregation the Count beheld—civilians—soldiers—nuns—monks—monks bearded, monks shaven, monks tonsured—monks in high hats and loose veils, monks in gowns scarce distinguishable from gowns of women—monks by the thousand. Ah, had they but dared a manly part on the walls, the cause of the Christ for whom they affected such devotion would not have suffered the humiliation to which it was now going! As to the mass in general, let the reader think of the rich jostled by the poor—fine ladies careless if their robes took taint from the Lazarus' next them—servants for once at least on a plane with haughty masters—Senators and slaves—grandsires—mothers with their infants—old and young, high and low, all in promiscuous presence—society at an end—Sancta Sophia a universal last refuge. And by no means least strange, let the reader fancy the refugees on their knees, silent as ghosts in a tomb, except that now and then the wail of a child broke the awful hush, and gazing over their shoulders, not at the altar, but toward the doors of entrance; then let him understand that every one in the smother of assemblage—every one capable of thought—was in momentary expectation of a miracle.

Here and there moved priestly figures, holding crucifixes aloft, and halting at times to exhort in low voices: "Be not troubled, O dearly beloved of Christ! The angel will appear by the old column. If the powers of hell are not to prevail against the Church, what may men do against the sword of God?"

The congregation was waiting for the promised angel to rescue them from the Barbarians.

Of opinion that the chancel, or space within the railing of the apse opposite him, was a better position for his charge than the crowded auditorium, partly because he could more easily defend them there, and partly because Mahommed when he arrived would naturally look for the Princess near the altar, the Count, with some trouble, secured a place within it behind the brazen balustrade at the right of the gate. The invasion of the holy reserve by the Berbers was viewed askance, but submitted to; thereupon the Princess and her suite took to waiting and praying.

Afterwhile the doors in the east were barred by the janitor.

Still later there was knocking at them loud enough to be by authority. The janitor had become deaf.

Later still a yelling as of a mob out in the vestibule penetrated to the interior, and a shiver struck the expectant throng, less from a presentiment of evil at hand than a horrible doubt. An angel of the Lord would hardly adopt such an incongruous method of proclaiming the miracle done. A murmur of invocation began with those nearest the entrances, and ran from the floor to the galleries. As it spread, the shouting increased in volume and temper. Ere long the doors were assailed. The noise of a blow given with determination rang dreadful warning through the whole building, and the concourse arose.

The women shrieked: "The Turks! The Turks!"

Even the nuns who had been practising faith for years joined their lay sisters in crying: "The Turks! The Turks!"

The great, gowned, cowardly monks dropped their crucifixes, and, like the commoner sons of the Church, howled: "The Turks! The Turks!"

Finally the doors were battered in, and sure enough—there stood the hordesmen, armed and panoplied each according to his tribe or personal preference—each a most unlikely delivering angel.

This completed the panic.

In the vicinity of the ruined doors everybody, overcome by terror, threw himself upon those behind, and the impulsion thus started gained force while sweeping on. As ever in such cases, the weak were the sufferers. Children were overrun—infants dashed from the arms of mothers—men had need of their utmost strength—and the wisdom of the Count in seeking the chancel was proved. The massive brazen railing hardly endured the pressure when the surge reached it; but it stood, and the Princess and her household—all, in fact, within the chancel—escaped the crushing, but not the horror.

The spoilsmen were in strength, but they were prudently slow in persuading themselves that the Greeks were unarmed, and incapable of defending the

Church. Ere long they streamed in, and for the first time in the history of the edifice the colossal Christ on the ceiling above the altar was affronted by the slogan of Islam—*Allah-il-Allah*.

Strange now as it may appear to the reader, there is no mention in the chronicles of a life lost that day within the walls of Sancta Sophia. The victors were there for plunder, not vengeance, and believing there was more profit in slaves than any other kind of property, their effort was to save rather than kill. The scene was beyond peradventure one of the cruelest in history, but the cruelty was altogether in taking possession of captives.

Tossing their arms of whatever kind upon their backs, the savages pushed into the pack of Christians to select whom they would have. We may be sure the old, sick, weakly, crippled, and very young were discarded, and the strong and vigorous chosen. Remembering also how almost universally the hordes were from the East, we may be sure a woman was preferred to a man, and a pretty woman to an ugly one.

The hand shrinks from trying to depict the agonies of separation which ensued—mothers torn from their children, wives from husbands—their shrieks, entreaties, despair—the mirthful brutality with which their pitiful attempts at resistance were met—the binding and dragging away—the last clutch of love—the final disappearance. It is only needful to add that the rapine involved the galleries no less than the floor. All things considered, the marvel is that the cry—there was but one, just as the sounds of many waters are but one to the ear—which then tore the habitual silence of the august temple should have ever ceased—and it would not if, in its duration, human sympathy were less like a flitting echo.

Next to women, the monks were preferred, and the treatment they received was not without its touches of grim humor. Their cowls were snatched off, and bandied about, their hats crushed over their ears, their veils stuffed in their mouths to stifle their outcries, their rosaries converted into scourges; and the laughter when a string of them passed to the doors was long and loud. They had pulled their monasteries down upon themselves. If the Emperor, then lying in the bloody alley of St. Romain, dead through their bigotry, superstition, and cowardice, had been vengeful in the slightest degree, a knowledge of the judgment come upon them so soon would have been at least restful to his spirit.

It must not be supposed Count Corti was indifferent while this appalling scene was in progress. The chancel, he foresaw, could not escape the foray. There was the altar, loaded with donatives in gold and precious stones, a blazing pyramidal invitation. When the doors were burst in, he paused a moment to see if Mahommed were coming.

"The hordes are here, O Princess, but not the Sultan."

She raised her veil, and regarded him silently.

"I see now but one resort. As Mirza the Emir, I must meet the pillagers by claiming the Sultan sent me in advance to capture and guard you for him."

"We are at mercy, Count Corti," she replied. "Heaven deal with you as you deal with us."

"If the ruse fails, Princess, I can die for you. Now tie yourselves as before—two and two, hand to hand. It may be they will call on me to distinguish such as are my charge."

She cast a glance of pity about her.

"And these, Count—these poor women not of my house, and the children—can you not save them also?"

"Alas, dear lady! The Blessed Mother must be their shield."

While the veils were being applied, the surge against the railing took place, leaving a number of dead and fainting across it.

"Hadifah," the Count called out, "clear the way to yon chair against the wall."

The Sheik set about removing the persons blockading the space, and greatly affected by their condition, the Princess interceded for them.

"Nay, Count, disturb them not. Add not to their terror, I pray."

But the Count was a soldier; in case of an affray, he wanted the advantage of a wall at his back.

"Dear lady, it was the throne of your fathers, now yours. I will seat you there. From it you can best treat with the Lord Mahommed."

Ere long some of the hordes—half a dozen or more—came to the chancel gate. They were of the rudest class of Anatolian shepherds, clad principally in half-cloaks of shaggy goat skin. Each bore at his back a round buckler, a bow, and a clumsy quiver of feathered arrows. Awed by the splendor of the altar and its surroundings, they stopped; then, with shouts, they rushed at the tempting display, unmindful of the living spoils crouched on the floor dumb with terror. Others of a like kind reenforced them, and there was a fierce scramble. The latest comers turned to the women, and presently discovered the Princess Irene sitting upon the throne. One, more eager than the rest, was indisposed to respect the Berbers.

"Here are slaves worth having. Get your ropes," he shouted to his companions.

The Count interposed.

"Art thou a believer?" he asked in Turkish.

They surveyed him doubtfully, and then turned to Hadifah and his men, tall, imperturbable looking, their dark faces visible through their open hoods of steel. They looked at their shields also, and at their bare cimeters resting points to the floor.

"Why do you ask?" the man returned.

"Because, as thou mayst see, we also are of the Faithful, and do not wish harm to any whose mothers have taught them to begin the day with the Fah-hat."

The fellow was impressed.

"Who art thou?"

"I am the Emir Mirza, of the household of our Lord the Padishah—to whom be all the promises of the Koran! These are slaves I selected for him—all these thou seest in bonds. I am keeping them till he arrives. He will be here directly. He is now coming."

A man wearing a bloody tarbousche joined the pillagers, during this colloquy, and pressing in, heard the Emir's name passing from mouth to mouth.

"The Emir Mirza! I knew him, brethren. He commanded the caravan, and kept the *mahmals*, the year I made the pilgrimage.... Stand off, and let me see." After a short inspection, he continued: "Truly as there is no God but God, this is he. I was next him at the most holy corner of the Kaaba when he fell down struck by the plague. I saw him kiss the Black Stone, and by virtue of the kiss he lived.... Ay, stand back—or if you touch him, or one of these in his charge, and escape his hand, ye shall not escape the Padishah, whose first sword he is, even as Khalid was first sword for the Prophet— exalted be his name!... Give me thy hand, O valiant Emir."

He kissed the Count's hand.

"Arise, O son of thy father," said Corti; "and when our master, the Lord Mahommed, hath set up his court and harem, seek me for reward."

The man stayed awhile, although there was no further show of interference; and he looked past the Princess to Lael cowering near her. He took no interest in what was going on around him—Lael alone attracted him. At last he shifted his sheepskin covering higher upon his shoulders, and left these words with the Count:

"The women are not for the harem. I understand thee, O Mirza. When the Lord Mahommed hath set up his court, do thou tell the little Jewess yonder that her father the Prince of India charged thee to give her his undying love."

Count Corti was wonder struck—he could not speak—and so the Wandering Jew vanished from his sight as he now vanishes from our story.

The selection among the other refugees in the chancel proceeded until there was left of them only such as were considered not worth the having.

A long time passed, during which the Princess Irene sat with veil drawn close, trying to shut out the horror of the scene. Her attendants, clinging to the throne and to each other, seemed a heap of dead women. At last a crash of music was heard in the vestibule—drums, cymbals, and trumpets in blatant flourish. Four runners, slender lads, in short, sleeveless jackets over white shirts, and wide trousers of yellow silk, barefooted and bareheaded, stepped lightly through the central doorway, and, waving wands tipped with silver balls, cried, in long-toned shrill iteration: "The Lord Mahommed—Mahommed, Sultan of Sultans."

The spoilsmen suspended their hideous labor—the victims, moved doubtless by a hope of rescue, gave over their lamentations and struggling—only the young children, and the wounded, and suffering persisted in vexing the floor and galleries.

Next to enter were the five official heralds. Halting, they blew a triumphant refrain, at which the thousands of eyes not too blinded by misery turned to them.

And Mahommed appeared!

He too had escaped the Angel of the false monks!

When the fighting ceased in the harbor, and report assured him of the city at mercy, Mahommed gave order to make the Gate St. Romain passable for horsemen, and with clever diplomacy summoned the Pachas and other military chiefs to his tent; it was his pleasure that they should assist him in taking possession of the prize to which he had been helped by their valor. With a rout so constituted at his back, and an escort of *Silihdars* mounted, the runners and musicians preceding him, he made his triumphal entry into Constantinople, traversing the ruins of the towers Bagdad and St. Romain.

He was impatient and restless. In their ignorance of his passion for the Grecian Princess, his ministers excused his behavior on account of his youth [Footnote: He was in his twenty-third year.] and the greatness of his achievement. Passing St. Romain, it was also observed he took no interest in the relics of combat still there. He gave his guides but one order:

"Take me to the house the *Gabours* call the Glory of God."

"Sancta Sophia, my Lord?"

"Sancta Sophia—and bid the runners run."

His Sheik-ul-Islam was pleased.

"Hear!" he said to the dervishes with him. "The Lord Mahommed will make mosques of the houses of Christ before sitting down in one of the palaces. His first honors are to God and the Prophet."

And they dutifully responded: "Great are God and his Prophet! Great is Mahommed, who conquers in their names!"

The public edifices by which he was guided—churches, palaces, and especially the high aqueduct, excited his admiration; but he did not slacken the fast trot in which he carried his loud cavalcade past them until at the Hippodrome.

"What thing of devilish craft is here?" he exclaimed, stopping in front of the Twisted Serpents. "Thus the Prophet bids me!" and with a blow of his mace, he struck off the lower jaw of one of the Pythons.

Again the dervishes shouted: "Great is Mahommed, the servant of God!"

It was his preference to be taken to the eastern front of Sancta Sophia, and in going the guides led him by the corner of the Bucoleon. At sight of the vast buildings, their incomparable colonnades and cornices, their domeless stretches of marble and porphyry, he halted the second time, and in thought of the vanity of human glory, recited:

"The spider hath woven his web in the imperial palace; And the owl hath sung her watch-song on the towers of Afrasiab."

In the space before the Church, as elsewhere along the route he had come, the hordes were busy carrying off their wretched captives; but he affected not to see them. They had bought the license of him, many of them with their blood.

At the door the suite dismounted. Mahommed however, kept his saddle while surveying the gloomy exterior. Presently he bade:

"Let the runners and the heralds enter."

Hardly were they gone in, when he spoke to one of his pages: "Here, take thou this, and give me my cimeter." And then, receiving the ruby-hilted sword of Solomon in exchange for the mace of Ilderim, without more ado he spurred his horse up the few broad stone steps, and into the vestibule.

Thence, the contemptuous impulse yet possessing him, he said loudly: "The house is defiled with idolatrous images. Islam is in the saddle."

In such manner—mounted, sword in hand, shield behind him—clad in beautiful gold-washed chain mail, the very ideal of the immortal Emir who won Jerusalem from the Crusaders, and restored it to Allah and the Prophet—Mahommed made his first appearance in Sancta Sophia.

Astonishment seized him. He checked his horse. Slowly his gaze ranged over the floor—up to the galleries—up—up to the swinging dome—in all architecture nothing so nearly a self-depending sky.

"Here, take the sword—give me back my mace," he said.

And in a fit of enthusiasm, not seeing, not caring for the screaming wretches under hoof, he rode forward, and, standing at full height in his stirrups, shouted: "Idolatry be done! Down with the Trinity. Let Christ give way for the last and greatest of the Prophets! To God the one God, I dedicate this house!"

Therewith he dashed the mace against a pillar; and as the steel rebounded, the pillar trembled. [Footnote: The guides, if good Moslems, take great pleasure in showing tourists the considerable dent left by this blow in the face of the pillar.]

"Now give me the sword again, and call Achmet, my muezzin—Achmet with the flute in his throat."

The moods of Mahommed were swift going and coming. Riding out a few steps, he again halted to give the floor a look. This time evidently the house was not in his mind. The expression on his face became anxious. He was searching for some one, and moved forward so slowly the people could get out of his way, and his suite overtake him. At length he observed the half-stripped altar in the apse, and went to it.

The colossal Christ on the ceiling peered down on him through the shades beginning to faintly fill the whole west end.

Now he neared the brazen railing of the chancel—now he was at the gate—his countenance changed—his eyes brightened—he had discovered Count Corti. Swinging lightly from his saddle, he passed with steps of glad impatience through the gateway.

Then to Count Corti came the most consuming trial of his adventurous life.

The light was still strong enough to enable him to see across the Church. Comprehending the flourish of the heralds, he saw the man on horseback enter; and the mien, the pose in the saddle, the rider's whole outward expose of spirit, informed him with such certainty as follows long and familiar association, that Mahommed was come—Mahommed, his ideal of romantic orientalism in arms. A tremor shook him—his cheek whitened. To that moment anxiety for the Princess had held him so entirely he had not once thought of the consequences of the wager lost; now they were let loose upon him. Having saved her from the hordes, now he must surrender her to a rival—now she was to go from him forever. Verily it had been easier parting with his soul. He held to his cimeter as men instantly slain sometimes keep grip on their weapons; yet his head sunk upon his breast, and he saw nothing more of Mahommed until he stood before him inside the chancel.

"Count Corti, where is"—

Mahommed caught sight of the Count's face.

"Oh, my poor Mirza!"

A volume of words could not have so delicately expressed sympathy as did that altered tone.

Taking off his steel glove, the fitful Conqueror extended the bare hand, and the Count, partially recalled to the situation by the gracious offer, sunk to his knees, and carried the hand to his lips.

"I have kept the faith, my Lord," he said in Turkish, his voice scarcely audible. "This is she behind me—upon the throne of her fathers. Receive her from me, and let me depart."

"My poor Mirza! We left the decision to God, and he has decided. Arise, and hear me now."

To the notables closing around, he said, imperiously: "Stand not back. Come up, and hear me."

Stepping past the Count, then, he stood before the Princess. She arose without removing her veil, and would have knelt; but Mahommed moved nearer, and prevented her.

The training of the politest court in Europe was in her action, and the suite looking on, used to slavishness in captives, and tearful humility in women, he held her with amazement; nor could one of them have said which most attracted him, her queenly composure or her simple grace.

"Suffer me, my Lord," she said to him; then to her attendants: "This is Mahommed the Sultan. Let us pray him for honorable treatment."

Presently they were kneeling, and she would have joined them, but Mahommed again interfered.

"Your hand, O Princess Irene! I wish to salute it."

Sometimes a wind blows out of the sky, and swinging the bell in the cupola, starts it to ringing itself; so now, at sight of the only woman he ever really loved overtaken by so many misfortunes, and actually threatened by a rabble of howling slave-hunters, Mahommed's better nature thrilled with pity and remorse, and it was only by an effort of will he refrained from kneeling to her, and giving his passion tongue. Nevertheless a kiss, though on the hand, can be made tell a tale of love, and that was what the youthful Conqueror did.

"I pray next that you resume your seat," he continued. "It has pleased God, O daughter of a Palaeologus, to leave you the head of the Greek people; and as I have the terms of a treaty to submit of great concern to them and you, it were more becoming did you hear me from a throne.... And first, in this presence, I declare you a free woman—free to go or stay, to reject or to accept—for a treaty is impossible except to sovereigns. If it be your pleasure to go, I pledge conveyance, whether by sea or land, to you and yours—attendants, slaves, and property; nor shall there be in any event a failure of moneys to keep you in the state to which you have been used."

"For your grace, Lord Mahommed, I shall beseech Heaven to reward you."

"As the God of your faith is the God of mine, O Princess Irene, I shall be grateful for your prayers.... In the next place, I entreat you to abide here; and to this I am moved by regard for your happiness. The conditions will be strange to you, and in your going about there will be much to excite comparisons of the old with the new; but the Arabs had once a wise man, El Hatim by name—you may have heard of him"—he cast a quick look at the eyes behind the veil—"El Hatim, a poet, a warrior, a physician, and he left a saying: 'Herbs for fevers, amulets for mischances, and occupation for distempers of memory.' If it should be that time proves powerless over your sorrows, I would bring employment to its aid.... Heed me now right well. It pains me to think of Constantinople without inhabitants or commerce, its splendors decaying, its palaces given over to owls, its harbor void of ships, its churches vacant except of spiders, its hills desolations to eyes afar on the sea. If it become not once more the capital city of Europe and Asia, some one shall have defeated the will of God; and I cannot endure that guilt or the thought of it. 'Sins are many in kind and degree, differing as the leaves and grasses differ,' says a dervish of my people; 'but for him who stands wilfully in the eyes of the Most Merciful—for him only shall there be no mercy in the Great Day.'... Yes, heed me right well—I am not the enemy of the Greeks, O Princess Irene. Their power could not agree with mine, and I made war upon it; but now that Heaven has decided the issue, I wish to recall them. They will not listen to me. Though I call loudly and often, they will remember the violence inflicted on them in my name. Their restoration is a noble work in promise. Is there a Greek of trust, and so truly a lover of his race, to help me make the promise a deed done? The man is not; but thou, O Princess—thou art. Behold the employment I offer you! I will commission you to bring them home—even these sorrowful creatures going hence in bonds. Or do you not love them so much?... Religion shall not hinder you. In the presence of these, my ministers of state, I swear to divide houses of God with you; half of them shall be Christian, the other half Moslem; arid neither sect shall interfere with the other's worship. This I will seal, reserving only this house, and that the Patriarch be chosen subject to my approval. Or do you not love your religion so much?"....

During the discourse the Princess listened intently; now she would have spoken, but he lifted his hand.

"Not yet, not yet! it is not well for you to answer now. I desire that you have time to consider—and besides, I come to terms of more immediate concern to you.... Here, in the presence of these witnesses, O Princess Irene, I offer you honorable marriage."

Mahommed bowed very low at the conclusion of this proposal.

"And wishing the union in conscience agreeable to you, I undertake to celebrate it according to Christian rite and Moslem. So shall you become Queen of the Greeks—their intercessor—the restorer and protector of their Church and worship—so shall you be placed in a way to serve God purely and unselfishly; and if a thirst for glory has ever moved you, O Princess, I present it to you a cupful larger than woman ever drank.... You may reside here or in Therapia, and keep your private chapel and altar, and choose whom you will to serve them. And these things I will also swear to and seal."

Again she would have interrupted him.

"No—bear with me for the once. I invoke your patience," he said. "In the making of treaties, O Princess, one of the parties must first propose terms; then it is for the other to accept or reject, and in turn propose. And this"— he glanced hurriedly around—"this is no time nor place for argument. Be content rather to return to your home in the city or your country-house at Therapia. In three days, with your permission, I will come for your answer; and whatever it be, I swear by Him who is God of the world, it shall be respected.... When I come, will you receive me?"

"The Lord Mahommed will be welcome."

"Where may I wait on you?"

"At Therapia," she answered.

Mahommed turned about then.

"Count Corti, go thou with the Princess Irene to Therapia. I know thou wilt keep her safely.—And thou, Kalil, have a galley suitable for a Queen of the Greeks made ready on the instant, and let there be no lack of guards despatched with it, subject to the orders of Count Corti, for the time once more Mirza the Emir.... O Princess, if I have been peremptory, forgive me, and lend me thy hand again. I wish to salute it."

Again she silently yielded to his request.

Kalil, seeing only politics in the scene, marched before the Princess clearing the way, and directly she was out of the Church. At the suggestion of the Count, sedan chairs were brought, and she and her half-stupefied companions carried to a galley, arriving at Therapia about the fourth hour after sunset.

Mahommed had indeed been imperious in the interview; but, as he afterward explained to her, with many humble protestations, he had a part to play before his ministers.

No sooner was she removed than he gave orders to clear the building of people and idolatrous symbols; and while the work was in progress, he made a tour of inspection going from the floor to the galleries. His wonder and admiration were unbounded.

Passing along the right-hand gallery, he overtook a pilferer with a tarbousche full of glass cubes picked from one of the mosaic pictures.

"Thou despicable!" he cried, in rage. "Knowest thou not that I have devoted this house to Allah? Profane a Mosque, wilt thou?"

And he struck the wretch with the flat of his sword. Hastening then to the chancel, he summoned Achmet, the muezzin.

"What is the hour?" he asked.

"It is the hour of the fourth prayer, my Lord."

"Ascend thou then to the highest turret of the house, and call the Faithful to pious acknowledgment of the favors of God and his Prophet—may their names be forever exalted."

Thus Sancta Sophia passed from Christ to Mahomet; and from that hour to this Islam has had sway within its walls. Not once since have its echoes been permitted to respond to a Christian prayer or a hymn to the Virgin. Nor was this the first instance when, to adequately punish a people for the debasement and perversions of his revelations, God, in righteous anger, tolerated their destruction.

To-day there are two cities, lights once of the whole earth, under curses so deeply graven in their remains—sites, walls, ruins—that every man and woman visiting them should be brought to know why they fell.

Alas, for Jerusalem!

Alas, for Constantinople!

POSTSCRIPTS.

In the morning of the third day after the fall of the city, a common carrier galley drew alongside the marble quay in front of the Princess' garden at Therapia, and landed a passenger—an old, decrepit man, cowled and gowned like a monk. With tottering steps he passed the gate, and on to the portico of the classic palace. Of Lysander, he asked: "Is the Princess Irene here or in the city?"

"She is here."

"I am a Greek, tired and hungry. Will she see me?"

The ancient doorkeeper disappeared, but soon returned.

"She will see you. This way."

The stranger was ushered into the reception room. Standing before the Princess, he threw back his cowl. She gazed at him a moment, then went to him and, taking his hands, cried, her eyes streaming with tears: "Father Hilarion! Now praised be God for sending you to me in this hour of uncertainty and affliction!"

Needless saying the poor man's trials ended there, and that he never again went cold, or hungry, or in want of a place to lay his head.

But this morning, after breaking fast, he was taken into council, and the proposal of marriage being submitted to him, he asked first:

"What are thy inclinations, daughter?"

And she made unreserved confession.

The aged priest spread his hands paternally over her head, and, looking upward, said solemnly: "I think I see the Great Designer's purpose. He gave thee, O daughter, thy beauties of person and spirit, and raised thee up out of unspeakable sorrows, that the religion of Christ should not perish utterly in the East. Go forward in the way He has opened unto thee. Only insist that Mahommed present himself at thy altar, and there swear honorable dealing with thee as his wife, and to keep the treaty proposed by him in spirit and letter. Doth he those things without reservation, then fear not. The old Greek Church is not all we would have it, but how much better it is than irreligion; and who can now say what will happen once our people are returned to the city?"

* * * * *

In the afternoon, a boat with one rower touched at the same marble quay, and disembarked an Arab. His face was a dusty brown, and he wore an *abba* such as children of the Desert affect. His dark eyes were wonderfully bright, and his bearing was high, as might be expected in the Sheik of a tribe whose camels were thousands to the man, and who dwelt in dowars with streets after the style of cities. On his right forearm he carried a crescent-shaped harp of five strings, inlaid with colored woods and mother of pearl.

"Does not the Princess Irene dwell here?" he asked.

Lysander, viewing him suspiciously, answered: "The Princess Irene dwells here."

"Wilt thou tell her one Aboo-Obeidah is at the door with a blessing and a story for her?"

The doorkeeper again disappeared, and, returning, answered, with evident misgivings, "The Princess Irene prays you to come in."

Aboo-Obeidah tarried at the Therapian palace till night fell; and his story was an old one then, but he contrived to make it new; even as at this day, though four hundred and fifty years older than when he told it to the Princess, women of white souls, like hers, still listen to it with downcast eyes and flushing cheeks—the only story which Time has kept and will forever keep fresh and persuasive as in the beginning'.

They were married in her chapel at Therapia, Father Hilarion officiating. Thence, when the city was cleansed of its stains of war, she went thither with Mahommed, and he proclaimed her his Sultana at a feast lasting through many days.

And in due time he built for her the palace behind Point Demetrius, yet known as the Seraglio. In other words, Mahommed the Sultan abided faithfully by the vows Aboo-Obeidah made for him. [Footnote: The throne of Mahommed was guarded by the numbers and fidelity of his Moslem subjects; but his national policy aspired to collect the remnant of the Greeks; and they returned in crowds as soon as they were assured of their lives, their liberties, and the free exercise of their religion.... The churches of Constantinople were shared between the two religions. GIBBON.]

And so, with ampler means, and encouraged by Mahommed, the Princess Irene spent her life doing good, and earned the title by which she became known amongst her countrymen—The Most Gracious Queen of the Greeks.

Sergius never took orders formally. With the Sultana Irene and Father Hilarion, he preferred the enjoyment and practice of the simple creed preached by him in Sancta Sophia, though as between the Latins and the orthodox Greeks he leaned to the former. The active agent dispensing the charities of his imperial benefactress, he endeared himself to the people of both religions. Ere long, he married Lael, and they lived happily to old age.

* * * * *

Nilo was found alive, and recovering, joined Count Corti.

* * * * *

Count Corti retained the fraternal affection of Mahommed to the last. The Conqueror strove to keep him. He first offered to send him ambassador to John Sobieski; that being declined, he proposed promoting him chief Aga of Janissaries, but the Count declared it his duty to hasten to Italy, and devote himself to his mother. The Sultan finally assenting, he took leave of the Princess Irene the day before her marriage.

An officer of the court representing Mahommed conducted the Count to the galley built in Venice. Upon mounting the deck he was met by the Tripolitans, her crew, and Sheik Hadifah, with his fighting Berbers. He was then informed that the vessel and all it contained belonged to him.

The passage was safely made. From Brindisi he rode to Castle Corti. To his amazement, it was completely restored. Not so much as a trace of the fire and pillage it had suffered was to be seen.

His reception by the Countess can be imagined. The proofs he brought were sufficient with her, and she welcomed him with a joy heightened by recollections of the years he had been lost to her, and the manifest goodness of the Blessed Madonna in at last restoring him—the joy one can suppose a Christian mother would show for a son returned to her, as it were, from the grave.

The first transports of the meeting over, he reverted to the night he saw her enter the chapel: "The Castle was then in ruins; how is it I now find it rebuilt?"

"Did you not order the rebuilding?"

"I knew nothing of it."

Then the Countess told him a man had presented himself some months prior, with a letter purporting to be from him, containing directions to repair the Castle, and spare no expense in the work.

"Fortunately," she said, "the man is yet in Brindisi."

The Count lost no time in sending for the stranger, who presented him a package sealed and enveloped in oriental style, only on the upper side there was a *tughra*, or imperial seal, which he at once recognized as Mahommed's. With eager fingers he took off the silken wraps, and found a note in translation as follows:

"Mahommed the Sultan to Ugo, Count Corti, formerly Mirza the Emir.

"The wager we made, O my friend, who should have been the son of my mother, is not yet decided, and as it is not given a mortal to know the will of the Most Compassionate until he is pleased to expose it, I cannot say what the end will be. Yet I love you, and have faith in you; and wishing you to be so assured whether I win or lose, I send Mustapha to your country in advance with proofs of your heirship, and to notify the noble lady, your mother, that you are alive, and about returning to her. Also, forasmuch as a Turk destroyed it, he is ordered to rebuild your father's castle, and add to the estate all the adjacent lands he can buy; for verily no Countship can be too rich for the Mirza who was my brother. And these things he will do in your name, not mine. And when it is done, if to your satisfaction, O Count, give him a statement that he may come to me with evidence of his mission discharged.

"I commend you to the favor of the Compassionate. MAHOMMED."

When the missive was read, Mustapha knelt to the Count, and saluted him. Then he conducted him into the chapel of the castle, and going to the altar, showed him an iron door, and said:

"My master, the Lord Mahommed, instructed me to deposit here certain treasure with which he graciously intrusted me. Receive the key, I pray, and search the vault, and view the contents, and, if it please you, give me a certificate which will enable me to go back to my country, and live there a faithful servant of my master, the Lord Mahommed—may he be exalted as the Faithful are!"

Now when the Count came to inspect the contents of the vault he was displeased; and seeing it, Mustapha proceeded:

"My master, the Lord Mahommed, anticipated that you might protest against receiving the treasure; if so, I was to tell you it was to make good in some measure the sums the noble lady your mother has paid in searching for you, and in masses said for the repose of your father's soul."

Corti could not do else than accept.

Finally, to complete the narrative, he never married. The reasonable inference is, he never met a woman with graces sufficient to drive the Princess Irene from his memory.

After the death of the Countess, his mother, he went up to Rome, and crowned a long service as chief of the Papal Guard by dying of a wound received in a moment of victory. Hadifah, the Berbers, and Nilo chose to stay with him throughout. The Tripolitans were returned to their country; after which the galley was presented to the Holy Father.

Once every year there came to the Count a special messenger from Constantinople with souvenirs; sometimes a sword royally enriched, sometimes a suit of rare armor, sometimes horses of El Hajez—these were from Mahommed. Sometimes the gifts were precious relics, or illuminated Scriptures, or rosaries, or crosses, or triptychs wonderfully executed—so Irene the Sultana chose to remind him of her gratitude.

Syama wandered around Constantinople a few days after the fall of the city, looking for his master, whom he refused to believe dead. Lael offered him asylum for life. Suddenly he disappeared, and was never seen or heard of more. It may be presumed, we think, that the Prince of India succeeded in convincing him of his identity, and took him to other parts of the world—possibly back to Cipango.

THE END.

Milton Keynes UK
Ingram Content Group UK Ltd.
UKHW030622061024
449204UK00004B/416

9 789362 096548

This book has been considered important throughout the human history, and so that this work is never forgotten we have made efforts in its preservation by republishing this book in a modern format for present and future generations. This whole book has been reformatted, retyped and designed. These books are not made of scanned copies of their original work and hence the text is clear and readable.

ISBN 978-93-6209-654-8

Alpha Editions

9 789362 096548